OAKVILLE GALLERIES
1306 LAKESHORE ROAD EAST
OAKVILLE, ONTARIO L6J 1L6

A CELEBRATION OF DEATH

By the same author

European Cities and Society. The Influence of Political Climate on Town Design (Leonard Hill, London 1970 and 1972)

The Victorian Celebration of Death (David & Charles, Newton Abbot 1972)

City of London Pubs. A Practical and Historical Guide (co-author Timothy M Richards) David & Charles, Newton Abbot 1973)

Victorian Architecture: its Practical Aspects (David & Charles, Newton Abbot 1973)

The Erosion of Oxford (Oxford Illustrated Press, Ltd., Oxford 1977)

English Architecture: An Illustrated Glossary (David & Charles, Newton Abbot 1977)

Nunhead Cemetery, London. A History of the Planning, Architecture, Landscaping and Fortunes of a Great Nineteenth-Century Cemetery. Originally printed in the *Transactions of the Ancient Monuments Society*, London 1977, edited by E. M. Yates, the paper was published by the Society in 1977 as a separate volume

Mausolea in Ulster (Ulster Architectural History Society, Belfast 1978)

Moneymore and Draperstown. The Architecture and Planning of the Ulster estates of the Drapers' Company (Ulster Architectural Heritage Society, Belfast 1979)

A CELEBRATION OF DEATH

An introduction to some of the buildings,
monuments, and settings of funerary architecture
in the Western European tradition

JAMES STEVENS CURL

CONSTABLE · LONDON

First published in Great Britain 1980
by Constable and Company Limited
10 Orange Street London WC2H 7EG
Copyright © 1980 by James Stevens Curl
Set in Monophoto Ehrhardt 11pt
Printed in Great Britain by
BAS Printers Limited
Over Wallop Hampshire

British Library cataloguing in publication data
Curl, James Stevens
A celebration of death
1 Tombs—Europe
2 Sepulchral monuments—Europe
I Title
726′.8′094   NA6162

ISBN 0 09 463000 3

Death is fortunate for the child, bitter to the youth, too late for the old
(*Mors infanti felix, juveni acerba, nimis sera seni*)

PUBLILIUS SYRUS: Sententiae No. 394

Death comes even to the monumental stones and the names
inscribed thereon (*Mors etiam saxis nominibusque venit*).

AUSONIUS: Epitaphs No. 32, 1, 10

But monuments themselves memorials need.

GEORGE CRABBE: The Borough Letter 2

Contents

Illustrations

Acknowledgements

... Who knows the fate of his bones,
or how often he is to be buried?
who hath the Oracle of his Ashes ...?

SIR THOMAS BROWNE (1605–1682): from the Dedication of *Hydriotaphia*

Many people have helped me to assemble the mass of material necessary for the compilation of this book. I am grateful to my publishers and to Miss Jacqueline Korn, whose encouragement got the whole project under way. I am extremely grateful to Miss Laura Grenfell and to the Ancient Monuments Society for enabling me to research the convoluted affairs of the London Cemetery Company. My thanks are due to Mr F. A. Wragg and to Mr Robert J. Cook of the Borough Engineer's Department, London Borough of Southwark, for invaluable help in making material available that was necessary for study. I am also very grateful to other members of the staff of the London Borough of Southwark, including Mr A. Vercouttere, Miss Mary Boast, and Mr Frank Nilan for assistance with documents, photographs, and other material.

Mr John Harris and his staff at the R.I.B.A. British Architectural Library Drawings Collection have been more than helpful, and I am most grateful. I should also like to thank Mr David Dean and the staff of the R.I.B.A. British Architectural Library; Mr John Hopkins and the staff of the Society of Antiquaries of London; the staffs of the Bodleian Library, Oxford; of the British Library; of the Department of Greek and Roman Antiquities in the British Museum; of the National Monuments Record; of the Courtauld Institute of Art; of the Public Record Office; of Guildhall Library, City of London; of the Bibliothèque Nationale, Paris; of the Library of the India Office; and of the various public libraries I have consulted. I owe especial thanks to Mr Ralph Hyde of Guildhall Library, City of London; to the Secretary of the Society of Antiquaries of Scotland; and to Mr Brian R. Curle of the Libraries of the Royal Borough of Kensington and Chelsea.

Signorina Luciana Valentini and the staff of the British School at Rome kindly assisted with illustrations, and I acknowledge help from Dr T. J. Cornell at the School. Miss Melanie Simo was kind enough to let me read her fascinating paper on J. C. Loudon, and I am most grateful to her for drawing my attention to certain aspects of Loudon's work that had escaped me. Dr Maurice Craig very kindly gave hospitality and much practical help with photographs and other information. My visits to Irish cemeteries in his company were entertaining and agreeable.

I acknowledge the Gracious Permission of Her Majesty the Queen to reproduce drawings in the Royal Collections. The Librarian of the Royal Library at Windsor Castle, Sir Robin Mackworth-Young, and the Hon. Mrs Roberts, Curator of the Print Room at Windsor Castle, have been most kind. The Archivist, The Aerary, S. George's Chapel, Windsor, also deserves thanks, and I acknowledge help from the Dean and Canons of Windsor.

Acknowledgments

Mr K. T. Groves of Sydney has been indefatigable in his help with photographs and information. Mr Howard Colvin has been his usual generous self with biographical facts about architects. Mr Charles E. Lee kindly let me have some hitherto elusive material concerning Highgate Cemetery and its architects. The Trustees of the Sir John Soane Museum gave permission to reproduce some drawings by Soane, and Miss Dorothy Stroud kindly helped me to select what I needed. Sir John Summerson generously granted me permission to quote from his work on Soane and the Furniture of Death. Mr Martyn Gregory and Mr Andrew Wyld kindly helped to trace a picture of Kensal Green Cemetery, and Miss Joan Pollard of the Museum of London also rendered assistance.

The Editor of *Country Life*, Mr Michael Wright, granted permission to reproduce material for which I am most grateful. Dr Francis Sheppard also very kindly granted permission to reproduce Mr John Sambrook's survey drawings of the Anglican chapel at Kensal Green, and assisted me in many other ways, as did Mr Peter Bezodis, Mr John Greenacombe, and Mr Victor Belcher. I am especially grateful to Mr John Greenacombe for help with Genoa and Brompton. Mr John Sambrook has also been most kind as have Mr C. E. B. Brett and the Ulster Architectural Heritage Society.

I am very grateful to Dr Franz Colleselli and the staff of the Tiroler Volkskunst-Museum, Innsbruck, for supplying information and photographs of Maximilian's great cenotaph; to Mr J. A. Wierzbicki, Marketing Services Manager, and to the Public Transport Commission of New South Wales, for photographs of the railway stations associated with Rookwood Cemetery; to Gen B. Pieralberto Galli and the Commissariato Generale Onoranze Caduti in Guerra of the Ministero della Difesa in Rome; to Dr Anders Hedvall; to Heer L. Constandt; to Mr John Gloag; to Mr Nicholas Penny; to M Georges-Henri Pingusson; to Dr Sten Åke Nilsson; to Mr Kenneth G. C. Prevette, General Secretary of the Cremation Society of Great Britain; to Professor Kristian Jeppesen; to Mr D. M. Bailey; to Miss Wendy Johnston for help with the Belfast cemeteries; to Mr F. H. Thompson of the Society of Antiquaries of London; to Mr David Walker; to Major Malcolm Voss; to Mr Denis F. McCoy; to Mr Mervyn Miller; to Mr Arthur Oldham; to Herr Albert Speer; to Dr H. Arntz; to Mr Desmond Hodges; to Dr Geoffrey B. Waywell; to Mr Laurence N. W. Flanagan; to Arkitekt Kirsten Andersen; to the Warden of St Mark's Institute of Theology, Canberra; to the Revd J. L. Tregea, Rector of All Saints Church, Canberra; to Mr Peter Clayton; to Mr John Morley; to Mr and Mrs Theon Wilkinson and to the British Association for Cemeteries in South Asia for assistance with pictures of Indian funerary architecture; to the Commissioners of Public Works in Ireland; to the late Mr T. G. F. Paterson; to Herr Björn Linn; to Professor Göran Lindahl; to Major G. C. S. Turner of the Memorial and Records Office, Scottish National War Memorial; to Mr Arnold Whittick; to The German National Tourist Office; to Mr John H. Lawrence; to Mr Collin B. Hamer, Jr., Head of the Louisiana Division of the New Orleans Public Library; to the Volksbund Deutsche Kriegsgräberfürsorge e. V.; to Mr John Gerrard; to Mr Edmund Esdaile; to Mrs Stella Howard; to Mr Gavin Stamp; to Dr Helen Rosenau-Carmi; to Mrs M.

van Baerle and the staff of the Commonwealth War Graves Commission; to Mr Michael Haškovec; to Mrs Pamela Johnson; and to Mr John Francis Marion.

I shall be indebted all my life to Mr Rodney C. Roach, who once again has done a splendid job not only in the processing of my own pictures, but in very kindly photographing documents for me. Mr A. H. Buck patiently read my typescripts and pithily made invaluable observations for which any words of thanks are inadequate. Mr Peter B. Bond generously gave me his permission to quote from his work on crematoria. Mr H. J. Malyon of the General Cemetery Company allowed me access to the Minutes of the Company, and kindly gave me facilities to photograph documents and buildings. I also owe thanks to the superintendents and staff of cemeteries and crematoria too numerous to list. With a few exceptions, they have been unfailingly helpful and courteous.

My brother, John, gave up a great deal of his time to help with the photography relating to Irish mausolea. His admirable driving, practical help, and amusing company were high spots in the writing of this book. My late father, George Stevens Curl, first stimulated my interest in funerary monuments for which I shall always be grateful. It is a source of particular sadness to me that he did not live to see this work completed, although I often discussed my ideas with him. He lies at Ballycairn near one of the most spectacular of all Irish monuments, the 'Giant's Ring'.

I owe Miss Helen I. Logan an especial debt for her kindness in helping with the collection of material in Paris, a task she accomplished with something approaching heroism. Mrs Penelope Jessel greatly assisted me in the building up of illustrations, and gave me much support, advice, practical help, and comment, for all of which I am most grateful. Mrs Stella Howard and Mrs Marguerite Johnston typed the book from a disreputable and unseemly manuscript. Their ingenuity in unravelling the convolutions of my text deserves praise and grateful thanks. Miss Astrid Curl, Mrs Judith Ashley, Mr Michael Brackenbury, Mr Stephen Heywood, and Mrs Penelope Jessel very kindly helped with that tedious task of checking the galleys against the original typescripts. My daughters, Astrid and Ingrid, helped me to check the pictures against captions. My wife accompanied me on many cemetery explorations over the years, and I am grateful to her for her patience. Many friends assisted me in one way or another, and without their kindness the task of writing the book would have been impossible.

JAMES STEVENS CURL

Oxford, London, St Albans, Leicester, and Winchester

1976–1979

Introduction

Oh, let me range the gloomy aisles alone:
Sad luxury! to vulgar minds unknown;
Along the walls where sparkling marbles show
What worthies form the hallowed world below.

THOMAS TICKELL: *On the Death of Addison*

The purpose of this book is to provide an introduction to funerary architecture, to cemetery design, and to memorials and monuments in the Western European tradition. It must be emphasized that the vastness of the subject precludes a full coverage. My chosen title underlines the point that this volume is essentially an introductory survey, for a comprehensive study would run to several large books. There is, however, a series of constant themes, and I have tried to pull the whole into a coherent story. The tombs of prehistory, of classical times, of the mediaeval period, and of the Renaissance have merited considerable attention by historians, but the cemeteries generally have been neglected. I have therefore drawn on studies by others when the subject has been adequately covered, and I have endeavoured to describe, through my own researches of many years, the later developments, such as those of the nineteenth century. A broad sweep, to tell the story as an entity, has been attempted, although I realise that the details of my sketchy mosaic will need detailed infill by others perhaps more specialised in their disciplines than I can hope to achieve.

European memorials, mausolea, cemetery designs, and monuments greatly influenced designers in North America, and, although the story is primarily European, examples from America will be discussed where they are appropriate. In a few instances, funerary architecture abroad and in the former British possessions is mentioned where relevant to the theme. Such a book seemed necessary, for funerary designs, architecture, and especially the whole subject of cemeteries, have suffered from a curious neglect at the hands of historians. Possibly this is because, unlike any other healthy and creative civilizations, we play down death, robbing it of its great significance. We treat the disposal of the dead in much the same way as that in which we rid our towns and cities of waste products. Nevertheless, there has been a revival of interest in the monuments, architecture, and trappings of death in recent years. The exhibition 'Death, Heaven, and the Victorians' at Brighton in 1970 heralded the publication of numerous articles and a few books on the subject, and in 1977 attention was focused on the architecture of war cemeteries in two exhibitions in London.

The buildings and landscapes associated with death are often most interesting. In particular, the strange melancholy of graveyards and of old cemeteries can be peculiarly moving. Nobody who has spent a childhood in Ireland can escape the remembrance of images of death, of sad decay, and of a haunting, almost unbearable beauty. The Irish tend to bury their dead in and around the sites of ancient abbeys and churches, thus the combination of crumbling architecture (usually overgrown with ivy and mistletoe), graveyards and monuments, yew trees and silence, could hardly fail to have a profound and indelible effect on the sensibilities. So it was in my own case, for since childhood I have been intensely aware of the nearness of death and of the dead. In Ireland it is likely that a Celtic sense of gloom and of desolation may have been strengthened in the presence of so many awesome structures from an ancient past, for the cult of death is still a powerful force in Irish life throughout the whole of that island.

The rarefied pleasures of the cemetery and of funerary architecture have been known to generations of travellers from the earliest of times. From Herodotus to Baedeker, the tomb has received honourable mention as an object for study and of reflection. The contemporary tourist misses much if he avoids the places where the dead are buried, yet such avoidance is symptomatic of the present attitudes towards death and remembrance. Tombs and monuments are often among the finest structures erected by man; the ancient necropoleis and burial-places have an almost tangible atmosphere; the great cemeteries of Italy and France are grand architectural experiences; and the leafy arbours of German and Scandinavian burial-grounds inspire a different kind of delight. However, the experience of exploring the cemeteries of London and of other great British cities, though interesting, can be profoundly disturbing today. The memorials and tombs placed within a landscape of evergreen and deciduous trees can often please, but widespread destruction is now distressingly usual. Monuments in such cemeteries usually carry inscriptions that insist on a remembrance that clearly does not hold true. The ephemeral nature of life, and the transience of kinship, of friendship, of fame, and of love, are obvious to the beholder of neglected graves and of vandalized monuments. Such structures, intended to commemorate in perpetuity, have become targets for youthful destroyers, and have barely survived a century. In the neglected cemeteries of Britain today are hundreds of thousands of such expensive memorials to families and to individuals. It is clear that the persons and the stones that are intended as their monuments have suffered an equal eclipse. Beliefs have changed with the times, for a great many gravestones are inscribed with references to a certain resurrection. Celestial bliss has proved less than a certainty, and the Victorian heaven seems infinitely remote. This change of attitude is reflected most poignantly in the graveyards of contemporary Britain.

Coherent and consistent threads run through the development of funerary architecture and the design of monuments. This book will attempt to describe and illustrate the riches that are to be found in the celebration of death within a tradition derived from early cultures in Europe and in the Middle East. These riches are rewarding, and should receive wider appreciation than has been the case in recent years.

JAMES STEVENS CURL

1979

The importance of the architecture and artefacts of death in ancient cultures.

*The funerary architecture of Ancient Egypt;
some funerary monuments of prehistoric
cultures in the British Isles.*

The tap'ring pyramid, the Egyptian's pride,
And wonder of the world whose spiky top
Has wounded the thick cloud.

ROBERT BLAIR: *The Grave*

Death, and the art, architecture, and landscapes inspired by it, are not
unworthy subjects for contemplation. Since mankind began to leave records
and traces of his civilizations, death has exercised his mind to no small
degree. The knowledge that every human being must die has undoubtedly
contributed to man's desire to commemorate his existence by building
monuments, erecting funerary architecture, and otherwise celebrating
death. The records that civilizations and craftsmen have left in funerary art
and architecture clearly express attitudes about the only experience in life
we may be absolutely sure will come to us.

Contemporary attitudes in Western Europe perhaps veer towards the
view propounded by Spinoza[1] that the correct study for a wise man is not
death, but how to live. Yet a life spent without any contemplation of death
is, in a sense, a denial of life, since death is the logical and inevitable end for
us all. The chief notions behind the *memento mori* principle were well-
known to authors of the past. Seneca[2] advises us to become familiar with
thoughts of death so that it ceases to be frightening; Cicero[3] said that
philosophers made a point of studying death; and the Psalmists[4] urged that
we may be taught to number our days in order to apply ourselves to wisdom.
The ancients were of the opinion that death is a natural law, and a corollary
of birth. Cicero, like many others, was also concerned with the philosophical
arguments about the doctrines of survival of the soul after the death of the
body. Death was considered by some to be a change or a migration, rather
than an extinction, but Cicero asked if anything more acceptable than
eternal sleep could be conceived if annihilation were the true nature of death.
To Socrates and Marcus Aurelius, either state of death would be acceptable,
while Epicurus and Lucretius[5] seem to have inclined to the view that death
was a privation of feeling: a dead person, having ceased to exist, could not
possibly be miserable, or experience any feelings whatsoever. Death, to such

philosophers, was simply an absence of life, a state of non-being. To other minds death was merely a converse of birth, and consequently held no terrors; it was a return to a state of unconsciousness, of which Pliny could say there was no more sensation in either body or soul than there was before life began.

Such admirably balanced ideas were believed in some circles, but the prevailing vanity of man possibly contributed to an even more widely held refusal to accept an end of existence. When the death of the body came to be considered, not as the fulfilment of some natural law, but as the result of the intervention of supernatural forces (even as a punishment for Original Sin), the stage was set for all manner of horrors to be unleashed. Eternal punishment for the damned soul was a potent weapon. Of course, beliefs in a future existence among even the Greeks and Romans were not always of a pleasant nature. Hades and Hell do not have much to recommend them, and a Mahometan Paradise or the Islands of the Blessed seem to offer more enticements than even the strongest of spirits could countenance in perpetuity.

Egyptian concepts are often found in the painted and incised interiors of tombs. The dead person is represented as he performs ritual acts, or is led to his destination by the strange gods of the culture. The symbolism associated with the sun often recurs in Egyptian funerary art in the form of solar discs, pyramidal shapes, or obelisks. The scarab beetle, as a symbol of immortality, was a favourite motif.

Labyrinthine patterns found in Celtic, Saxon, and other cultures may also symbolize eternity. Etruscan painted tombs often depict scenes from Greek mythology, banquets, hunts, and other common human pursuits. However, during Roman banquets, miniature jointed skeletons were often introduced, presumably to encourage enjoyment. Where reminders of death were introduced at Egyptian feasts, the idea was to encourage friendship and to provide a deterrent to wickedness. Representations of skulls were not unknown on the walls of Pompeian dining-rooms. Some fine Roman wine-cups are decorated with skeletons, or *larvae*, presumably as part of the exhortation: *edite! bibite! post mortem nulla voluptas!*

The familiar symbols found in funerary architecture all express real ideas. The classical use of inverted torches to decorate tombs is, of course, symbolic of the extinction of life. The serpent eating its own tail symbolizes eternal life, while other motifs, such as weeping *putti*, shrouded urns, skeletons (often realistically animated and armed), and skulls and crossbones have obvious allegorical meaning. The weeping female mourner beside a shrouded urn is a familiar subject for Neoclassical sculptors.

In mediaeval Europe, representations of the terrors of death and hell began to appear in the most horrifying manner. Mediaeval 'Dooms' decorated many parish churches, while the Dance of Death was a popular subject, spurred on, no doubt, by frequent visitations of the plague. Death, as a partially draped skeleton, is seen gleefully grasping maidens, kings, popes, and every type of human being. Death is depicted as a hunter, a warrior, and even as a mischievous clown-like figure who fears nobody. During the Black Death there were outbreaks of dancing mania, possibly connected with pictorial representations of the Dance of Death. The Dance originated in the thirteenth and fourteenth centuries as a morality tale consisting of dialogues between Death and living characters typical of the various stations in life. The power of death could thus be impressed upon the minds of all. Images of three kings confronting three skeletons of themselves obviously contained a strongly moral message. The mediaeval morality play of *Everyman* has Death as a central figure. However, there is a strong tie between mediaeval representations of a malevolent dancing skeleton to represent Death, and the late-Roman and Graeco-Roman method of representing *larvae* as skeletons. It was hardly surprising that the grim realities of death should have been used by the designers of tombs, monuments, and other works of art for the purposes of religious teaching. The admonitory, *memento mori*, and *gisant* type of funerary monument will be discussed in subsequent chapters. Skulls, hour-glasses, and scythes were constant reminders of the fleeting nature of life, and were often used in paintings, engravings, sculptures, and funerary art from Renaissance times.

The type of memorial inscribed with humorous bravado existed in classical times as it did in the eighteenth century. Most memorials, however, are clearly designed to commemorate, console, praise, or record, where there is an inscription. It is clear that the architecture and artefacts of death have been important in all civilizations as a canalization and formalization of loss, and as a reflection of social, religious, and artistic tendencies in cultures.

Many vanished civilizations have left us their tombs, cenotaphs, mausolea, and cemeteries from which we can gain much knowledge about the aspirations and tastes of the people who are thus celebrated. Civilizations have expended much wealth and effort on an architecture of death. The great prehistoric cemeteries have been perhaps the only sources of information concerning some peoples, while the huge cemeteries of classical times augment what we already know of the cultures of Greece and Rome. Those who have visited the cemeteries of Ancient Egypt, of the Kedron Valley, and of Petra; or who have experienced the extraordinary beauty of the tomb-lined Via Appia Antica in Rome; or who have ventured into the catacombs, will understand more of those who laid their dead to rest there. In Britain, our parish churches and cathedrals are full of memorials and tombs, and nearly all parish churches have stones in the churchyard that are valuable sources of genealogical information as well as providing a setting for the church. it is outrageous that so many churchyards are being vandalized by misguided zealots who imagine that sweeping away the stones or stacking them somehow tidies or improves a churchyard. In current British culture, it seems, death must not be thought of, and no reminder of death should ever impinge upon the cosy world of plastic flowers and hygienic, antiseptic places that rid us of our unwanted dead.

In a sense, funerary architecture is the purest form of the Mistress of the Arts, for many of the greatest examples are objects in space, unchanging, with no problems of having to acquire a new use to survive. The great mausolea and tombs of ancient Roman civilization, indeed the mausolea of

3

all periods, are there as statements of architecture, complete, and silent. The nobleman's mausoleum in the park, for example, as at Castle Howard, is magnificent in its finality, alone in the landscape, undisturbed by daily use by the mere living. The successful mausoleum must appear to be an edifice for the housing of the dead, and here symbolic aspects of shape appear to be consistently important. Simple geometrical forms such as the pyramid, drum, and cone, or the house-tomb, temple-tomb, and the obelisk make the most immediately recognizable tombs. The formality of so much funerary architecture reflects the need to provide a suitable setting for the dead to lie, and the balanced, serene plans of so many mausolea mirror the repose of a dead body lying still for eternity. The formal tomb, like the perfect urn, or sarcophagus, is truly a 'Sylvan historian', with an 'Attic shape' and 'silent form' that can 'tease us out of thought' like eternity itself.

There are other, more discreet tombs, however. The rock-cut tombs, catacombs, and others, all depend for their effects on their interiors and, sometimes, on their façades. Barrows, tumuli, tombs of the *tholos* type, pyramids, and other geometrical structures, have certain similarities of architectural form. To a certain extent, these forms had their origins in the houses of the living, for in Ancient Egypt the change from circular huts to rectangular houses was followed by similar changes in tomb plan.[6] Façades of some more elaborate Egyptian tombs were modelled on domestic prototypes. Clay urns of Etruscan and pre-Etruscan cultures are often in the form of rectangular houses or circular huts. The circular tumulus-tomb and the later circular imperial tombs of Rome may have their origins as round houses or primitive huts. Neolithic long barrows, such as those found in the British Isles, may be derived from contemporary house-types, while the hog-back monuments of northern Britain may represent houses of the Viking period.[7] It may well be that the similarity of tombs to contemporary houses reveals a tendency to provide the dead with domestic comforts.

Many prehistoric civilizations favoured inhumation of the whole body, very often laid in a contracted posture: on the side, with the thighs bent at right angles to the spinal cord, to resemble an attitude of sleep. A more formal posture is when the body is laid on its back, known as the extended posture. When wooden coffins, stone sarcophagi, and mummification became usual in Egypt the extended posture was, of course, the position that suited the custom of placing the body in a coffin. This posture became normal in late-Neolithic, Bronze and Iron-Age times where inhumation was favoured, and would lend itself to a formal layout of grave furniture and tomb design.

Cremation appears to have been practised first in the Neolithic period, and was sometimes communal in character. From the Bronze Age it was individual rather than communal. After the pyre had cooled, the bones were broken and placed in a container. Cremation appears to have been the favoured rite in Europe from the Middle Bronze Age, but inhumation and cremation have both been practised at the same periods. Where cremation was usual, clothes and personal belongings were also consumed on the fire. Herodotus tells us that the ghost of Melissa appeared to Periander[8] to say that she was cold, since her clothes had been buried rather than burned. As a result the women of Corinth were relieved of their clothes which were then burned to provide Melissa with a wardrobe. The dead who were cremated could only take objects into an after-life if those objects were also consumed on the pyre.

In Egypt, many objects were placed with the mummified corpse in the tombs, and several cultures appear to have buried or burned their dead with clothes and other objects for use in the after-life. We have learned much about the clothes and the ephemera of various periods through the survival of tombs, though much has been lost to grave-robbers. Important finds of Bronze-Age clothing have been made in Jutland,[9] where they were preserved in oak coffins in waterlogged barrows and mounds. The famous Iron-Age victims of sacrifice found in the Danish bogs are not to be confused with the mound—burials of Jutland at the end of the second millennium BC. The oak-coffin finds at Egtved and Skrydstrup are important, for they provide examples of the burial of two high-born young women, with their clothing and jewellery preserved almost intact through the preservative qualities of the acidic soil. Aromatic flowers were buried with the bodies, and the burned bones of a young girl, possibly a servant, were found associated with the Egtved burial. These burials were within large artificial mounds. The treasures found in tombs in Egypt, Ireland, Crete, and in other places are indicative of the extraordinary importance the after-life occupied in so many civilizations. Significant personages were often accompanied to the after-life by servants, wives, concubines, and animals, all slaughtered and buried at the same time. In Egypt, royal burials were augmented by subsidiary burials until the end of the First Dynasty. Another curious feature of royal burials at this time was the erection of a tomb in one part of Egypt, and a cenotaph in the other, perhaps to emphasize the unity of the Kingdoms. In some cultures, servants and retainers seem to have been buried alive. The royal tombs at Ur[10] of the second millennium BC are noted for the large numbers of sacrifices of humans and animals. It was the Indo-European custom from the Neolithic period to slay wives and dependent children on the death of the husbands and this is proved by the large numbers of burials of men and women together. The Hindu custom of *Suttee*, or burning of a widow on her husband's pyre, is a survival of this. When Patroclus was cremated, a dozen noble Trojans were slain as sacrifice, and similar customs appear to have survived in Cyprus during the seventh century BC, in Scythia until the third century BC, and even in certain areas where the Vikings established themselves as late as the tenth century AD.[11] The killing of animals also provided fat which was smeared on the body to assist the combustion. Animal and human fat was also sometimes used to seal the lid of the urn containing the cremated remains.[12] Many dogs, horses, bulls, goats, cattle, and sheep were slaughtered and buried to accompany the worthy dead to a rich after-life. Some magnificent bridles and pieces of chariot have been found associated with Scythian barrows, and the practice of killing animals seems to have been widespread over most of Europe.

Food, drink, clothing, weapons, money, and jewellery were also taken into the after-life in considerable quantities. The stores of the pyramid of

Zoser contained about 8,000 vases.[12, 13] Often, means were provided for pouring libations into a grave or coffin, notably at Roman Colchester, where a lead coffin was fitted with a pipe for libations to be admitted to the body. Quite apart from the remarkably widespread practice of providing the dead with all the comforts for a future life, there appears to have been considerable fear of the dead and of the spirit-world in many ancient civilizations. The provision of a securely-built tomb, stocked with goods, may have been a form of inducement or bribe to the dead to remain in the tomb. Fear of the ghosts returning to demand food, clothing, money, or appropriate rites to secure peace and rest, seems to be a recurrent theme. Even in sophisticated Rome, regular ceremonies to pacify the dead were held, and libations were offered to the departed.

A curious feature of burial customs appears to be that the sparser the furnishing of the graves, the richer and more economically developed a culture actually was. According to Childe,[20] this was because grave-goods became largely regulated by custom. Certainly, as early as the predynastic period of Egypt, substitute offerings, models, and the like, made do for the customary objects in many cases. This was more economical and was less attractive to a potential grave-robber. Adult males, for example, were entombed with statuettes of women in order to provide companions for sexual pleasure, while model armaments, imitation food and drink, and *ersatz* jewellery proved admirable substitutes for the real thing. Often, pottery and other objects were 'killed' by breaking them so that their 'spirits' would accompany the dead to the other world. This custom had the added advantage of rendering grave-goods useless to tomb-robbers, and also prevented squabbles over property among relatives. There also appears to have been a sense of decorum concerning funerary objects, in that it was thought unfitting to use them for any other purpose, and because they were associated with the deceased. Bronze bowls have been found, deliberately holed, while swords have been bent and chariots dismantled.[14] In late Hellenistic times more appropriate gifts, such as frankincense and saffron, for remembrance, were given to the dead.

It is clear that the scale and importance of funerary architecture can vary greatly from one culture to another. The Egyptians were very concerned to build imposing tombs, since they placed so much more importance on an after-life. The Egyptian tomb had to be a solid, secure, and lasting house for the mummified body and all its parts, for, when the spirit of the deceased finished wandering the world in animal form, it would return to the tomb and reclaim the corpse. Thus life would begin anew. The loss, theft, or destruction of the body was a singular disaster to the Ancient Egyptian, and so the architecture of his tombs reflected the importance of its function. The Iron-Age Britons, however, built elaborate tombs only for their chiefs. Egyptian tombs had to have facilities for periodical performance of ritual, communing with the dead, and other ceremonies. The tombs therefore had a chapel attached to the burial-chamber where such events could be celebrated. The interiors were richly decorated with paintings of mourners and representations of the deities. Mycenaean tombs were often of a *tholos* type, with a circular domed chamber, and a long *dromos* or passage leading to it. Funerary games, ritual mourning, and fumigation with burning of incense appear to have been usual in Mycenaean tombs.

In Egypt, the problem of the upkeep of tombs had to be faced. It appears that many tombs, notably the pyramid complexes, were endowed to enable priests to make offerings and to perform rituals. The practice is not dissimilar to the endowment of chantries in the Middle Ages or to the provision for the upkeep of tombs by wealthy Romans. The great royal tombs, such as the pyramid complexes, also provided mausolea for wives and relatives. Families were often entombed in the one building, and not infrequently tombs were enlarged with extra chapels and burial-chambers. Heads of Egyptian families built the tombs, which were subsequently completed or enlarged by their descendants. Minoan and Mycenaean vaulted tombs appear to have been family or even tribal mausolea, as many contain several hundred bodies. Many Etruscan tombs were family mausolea, and it seems fairly clear that the Orcadian cairns were family tombs.

Great ingenuity had to be shown to evolve ways of protecting tombs from robbers. Fear of robbery seems to have been a common feature of most cultures, and not even the most bloodcurdling curses were adequate deterrents. Architects produced complex labyrinthine passages leading to well-protected tomb-chambers. The entrances were often concealed, or fake portals were constructed to cause confusion. The famous royal necropolis in the Valley of the Kings at Thebes appears to owe its origins to the necessity of hiding the rich mausolea of the kings and nobility. The fact that Tutankhamun's tomb lay undiscovered for so long is an example of the cunning that had to prevail. Inscribed curses, massive sarcophagi, and heavy fines for tomb-robbers were features of other civilizations, including the kingdom of Sidon, the Hellenistic cultures of Asia Minor, and the Nabataeans at Petra. Sculpted animals, such as lions, guarded tombs in Etruria and in other parts of the Mediterranean lands.

Egyptian culture, by the importance it placed on the housing and protection of the dead, has left the most extensive and famous tombs of all time. The pyramids of Egypt are celebrations of death on a powerful scale, and are themselves associated with the symbolism of the solar cult of Heliopolis. The pyramids, sphinxes, obelisks, and even the architectural details of Egyptian buildings, provided sources of inspiration to the designers of monumental buildings in eighteenth- and nineteenth-century Europe.

Religion and architecture were closely connected. The powerful priesthood was equipped with learning and considerable authority. The traditional, conservative, and mysterious rites of the Egyptians were reflected in the architecture of tombs and of temples. Worship of the sun and of Osiris, the man-god who died and was resurrected, was perhaps the key to the understanding of the basic philosophy of an expectancy of resurrection of the body. Indeed, the outstanding feature of the Egyptian religion was the belief in an after-life, and this involved the protection of the body for future use. The embalmed bodies of the dead were carefully wrapped and coffined, while the canopic jars containing the internal organs were placed convenieniently to hand. Furniture, money, and useful objects were set aside for future use when the corpse came to life once more. Herodotus tells us that in Egypt the dwelling-house was a temporary lodging, while the tomb was regarded as the permanent home until the resurrection. The tomb, as the house where one would dwell longest, was therefore, quite logically in such a society, the more splendid.

Social conditions were largely determined by the despotism of the centralized government. There was no danger of religion and state being opposed to each other, since kings were frequently priests, and the priesthood was closely allied to royalty and to government. At times of inundation by the Nile, the agricultural workers were employed to build monumental structures, usually royal tombs. Prisoners-of-war and captive peoples were similarly engaged. Under Rameses II there were so many captives in Egypt that the nation grew uneasy at their numbers. Exodus[15] tells us that the new Pharaoh observed 'the children of Israel' were 'more and mightier' than the Egyptians, and that it would be wise to deal with them so that they would not join forces with the Pharaoh's enemies. 'And the Egyptians made the children of Israel to serve with rigour', including presumably on building-works associated with funerary architecture.

Craftsmanship was greatly prized in Egypt, and high degrees of prosperity were achieved by those versed in weaving, glass-making, pottery, metalworking, and in the manufacture of musical instruments, jewellery, and furniture. Everyone, however, aspired to a permanent home once dead, and even the poorest (whose bodies were merely pickled in natron) were given shelter of a primitive sort that has probably survived the incursions of time and robbers far better than the richer tombs of kings, priests, and the nobility.

The development of the Egyptian tomb led to a type of *mastaba*, or rectangular tomb, with battered sides. The *mastabas* were flat-roofed, with sides sloping at about 75 degrees. They consisted of an outer chamber, usually decorated, where ritual was performed; an inner secret chamber where stood statues of the family; and an underground tomb-chamber reached by a shaft. The *mastaba* of the architect Thi at Sakkara is a particularly fine example, and contains mural reliefs depicting everyday scenes of craftsmen's lives. The famous step-pyramid of Zoser at Sakkara of about 2650 BC started life as a *mastaba* that formed the basis of the first step. This base was extended, and three more steps were added. The pyramid was later enlarged to make it a rectangle on plan, and two further steps were added. Like all pyramids, it was surrounded by a wall, and had associated buildings and courts (Pl. 1). The pyramid and its complex housed the bodies of the king and his family, while various temples for acts of re-dedication and other rituals occupied one side of one of the great courtyards. The architect of this earliest known pyramid was Imhotep.[16]

The great complex of buildings at Maidum also contains a pyramid that started life as a stepped form. Blocks of stone were later added to conceal the stepped shape and formed a true pyramid. As with other pyramids, an entrance was formed some distance up one of the sloping faces, and access to the vaulted burial-chamber was by a long shaft. The southern pyramid of

Plate 1 The step pyramid of King Zoser at Sakkara, with the Heb-sed pavilion seen across the Heb-sed court. The state of restoration of the pavilions in February 1977 can be seen (*Peter Clayton*)

Snefru at Dahshur has the upper and lower parts with sides of differing slope, probably owing to construction difficulties. The pyramid was set in a walled court, with a long causeway leading to it from a temple.

The greatest pyramid complex of all is that at Giza, where Kheops built the Great Pyramid. This, with the pyramids of Khephren and Mycerinos, together with the Sphinx and smaller tombs, forms a celebrated regal necropolis (Pl. 2). Each pyramid had an associated temple linked to the pyramid complex by a causeway. The interior of the Great Pyramid has three tomb-chambers, with an enormous grand gallery that gives access to the main chamber. This gallery has a corbelled roof. The main tomb-chamber is roofed with granite slabs, above which are five more chambers, each roofed with granite. The small pyramids to the east of the Great Pyramid were probably the tombs of the wives of the pharaoh. The Sphinx is carved from solid rock, and appears to have had as its head a portrait of Khephren facing the east. This was a grand sculptural object by the side of the causeway and temple leading to Khephren's pyramid. The great Giza complex is dated from about 2580 BC to 2490 BC.

The mortuary temples associated with Egyptian tombs reached their apotheosis on the left bank of the Nile in the great mausoleum at Dëir-el-Bahari. This was built on rising ground on the side of the hills as the mortuary temple of Queen Hatshepsut and needs special mention as it has a plan and architectural character that are unique. The temple is built in and partly against a recess of the hills opposite Karnak and Luxor (Pl. 3). It is closely bounded on three sides by cliffs, and is only open to the east. It is

9

Plate 2 The Sphinx and the pyramid of Kephren (*Michael Wright*)

formed of three courts that rise one above the other, each being reached by great ramped causeways built up the centre-line of the lowest and middle court. Each wall facing the court is lined with a double colonnade of the severest style. Some of the columns are square on plan, but sixteen-sided columns similar to those of the rock-cut tombs at Beni-Hasan are also found. The sanctuary was cut into the rock behind this noble complex. The severity of the stripped-down colonnades recalls some of the work of Troost and Speer during the Third Reich in Germany. The temple of Queen Hatshepsut was designed by her architect Senmut in 1520 BC to stand beside the funerary temple of Mentuhetep of some five hundred years previously. The latter had certain similarities of design, but was crowned by a small solid pyramid standing over a dummy burial-chamber.

There were later pyramids, all more or less following similar lines. Some pyramid-tombs were very small, and were adopted by the well-to-do after the form had been abandoned by the pharaohs. This decline in favour was due to three causes: the staff and upkeep needed for each pyramid put a great strain on the finances of Egypt; the Heliopolitan cult waned in popularity; and pyramids, by their very nature, were conspicuous targets for robbers. Certainly the form of the pyramid seems to have appealed to later designers of tombs. The pyramid of Cestius in Rome is a very curious survival of the form, while the Neoclassical architects of the eighteenth century favoured pyramids as motifs for their designs for cemeteries, tombs, and cenotaphs. It appears that the pyramid was a symbol of the sun's rays, and each side was inscribed with solar discs. The buildings also reached towards the heavens, so facilitating the ascension of the dead monarch.

The success of the robbers prompted the pharaohs to seek more discreet forms of burial. The great royal necropolis of the Valley of the Kings largely consists of tombs with modest entrances, usually rock-cut, but with subsidiary building work. These tombs were usually planned in a formal manner, with corridors cut into the rock, each leading to an antechamber beyond which lay the sepulchral room containing the magnificent sarcophagus. Sepulchral temples were attached to the tombs for funeral rites and offerings. Most of these tombs date from about 1554 BC to about 1080 BC. The rock-cut tombs of Seti I and of Rameses IX are particularly fine examples (Pl. 4). The very remarkable group of rock-cut tombs at Beni Hasan contains one example with an entrance that incorporates two sixteen-sided columns, fluted and tapered, that are singularly like prototypes of the Greek Doric Order (Pl. 5). The interiors of Egyptian rock-cut tombs were elegant, and often incorporated architectural motifs, as in the Middle-Kingdom tomb number 17 of Beni-Hasan.

The so-called Tomb of Darius at Naksh-i-Rustam, some eight miles north of Persepolis in what was ancient Persia, is one of the four rock-cut sepulchres of the great Achaemenian kings, and the type may have been suggested to Darius by the tombs in Egypt which he had seen when serving under Cambyses. The façade of this tomb reproduces the front of the small palace of Darius at Persepolis, with four columns with double-bull-head capitals carrying a cornice over which is a bas-relief showing the king before an altar of the sun-god. In the centre of the façade is a doorway of strongly

Egyptian form. The Persians were not averse to an eclectic use of antique elements. The Tomb of Cyrys at Pasargadae (*c.* 529 BC) had a single chamber on a stylobale of six steps, not unlike the Lycian tombs. This tomb was described by Strabo, Herodotus, and Pliny, and was visited by Alexander the Great, who saw the treasures, including the gilded sarcophagus.

Egyptian architecture was essentially conservative, with relatively uninterrupted traditions. The solemnity, massiveness, and gloom associated with Egyptian buildings suggest structures intended to last for eternity, while the awesome funerary architecture, with the geometrical forms and massive sarcophagi, is admirably suited to the performance of funerary rites and for the protection of the bodies to await the return of souls. To the Ancient Egyptians, death was the real beginning of life, and so the process of mummification, entombment, and the building of necropoleis was central to the culture.

Obelisks, like pyramids, were associated with the sun cult at Heliopolis, and were essentially monoliths decorated with incised hieroglyphics. Although not funereal in origin, their shapes became popular among Renaissance, Baroque, and Neoclassical designers as objects to flank entrances, dignify upperworks, and otherwise embellish the architecture of death. Egyptian doorways, window details, and other motifs became widely used in Neoclassical architecture, sometimes curiously intermingled with Greek elements, as at Highgate Cemetery, for example.

A very large part of the Egyptian economy was thus taken up with the building, furnishing, upkeep, and servicing of tombs and funerary architecture. No subsequent culture was to expend as much comparative wealth on the building of necropoleis, although there were to be individual tombs of great importance architecturally in later civilizations. The Romans were fascinated by some aspects of Egypt, and they embellished Rome with obelisks taken from Heliopolis and other places. The possibilities of Egyptian funerary architecture were not to be fully exploited by designers again until the eighteenth century of our era.

Elsewhere, in Europe, such a high degree of cultural achievement had not been reached. Yet the funerary monuments of early civilizations sometimes provide the most astonishing architectural experiences, and bear testimony to how very similar the built solutions actually were to the problem of providing permanent houses for the dead. A formal arrangement of elements about a central space; a degree of protection; the covering of a structure with a mound of earth; and the degree of sophistication displayed in the building of necropoleis, funerary monuments, and tombs are apparent in the great legacy of how man has celebrated death. This sophistication is amply demonstrated by the riches of the tombs and monuments such as Maes Howe on Orkney. The outside of this famous tomb, the supreme example of the type in the British Isles, is a dome-shaped mound, about eight metres high, and thirty-five metres in diameter at the base. It is surrounded by a broad ditch, some fifteen metres in width, and one metre deep.

The entrance to the interior is by a long passage that rises gently to the

Plate 4 Exquisite decorations in the tomb of Seti I in the Valley of the Kings. Such sumptuous décor was a fit setting for the permanent house of the dead (*Michael Wright*)

Plate 5 The entrance to a Middle Kingdom tomb of Khumhotep III at Beni-Hasan. Note the resemblance of the columns to those of the Doric Order (*Peter Clayton*)

centre of the mound. There are door-checks of upright stones, and the first two metres or so of the passage are lined with coursed masonry. For the rest of the length of the passage, the walls and roof are formed of single slabs of stone that average six metres long, and are just over one metre wide and about fourteen centimetres thick. The lofty central chamber, once reached via the passage, is breathtaking in its grandeur (Pl. 6). It is nearly five metres square, with walls that rise vertically for the first one and a half metres. The four sides then converge in overlapping courses, laid flat, and pinned where necessary. At the four corners of the chamber there are projecting piers, and one side of each of these is formed of a carefully plumbed monolith, the longest being about three metres. These piers supported the converging roof or pseudo-vault, and restrained lateral movement.[17] In each of the walls, except the one leading to the passage, is an opening, giving access to a cell. These openings were sealed with large stones. Each cell was therefore a burial-chamber. It is likely that Maes Howe was a great family mausoleum.[18]

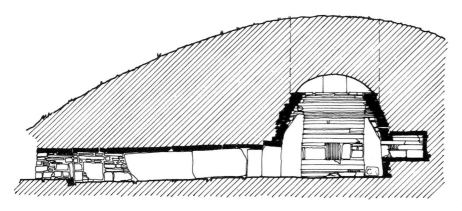

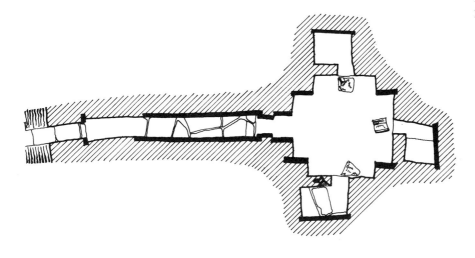

Fig. 1 Section and Plan of Maes Howe, Orkney. Note the long passage lined with huge stones, and the rectangular chamber with pseudo-vault. (*The Author*)

0 1 2 3 4 5 6 m.

Plate 6 The lofty central chamber of Maes Howe, Orkney. To the right is the entrance to one of the tomb-chambers, to the left is the entrance to the passageway. Note the corbelled pseudo-vault (see Fig. 1), corner pier, and large monolith (*Crown Copyright: reproduced by permission of the Department of the Environment*)

The tomb's stone structure was made possible by the ease of quarrying the curious laminated stone of Orkney. The interior is of very considerable interest because of the existence of Viking Runic inscriptions, probably incised in the twelfth century of our era.

The formal, symmetrical arrangement of Maes Howe, like many chamber-tombs in other parts of the world, is an essential part of architectural designs for a celebration of death. The serenity, the sense of repose, and the wholeness of such works of architecture are contributory factors to the success of monumental design. There is no hint of the trivial, no mawkish sentimentality, in the greatest works that celebrate death.[19] A completeness, a balance, a stillness, and an ineffable perfection in the finished work characterize the best of funerary architecture (Fig. 1).

Orkney is exceedingly rich in the architecture of death, and cairns of considerable variety exist. These have very similar features including stone-built burial-chambers divided into compartments, with an entrance passage of varying length, but normally very constricted. The whole tomb was covered with a grassy mound. Generally, the walls of the chambers converge as they get higher, by a system of corbelling. Two main types of cairn exist, of which Maes Howe is one example. The first type has a main chamber, with side-chambers or cells opening off it, approached by a long passage within the earth mound; the second main type consists of a narrow, elongated chamber subdivided by upright slabs of stone, and is known as a 'stalled cairn' (Figs. 2, 3). Burial in Orkney was generally by inhumation, but cremation was not unknown. The Orcadian tombs are products of a widespread megalithic culture, and are similar to burial-chambers found throughout southern Europe, especially in the Mediterranean lands. However, this does not mean that there was any direct connection. It would seem that many ancient cultures found similar architectural solutions to an identical problem: that of housing, commemorating, and protecting the dead and giving them shelter in preparation for some future existence.

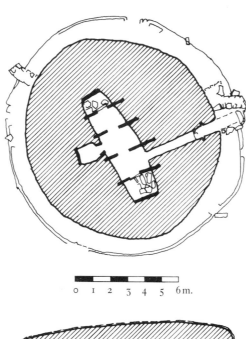

Fig. 2 Plan of Onston Chambered Cairn, Orkney. Note the subdivision of the main chamber by large upright flagstones (*The Author*)

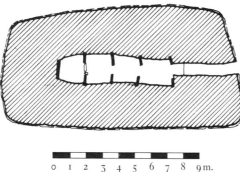

Fig. 3 Plan of Yarso Stalled Cairn, Rousay. The interior is subdivided by upright stones (*The Author*)

    The impact of ancient tombs in the haunting landscapes of Ireland is considerable, and a sense of another remote, invisible world is hard to overcome when visiting such burial-places. Many portal-dolmens can be seen throughout Ireland, consisting of upright stones on which is a monolithic slab-roof. These dolmens are the central single chambers of what were once burial-mounds. The earth mounds have disappeared, leaving only the stark architecture of the tomb-chambers themselves. A fine example of a portal-dolmen can be found at Proleek, Co. Louth. Such dolmens are now thought to date from the end of the Neolithic period (Pl. 7).

Plate 7 The portal-dolmen at Proleek, Co. Louth (*Commissioners of Public Works in Ireland*)

The court-graves and passage-graves appear to be earlier, dating from about the third millennium BC. The long wedge-shaped or trapezoidal barrows may have been introduced from the Continent in about the second millennium, but before that, even in the fourth millennium, the distinctive court-graves of Ulster and Connacht were being built. They consist of galleries, usually divided, built of stone slabs, set in elongated cairns. These galleries open to a central unroofed court, usually roughly pear-shaped in plan, round which is stonework. These graves functioned not only as burial-places, but as holy shrines for fertility rites. Sometimes the courts were only semi-circular, and were placed at one or both ends of the cairn. The long shape of these cairns may derive from the long barrows of England or from some ancestry common to both Irish and English cultures of prehistory. Fine court-graves are found at Malinmore, Co. Donegal, and at Browndod, Co. Antrim.

Many of the finest Irish tombs are in the magnificent necropolis known as the Bend of the Boyne, in Co. Meath. This megalithic cemetery had a type of tomb that was very different from the court-graves. Generally, the best of

the Bend of the Boyne tombs are roofed with high corbelled vaults, are constructed to a cruciform plan, and have long entrance-passages. The whole structure is protected by a large circular mound, and is usually sited on high ground. The best of these passage-graves have considerable numbers of stones carved with spirals, circles, lozenges, and other designs that suggest the intricacies of Irish Celtic art of a much later date. These roofed structures are not dissimilar to other tombs in Spain and in Brittany, but are unique in their profusion of decoration.

Irish passage-graves seem to have been built mostly between 2500 and 2000 BC, and the best examples number about three hundred. While New Grange is the most splendid, Fourknocks, in the Delvin Valley, Co. Meath, is of considerable interest. It is a passage-grave within an elliptical mound that is contained by a low rubble wall. A passage leads to the central chamber off which are three recesses, in the cruciform plan-shape usual in such tombs. The size of the central chamber (6.5 × 5.5m.) precluded a corbelled vault over the whole room. A timber scaffold was probably erected in the centre to support some corbelling that sprang from the perimeter of the chamber. The whole was probably roofed with turf (Pl. 8).

New Grange is the grandest of these passage-graves, and has a mound

Plate 8 The interior of the mound of Fourknocks, Co. Meath. This pear-shaped chamber has subsidiary chambers opening off it (*Commissioners of Public Works in Ireland*)

some eighty-five metres in diameter. This mound was surrounded by a circle of standing-stones. A passage led to a main chamber with three subsidiary rooms off it, a similar plan to that of Maes Howe and other passage-graves. The passage itself is lined with dressed stone, and there is much carved decoration. The main chamber has a corbelled vault, some six metres high, built with an architectural verve and mastery that are unusual (Pl. 9). The stone that originally closed the tomb is elaborately carved with spiral decorations that resemble those in the main chamber itself. Over the entrance is a decorated lintel. Other similar tombs exist in the vicinity of New Grange, the finest of which is probably Knowth, with its magnificent central chamber.

The best of the ancient tombs in the British Isles are of the tumulus (circular) kind, not dissimilar in basic arrangement to Mycenaean *tholoi* types. Many round barrows exist in Wessex, in Wiltshire, and in Dorset, where there is an especially fine group of circular barrows at Oakley Down. The best examples of chamber-tombs in England are those of the West Country, and the internal arrangement of passages lined with stones, with chambers on either side, seems to be a variant of previous types discussed. The finest barrows in England containing built structures of tombs and passageways are the long barrows of Somerset, Berkshire, Wiltshire, and Gloucestershire. At Stony Littleton in Somerset there is an excellent example of a trapezoid long barrow with three pairs of chambers off a central passage, and one chamber at the end of the passage.

Wayland's Smithy in Berkshire is another example of a long trapezoidal barrow-tomb. In the centre is a large enclosure floored with stone slabs. This enclosure was a wooden structure that protected fourteen burials. This was covered with a small mound. At a later date, a trapezoidal barrow was constructed over this, with a retaining boundary of stone slabs. At the southern end was a gallery with three chambers arranged in a cruciform pattern, not unlike the plan of other tombs, but less sophisticated than Maes Howe. The entrance had a grandly impressive façade, some three metres high, made of stone slabs.

Belas Knap in Gloucestershire has a huge long barrow ($55 \times 18 \times 14$ m.) with a horned northern end containing a false entrance. The real chambers are on either side of the barrow.[20] It would therefore appear that grave-robbing was not unknown even to the Neolithic peoples of Britain. A feature of funeral practices in several cultures seems to have been the placing of a statue or stone or inscription to guard the tomb. Egyptian tombs often held guardian warriors, while standing stones are found by megalithic tombs in parts of Europe. Some standing stones may represent figures, and so may form a guardian group around a tomb, as at New Grange in Ireland. The Ogham-inscribed stones of pre-Christian Ireland seem to have had some commemorative or even guardian purpose, and were superseded, like other standing stones, by Christian crosses. The High Crosses of Ireland are supreme examples of this transfiguration, and, though not tombstones themselves, have a significance of guardianship, casting an aura of hallowedness round them. In many cases in parts of Europe pagan standing stones were 'Christianized' by having the cross and other symbols inscribed on them.

19

The earlier stone circles often surround burial-places and frequently have associated ditches and banks. The Giant's Ring near Ballycairn, in Co. Down, has a dolmen in the centre of a spectacular earthwork ring. However, such monuments, like court-graves, also doubled as places for ritual. In later times, standing stones became recognizably anthropomorphic, like the curious two-sided stones that guard the graveyard at Boa Island, Co. Fermanagh. While these Janus-headed stones may be idols, they could conceivably be developments of the guardian stone, and are suitably sinister to deter intruders.

Throughout early civilizations, the celebration of death has left many superb buildings and monuments. In some cases the tombs have been the most substantial survivals of ancient cultures. Man has lavished wealth and art on providing tombs for himself and his family in many periods. One of the richest developments was that of the Graeco-Roman world, and it is to those cultures that I now turn.

Plate 9 The main chamber of New Grange, Co. Meath, showing the passage-entrance, corbelling, and spiral decorations that resemble those on the stone marking the entrance (*Commissioners of Public Works in Ireland*)

2

The buildings, cemeteries, gardens, and sculptures associated with death in the Graeco-Roman world.

Mycenae; Attica; the Hellenic and Hellenistic periods; Xanthos; the great mausolea; Etruscan funerary; architecture; and a celebration of death in Rome and in the Roman Empire

Painting and Sculpture are but images,
Are merely shadows cast by outward things
On stone or canvas, having in themselves
No separate existence. Architecture,
Existing in itself, and not in seeming
A something it is not, surpasses them
As Substance shadow.

LONGFELLOW *Michael Angelo*. i, sec. 2, l. 54

Greek culture profoundly influenced the development of European funerary architecture, notably that of the Etruscans, and, later, that of the Romans. Greece is thus one of the main sources of architectural inspiration throughout Western European history, although Egyptian motifs began to recur from Renaissance times.

Some of the most remarkable funerary buildings are found among the *tholoi* tombs of Mycenae. Each building is of stone, and consists of a circular chamber with a corbelled roof known as the *tholos*, the grave-pits being in the floor. In two such tombs there are subsidiary chambers attached to the *tholos*, which was usually covered with a great mound of earth contained within a retaining wall. There was a long corridor called the *dromos* that led into the chamber. This *dromos* was filled after each funeral. The door to the *tholos* was usually grand, and is especially monumental at the so-called Treasury of Atreus.

Most Mycenaean *tholoi* tombs date from the sixteenth century BC, usually from about 1600 to 1200. The large tombs are thought to be for royalty or for important families of the ruling classes. Like most large tombs of antiquity, these great buildings have been denuded of their contents by robbers. The Minoan civilization of Crete may have influenced the development of the Mycenaean tombs.

The nine celebrated *tholoi* tombs of Mycenae are placed fairly close together. According to Wace[1] these can be divided into three groups. The first has tombs with a rock-cut *dromos*, unlined with any additional material. Lintels are the straight type, with no relieving structures above. The *tholos* itself is constructed of rubble. The second has a rock-cut *dromos* lined with ashlar and/or rubble. Lintels have a relieving triangular 'arch' above them. The *tholos* is built of rubble, with dressings of ashlar at door-jambs and at a plinth level. The third has a *dromos* lined with ashlar, and doorways are

Fig. 1 Reconstruction of the decorative treatment at the entrance to the *Tholos* of the 'Treasury of Atreus' at Mycenae (*Trustees of the British Museum*)

Plate 1 *Dromos* and entrance to the Treasury of Atreus at Mycenae. Note the triangular corbelling above the lintel (*Peter Clayton*)

finely dressed and monumental. Two tombs had engaged columns flanking the doorcase. Lintels were surmounted by a relieving triangular 'arch', richly decorated. The *tholos* itself is built entirely of ashlar.

The finest of all tombs at Mycenae is the Treasury of Atreus, also known as the Tomb of Agamemnon. The *dromos* faces east, and is heroic in scale, being six metres wide and thirty-six metres long (Pl. 1). The doorcase is exceptionally impressive. Like Egyptian openings, the doorway is battered, and is narrower at the top. Above the lintel is a relieving triangle enriched with scroll designs and strings. On either side of the doorway were engaged marble columns decorated with a zigzag motif not dissimilar to later Norman work (Fig. 1). The doors were probably of bronze, or of timber clad with bronze.[2] The *tholos* itself (about 14m. in diameter, and 13m. high) is constructed of finely cut stone. The central chamber is covered with a pseudo-dome of rings of stone corbelled inwards, a familiar method found in tombs from Orkney to Asia Minor (Fig. 2). Off the central chamber is a square tomb-chamber. The interiors of these tombs were decorated with rosettes of bronze. The whole tomb was covered with a mound at the base of which was a retaining wall. Wace says that the 'unknown master of the Bronze Age who designed and built the Treasury of Atreus deserves to rank with the great architects of the world'.[3]

Tholoi tombs of considerable grandeur, as well as rock-cut chamber-tombs, were known throughout the Mycenaean world. Kurtz and

23

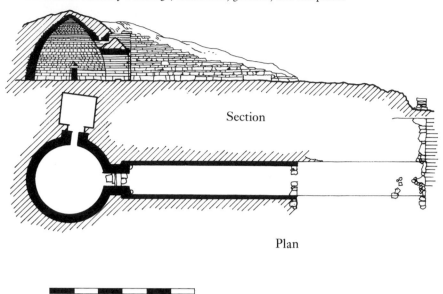

Fig. 2 The *tholos* tomb, known as the 'Treasury of Atreus', Mycenae. Note the long passage, or *dromos*, and the circular chamber with pseudo-dome (*The Author*)

Section

Plan

0   5   10   15   20   25   30 m.

Boardman have noted that although offerings of food, drink, weapons, jewellery, and other objects were placed in tombs, the Mycenaeans do not appear to have been afraid of the dead, for tombs were re-opened, bodies were moved, and, after rites of fumigation, further burials took place.[4] The dead were buried in the floors of the main chambers and in the *dromoi*. Any rites were carried out at the time of burial, and not subsequently, for there does not appear to have been a cult of the dead. Re-use of graves seems to have been usual in Greek cemeteries, but always offerings were left as a mark of respect.[4]

Earth-graves, lined and covered with stone slabs, were known in the Bronze Age, and single inhumations were known as well as the multiple burials in *tholoi* tombs. By the tenth century BC, cremation was usual in Greek burial customs, and burial of the ashes was in an urn. The spot was marked by a small mound. Athens developed a series of roads that linked settlements in Attica, and burials were near these roads, with concentrations of graves near gates. From the ninth century BC cremation and inhumation were practised. Often, graves were marked by vases or urns, but these had a limited life, and were the models for later stone urns on plinths or other pedestals. Graves in Ancient Greece were also marked by upright slabs of stone, or *stelai*, plain or decorated. The so-called Archaic period in Attica was a time during which funerary art and architecture flourished, and cremation usually took place in the actual grave. Earth mounds over graves were of considerable size, and were erected over both cremations and inhumations. Crowning markers were built on top of the mounds, usually of the *stelai* type. Built tombs are also known from the Archaic period, but these were usually of simple form. Gravestones consisted of *stelai* or of sculptured figures, and usually incorporate short inscriptions. Before the end of the sixth century, however, funerary art became much more modest, probably because of economic reasons that required legislation to restrict expenditure on memorials. Indeed, gravestones with relief decoration incorporating figures were not generally made after the sixth until the end of the fifth centuries. Cicero tells us that laws were passed expressing limits on the size and type of monuments to discourage Athenian display.

During the Classical period of Greek culture, both cremation and inhumation continued. Cenotaphs were erected to those whose bodies could not be recovered, and elaborate tombs and cenotaphs were built to commemorate state celebrities. Offerings of a personal nature became common, and pedimented gravestones with sculptured reliefs were usual. Rectangular built tombs surmounted by *stelai* and by gravestones became common, and lined the roads. An Athenian burial of the fourth century BC was commemorated by a stone monument that consisted of a circular drum supporting a *loutrophorus* (marble vase) flanked by two projecting wings at the ends of which were two guardian dogs. Although this is grand enough to be a state burial, and is in an area where state burials abound, it is apparently not one of them. State burials were elaborate affairs, and were commemorated each year.

Stelai decorated with vases, columns supporting urns, sculpture in the round, and pedimented gravestones were other types of classical marker that were to have great influence on later European developments in funerary art. Beautiful capitals incorporating volutes, palmettes, and acanthus leaves are found on *stelai* (Pl. 2). Family graves were often enclosed with walls or other markers.[4]

After battles, the dead were usually buried on the spot, and were commemorated by a mound on which *stelai* with inscriptions were set up. If a General in war failed to provide for the burial of the slain, he was deemed guilty of a capital offence. Burial of the dead was not refused, even to an enemy, for an unburied body was an offence to man and to god. Athenians in the Classical period brought the bodies or bones of heroes back to Athens for burial. A seated lion marks the communal grave of the victims of the battle of Chaeronea of 338 BC. In this case the bodies had been neatly laid out in rows, with offerings, within an enclosure. Where individuals died abroad, the body might be cremated and the ashes brought home. Where no body existed, a ritual burial of a statue or bust might take place within a cenotaph.

Early sarcophagi appear to have derived from stone cists, or even from wooden coffins in some instances. Some early Greek sarcophagi have affinities with Egyptian prototypes, and indeed sarcophagi were commonest in the eastern part of the Greek world. The celebrated sarcophagi of Sidon are perhaps the finest of all those decorated by Greeks, but different types of sarcophagi exist. The Lycian type was in the form of the famous and distinctive house-tombs of Lycia, with their pitched convex roofs. Anthropoid sarcophagi, temple-sarcophagi, and other types are also found. It should be noted that the term *sarkophagos* means 'a flesh-eater', and described a limestone coffin which dissolved flesh quickly, although it was not a word used in Classical times.

During the Hellenistic periods, monumental funerary architecture became common, usually in the form of ambitious chamber-tombs. From this period, belief in the immortality of the individual gained ground, and the example of Alexander the Great even encouraged a claim to divinity that owed much to Egyptian religion. Alexander's own background was Macedonian, and the tombs of that area were covered with earth mounds incorporating a *dromos* approach. The façades of tombs had monumental doorcases, and often have columnar arrangements with pediments despite the fact that they were concealed with earth. Plans of tombs usually included an antechamber behind the façade, with a burial-chamber behind that. The dead were laid out on *klinai*, or couches, that sometimes had lids. The

Plate 2 Various Greek tombstones and *stelai*. These became the inspiration for many Neoclassical designs of the nineteenth century. (*Author's Collection*)

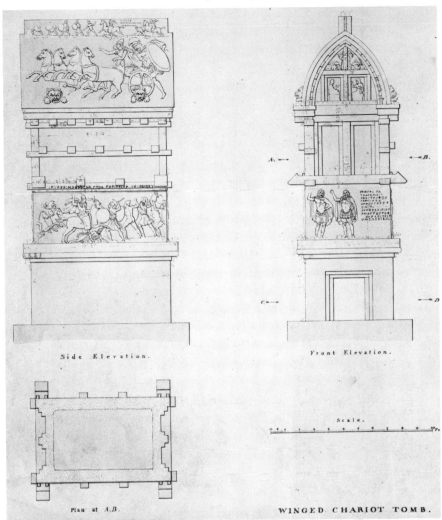

Side Elevation.

Front Elevation.

Scale.

Plan at A.B.

WINGED CHARIOT TOMB.

Plate 3 Drawing by George Scharf of the tomb of Payava at Xanthos of the first half of the fourth century BC. Note the high curved roof, the whole form being reminiscent of later Gothic tombs (*Trustees of the British Museum*)

burial-chambers were usually vaulted, and the decorations and layout recall aspects of domestic architecture. The couch on which the dead lay suggests the *koimeterion*, or sleeping-place. Thessalonian tombs often had pseudo-vaults not unlike Mycenaean *tholoi* tombs, and similar forms may be found in Thrace and elsewhere in the Greek world. Hellenistic tombs often had monumental fronts with sophisticated architectural façades.[5]

The Hellenic style of architecture that followed the Mycenaean period is generally recognized as the true 'Greek' architecture, and is essentially columnar and trabeated. It thus had a character in which the structural system was obvious, and was uncomplicated by arches, by vaults, and by domes, unlike the pseudo-vaulted tombs of Mycenae. Early Hellenic architecture is archaic and severe, strongly influenced by Mycenae. Gradually, however, further refinements took place, and columns, capitals, mouldings, and details reached an astonishing degree of inspiration and delicacy.

Architectural developments in later Hellenistic times, however, were considerable, and tombs in Asia Minor were often constructed above

27

ground. These tombs usually consist of a large podium carrying a decorated upperwork, and a gabled roof. Pyramidal roofs are not uncommon. This type of tomb in its basic form is simply an elevated sarcophagus with a roof, and in its elaborate metamorphosis is an ornate mausoleum of the Halicarnassos type.

The Lycian tombs of the Persian period were decorated by Greeks. The best examples of these Lycian tombs are from the great necropolis at Xanthos, and consist of chambers set on top of a high podium. From about the fifth century BC, Lycian sarcophagi were built on podia which were constructed in the form of timber buildings. The Harpy tomb of c. 470 BC consisted of a funerary pier in the form of a large pedestal, with a frieze around the top under a heavy cornice. The chamber containing the burial was at the top of the pier. The tombs of Merehi of Lycia (400 BC) and of Payava (c. 360 BC), both at Xanthos, are of the typical Lycian type, that is with a high rectangular base surmounted by a tomb-chamber. Over this is a convex-sided roof meeting at a ridge, with gable-ends (Pl. 3).[6]

The Nereid tomb from Xanthos (c. 400 BC) was the tomb of a Lycian chieftain and took the form of a small Ionic temple on a high podium. It was the largest of the Lycian tombs brought to London by Charles Fellows in the nineteenth century. There was a *cella* (containing *klinai*) with a peristyle of six columns on each side, and four at each end. This was similar in basic arrangement to later Roman temple-tombs such as that shown on a marble relief from the Haterii tomb. Round the top of the podium were two friezes depicting battle-scenes between Greeks and others, possibly Persians. The cornice of the podium is enriched with egg-and-dart mouldings. Above this cornice stood the Ionic peristyle which carried a sculptured frieze without an architrave. The pediments also contained sculptured reliefs, and statues of female figures stood between the columns. These figures included the Nereids, from which the tomb derived its name. The pediments were also surmounted by sculptured groups (Pl. 4). This exquisite tomb helped to establish a pattern for later tombs in Asia Minor, and its most celebrated derivative at Halicarnassos was known as one of the Seven Wonders of the ancient world.[7]

The Mausoleum at Halicarnassos was erected in memory of King Mausolos of Caria by his sister-widow, Artemisia, in about 353 BC. From the king's name the title 'mausoleum' is derived to describe any monumental tomb. It consisted of a rectangular podium that supported a tomb-chamber or upper structure with a peristyle of thirty-six columns. It was surmounted by a pyramidal stepped roof at the apex of which was a quadriga and group of statues. The architects were Satyros and Pythios, and the sculptors are thought to be Scopas (east frieze), Bryaxis (north frieze), Timotheos (south frieze), and Leochares (west frieze), but the attributions are largely subjective. Pythios was responsible for the chariot. The vigour and splendour of this tomb may be understood from the fragments of sculpture in the British Museum. The Knights of St John used the stones of the Mausoleum to repair their castle in AD 1522. No further comment on the philistinism of many of the orders of Christian knights is necessary, especially when we recall the earlier sacking of Constantinople by

Plate 4 Reconstruction of the façade of the Nereid Tomb at Xanthos in Lycia of about 400 BC. This is one of the most refined of all classical tombs of the Graeco-Roman world (*Trustees of the British Museum*)

Crusaders. The Mausoleum at Halicarnassos has been the subject of many attempts at reconstruction. Descriptions by Pliny and by Vitruvius are strangely ambiguous and unsatisfactory, but evidence was obtained when the site was excavated by C. T. Newton and by Biliotti between 1857 and 1865. The whole site was eventually studied in depth by a team of Danish archaeologists under Kristian Jeppesen[8] in the 1950s. It appears that there were nine columns at each end, and eleven along each side. The Mausoleum was richly decorated with sculptures. The friezes depict battles between Greeks and Amazons, and between Lapiths and Centaurs. The third frieze shows a chariot-race, possibly part of funeral games. Jeppesen's researches indicated that the Amazon frieze was placed at the top of the podium, and so corresponds with the position of the battle-friezes of the Nereid monument. The Centaur-frieze may have enriched the base of the crowning chariot-group, while the chariot-frieze could have been inside the buildings or perhaps around the *cella* itself. It was this great Mausoleum, perhaps one of the finest tombs the world has ever seen, that set a fashion in Asia Minor for monumental tombs with a crowning stepped pyramid carried above a peristyle (Pl. 5).

Derived from the Mausoleum is the Lion Tomb at Cnidos, which was about half the height of the Halicarnassos tomb. It was built about the middle of the fourth century. Though much later than the *tholoi* tombs at Mycenae, it is related both to them and to the celebrated Mausoleum. The Cnidos tomb consisted of a square podium on which stood a square compartment surrounded by a Doric colonnade of engaged columns. Above

Plate 5 Reconstruction of the Mausoleum at Halicarnassos by the Danish Halicarnassos Expedition of 1977. Note the immense podium and the Ionic peristyle (*Professor Kristian Jeppesen*)

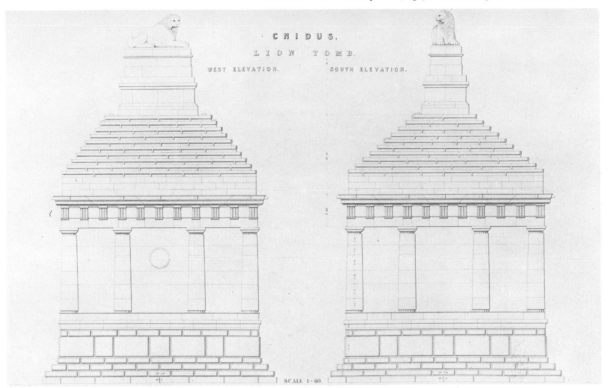

CNIDUS.

LION TOMB.

WEST ELEVATION.   SOUTH ELEVATION.

SCALE 1:60.

Plate 6 Reconstruction of the Lion Tomb at Cnidos. The Doric Order is engaged, and the pyramidal form is still evident (*Trustees of the British Museum*)

the entablature was a stepped pyramidal roof crowned with a recumbent lion (Pl. 6). The circular interior was roofed with a corbelled pseudo-dome. It is interesting to note that although the basic arrangement of this tomb is Hellenistic, certain archaic features survive, notably the pseudo-vault reminiscent of Mycenaean examples, and the stepped pyramid recalling both a tumulus and an Egyptian pyramid to mind. The sarcophagus from the Cnidos tomb is an exquisite object hewn from a solid block of marble. Other supreme examples of Greek sarcophagus design are the celebrated 'Alexander' sarcophagus, with panels of vigorous sculpture, and the beautiful 'Tomb of the Weepers' at Sidon. The latter is in the form of a miniature Ionic temple, with statues of mourners between the columns of the peristyle; it is not dissimilar in design to mediaeval altar-tombs where 'weepers' stand in niches under elaborate tabernacle-work (Pl. 7).

The Mausoleum at Halicarnassos, like the Cnidos tomb, seems possibly to have retained vestiges of the Mycenaean pseudo-vault for the interiors. This may have been partially from respect for tomb-design of the past, and partly from a consideration of structural expediency. The echoes of a pyramid-tumulus effect of the roof are also interesting.[9]

Another derivative of the Mausoleum was the tomb of Antiochus II at Belevi near Ephesus. The tomb-chamber was again vaulted, and there was a Corinthian peristyle. Elsewhere in Asia Minor, there were many tombs that owed something to the Halicarnassos prototype. Rock-cut tombs with classical façades derived from Macedonian tombs were also known in great numbers, but the façades were exposed rather than covered by tumuli, as

31

was the case in Macedonia itself. In some Macedonian examples, the architectural features were painted on the façade, as in the Lefkadia tomb, and the tumulus helped to preserve the decoration.

Rock-cut tombs of Asia Minor had their origins before any Greek influence was felt. The Persian rock-cut façades have already been mentioned. Columnar treatments are known in Asia Minor from the sixth century. In Lycia the emulation of timber construction is common, especially where the tall sarcophagus-tombs are encountered. Xanthos boasts only one façade with columns, but rock-cut columnar façades are found at Telmessos and elsewhere in Lycia. These façades incorporate antae, columns, entablatures, and pediments, with enrichments (Pls. 8, 9).

Apart from these tombs and the humbler burials, the *heroon* was not unknown, especially when the state elevated the dead to positions where their celebration was essential.[10] Cenotaph *heroa* were not unusual, but where *heroa* contained bodies, there was also a planned area for ritual purposes. Normally, the *heroon* consisted of the enclosed tomb within a walled sanctuary. At Miletus the burial chamber consisted of a vaulted room set within a tumulus. This mound was within a courtyard that was surrounded by rooms. The *heroon* for the family of Charmylos on Kos consisted of a two-storey building. The burial-chamber was on the ground floor, and the rooms for ritual were on the first floor. This *piano nobile*

Plate 7 Sarcophagus of the Weepers from Sidon. One of the most refined examples of a sarcophagus in architectural form (*Hirmer Fotoarchiv München*)

.*Opposite above*
Plate 8 Drawing by George Scharf of Lycian rock-cut tombs at Pinara of the fourth century BC. Note how structural elements, like beams, are expressed in the façade (*Trustees of the British Museum*)

Opposite below
Plate 9 Drawing by George Scharf of Lycian rock-cut tombs at Pinara of the fourth century BC (*Trustees of the British Museum*)

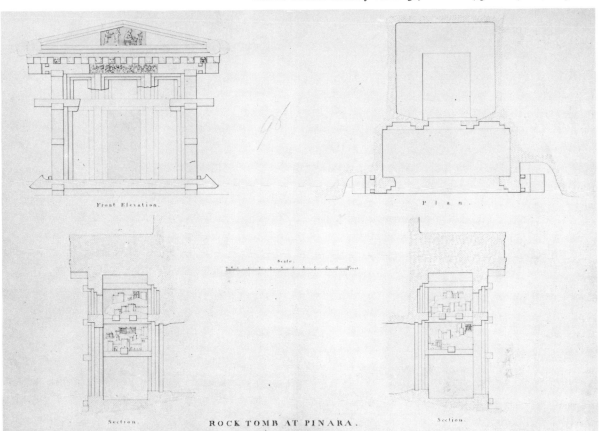

Front Elevation.

Plan.

Scale.

Section.

Section.

ROCK TOMB AT PINARA.

arrangement was rare.[11] As the dead achieved a new status in late-Hellenistic times, altars were set up at tombs, and sometimes tombs took the forms of altars. Several altars were set up in Alexandrian tombs, and the practice became common in Roman times. Indeed, Alexandria had extensive cemeteries, and these were the first to be called necropoleis. Monuments were generally of the *stelai* type, often painted, but tower-tombs were also common. Egyptian influences were only obvious at the end of the Ptolemaic period. Unquestionably the finest of Alexandrian necropoleis were underground, and combined elements of Macedonian tombs with those of the rock-cut tombs of Asia Minor.[6] The plans of these underground tombs were similar to those of houses of the period, and often featured open courtyards or light-wells. Sarcophagus-burials were made in great numbers, but most of the tombs have walls lined with *loculi* for the placing of ash-chests or urns. Painted decorations were common, and these Alexandrian tombs appear to have been the models for later Roman *hypogea* and catacombs. Rock-cut tombs with peristyles are also found in Cyprus. Occasionally, monumental tombs took the form of giant sarcophagi. At Cyrene, such a building contains a number of compartments for burial.

As Greek society became stable, fewer valuables were placed in graves or burned on pyres. Yet the Greeks concerned themselves with funerary architecture to a remarkable degree throughout history, and have left an incomparable legacy. The interesting fact about Greek burial custom is that the emotional aspects of severance were satisfied within observances that were essentially traditional, and which enabled grief to be expressed ritualistically. The house where a death had occurred, and those who inhabited it, were purified by ritual water after the funeral. The classical world of Greece appears to have had an attitude to death that satisfied basic emotional and aesthetic problems, while celebrating the fact of death in architecture and art of rare perfection. Quite apart from funerary architecture, the Greeks invented other monuments of considerable beauty to commemorate victories, events, or festivals. The Choragic Monument of Lysicrates in Athens (*c.* 335 BC) is a type of monument erected to support a tripod, as a prize for the winners of festivals of games, music, or theatre. It has a rusticated podium supporting a drum that is surrounded by Corinthian columns. These carry an entablature crowned by a saucer-shaped roof that is capped by a floral ornament. The capitals have a curious variation of an Egyptian lotus instead of the more conventional type of Corinthian cap. This building was to be an inspiration to designers of monuments from the eighteenth century onwards, and is typical of the potency of Greek invention in monumental architecture.[12]

Greek *tholoi* were built for a variety of structures. The celebrated *tholos* designed by Polycleitos at Epidauros in about 360 BC was perhaps the most famous. The Philippeion at Olympia (*c.* 335 BC) housed statues of the Macedonian royal family, so had something of the character of a commemorative building, as did the Arsinoeon at Samothrace of about 270 BC. *Tholoi* were in vogue in the Roman Empire following the construction of the mausoleum of Augustus, and late-Hellenistic and Graeco-Roman tombs followed the fashion. The most spectacular *tholoi*

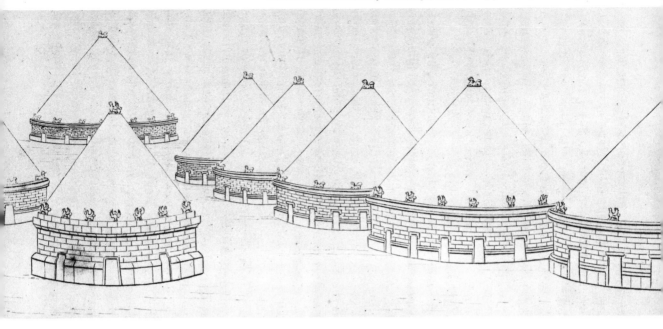

Plate 10 Restoration of the Etruscan Necropolis at Tarquinia. From Gray, Mrs Hamilton *Tour to the Sepulchres of Etruria in 1839* London 1841 (*Author's Collection*)

tombs of a late-Greek influence are found in Algeria. The great circular tomb at Medracen has an Order of engaged Doric columns all the way round it, but much larger still is the Tombeau de la Chrétienne near Cherchel, the capital city which Juba II started to build in AD 25. This, too, has an Order of engaged columns reminiscent of the arrangement at Epidauros.

Both cremation and inhumation were practised by the Etruscans. One of the earliest of tomb-forms used for the burial of cremated remains by the Etruscans was a cylindrical shaft at the bottom of which was an urn. Early trench-graves, usually associated with interment, but sometimes involving cremated remains, were rectangular, and often contained furniture and effects. From this trench-tomb probably evolved the characteristic Etruscan chamber-tomb.[13] These rectangular or sometimes circular compartments were often covered by conical mounds, and were usually partly rock-cut and partly constructed of masonry. They were often surrounded by several smaller rooms that opened off them, and were approached from the edge of the earth mound by a long *dromos* or corridor. These monumental tombs, each covered by a tumulus, had masonry ring-walls, with plinths (Pl. 10). They are architecturally of great significance as a model for the imperial tombs of Hadrian and Augustus, and are not unrelated to burial-chambers elsewhere in Europe, as was seen in the previous chapter. The great Etruscan cemeteries at Tarquinia, Volterra, and Caere (Cerveteri) must have been extraordinary sights in their pristine state, with several large-scale tumuli surmounting the tombs themselves. From the centuries before 400 BC, when Etruscan city-states dominated central Italy, the Po valley, and Campania, the huge tumuli of the cemeteries were erected. They changed the landscapes around the cities dramatically. It is interesting to note that the corridors of these tombs were often roofed with primitive vaults of corbelled courses of masonry. The disposition of tomb-chambers around the central chamber or on either side of the corridor was always symmetrical, and the plans are severely formal, a characteristic of much funerary architecture, even when developed by relatively early cultures. Often, the tomb-chambers were decorated with frescoes, and the interior décor was similar to that of rooms for the living. Clearly, the Etruscans wanted to make their dead feel as comfortable as possible, a not unusual desire in ancient civilizations, as we have seen. At Vulci, for example, many elaborate tombs exist, while one extraordinary monument, known as the Cucumella, consisted of a vast cone of earth that was encircled at its base by

Plate 11 Etruscan tombs at Vulci. *Top*: the Cucumella, with the two towers that probably originally carried the statuary; *middle*: plan of a chamber-tomb; *bottom*: a section through a chamber-tomb. From Gray, Mrs Hamilton *op. cit* (*Author's Collection*)

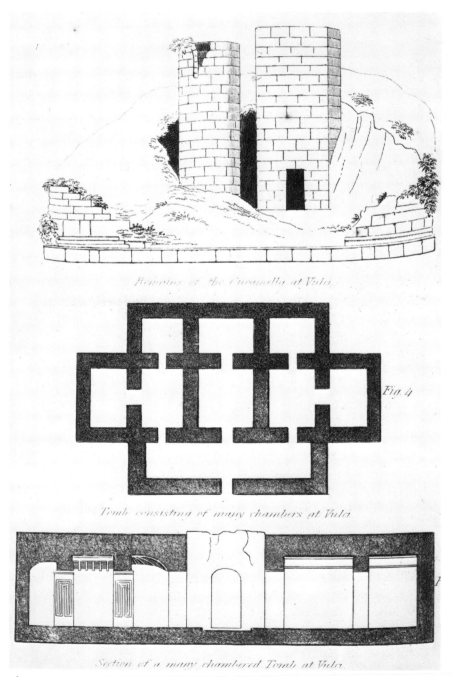

Remains of the Cucumella at Vulci.

Fig. 4

Tomb consisting of many chambers at Vulci.

Section of a many chambered Tomb at Vulci.

a girdle of masonry. Inside the cone of earth were coarsely built towers of masonry, probably built as supports for crowning statuary (Pl. 11).[14] Mrs Hamilton Gray described the remains in 1841.[14]

Tombs not covered with mounds often stood, alone or in groups, within walls, and give the appearance of planned villages. The cemetery at Caere (Cerveteri) has a principal street, and the plan of the necropolis is not unlike that of the Roman city of Ostia. Vulci has regular rows of tombs, and has a recognizable plan and layout, similar to towns for the living. Plans of individual tombs were usually formal in arrangement, and interiors were elaborately decorated.

Etruscan tombs offered grand receptacles for the dead. Often, ashes were deposited in terracotta containers with anthropomorphic shapes, the so-called 'Canopic' urns. Terracotta or bronze cinerary urns were also made to resemble houses, figures, or even circular tomb-like shapes. From the fourth century, ash-chests of stone or terracotta, highly decorated with reliefs, and surmounted by reclining figures, were usual. The tomb of the Atian family at Volterra is an interesting specimen of a large family tomb, with terracotta ash-chests placed around the wall and the central column of this circular rock-cut enclosure. The high level of sophistication is here apparent. Indeed, Volterra has several examples of the circular, or *tholos* type of tomb, with the roof carried on a central pier. Some of these are wholly rock-cut, while others are of masonry. In the latter case the walls are built up, and corbelled pseudo-vaults are constructed of concentric rings of stone slabs. The centre is carried on a column of roughly hewn stone. One of the best examples is the *tholos* tomb at Casal Marittimo. The phallic imagery may have no significance, and the column is simply a reinforcement at the centre. Similar *tholoi*, or beehive tombs are found in Greece, and I have already mentioned some of the most important examples.

Another fine Etruscan tomb of the tumulus type, with a long *dromos*, and a *tholos* with a central pillar, occurs near Vetulonia at the Pietrera tomb. This had a pseudo-vault of corbelled stone, with squinches to enable a circular dome to be placed over a square compartment. The upper chamber was decorated with Etruscan reliefs showing the dead in antique Greek style.

The Etruscan necropolis at Orvieto has tombs above ground in a terrace of small mausolea. These have doors and very simple façades. The roofs had a light layer of earth superimposed, and cone-shaped structures were erected on the roofs. Rectangular tombs with pitched roofs, and also circular tombs were known in Etruscan times, undoubtedly being models for later Roman developments. Rock-cut tombs were often plain on the outside, but occasionally had façades decorated with columns and entablatures. Although the Romans in central Italy cut similar tombs for themselves the façades were usually very simple. Lavish display at the entrances to rock-cut tombs is found in the later Roman sepulchres on the eastern fringes of the Empire, and some of these will be mentioned later.

One of the finest Etruscan rock-cut tombs is that of the Volumnii near Perugia. The tomb is approached through a simple aediculated opening, and the plan is similar to that of a Roman house. Timber beams and rafters

are simulated in the carved stone. The accommodation consists of an *atrium*, a main room or *tablinum*, and other small chambers. This tomb was intended to function for several generations, but the decorations were not completed, and burials only took place in the *tablinum*. Marble and stone ash-chests, of rare beauty, rest in the *tablinum* (Pl. 12).

Etruscan tombs and cemeteries were always outside the towns and cities. The cemeteries near Tarquinia have numerous tumuli. Like other cemeteries in Asia Minor, the Tarquinia tumuli have retaining walls and a *dromos*. One of the largest cemeteries at Tarquinia is about five kilometres long and one kilometre wide. Many painted tombs feature trees, plants, animals, and other soothing images from daily life. From about 550–470 BC a number of these tombs with exquisitely painted interiors was erected. The Tomb of the Bulls is one of the earliest, and features Achilles ambushing Troilus as the main subject. The tomb is named from the representation of bulls on the frieze, beside which are paintings of couples enjoying copulation. The internal arrangements of these tombs were simple, and consisted of entrance chambers with smaller chambers behind.

From 470 BC refinements in Etruscan art produced some exquisite tombs, of which one of the most elegant is the Tomb of the Leopards, named from the two leopards that decorate the pediment of the wall of the burial chamber. The main scene is of a banquet, with musicians and bearers. Other fine mural decorations have survived. Mrs Hamilton Gray arranged for

Plate 12 Tomb of the Volumnii, Perugia. The ash-chests are in the *tablinum*. Note the emulation of a timber roof (*Mansell-Alinari Collection*)

Opposite above Plate 13 The enchanting decorations of the interior of the Grotta della Querciola at Tarquinia. From Gray, Mrs Hamilton. *op. cit.* (*Author's Collection*)

Opposite below Plate 14 The beautiful painted interior of the Grotta del Triclinio at Tarquinia. From Gray, Mrs Hamilton *op. cit.* (*Author's Collection*)

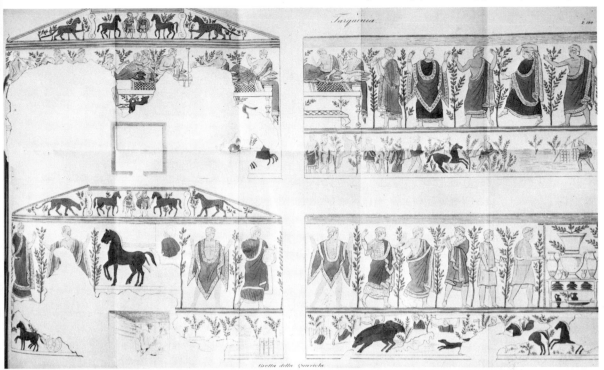

illustrations of some of these to be produced for her celebrated book, and examples of two tomb-interiors are illustrated here. The first, the Grotta Querciola, is ravishingly beautiful, and features a banquet with musicians and dancers, a boar-hunt, and other sports. The Grotta del Triclinio also features a banquet with somewhat more animated dancers (Pls. 13, 14).

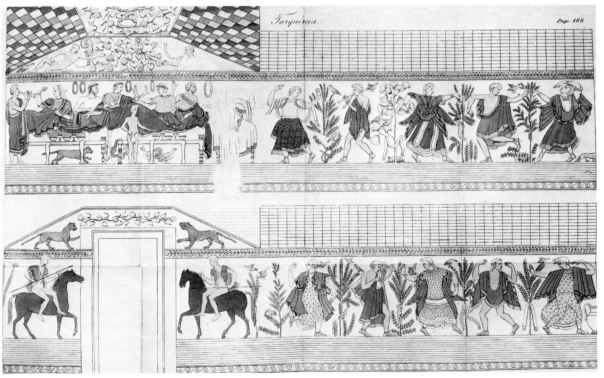

At the neighbouring city of Cerveteri were several necropoleis of very considerable importance. One of the finest tombs is the Regolini-Galassi tomb of about 650 BC. This was a great tumulus containing several burial-chambers with a diameter of forty-seven metres. The passages were roofed with pseudo-barrel-vaults. This tomb contained bodies on beds, with gold and silver jewellery, dishes, tripods, a chariot, weapons, vases, and shields. Many of the bronze objects had a markedly Neoclassical style with Egyptian influences in the ornament. The Banditaccia cemetery at Cerveteri contains many tombs of the tumulus type strung along the principal sepulchral way. Many of these tombs were finely furnished, and contained painted reliefs.

Greek architecture, in its purest form, was to influence the designers of tombs in the eighteenth and nineteenth centuries, but it was Rome that led the field in example for two millennia. Egypt, too, had its influence, and, like Greece, was to provide potent models for architects and artists of the later times. Motifs, such as pyramids, obelisks, and sphinxes, though known to the Romans, became part of the language of Neoclassicism as a whole, and were features of many designs for a celebration of death during the late-eighteenth and early-nineteenth centuries.

Death, and the disposal of the dead, have been aspects of social life that played an important part in the lives of all peoples who lived under Roman rule or who were under the influence of Rome, and so it has been ever since. The inheritors of Rome, in Europe and in the New World, all owe an immense debt to Roman culture for the great legacy of funerary architecture that has been handed down. Roman funerary ritual and customs, the planning of Roman cemeteries, the design of tombs, and the art of monumental sculpture were important aspects of Graeco-Roman civilization. Roman culture, in funerary matters, perhaps owed more to Etruscan culture than to the Greeks. There were, however, many aspects of Greek art and architecture that influenced the Roman world in the design of funerary artefacts, notably the sarcophagi.

Roman tombs were places where the dead 'resided', in a sense, and so, like Etruscan tombs, they sometimes resembled the houses of the living. Cicero and Pliny both tell us that inhumation, rather than cremation, was the rite of early Rome, but by the fifth century BC both methods were used. Lucretius mentions that embalmment was also practised in the era of the late Republic. Many families favoured earth burial long after cremation had become the commonest method of disposal of the dead, including the Gens Cornelia, of which Sulla was apparently the first member to be burned. In several family tombs, sarcophagi and ash-chests are found together. When the Empress Poppaea was buried, it was regarded as extraordinary, for cremation was the Roman custom during the first century of our era. From the second century AD, inhumation gradually ousted cremation as a favoured method, and the art of carving elaborate sarcophagi developed to a great degree.[15] A growing belief in an agreeable after-life (not confined to Christians) tended to favour the placing of bodies in sarcophagi rather than to encourage drastic destruction by burning. Embalming, though known, was regarded as a foreign, un-Roman custom, and was not favoured, though Poppaea was embalmed. Other preserved bodies have been found, and it may be that the cults of Isis and other Egyptian deities encouraged preservation of bodies in this way, especially among Romans who had seen service in Egypt.[15]

The disposal of Roman dead took place outside the cities, although emperors and important personages could receive special treatment. The majority of Romans had their remains buried in tombs strung along the roads beyond city gates. The poor were deposited in the earth. Semitic peoples, early Christians, and some others were laid on shelves known as *loculi* cut in the rock of catacombs. Richer persons were placed in sarcophagi of lead, marble, stone, terracotta, or timber, and the sarcophagi were themselves laid in chamber-tombs or were buried. In the case of cremations, the corpse and bier were consumed by fire at a cremation-ground known as the *ustrinum*, or at the tomb where the ashes were to be placed.[15] A last valediction was thrice uttered by the attendants. This usually took the form of '*Vale, vale, nos te ordine quo natura permittet sequamur.*' (The early Christians sprinkled earth three times on the body before inhumation.) After the *rogus* or pyre had burned down, the remains were cooled with wine, collected, and placed in ash-chests of marble, stone, lead, terracotta, or wood. Vases, urns, and pots also served as receptacles. These containers were either placed in niches in columbaria, within chamber-tombs, or simply buried. The *funus imperatorium* was a lavish affair, and culminated in the burning of the body on a huge decorated pyre, often built in stages, and decorated with hangings, paintings, statuary, and other enrichments.

An important aspect of Roman practice was the cult of the dead. Roses, food, and drink were offered at the tombs; family occasions, such as the birthday of the dead, were celebrated at the grave. Lamps were lighted at the grave on the kalends, ides, and nones of each month, a practice that has been transmogrified into common use at Roman Catholic cemeteries in southern Europe today. Festivals of the dead were held in February and May, when gifts were brought to the tomb and rituals were carried out to ensure that hungry ghosts with no relatives, as well as the dangerous *larvae*, were pacified.

Roman cities had necropoleis, always outside the walls. These usually were developed in association with the roads that led from the gates to the open country. Roadside cemeteries, like those of the Via Appia Antica outside Rome, were a familiar feature of the approaches to Roman cities. The Vestal Virgins could be buried within the city, although those who violated the oath of chastity were buried alive. The Law of the Twelve Tables forbade the burial or burning of dead bodies within the city. The Romans built elaborate necropoleis similar in layout to those of the Etruscans, and also laid out more compact cemeteries. One such necropolis was that of Isola Sacra, the cemetery of Portus Augusti, dating from the second and third centuries AD. The tombs are built on either side of the coast-road between the town and Ostia, and the appearance of the cemetery was not dissimilar to that of an Etruscan necropolis. Most of the tombs are rectangular buildings of brick and stone, sometimes with vaulted roofs, erected in blocks to form *insulae* with roads between. The façades are often pedimented and in the centre of the wall is an entrance doorway above which is a panel for the inscription. Barrel-vaulted tombs are often capped with segmental pediments, or have pediments set back behind the crowning cornice (aesthetically a curiously unsatisfactory device). Most of the tombs in Isola Sacra are of one storey. The doors lead to a *cella* or main chamber, the walls of which are lined with niches, often aediculated, containing ash-chests or urns. Burial of whole bodies was sometimes in *loculi*, sometimes within arched niches known as *arcosolia*.

Very similar to the Isola Sacra cemetery was that under the Basilica of S. Peter in the Vatican, though the majority of these tombs were cross- rather than barrel-vaulted. Much interior decoration survives in this cemetery, and gives us a surprisingly vivid glimpse of what a middle-class graveyard of the period was like. The painted and stuccoed tomb in the Vatican cemetery, for example, is richly decorated. The vaults, niches, and apses are decked out in sumptuous taste, the whole coloured with great refinement. The effect is almost Baroque.

Many walled cemeteries existed in Roman times, usually with a central monument of some importance. Other walled enclosures associated with tombs, however, were funerary gardens laid out and planted to provide fruit, flowers, and wine to honour the dead. Wealthy Romans left endowments to ensure the continuity and inviolability of such gardens. Summer-houses and dining-areas were provided where families could feast during days of commemoration. These funerary gardens were laid out to formal plans, and must have been delightful oases of peace and beauty, with vines and roses in abundance. Sir Thomas Browne tells us that, 'in strewing their Tombs, the *Romans* affected the Rose, the Greeks *Amaranthus* and myrtle; that the Funerall pyre consisted of sweet fuell, Cypresse, Firre, Larix, Yewe, and Trees perpetually verdant, lay silent expressions of their surviving hopes.' Wells, pools, statuary, and shady walks ensured that the gardens were charming places where the dead could not only be commemorated, but could themselves experience, as they were thought to be capable of feeling. The ideal landscape of an Elysian after-life could be enjoyed on earth, for the funerary garden symbolized the gardens of the other world. Sepulchral gardens were known throughout the eastern part of the Graeco-Roman world, and it seems that their produce helped to finance the upkeep of the gardens and even of the tombs. The funerary garden was also an added amenity for the furnished tomb, and was laid out for perpetual enjoyment. Some funerary gardens contained vineyards that ensured continual supplies of libations for the dead as well as a profitable piece of real-estate to maintain the mausolea themselves. Ausonius produced a number of epitaphs of singular beauty in which he refers to roses and to other flowers. The famous Epitaph XXXI, known as *In Tumulo Hominis Felicis* (on the tomb of a happy man), reads:

> *Sparge mero cineres bene olentis et unguine nardi,*
> *hospes, et adde rosis balsama puniceis.*
> *perpetuum mihi ver agit inlacrimabilis urna*
> *et commutavi saecula, non obii.*

The exquisite beauty of these lines is the essence of classical poetry. No translation can do them justice, but the meaning might be rendered thus:

Sprinkle my ashes with good wines and with perfumed oils of spikenard;
stranger, add balsam and crimson roses.

Ever, without tears, my urn knows spring,
for I have not died. I have changed my state.

Such an epitaph might have graced a tomb set in a delightful garden. There,
the garlanded urn could be, enclosing the grey ashes cool now after the fire,
and surrounded by vines, by roses, and by all manner of sweet-smelling
flowers. A pool of water, the antidote to fire, would have emphasised a
perfect balance: the sense of repose was completed. Ausonius concluded:

nulla mihi veteris perierunt gaudia vitae,
seu meminisse putes omnia, sive nihil.

These words are valedictory, yet untinged with sentimentality. In English
they become:

I have not lost a single joy of my old life,
whether you think I remember everything or nothing.

Plate 15 Sarcophagus of
Cornelius Lucius Scipio
Barbatus, with Doric frieze,
dentils, and Ionic scrolls
(*Author's Collection*)

Extremely large tombs also were built. The tombs of the Scipios were
hollowed out of the tufa, and contained sarcophagi, as this family (the Gens
Cornelia) generally buried their dead. The sarcophagus of Cornelius Lucius
Scipio Barbatus, the first member of the family to be buried in the tomb by
the Via di Porta San Sebastiano, is a fine example of the art of Roman
monumental design of the third century BC (Pl. 15). It has a Doric frieze,
dentils, and Ionic scrolls above the cornice, and was a favourite prototype of
many eighteenth- and nineteenth-century designs for funerary monuments.

Cremation was more usual in Republican Rome, however, and
columbaria (large tombs, usually underground, in the walls of which are
niches known as *loculi* like those in dovecots) were built in large numbers,
although only a handful are preserved today. A huge columbarium (known
as No. 1 of the Vigna Codini series) of the first century AD, near the Porta di
San Sebastiano, was constructed for the remains of the freedmen, slaves, and
servants of the Caesars. It has a massive rectangular pier in the centre,
containing many niches (Pls. 16, 17). Mostly, these *loculi* are semi-circular
in elevation, are horseshoe-shaped on plan, and contain urns. The walls, of
opus reticulatum, are stuccoed and painted. About 450 cremation burials

Plate 16 Section through a columbarium for the first century near the Porta di San Sebastiano for the servants of the Caesars (*J. H. Parker Collection, British School at Rome No. PA 1297*)

were made here, mostly of persons who died during the first century of our era. A tomb built also of *opus reticulatum* of about 60 BC in the Thermae of the Gordiani contains a columbarium arrangement (Pl. 18) typical of the period.

A very remarkable columbarium found in 1886 in the grounds of the Villa Wolkonsky has been measured and drawn (Pls. 19, 20, 21). It was a partly subterranean structure of three storeys, built for Tiberius Claudius Vitalis by his family, which included architects. The columbarium adjoins the Aqua Claudia, the mighty arches of which tower above it. The top storey was vaulted. Stairs led down to the middle storey. This middle

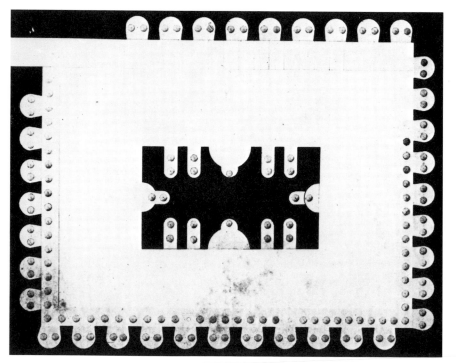

Plate 17 Plan of a columbarium of the first century near the Porta di San Sebastiano for the servants of the Caesars (*J. H. Parker Collection, British School at Rome No. PA 1298*)

section had a door from the street, and the lowest storey was totally underground. Another columbarium near the Porta di San Sebastiano contains *loculi* with many urns, ash-chests, and busts. It is typical of late-Republican and early-Imperial columbaria (Pl. 22). A more elaborate arrangement of niches and types of *loculi* exists in the columbarium of the Villa Campana, where elaborate vaulting is painted, and the decorations of the interior enhance the architectural effects (Pl. 23). The ceiling is especially fine, with its light and pretty paintings of vines, birds, torches, and other subjects.

While many early-Imperial tombs were hollowed out of the tufa in and around Rome, contemporary tombs in other parts of the Empire were constructed above ground. At Ostia, rectangular tomb-enclosures were common, and consisted of high walls of *opus reticulatum* with brick and stone dressings. Sometimes the enclosures were roofed, and sometimes left open to the sky. The walls of the interior were fitted out as a columbarium, and often one part of the interior was set aside as a cremation platform. Columbaria are often impressive works of architecture, and frequently the niches contain elaborate ash-chests or urns. Busts of the dead are often present. Inscriptions are sometimes on the urns themselves, or sometimes on panels above or below the niches. Niches may be open or sealed with a slab. There are several columbaria associated with the freedmen of the emperors, the best perhaps being that already referred to. The Vigna Codini

Plate 18 Tomb of 60 BC with a columbarium of *opus reticulatum* in the Thermae of the Gordiani (*J. H. Parker Collection, British School at Rome No. PA 932*)

Plate 19 Columbarium of Tiberius Claudius Vitalis by the Aqua Claudia. Section drawn by the architect Cicconetti (*J. H. Parker Collection, British School at Rome, No. PA 354*)

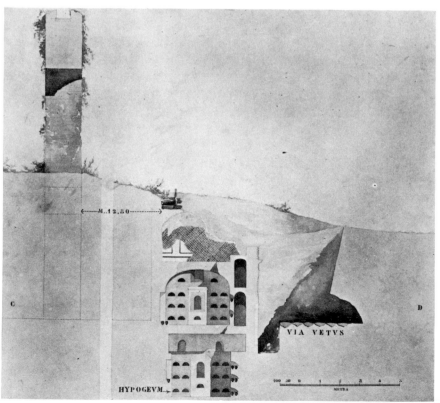

Plate 20 Columbarium of Tiberius Claudius Vitalis. Section drawn by the architect Cicconetti (*J. H. Parker Collection, British School at Rome, No. PA 355*)

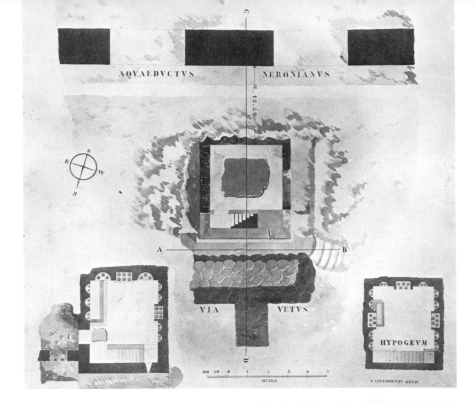

Plate 21 Plan of the columbarium of T. Claudius Vitalis, drawn by the architect Cicconetti (*J. H. Parker Collection, British School at Rome, No. PA 353*)

Plate 22 Typical columbarium arrangement with *loculi* horseshoe-shaped on plan with semi-circular arches over, containing urns and ash-chests. This columbarium is near the Porta di San Sebastiano (*J. H. Parker Collection, British School at Rome No. PA 1769*)

columbarium has one compartment where most of the niches are rectangular rather than arched, and there is a considerable use of marble both for ash-chests and for embellishment.

We know much about Pompeian funerary architecture because so much was preserved by the volcanic eruption. A common type consisted of a vast podium of elegant design set on steps. This podium was decorated with ornament of the greatest refinement, and capped by a crowning cornice. These bases often were surmounted by canopied upper works (Pl. 24). Individual tombs of similar design with massive bases and superstructures survive on the Via Appia (Pl. 25). Often, the most elegant tombs, with a full classical treatment of plinth, pilasters, and entablature, contain bust-sculptures. A charming example lies on the Appian Way at the tomb of C. Rabirius Libertus of Posthumius Hermodorus, of Rabiria Demaris, and of Usia, first priestess of Isis. This tomb of the first century has a Grecian design above the cornice. The whole has an Alexandrian elegance unusual for its site (Pl. 26).

Plate 23 Niches in the columbarium in the Villa Campana. Note the sumptuous painted decoration (*J. H. Parker Collection, British School at Rome No. PA 1945*)

One of the best preserved of all tombs in Rome is that of Gaius Cestius, of the time of Augustus, which stands on the line of the Aurelian Wall near the Porta Ostiensis. This is a large pyramid of brick-faced concrete covered in marble slabs. Clearly, Egyptian prototypes may have suggested this curious monument that stands sentinel over the Protestant Cemetery in Rome. This is one of the loveliest spots in the Eternal City, though full of sadness, for here many young men of promise are laid to rest. Eugene Lee-Hamilton wrote:

Sweet are the gardens of Rome; but one is for Englishmen sacred;
Who, that has ever been there, knows not the beautiful spot

Plate 26 Tomb of C.
Rabirius Libertus of
Posthumius Hermodorus, etc.
(*J. H. Parker Collection,
British School at Rome, No.
PA 2332*)

Where our poets are laid in the shade of the pyramid lofty,
Dark grey, tipped as with snow, close to the turreted walls?

Samuel Rogers observed that the cemetery 'is a quiet and sheltered nook,
covered in winter with violets; and the pyramid, that overshadows it, gives it
a classic and singularly solemn air . . . it is a stranger among strangers'.[16]
The vaulted tomb-chamber of the pyramid was decorated with figure-
paintings.

During the first century AD tombs sometimes took the form of temples,
built on podia, with Giant Orders of Corinthian pilasters carrying a massive
entablature (Pl. 28). They consisted of a mortuary chapel with a portico,
peristyle, or Order of engaged columns or pilasters. The podium contained
the sepulchral vaults. The chapel housed the niches for statues of deities or

Plate 27 The 'tomb of
Herodes Atticus called Dio
Redicolo', AD 143. This tomb
is actually that of Annia
Regilla (*J. H. Parker
Collection, British School at
Rome No. PA 909*)

Plate 28 Tomb of the first
century on the Via Latina,
Rome (*J. H. Parker
Collection, British School at
Rome No. PA 1430*)

Plate 29 The Castel Sant'
Angelo, Rome, formerly the
mausoleum of Hadrian (*The
Author*)

portrait-busts of those buried. The niches were also used to house cinerary urns. The so-called tomb of Herodes Atticus, sometimes referred to as the tomb or temple of Dio Redicolo, is such an example. The tomb-chamber was underground, and the rooms above ground were for funerary cults and celebrations. This tomb is not that of Herodes Atticus at all. Herodes Atticus was professor of rhetoric to Marcus Aurelius and Lucius Verus. He became Consul in AD 143. He married the wealthy heiress Annia Regilla (who died shortly before the birth of her fifth child) and was accused by her family of poisoning her. He demanded a trial and was acquitted. He built this magnificent tomb for his wife in a sepulchral field within the precincts of the villa dedicated to Minerva and Nemesis. It was made an act of the highest sacrilege for any but her own descendants to be buried within. The front, facing north, was approached by a flight of steps. The pilasters, strings, and entablature are of red brick, and the flat surfaces are of yellow brick. The interior is vaulted.

A variation of this type consisted of two storeys, with pilasters at the corners, and an entablature at the first stage. Orders were superimposed rather than carried up full height in a Giant Order (Pl. 29). The roofs of these rectangular mausolea were usually barrel-vaulted, and the interiors were richly decorated. Capitals were sometimes of terracotta and sometimes of marble. This type of tomb is known as a house-tomb, although many are of an impressive size, with considerable architectural grandeur.

Circular and polygonal tombs are among the most impressive of Roman monuments. This type of tomb grew in favour from the time of Augustus, and clearly owes a debt to Etruscan tumulus-tombs with their ring-girdles of masonry. The huge imperial mausoleum of Augustus in the Campus Martius may be the first of the Roman circular tombs. It dates from about 28 BC, and is about eighty-eight metres in diameter. Inside, centrally placed, was a mighty pier that supported the statue of the emperor at the top of the monument. Around the centre were five gigantic ring-walls linked by vaults that decreased in height towards the circumference. The outer wall retained an earthen mound that covered the whole structure. It is likely that rings of cypresses were planted round the outer parts of the mound.

Merivale[17] described the mausoleum as having 'three retiring stages, each of which had a terrace covered with earth and planted with cypresses. These stages were pierced with numerous chambers, destined to receive, row within row, and storey upon storey, the remains of every member of the imperial family, with many thousands of their slaves and freedmen. In the centre of that massive mound the great founder of the empire was to sleep his last sleep, while his statue was ordained to rise conspicuous on its summit, and satiate its everlasting gaze with the view of his beloved city.' In AD 14 Augustus died, and was cremated on a funeral pyre so huge that the widowed Livia, attended by the principal senators, had to watch it for five days and nights before it had cooled sufficiently for them to collect the ashes of the emperor.

Plate 30 Model of a conjectural restoration of the mausoleum of Hadrian in the Castel Sant' Angelo (*The Author*)

The imperial mausoleum of Hadrian differs greatly from that of Augustus, although it was clearly inspired by it. It consists of a drum some seventy metres in diameter above which there may have been further drums of decreasing diameter. At the top was a cypress-planted mound and a statuary group. The interior had a circular ramp that wound up to the central sepulchral chamber. A great square wall, possibly added later, surrounded the drum (Pl. 30). The mausoleum was built by Hadrian after the last niche in the imperial mausoleum of Augustus was filled when the

Plate 31 Restored model of the Augustan tomb of Lucius Munatius Plancus at Gaeta. This dates from about 20 BC, and owes its origins to Etruscan circular tombs. It was similar in structure to the mausoleum of Augustus (*Mansell–Alinari Collection*)

ashes of Nerva were placed there. Procopius described the mausoleum of Hadrian in the sixth century as being 'built of Parian marble; the square blocks fit closely to each other without any cement. It has four equal sides, each a stone's throw in length. In height it rises above the walls of the city. On the summit are statues of men and horses, of admirable workmanship, in Parian marble.' Merivale wrote that the mausoleum of Hadrian 'far outshone the tomb of Augustus, which it nearly confronted. Of the size and dignity which characterized this work of Egyptian massiveness we may gain a conception from the existing remains; but it requires an effort of imagination to transform the scarred and shapeless bulk before us into the graceful piles of antiquity.'[17] The tomb of Lucius Munatius Plancus was also circular on plan, and was dressed externally with blocks of travertine (Pl. 31).

One of the most celebrated circular tombs is that of Caecilia Metella, which consists of a drum set on a square podium by the Via Appia Antica. It appears to date from the middle of the first century BC. The exterior of this brick-built tomb was covered with travertine marble blocks. The elegant entablature contains panoplies and festoons suspended from *bucrania*. It is probable that the mediaeval work above the cornice contains part of the Roman *cippi*, or small columns used as funerary monuments sometimes found around the top of circular tombs (Pl. 32). Caecilia Metella was the daughter of Quintus Metellus Creticus, and wife of Crassus. The *bucrania* gave it the popular name of Capo di Bove. The marble cladding of the base was removed by Pope Urban VIII for incorporation into the Trevi fountain. Byron wrote of this tomb:

There is a stern round tower of other days,
Firm as a fortress, with its fence of stone,
Such as an army's baffled strength delays,
Standing with half its battlements alone,
And with two thousand years of ivy grown,
The garland of eternity, where wave
The green leaves over all by time o'erthrown;
What was this tower of strength? within its cave
What treasure lay so lock'd, so hid?—A woman's grave.

It is at the tomb of Caecilia Metella that the beauties of the Appian Way truly begin. A short distance further on, the road emerges from the cavernous walls that shut it in, and splendid views are to be had over the Latin plain to the Sabine and Alban mountains.

Most of the tombs, both on the Appian Way, and in other linear cemeteries, had an inscription, or *titulus sepulchralis*, stating the size of the

Plate 32 Tomb of Caecilia Metella, on the Via Appia. The upper works are mediaeval, but appear to incorporate *cippi* (*The Author*)

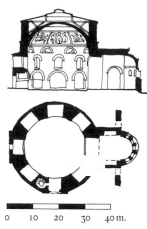

0   10   20   30   40 m.

Fig. 3 Church of S. George, Salonika, formerly the mausoleum of Galerius (*The Author*)

Plate 33 Tomb of S. Helen of AD 330 (*J. H. Parker Collection, British School at Rome No. PA 207*)

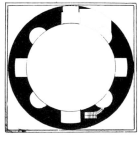

0   5   10   15 m.

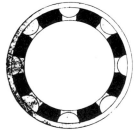

Fig. 4 Plan of the tomb of S. Helen (*J. H. Parker Collection, British School at Rome No PA 206*)

plot on which the monument stood. Horace mentions an inscription that stated the plot measured a thousand feet in front and three hundred in depth, while the tomb ownership was not to be hereditary.[18]

The Rotunda of S. George, Thessalonica, was originally built about AD 300 as a mausoleum for Galerius. This circular brick structure has a hemispherical dome (Fig. 3) and eight vaulted niches above which are windows. Thessalonica was already important when Galerius (293–311) chose it to be his capital. Galerius's tomb was approached along a processional way that was lined by colonnades. The great rotunda was surrounded by an octagonal wall in which were apsidal *exedrae*. The great rotunda was freestanding, and was not unlike the *caldarium* of the Baths of Caracalla in Rome, with eight barrel-vaulted rooms at ground-floor level above which were eight smaller recesses to allow light to enter from the windows. The interior was decorated with a veneer of marble. The vaults were enriched with mosaics. Not unlike this structure, but much less well preserved, is the mausoleum of the Empress Helena on the Via Labicana outside Rome, dating from about AD 330 (Fig. 4 and Pl. 33). This fine mausoleum contained a sarcophagus that is now preserved in the Vatican. The building incorporated a later small church of Santi Pietro e Marcellino, and was named the Torre Pignattára by the Italians from the use of *pignatte*, or earthenware pots, used in the construction of the concrete vaulting, as was customary during the later Imperial period. Another circular tomb, once associated with the Gordiani, has remains of frescoes and large apsidal niches (Pl. 34). This Torre de' Schiavi on the Via Praenestina dates from the

Plate 34 Tomb with
paintings of about AD 240
associated with the Thermae
of the Gordiani (*J. H. Parker
Collection, British School at
Rome No. PA 923*)

time of Diocletian. It was modelled on the Pantheon and consisted of a
domed drum with two cornices set on a podium. A pedimented portico
marked the entrance.

Much more elegant, sophisticated, and nobly proportioned is the
building now known as the church of the Santa Costanza in Rome. This was
erected about AD 330 by Constantine as a mausoleum for his daughters, and
was converted into a church in 1256. The entrance leads to a central space
encircled by twelve pairs of granite columns that support the drum and
dome, and this central space is surrounded by an aisle covered with a barrel
vault. The pairs of columns are placed radially to the circumference. The
drum has clerestory windows (Fig. 5). In the thickness of the outside wall of
the aisle are three large and twelve small niches, originally intended to
contain sarcophagi. The vaulting is covered with beautiful fourth-century
mosaics of an arabesque pattern (Pl. 35).

The step from these great Roman mausolea to that of Theodoric the Goth
at Ravenna (*c*. AD 530) is considerable, for here is a tomb of outstanding
modernity that looks as though it could almost be a creation of Hawksmoor.
It is of two storeys, of which the lower is a decagon enclosing a cruciform
vaulted crypt of stone, and the upper is circular internally, with a decagonal
exterior. The upper part of the upper storey is a drum that carries one huge
slab of stone hollowed out into a saucer dome. This slab has stone fixing
points from which it was lifted into position. There is a crowning cornice at
the top of the drum, and a string-course below the frieze. Under this string-
course are traces of an arcade, so there may have been a peristyle carrying an

57

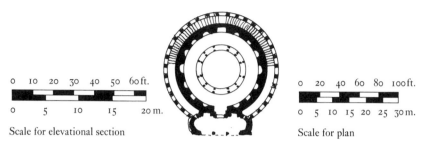

Fig. 5 Elevation, section and plan of Santa Costanza in Rome (*The author*)

Scale for elevational section

Scale for plan

open arcade all the way round this marvellous building (Pl. 36). The mausoleum was renamed Santa Maria della Rotonda after the remains of Theodoric were dispersed by Belisarius.

The road which leads by the Aqua Bollicante, where the Arvales sang their hymn, leads to the Torre de' Schiavi. To the right of the Via Gabina is a tomb of *opus latericium* of the first century that is vaulted (Pl. 37). This simple square tomb is of a not uncommon type. However, the use of a square compartment, with arms to provide a cruciform plan, was a new departure, and is found in the tomb of Galla Placidia in Ravenna of about AD 440. This extremely interesting building is of brick, and each arm of the cross has a pedimented end façade decorated with blind arcades. Over the crossing is a square tower. The sarcophagi are in their original positions in the arms of the cross. The arms are roofed with barrel vaults, and the square tower is covered by a dome (Fig. 6). This mausoleum was founded by the empress Galla Placidia beside the church of Santa Croce. The interior is adorned with sumptuous mosaics on a dark blue ground. The two other sarcophagi are reputed to be those of Constantius III and either Honorius or Valentinian III (Pl. 38).

Another type of Roman tomb was the tower-tomb, usually square or rectangular, rising from a podium or steps. Tower-tombs are often found in the provinces, usually on the eastern fringes of the Empire, although one of the most famous of all such tombs is Trajan's column, the monument and mausoleum of the Emperor. It is the largest and best preserved example of relief-sculpture as practised by the Romans, and is constructed entirely of Parian marble. The ashes of Trajan, who died in Cilicia in AD 117 were placed in the tomb-chamber in the pedestal of the column. Several tombs on the Via Appia have mediaeval towers on top, and may originally have been varieties of tower-tombs (Pl. 39). The finest surviving Roman tower-tomb is that of the Secundinii which stands almost intact in the tiny village of

Plate 35 Imperial mausoleum
erected around AD 330. It is
now the Church of Santa
Costanza, Rome. From
Piranesi's *Le Antichità
Romane* Rome 1756 (*Society
of Antiquaries of London*)

Plate 36 The mausoleum of
Theodoric the Goth at
Ravenna (*The Author*)

Plate 37 First-century tomb of *opus latericium* to the right of the Via Gabina at Aqua Bollicante (*J. H. Parker Collection, British School at Rome No. PA 1639*)

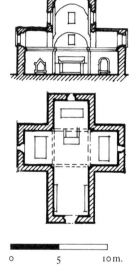

Fig. 6 Section and plan of the mausoleum of Galla Placidia in Ravenna (*The Author*)

Igel[19] near the city of Trier in Germany. It is known locally as the Heidenthurm, and is a sandstone pier, square on plan, some twenty-three metres high, that celebrates the cloth-making family of Secundinii. The pier sits on a podium enriched with mythological scenes that offer a piquant contrast to the carvings showing scenes from the daily life of the family in business. The podium is crowned by a cornice. Over this is the pier at the angles of which are Corinthian pilasters with shafts decorated in sumptuous style. At the top of the pier is an entablature with a sculptured frieze over which is an attic stage with a sculptured face on each side. The pyramidal roof is crowned by a pineapple carrying a sculptured group of the Rape of Ganymede. This is a particularly beautiful Roman funeral monument, and dates from the third century of our era. It is one of the most interesting Roman tombs north of the Alps (Pl. 40).

The tomb of the Julii at St Rémy in Provence is another interesting example of the tower type of monument. It consists of a high pedestal supporting engaged Corinthian columns with arched openings between. Above the entablature is a circular Corinthian peristyle with a conical roof. Another elegant tower-tomb is found in the Lebanon, at Hermel. It is of two stages with a slight inward batter, and has a base ten metres square constructed on three steps of black stone. The lower stage has angle pilasters between which are carved reliefs, while the upper storey has four pilasters on each face. Above the crowning cornice is a pyramidal roof of similar proportions to those of the pyramid of Cestius in Rome. This tomb probably dates from the first century BC. Tower-tombs contained vaulted chambers with *loculi* in the wall, and spaces for sarcophagi (Pl. 41). The tombs at Hermel and at Igel have obvious similarities of design to Greek tombs such as the Lion Tomb at Cnidos and the Halicarnassos Mausoleum. Familiar motifs recur in classical funerary architecture.

Yet another type of tomb is found in present-day Yugoslavia, near the Roman town of Celeia. Fairly typical of this type is the monument of the

Plate 38 Tomb of Galla
Placidia, Ravenna (*The
Author*)

Plate 39 Tomb on the Via
Appia, with a mediaeval
tower superimposed (*J. H.
Parker Collection, British
School at Rome No. PA 1628*)

Far Right Plate 40
Monument to the
Secundinii family at Igel near
Trier (*Author's Collection*)

Plate 41 Tomb at Hermel in the Lebanon, lithographed by Jacottet and printed by Lemercier (*Author's Collection*)

Prisciani family, composed of three steps, above which is a rectangular base enriched with sculpture. This base, or podium, has a carved string-course more than half-way up its face. The podium has a crowning cornice above which is an aediculated opening flanked by Corinthian columns with barley-sugar fluting. The aedicule is linked to the structure behind by arches. The structure is pedimented, with exaggerated eaves-cornices. A Medusa mask crowns the apex of the pediment. Within the apsidal niche at the back of the aedicule are statues of the family in high relief.

The eastern fringe of the Empire contained remarkably rich tombs, some of which are rock-cut. Often, as was the case at Beni-Hasan and derivative Persian examples, façades were cut in the vertical face of the rock cliffs, with burial-chambers tunnelled behind. The influence of the Graeco-Roman architectural traditions was such that often Semitic customs merged with a classical language of architecture, as at the Kedron Valley complex and at Petra, the Nabataean capital.[20] The grandest tombs were those in the Kedron Valley near Jerusalem and at Petra. One of the most interesting examples is the large square block, cut free from the rock-face, known as the 'Tomb of Absalom' (Pl. 42). This marks the entrance to a large rock-cut tomb behind it. The 'Tomb of Absalom' contains a burial chamber, and so is a tomb as well as an entrance. A cube stands on a rock-cut base that is surrounded by engaged Ionic columns and corner piers surmounted by a Doric frieze; this in turn is overhung by a heavy cornice of curiously Egyptian character. Over the base is an ashlar plinth, above which is a circular drum. On this sits a cone of concave section surmounted by a finial. The 'Tomb of Zechariah', in the Kedron Valley complex, is also rock-cut, and has engaged Ionic columns with corner-piers. Above is a heavy cornice

Graeco-Roman funerary buildings, cemeteries, gardens, and sculptures of the Egyptian type, the whole crowned by a pyramid, basically a similar arrangement to that of the Hermel tower-tomb. Plate 42 shows a curious mixture of tombs, some of which are from the Kedron Valley complex, with sarcophagi in the foreground. The pyramids in the background may not be the Egyptian variety, but may be attempts to show the pyramids set up by Helena beside the tomb of Izates and of herself in the first century AD.

The celebrated tombs of Petra have façades cut from the rock. While some façades have an architectural treatment that is unclassical, others are grandly Roman, even Baroque. It appears that architectural treatment in the Kedron Valley, at Petra, and elsewhere in the Middle East, was largely derived from Graeco-Roman precedent, yet occasionally the handling of classical motifs can be curiously perverse. In the Jewish world, non-figurative ornament only was permitted, so the floral rosette and continuous scroll were popular decorative features of sarcophagi and tombs. Many Petran tombs rise in tiers up the faces of the cliffs, having plain façades with entrances flanked by pilasters not unlike the Persian rock-cut tombs mentioned earlier. Other Petran tombs have more elaborate façades with heavy cornices derived from Egyptian prototypes. The temple-tombs of

Plate 42 An architectural phantasy of the early nineteenth century, showing sarcophagi in the foreground. *Centre*, the 'Tomb of Zechariah', *behind* it the 'Tomb of Absalom'. Other rock-cut tombs are shown, while the pyramids (perhaps an attempt to show the structures erected by Helena, Queen of Adiabene, beside her tomb in the first century AD) loom incongruously in the background (*Author's Collection*)

Petra have a more clearly defined Graeco-Roman character, and sometimes incorporate sculptures of lions, obelisks, and other motifs. The finest of all Petran tombs are unquestionably those that derive from Hellenistic sources. The six great tomb-façades including the Khazne are among the most impressive of all tombs in the former Roman provinces, and incorporate a degree of architectural sophistication and invention that was hardly surpassed in later funerary architecture. The Khazne itself has a façade of two storeys set in a deep recess. The lower storey has a portico of Corinthian columns with an entablature and pediment, behind which is the podium of the second storey. In the centre is a pavilion of circular plan with engaged Corinthian columns and a conical roof. On either side of this circular pavilion is a piece of broken pediment (Pl. 43). The whole effect is Baroque in its daring inventions, and the influence of Graeco-Roman design is at once apparent, despite the fact that the Romanization of the Nabataeans only began in the first century BC. A not dissimilar Baroque façade is also found at the Deir Tomb at Petra. Petran tombs housed sarcophagi, rather than cremated remains, as might be expected where Semitic burial customs were associated with Graeco-Roman architectural treatment. Bodies were placed in *loculi* cut deep into the walls, or placed in *arcosolia* cut parallel to the walls. Lids of sarcophagi in this part of the Roman world were usually segmental in section (Pl. 42). The date of the Petran tombs is probably around the first century BC. They are of great importance, for they are examples of how local customs mingled with Graeco-Roman art, and indicate how potent Roman example was even on the outskirts of the Empire.[21]

No introductory survey of Roman funerary architecture would be complete without mention of the *hypogea* and catacombs. Both terms denote underground sepulchres. A *hypogeum*, however, was a compact underground tomb, usually for use by one family or by a particular sect or group. A catacomb, on the other hand, was a large underground necropolis used by groups such as Jews or Christians, although other groups may have enjoyed burials there. Catacombs tended to be irregular in layout, of many levels, and they covered an extensive area. A *hypogeum* was compact, usually on one level, and was often formally planned.

The *hypogeum* of Yarhai in the Valley of the Tombs at Palmyra is a typical example, cut into the rock, with an open vestibule leading to a single door on the south, but it is sumptuously decorated. It has been fully described by Toynbee. The main doorway has a classical entablature, and contains stone doors. From it, steps lead down to the hypogeum, which consists of a long gallery running north–south, with two *exedrae* running west–east. The western *exedra* is very grand, almost Baroque in its splendour, and is enriched with architectural and sculptural detail. The barrel-vaulted gallery is also cut to resemble correct classical detail, with a dado, pilasters, entablature, and arches. There is space for two hundred and nineteen bodies in *loculi*. The southern end of the *hypogeum* was enriched with niches over which was a scallop decoration. This hypogeum appears to date from AD 108, and probably owes its richness of architectural treatment to the fact that the dead were venerated and so the chambers were used

Plate 44 Catacomb of SS. Nereo and Achilleo. Painted chamber of AD 523 (*J. H. Parker Collection, British School at Rome*)

regularly for ritual purposes. The tomb was very likely intended for wealthy and cultivated persons.

Public catacombs were very different in character. The term 'catacomb' has its origins in the *Coemeterium ad Catacumbas* under the church of San Sebastiano on the Via Appia. The basilica above was rebuilt in 1611 by Ponzio for Cardinal Scipio Borghese, on the site of a church that had been founded by Constantine. On this site stood the house and garden of the matron Lucina in which she buried the body of Sebastian after his second martyrdom under Diocletian. The chapel of S. Sebastian has a statue designed by Bernini.

The entrance to the catacombs is marked with an inscription to the effect that in this most holy of places, called *ad Catacumbas*, the bodies of some 174,000 martyrs were buried. This catacomb was the only one still open in the fifteenth century, and was a place of pilgrimage, owing to the desire in the early Church of saving the graves of the first confessors. The relics of the Apostles Peter and Paul rested here, for surety and safety. The body of S. Peter was translated to the catacombs of San Sebastiano for a second time during the reign of Heliogabalus. In AD 257, S. Stephen, the Pope, was martyred in the cemetery, and the bones of S. Peter were once more restored to the tomb in the Vatican.

The subsoil around Rome was admirably suited to the construction of *hypogea* and catacombs, as it consists of deep layers of tufa which was easy to work, yet very stable. Both the Christian and Jewish communities acquired land for constructing catacombs. The catacombs were begun by cutting a stair into the ground, and then a gallery parallel to the surface of the earth. Further galleries were then cut at right angles to the main gallery, and these were linked by more galleries parallel to the first one. When more ground was needed, further levels were excavated deeper in the tufa. The dead were laid in *loculi* cut parallel to the walls, rather like bunk-beds. It is rare to find Roman catacombs with *loculi* cut deeply into the walls, with the length at right angles to the passage. After a body had been deposited, the shelves were sealed with tiles, slabs of stone, marble, or terracotta. Sometimes symbols or inscriptions were placed on the surfaces of these sealing panels, but more often identification was by medallions, glass, or even coins which were set in mortar beside the *loculi*.[22] More sophisticated shelves were cut as troughs in the walls within *arcosolia* or arched recesses and covered with a flat slab, rather like a mediaeval table-tomb within a canopied niche.

Most catacombs date from the third and fourth centuries of our era, and are found beside the main roads radiating from Rome. Many contain *cubicula*, or small rooms off the galleries, probably intended for celebrations of the rites of the dead—a relic of earlier, classical customs observed in the funerary gardens and cemeteries of pagan Rome. Many *cubicula* were vaulted and magnificently decorated, and often the *arcosolia* were sealed and adorned with inscriptions (Pl. 44).

Some of the finest catacombs outside Rome are in Naples and Syracuse. The Neapolitan catacombs are two-storeyed, and contain both *arcosolia* and *loculi*, with considerable areas of painted decorations (Pl. 45).[23] Truly it may be said of the catacombs that:

Hic congesta jacet quaeris si turba Piorum,
Corpora Sanctorum retinent veneranda sepulchra,
Sublimes animas rapuit sibi Regia Coeli.[24]

The architectural unity of the Catacombs of the Aruntii had a Piranesian splendour. The drawing by Metz shows the arrangements of vaults,

Plate 45 General view of the catacombs in Naples showing frescoes. Note the *loculi* and *arcosolia* (*J. H. Parker Collection, British School at Rome No. PA 2146*)

arcosolia, *loculi*, and individual galleries of a consciously architectural scheme. (Pl. 46).

Plate 46 Catacombs of the Aruntii, drawn by Metz (*Author's Collection*)

The tombs, cemeteries, and catacombs of the Roman Empire are among the most moving and interesting works of man. The Via Appia, most enchanted of ancient cemeteries, is infinitely evocative, haunted by the past. Near the church of Domine Quo Vadis?, for example, are many catacombs, notably those of S. Calixtus, but the walls of tavern gardens, orchards, and private enclosures give an air of peaceful country seclusion. Many of these walls are hung with the rare yellow-berried ivy, often represented in mosaics. Roman pines shade the way, until the road opens out and gives vistas over the plain, where one can watch the cloud-shadows dapple the landscape. The tombs, set among pines and cypresses, create an unforgettable, essential Arcadian landscape that is mirrored in the mind for ever. The Arcadians may have been chestnut-eaters, but it is the pines, myrtles, cypresses, and roses that are remembered, together with the resigned beauty of the ruined tombs.[25]

3

The flowering of funerary art in the Middle Ages.

The development of funerary architecture from early prototypes; the great tombs, effigies, and chantry chapels; the change of emphasis.

All things that we ordained festival,
Turn from their office to black funeral;
Our instruments to melancholy bells,
Our wedding cheer to sad burial feast,
Our solemn hymns to sullen dirges change,
Our bridal flowers serve for a buried corse,
And all things change them to the contrary.

WILLIAM SHAKESPEARE: *Romeo and Juliet*

We have noted how, from Hellenistic times, altars were set up in hypogea and in catacombs. Altar-tombs became not uncommon, and altars were erected in Christian catacombs. It appears that, as far as burial-custom was concerned, Christians complied with Roman laws, and under the Empire buried their dead in the catacombs (Pl. 1). These underground cemeteries took on especial importance as the burial-places of the early martyrs, and some burial-rites of Roman dead, together with ritual at the tomb, became combined in Christian observances. The presence of altars near the tombs in catacombs ensured a church-like quality in many parts of the cemeteries. When churches were later built over the places of burial, or near the places where martyrs had died, altars were erected that contained fragments of bone from the catacombs. This practice of placing relics within the altar has been continued to this day, and derives from the early worship in the catacombs.

As more churches were built where they were needed, rather than over places of burial, the dead were buried under or beside the churches. The eminent in Christian society were buried in the churches as a privilege, and, as the custom became widespread, the practices of the few were extended to the burials of the many. 'The emanations from the bodies of Saints exercised a peculiar virtue upon all those who lay near them.'[1] The odour of sanctity clearly had a commercial value, and relics became widely sought after to give authenticity to a church or an altar. Christians thus inherited a guardianship of the dead, and control of cemeteries passed to the Church. This control had many repercussions in later times, for a considerable part of the income of clergy derived from fees charged for interment.

It is interesting that the early Christians adopted some of the customs of the Romans themselves in the disposal of their dead. I have already noted how the art of sarcophagus carving reached new heights in the early days of the Empire. A typical Roman tomb on the Via Claudia (Pl. 2) is not so different from the Early-Christian sarcophagi such as those found in the Sepolcreto di Braccioforte, Ravenna.

Early-Christian burial up to the end of the fourth century of our era generally took place in tombs of the catacomb or hypogeum type, although in various parts of the Empire individual tombs were also known, and many Early-Christian sarcophagi survive. Cremation was prohibited by the Church, although catacombs containing *loculi* for cremated remains became used by Christians as the new religion spread. At the commencement of the fifth century, however, the first cemetery inside the walls of Rome appears to have been formed, and from the seventh century, burial within the city

Plate 1 The catcombs of Naples. An eighteenth-century view by A. Sand; (*Author's Collection*)

Plate 2 Tomb at the sixth
mile on the Via Claudia, with
an inscription to P. Vibius
Marianus, of the time of
Severus (*J. H. Parker
Collection, British School at
Rome, No. PA 1634*)

became customary, for the old laws against intramural interment were no
longer enforced, as the population had decreased to a very great degree.
Imperial Rome was now a quarry from which Christian builders pillaged
columns, entablatures, and details, with little sense of what they were
destroying. Monumental designs for tombs of the Christian era have already
been noted at Rome, Ravenna, Thessalonica, and elsewhere.

The demand for burial-space adjacent to churches was great, and in 752
S. Cuthbert obtained papal permission to add churchyards to churches.
These churchyards were enclosed by walls and were consecrated by a bishop
to ensure all evil influences that might disturb the dead would be expelled.
Enclosure was important, for the use of the churchyard for any purpose
other than burial was frowned upon. In 1267 Bishop Quevil ordered that all
churchyards in his diocese should be carefully enclosed, and that no animals
should have access to them.

During the Middle Ages burial was directly in the ground, in sarcophagi,

or in vaults. The corpses were wrapped in shrouds that were knotted at the top and bottom. Often, bodies were laid in the earth, but from early times wooden, lead, or stone 'chests' were used. It appears that the boxing of a body in a coffin originated in an attempt to contain the corpse and to protect it from complete dispersal, a desire that was encouraged by a Christian belief in a material resurrection. Of course, funerals of important persons often took some time to arrange, and if a body had to be carried far, its encapsulation was essential in the interests of health and decency. It would seem, however, that the poor tended to look on a coffin as a luxury which was sometimes even denied them by law. Indeed, the quality of a coffin was a symbol of respectability and social status in Britain until fairly recently, and is still important in many other European countries. The placing of bodies in coffins within churchyards retarded the process of dissolution, and this process was further slowed when corpses were elaborately buried. Money was sometimes placed in coffins, usually on the eyes of the corpse, a relic of the old superstition that money would be necessary to pay the fare to the other world. Churchyards were regularly cleared of bones which were stored in charnel-houses, leaving the ground free for more burials. This practice is usual in Alpine and Central-European churchyards, where the land used for burial cannot be extended. Today, many of the great European cemeteries have graves and places in catacombs that are leased for a limited period, so they never become full, and the economic basis of the cemetery is not harmed.

It is worthy of note that the classical tradition persisted in Early-Christian times. A tomb in the narthex of the church of San Lorenzo fuori le mura in Rome is in the form of a temple, though with coarse detail, but the ancestry of Hellenistic and Roman pagan tombs is absolutely clear (Pl. 3). The marble sarcophagi of the fifth to the eighth century of our era in the church of Sant' Apollinare in Classe at Ravenna are extremely interesting examples of the

Plate 3 Canopied monument in the narthex of the church of San Lorenzo fuori le mura in Rome (*Author's Collection*)

manner in which the classic Greek sarcophagus, as epitomized in the Tomb of the Weepers at Sidon (Chapter II Pl. 7), had become transmogrified. One example has a complete arcade of stumpy Corinthian columns all round it, while the lid, semicircular in section, is carved to resemble a tiled roof. Instead of weepers, Christian symbols of the cross and the palm decorate the spaces between columns (Pl. 4). Roman sarcophagi of the Early-Christian period from Arles are beautiful examples of variations on the frieze and colonnade themes (Pl. 5).

Soon, the churches themselves became burial-grounds, and the floors filled with bodies. Churchyards, crypts, and the churches became the only possible places of sepulture for Christians. There were various attempts to prevent abuses, notably when the seventh-century Council of Nantes had expressly prohibited burials in churches, although corpses could be interred

Plate 4 Sarcophagus of Greek marble of the sixth century in the church of Sant'Apollinare in Classe, Ravenna (*Author's Collection*)

Plate 5 Early-Christian sarcophagus from Arles. *Top*: note the arcade with figures in Roman dress, and the larger figure of Christ; *middle*: a frieze of figures serves as the colonnade; *bottom*: the colonnade has become formalized trees, with figures and Christian symbolism (*Author's Collection*)

in the atrium or porticus in very special cases: *Prohibendum est etiam secundum majorum instituta, ut in ecclesia nullatenus sepeliantur sed in atrio aut porticu aut in exedris ecclesiae.* Power and influence could overcome such rulings, however, and burial continued in the churches, especially of the nobly born. Much later, particularly in the seventeenth century and afterwards, burial in church was fashionable among the better-off members of society, as the vault-covers of thousands of churches can indicate.

Mediaeval graves inside churches were usually in the form of a shaft in the earth, lined or unlined with masonry, and covered with a slab set in the floor. Grave-slabs were oriented towards the altar, a symbolic principle that was unambiguous. Where burial took place in the churchyard, the most desirable plots were those near the chancel, so the boundaries of the churchyard were in reality extensions of the walls of the church for purposes of interment. The layout of a mediaeval churchyard seems to have consisted of long strips, the widths corresponding to the length of a grave, running at right angles to the long axis of the church. The strips recall the distribution of farmland within the parish.

It would appear that, after the turmoil of the collapse of the Roman Empire in the west, and the great movement of peoples, Europe began to stabilize itself around the beginning of the twelfth century. The Normans had established themselves in England, and France became a rival kingdom. The Emperor Henry IV was strengthening the great Empire based on Germany, while the Eastern Empire was about to suffer at the hands of Normans and Crusaders. Power was shifting westwards, and feudalism, monasticism, and ecclesiastical growth ensured the establishment of the Church in a central rôle.

As I have already mentioned in Chapter I the terrors of death and of hell were constantly paraded before the populace. A considerable part of the effort of mediaeval man was devoted to ensuring the avoidance of eternal damnation, for an after-life was as real to him as to his Egyptian predecessor. The torments of hell were shown in murals, sculpture, illuminations, and stained glass in order to encourage greater zeal among the faithful. The skeletal figure of Death assumed a new and menacing horror in the Middle Ages, and was both allegorical and admonitory in intent. Ghastly images of torment were being made from the eleventh century, and there is something of the lurid and the sensational in them.

The spread of Christianity throughout Europe encouraged the growth of funerary architecture, and pagan monumental memorials became adapted for Christian burial. Marker-stones of pagan origin were inscribed with the Cross and with other Christian symbols to make them benign and acceptable. The cross at Govan has pagan designs on one side and Christian on the other. Crosses were sometimes set up on pagan monuments to cast an aura of beneficence around them. Ireland and Scotland are especially rich in crosses. Some of the most sophisticated of crosses are those at Monasterboice in Co. Louth, and these are elaborately sculpted with figure reliefs (Pl. 6). The upper part of the cross is akin in design to a reliquary, although the purpose of a High Cross was not sepulchral but to indicate a place hallowed by Christianity, consecration, and custom. As burial of the eminent began to take place in churches the growth of the architecture of death was encouraged. From the practices of Greece and Rome, burial in stone sarcophagi appears to have been common among persons of wealth and eminence, and many stone coffins exist from Early-Christian times, some of them highly sophisticated and beautiful objects in themselves. During the Middle Ages stone coffins were built into floors of churches so that the solid covers formed part of the pavement. The lids were frequently adorned with swords, croziers, arabesques, and other ornament. The most usual decoration is a cross, the whole length of the slab. Stone coffins were also placed in churchyards, the lids being raised above the ground. Coffin-lids were often coped, or ridged, and were termed *en dos d'âne* (incised slabs form a study in themselves, and are beyond the scope of this book, but their development gave rise to the grander tombs that can be termed 'architecture'). The remarkable hog-backed monuments of Penrith, Govan, Heysham (Pl. 7), and other places are single stones the length of the grave, and appear as crouching armadillos, or even as tiled houses, obviously protecting the dead.[2] The finest hog-backs are undoubtedly those in Govan.

A steeply pitched coffin-lid exists in Bakewell, Derbyshire, probably of Saxon origin. The finest coffin-lids of incised work are those of the Saxon and mediaeval periods. A tradition of incised slabs was carried on into the sixteenth century in the western isles of Scotland, notably the slabs of Islay, where curious anthropomorphic slabs are found with slabs of the more conventional type. In Europe generally, slab-covers give evidence of a long and undisturbed tradition, extending from the twelfth to the sixteenth centuries. The commonest ornaments are crosses, sometimes designed in the form of a tree of life. From the mid-mediaeval period full-length figures began to appear. Heraldic devices on tombs indicate the organization of the nobility on the main European pattern; in Sweden, such devices only appear from the beginning of the fourteenth century.

In England, coffins of the ridge type, with a cross, sometimes have gabled wings on the short branches of the arms of the cross. Semi-effigial monuments, in which only parts of the human figure are represented, such as the head and bust, derive their origins from endeavours to combine an effigy with a monumental cross, and date from the thirteenth century. The head and bust are frequently found within a *vesica piscis* figure, or inside a circle or quatrefoil. From the fourteenth century, busts are frequently found within an arched opening. In the twelfth and thirteenth centuries, burials within churches were relatively few in number, as this privilege was reserved for founders or benefactors. Tombs were usually recessed under low arches in the north wall of the chancel or presbytery. Bishops and abbots were usually interred in chapter-houses. Decorated coffin-lids were sometimes incised with whole figures representing the persons buried, and these incised figures later developed into complete three-dimensional effigies. Tombs usually told something of the deeds and fame of the person commemorated. Effigies, especially those of ecclesiastics, depicted vestments and certain aspects of power. The celebrated tomb of the Archbishop of Mainz, Siegfried III, shows the cleric crowning two Emperors, while later Archibishops are depicted as very much alive, rather than as recumbent effigies. Tombs of warriors show the figure in armour, with heraldic devices, while tombs of royalty often give us an excellent picture of the richer type of dress of the period. It is clear, despite Christian emphasis on humility and all being equal in the sight of God, that political or ecclesiastical power ensured splendid tombs would be erected to preserve the bodies of those who had enjoyed such power in life. Fine monuments on choice sites in churches would mark the resting-places of the rich and powerful until the Resurrection. The poorer people would have to be content with temporary graves in the churchyards marked with simple stones or wooden crosses, after which their remains would be stored in the parish charnel-houses with all the rest of the poorer social castes.

Monuments fell into the two main types: those sculptured in the round, or in medium or low relief; and engraved monuments, where the design is cut into the gravestone, or into flat inlays of bronze, brass, stone, or even mortar. Brasses were often enriched with inlays of enamels. As F. A. Greenhill has pointed out in his comprehensive work on incised slabs,[3] monumental brasses have long received the lion's share as the representative

Plate 6 The great cross of
Abbot Muiredach at
Monasterboice, Co. Louth; it
is of the tenth century (*The
Author*)

Plate 7 Hog-backed tombs
from Heysham, Lancashire.
The forms are not dissimilar
to those of Viking houses
(*Author's Collection*)

of the second type of commemorative slab, despite the fact that incised slabs as a whole are far more numerous, and far transcend brasses in importance. Throughout Europe, incised slabs are of immense significance as works of art and as historical records. An incised slab is any flat memorial with an effigy, a cross, or other designs cut into it. Greenhill's book is illustrated with various types of incised slab, and he rightly draws attention to the superb slabs of the Western Highlands.

Plate 8 Monument of Can Grande della Scala at Verona, over the door of the church of S. Maria Antica (*Stephen Thompson, Author's Collection*)

During the Middle Ages, the most sumptuous decoration was applied to the shrines of saints. The shrines of S. Alban, S. Edward the Confessor, S. Sebald in Nürnberg, and others testify to this. Although the best English examples have suffered at the hands of over-zealous reformers, several European shrines still exist that demonstrate the richness and inventiveness of Gothic art. The shrine of S. Peter in the church of Sant' Eustorgio in Milan, and the Arca of S. Augustine in Pavia Cathedral are two superb shrines of the Middle Ages. Perhaps the loveliest of all mediaeval shrines is that of S. Ursula in the Hospital of S. John in Brugge, dating from 1489. It was made in the form of a miniature chapel, with a steeply pitched roof, arcaded sides, buttresses, pinnacles, and crockets. The panels within the architectural framework are exquisite paintings by Memlinc. The effigies, tombs, chantry-chapels, and memorials of the mediaeval period provide perhaps the richest repository of art of the period. The memorial chapels and canopied tombs have, to a very great extent, survived. They provide complete records of costume, of armour, of heraldry, and of the crafts of the sculptor, of the metal-worker, of the smith, and of the architect. The superb craftsmanship and lavish materials of the shrines and reliquaries of saints ensured that they were venerated during the Middle Ages, and pillaged during the Reformation and Revolutionary periods in Europe. The shrine of S. Thomas of Canterbury provided Henry VIII with many precious stones and metals.[4] Peter Vischer's shrine of S. Sebald in Nürnberg of 1519 is a supreme example of funerary art for a particular set of holy relics. The great shrines of Italy, notably the tomb of S. Anthony of Padua, are overwhelming in their richness. Italian tombs of the period usually have Gothic gabled canopies and sarcophagi, while the group of tombs of the Scaliger family in Verona have not only walled screened enclosures, but canopied tombs that were to be the model of that last word in Victorian commemorative architecture, the Albert Memorial in Kensington.

The Scaliger monuments at Verona, near the Church of Santa Maria Antica, are celebrated for a splendid sequence of Gothic tombs. The first is that of Can Grande I della Scala (ob. 1321) which consists of a sarcophagus and effigy set within a bold arched canopy that is carried on colonettes. This canopy and the sarcophagus are carried on a shelf that is supported on brackets over a door to the church. On top of the whole ensemble is a truncated pyramid on which is an equestrian statue (Pl. 8). Ruskin called this tomb of 1335 the 'consummate form' of the Gothic tomb. The second of these great Scaliger tombs is that to Mastino II della Scala by Perrino da Milano of 1355. It stands next to the monument of Can Grande, and consists of a raised sarcophagus bearing a recumbent effigy over which is a huge protective canopy of three stages on four columns. Another truncated

Plate 9 Tomb of of Mastino II della Scala at Verona (*Stephen Thompson, Author's Collection*)

pyramid caps the composition (Pl. 9). Close to the monument of Mastino II is the most sumptuous of the trio of tombs: that of Can Signorio della Scala of 1365, designed by Bonino da Campione. There is a low wall surmounted by exquisite ironwork held between four corner-piers over which are canopied niches. The tomb itself has three stages, the effigy and sarcophagus being on the second stage, protected by the gabled canopy (Pl. 10). The upperworks of these tombs, with their truncated spires and equestrian groups, are reminiscent of the pyramidal forms from Halicarnassos and elsewhere. These tombs are unusual, for most Italian memorials are placed against walls, as in the cloisters at Padua, but common features are the gabled Gothic canopies, the carved sarcophagi, and the supporting columns or caryatides. The stern Gothic forms of the Scaliger tombs commemorate the genius of a powerful dynasty whose crest, the ladder, recurs as a motif in the ironwork of the tomb-enclosures.

As funerary art developed, full effigies were created instead of incised

Plate 10 Tomb of Can
Signorio della Scala, the most
sumptuous of the fourteenth-
century Scaliger tombs in
Verona (*Stephen Thompson,
Author's Collection*)

Plate 11 Canopied tomb of S. Etienne, of the mid-thirteenth century, at Aubazine, Corrèze (*Author's Collection*)

designs or low reliefs, and these effigies were protected within niches or under canopies, and were supported on a raised base. A beautiful example is the canopied tomb at Aubazine, Corrèze, of 1250, which incorporates a Gothic arcade that surrounds the effigy. Above, the roof also has an arcade, the spaces between columns being busy with figures. The form is still basically that of the temple, but the entire work becomes an original and lovely work of Gothic art (Pl. 11). Some early bronze effigies exist, the finest perhaps being that of Eleanor, Queen of Edward I, of 1292. This is among the most superb bronze effigies existing in Europe; the figure of the queen is sheer perfection, an unquestioned masterpiece of late-thirteenth-century art (Pl. 12). The Queen died in Nottinghamshire, and the progress of her funeral to London is celebrated. At each spot where her bier rested the King caused a cross to be erected, and the three surviving crosses are acclaimed as great works of thirteenth-century architecture. These crosses were not only memorials: they were intended to inspire those who saw them to pray for the soul of the Queen. It is less well known that such a long progress to London necessitated the embalming of the body, and indeed most persons of wealth were partially embalmed from the Middle Ages until the eighteenth century. The Queen's bowels were buried in the Lady Chapel of Lincoln Cathedral, and another effigy was erected over the spot, finely executed in latten, gilt, and enamels. The inscription boldly read:

Hic sunt sepulta vicera Alionore quondam Regine Anglie,
Uxoris Regis Edvardi Filii Regis Henrici. Cujus anime propitietur Deus.
Amen. Pater Noster.

Unfortunately, this extraordinary monument has been destroyed. Queen Eleanor's sumptuous funeral, and the immense amount of wealth (including gifts of twenty-two manors) necessary to ensure that religious observances would be continued, set something of a fashion among the well-to-do. Families vied with each other to provide suitable endowments for funerary and post-funerary purposes. The parallels with Ancient Egyptian and Roman practices will be obvious. Eleanor was buried in Westminster Abbey

Plate 12 Effigy of Queen Eleanor, Westminster Abbey, drawn by Blore and engraved by Le Keux (*Author's Collection*)

'in the chapell of seynt Edwarde, at ye fete of Henry the thirde, where she hathe ii wexe tapers brennynge upon her tumbe both daye and nyght, which so hath cotynued syne the day of her buryinge to this present daye'.[5]

Queen Eleanor's monument is on the north side of the Confessor's chapel, under one of the arcades that separates it from the aisle. It consists of an altar-tomb of grey marble, relieved with Gothic gabled niches, cusped, crocketed, and with finials. It was executed by Richard Crundale. Within each opening is a heraldic shield (Pl. 13). The effigies of the Queen and of Henry III were the work of Master William Torel, a goldsmith who produced shrines and images for the Church. He employed a system of casting based upon the waste-wax method, which involved the spreading of wax over a core, its modelling, and replacement with metal. The surface of the metal was then engraved and enriched. Queen Eleanor's effigy is a work of serene beauty. She lies, with her head on patterned cushions, decorated

Plate 13 Monument of Queen Eleanor in Westminster Abbey, drawn by Blore and engraved by Le Keux (*Author's Collection*)

with the arms of Castile and Leon, her eyes open, and her long locks framing her noble face. Her left arm lies over her breast, and her right hand is relaxed, poised over her right side. It once held a sceptre. Over her crowned head is a canopy. A fine iron grille protects the effigy. The drapery is long and flowing, and beautifully arranged. Valuable ornaments were once fixed to the sleeves and to the coronet.

The gabled niches on the altar-tomb of Queen Eleanor were the usual form of decoration on fourteenth-century tombs of substance, but gradually gave way to niches topped by little vaulted canopies enriched with tabernacle-work. During the fourteenth century tomb-decoration assumed a form that remained more or less constant for the next century, and it achieved complete expression in the monument of Edward III in Westminster Abbey (1377). The base of the altar-tomb is enriched with square panels of cusped quatrefoils containing heraldic shields. The altar-tomb itself, of Petworth marble, has six niches on each side under vaulted canopies enriched with tabernacle-work. In the niches were beautifully wrought figures of gilt latten, and under each niche are quatrefoils. Between

Plate 14 Monument of Edward III in Westminster Abbey, drawn and engraved by Blore (*Author's Collection*)

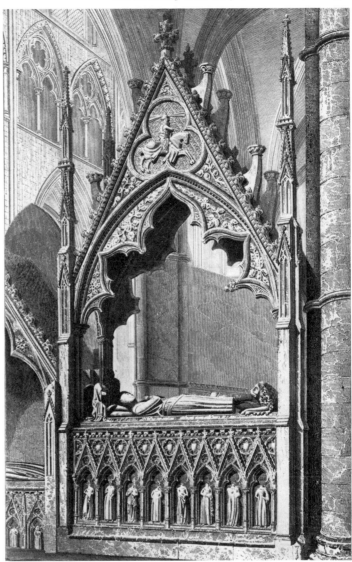

the niches are blind panels of tracery surmounted by crocketed gables. Flanking each niche are buttresses capped by crocketed finials (Pl. 14). The top of the table-tomb is of gilt latten and the effigy lies on it within a canopied shrine, the sides of which are enriched with tabernacle-work and other effigies (Pl. 15). Over the tomb is a wooden canopy or tester.

The chief characteristics of tomb-design in the fourteenth century were the use of the gable as an architectural element, freely enriched with crockets, finials, and foliate decorations. Plain spaces were eschewed, and niche-work became fashionable. Towering canopies were developed in tiers from the second quarter of the century, and canopies almost overwhelmed the tombs by their intricacy and size. The tomb in Westminster Abbey of Aymer de Valence, Earl of Pembroke (died 1324), is an excellent example, and consists of a single gabled canopy over a cinquefoiled arch that shields an altar-tomb enriched with gabled niches containing weepers (Pl. 16). Canopies were often of exquisite workman-

85

ship; the mid-fourteenth century canopy over Bishop Drokersford's tomb in Wells Cathedral displays tabernacle work of a high order, carrying stonecarving to lace-like extremes (Pl. 17). By the third quarter of the century, tomb design assumed a form that remained more or less constant for the next hundred years, and is shown in its complete form in the monument of Edward III (Pl. 14).

Plate 17 Tabernacle-work above Bishop Drokersford's tomb in Wells Cathedral (*The Author*)

Plate 18 Monument of
Edward the Black Prince in
Canterbury Cathedral, drawn
and engraved by Blore
(*Author's Collection*)

The monuments of Thomas Beauchamp, Earl of Warwick, and his
Countess date from 1370. The usual arrangement of weepers in niches
adorns the altar-tomb. The effigies are shown holding hands in a display of
marital affection. The tomb is in the choir of S Mary's Church in Warwick.
To some extent the whole church might be regarded as the mausoleum of
the Beauchamp family, for three Earls are interred there.

The effigy of Edward the Black Prince of 1376 in Canterbury Cathedral
is particularly fine, for it shows the Prince in armour, resting on his helm.
The effigy is of gilt latten, set with coloured stones and enamelled. The tomb
is situated under an arch dividing the nave from the south aisle of the
Trinity Chapel. The altar-tomb is of Sussex marble, the top of which is set
with brass. The sides of the tomb are enriched with square compartments
containing shields. A wooden canopy protects the whole monument
(Pl. 18).

The tomb of Philippa of Hainault, Queen to Edward III, stands in the
south side of the Chapel of the Confessor in Westminster Abbey. It consists
of an altar-tomb of black marble on a high base, surmounted by a simple
wooden canopy. The sides of the tomb were enriched with a great profusion
of canopy work in pierced alabaster of the most exquisite workmanship. The
canopies were three large and three small on each side, and two large and one
small at each end. Each large canopy contained two figures, and each small

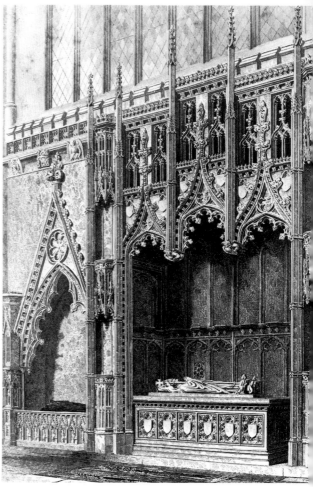

canopy contained one figure. The effigy of 1369 was the work of Hawkin of Liège, a Frenchman. The seventy-odd smaller figures around the tomb were made by John Orchard, Latoner.[6] These small figures were called 'weepers', and most have been destroyed (Pl. 19).[7] About the year 1290 tombs became adorned by these little figures set in canopied niches or arcades. The tomb of Archbishop Peckham in Canterbury is one of the first examples where Gothic weepers appeared, and was set beneath a richly ornamental gabled arch. It contrasts with the contiguous monument of Archbishop Warham, of the first half of the sixteenth century (Pl. 20). The effigy of Bishop Walter Bronescombe in Exeter Cathedral (1280) is typical of ecclesiastical effigies of this date. Bishops hold a crozier in the left hand, and bless with the right. The figures that very commonly stood around mediaeval tombs within arrangements of canopies, niches, and Gothic ornament had predecessors in the 'weepers' that stood between the columns of Greek sarcophagi and tombs. The celebrated 'Tomb of the Weepers' at Sidon is an exact classical equivalent of the Gothic altar-tombs surrounded by 'weepers'. The tomb of Louis of France, heir of Louis IX, at Saint-Denis, has an effigy on a fully colonnaded sarcophagus. Between the columns of the Gothic arcade are figures in procession following the prince's bier. The effigy itself has open eyes and hands pressed together in prayer, a common type of figure that survived in popularity long after the Reformation and the Renaissance. Weepers are often shown heavily cowled, as in the tomb of Philippe le Hardi, Duke of Burgundy, and in the tomb of Philippe Pot, Grand Seneschal of Burgundy, formerly in the Abbey of Cîteaux. The Pot tomb, of the late-fifteenth century, is a remarkable work, for the weepers have become pall-bearers, and carry the slab on which the effigy lies.

During the thirteenth and fourteenth centuries, water was the main form of transport in England. Many tombs of the period were carved in dark limestone from the Isle of Purbeck, and were transported by sea. Stone was also imported from France. There were other regional stones used in the period, notably sandstones, chalk-stones, and freestones. The general use of freestones from the fourteenth century was caused by the fashion of covering effigies with coatings of *gesso* (a mixture of size and whiting) and paint, which made the choice of stone immaterial for effigies, though not, of course, for the architectural work. These materials continued in use until the end of the Middle Ages, although from the mid-fourteenth to the sixteenth century Derbyshire and Staffordshire alabaster greatly increased in popularity, and largely displaced the stones favoured earlier. Timber was also used for effigies, and was coated with *gesso*. The details of the mail and armour were pressed by dyes onto the *gesso* while still plastic, and the effigies were afterwards gilded and coloured. Shields and swords were added. Wooden and stone effigies were often further embellished with enamels, coloured stones, and metals. Alabaster became fashionable from 1300, and by the end of the century had largely replaced other materials for tombs and effigies. It is easily carved, and has an agreeable translucent quality. Against dark marble it is most attractive.

Bronze or latten was used throughout the period, but many examples have been stolen through the centuries. From the time of the effigies of Edward III and the Black Prince (the last quarter of the fourteenth century) workmanship of funeral monuments was exceedingly fine; metal workers, carvers of alabaster, and enamellers produced designs of great refinement.

The styles of the mediaeval period are often best expressed in surviving tombs and chantry-chapels, as these structures are of comparatively small size. When tombs were placed away from walls, and had no canopies, they lost their coffin-form and became altar-like, usually decorated with quatrefoils or arcades. Heraldry was in vogue as decoration by the mid-thirteenth century. Canopies began to appear over tombs at this time. In the last decades of that century, Abbot Richard Ware brought Italian artists in *Cosmati*-work (mosaics and marble inlays) to assist in the decorations of Edward the Confessor's shrine in Westminster. The tombs of Henry III and of his children were also embellished with Italian *Cosmati*-work of peculiar richness.

There appears to have been a regular exchange of craftsmen and materials between England and continental Europe during the Middle Ages. Richard Ware arranged for Peter and Odoric, workers in Roman *Cosmati*, to visit

Far left Plate 19 Monument of Philippa of Hainault, Queen of Edward III, in Westminster Abbey, drawn and engraved by Blore (*Author's Collection*)

Left Plate 20 Monuments of Archbishops Peckham and Warham in Canterbury Cathedral, drawn and engraved by Blore (*Author's Collection*)

England when he was in Rome in 1267. Certainly the lovely *Cosmati*-work of the tomb of Henry III is very similar to that of the monuments to Hadrian V and Clement IV, both in the Church of San Francesco at Viterbo. Odoric is credited with the work on the tomb of Clement IV (died 1268). Perhaps one of the most interesting of tombs of this *genre* is that of Cardinal Giovanni di Brago (died 1282) by Arnolfo di Cambio in the Church of San Domenico in Orvieto (Pl. 21). The designs of *Cosmati*-work in the base of this tomb are typical of the period.

No consideration of the mediaeval period would be complete without taking into account the effects of the Black Death, which effectively divided the epoch. The plague made its terrible visitation in the middle of the fourteenth century, and such was the toll that many religious houses were emptied, and many persons unfitted to religious life were admitted to formerly august establishments. The scarcity of masons changed the character of Gothic architecture, which began to lose its soaring verticality, and detail became repetitive and more rectangular in character. Despite the death-toll, however, England made a rapid economic recovery. Merchants, often in the wool trade, became wealthy, and were ennobled for services to the King. The increasing power of the merchant-classes, and the weakening of the old nobility, were now factors in the architecture of death. Comfort and amenities were more prized by the powerful new classes, who also spent freely to enlarge and enrich the churches. The great churches of East Anglia, the Cotswolds, and Devon are typical of the period. Often, chantry-chapels were added to the church, either as extensions or as screened enclosures within the churches.

When the notion of Purgatory became respectable, prayers for the dead became an essential part of religious devotion. Donations and gifts to the great abbeys and churches ensured prayers for the living but the emphasis gradually changed to encourage prayers for the dead. These observances were known as chantries, and royal example ensured nationwide popularity. Benefactors, founders, and pious persons desired that intercession would be made for their souls, and prayers for them were carried on in perpetuity by grateful institutions. *Obits*, or Masses on the anniversary of a founder's death, were said for a limited time or in perpetuity, depending on the size of the donation, and indeed there appear to have been recognised scales of charges for *Obits*. The rich and powerful endowed chantries, and in many cases caused individual chapels around their tombs to be erected, where prayers would be said for the repose of their souls. Often those chapels were themselves canopied, and are almost miniature churches within churches. England has a great number of surviving chantry-chapels; the cathedral of Winchester and Westminster Abbey contain the finest examples. Intercession for one's soul became desirable, for the horrors of hell were depicted with such ferocity. As a result chantries generally became part of the economy of the mediaeval Church.

From the fifteenth century, ornate fittings and exquisite carving became usual in funerary architecture. Chantry-chapels began to play an important part in the architectural elements of churches and cathedrals, and were enclosed by screenworks of stone, wood, and metal. They often formed

Plate 21 Tomb of Cardinal Giovanni di Brago in the church of San Domenico in Orvieto. Note the Cosmati-work in the base (*Author's Collection*)

small complete buildings in themselves, with their own altars and even sacristies, the enclosures generally taking the form of open tracery-work. The niche-work was finished with cresting. Often such chantry-chapels had elaborately vaulted roofs; that of Isabel, Countess of Warwick, of 1422 is a fine example (Pl. 22). Gabled arches were sometimes favoured, usually in threes, as in the very refined and delicate chantry-chapel of William of Wykeham in the nave at Winchester Cathedral (1404) (Pl. 23). Inside is an effigy of the bishop on an altar-tomb around which is an inscription on enamelled brass.

Elaborate screenwork was also found above tombs, such as the exquisite

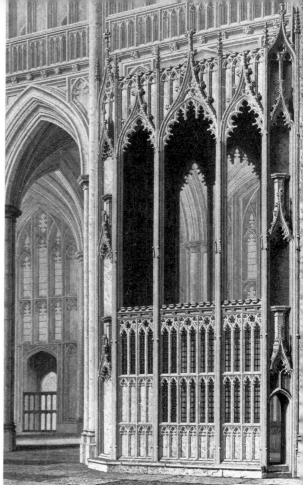

mid-fourteenth century work over the vault of Humphrey, Duke of Gloucester, in St Alban's. During this period, four-centred arches came into fashion, although the ogee was often found in canopies. Flattened arches were a special feature in south-west England, as in the canopy over the tomb of Bishop Stafford (died 1419) in Exeter Cathedral. The effigy is delicate and beautiful, and the canopy was the model for Bishop Bronescombe's monument (Pl. 24).

The majority of tombs follows the niched and tabernacled form of the centres of the alabaster industry. The tomb in Canterbury of Henry IV and his Queen, Joan of Navarre, is a fine example (Pl. 25). The effigies themselves lie under canopies of the greatest of delicacy, and are formalized to harmonize with the architectural decoration. Similar head-canopies are found on the alabaster tomb of Thomas Fitz-Alan, Earl of Arundel, in Arundel, Sussex. The monument dates from 1416, and has effigies of the Earl and his wife under head-canopies, on an altar-tomb enriched with niches and weepers (Pl. 26). Exquisite though these effigies with elaborate canopies are, the Fitzalan Chapel contains chantry-chapels and tombs of even greater interest. The chantry-chapel and tomb of William, the ninth Earl, and his wife, of the late fifteenth century, has more than a hint of the Renaissance; but in the tomb of Thomas, the tenth Earl, and his wife, late-Gothic and Renaissance motifs mingle in the oddest fashion. The tomb consists of a tripartite canopy carried on columns that have Perpendicular

Far left Plate 22 Chantry-chapel of Isabel, Countess of Warwick, (*ob.* 1439) at Tewkesbury, drawn by Carter (*Author's Collection*)

Above Plate 23 Chantry-chapel of William of Wykeham, Bishop of Winchester, in Winchester Cathedral, drawn by Blore and engraved by Le Keux (*Author's Collection*)

Plate 24 Tomb of Bishop Stafford (died 1419) in Exeter Cathedral (*The Author*)

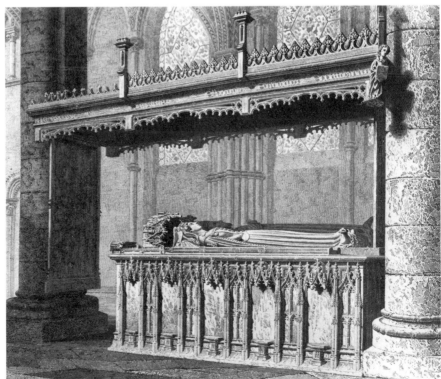

Plate 25 Monument of Henry IV and Joan of Navarre in Canterbury Cathedral, drawn by Blore and engraved by Le Keux (*Author's Collection*)

Plate 26 Monument of Thomas, Earl of Arundel, and his countess, Beatrix, in Arundel Church, drawn by Blore and engraved by Le Keux (*Author's Collection*)

and Renaissance elements. Squat ogees with cusps carry panelled spandrels over which are panels of coats of arms (Pl. 27). The head-canopy and effigy of the tomb of Alice, Duchess of Suffolk, of 1477 in Ewelme Church, Oxfordshire, gives some idea of the supreme delicacy of funerary art in this period. This alabaster effigy lies on a tomb-chest supported on an arcade. Behind the traceried openings on which the tomb-chest stands is a *memento mori*, a wizened cadaver, partially covered by a shroud, a grim example of late-Gothic love of the macabre. The decomposing corpse is depicted in great detail. It lies on a shroud, the long tresses falling from the skull. The

Plate 27 Canopied tomb of Earl Thomas in the Fitzalan Chapel, Arundel (*Author's Collection*)

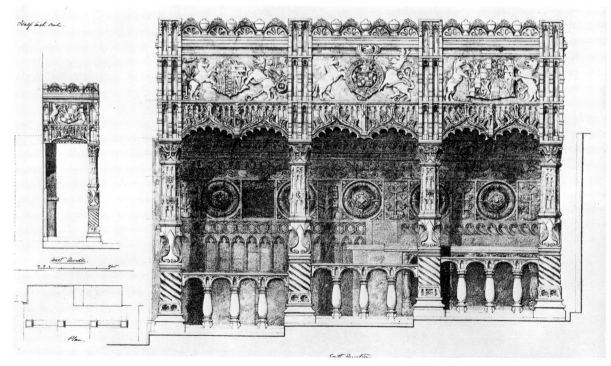

Plate 28 Tomb of Bishop
Beckington (1451) in Wells
Cathedral, with mediaeval
ironwork (*The Author*)

contrast with the beauties of the alabaster figure above is infinitely painful.
The tomb of Bishop Beckington in Wells Cathedral of 1451 has two tiers:
this time the slab on which the effigy rests is a table supported on slender
colonnettes. This arrangement leaves the cadaver displayed under the table.
The iron screen is particularly fine (Pl. 28).

In northern Europe, the physical facts of death had entered into funerary
art. Besides the grim business of war and violent death, plague and disease
had been constant visitors. The Black Death was horrific in its fury and
effects, and emphasized the transience of life. Earthly splendour and
physical beauty began to be contrasted, almost obsessionally, with the
horrible realities of decay and corruption in the tombs of the great. At
S. Denis the effigies of Louis XII and his Queen are shown with the
incisions and stitches made by the embalmers. Often entrails, hearts, and
other parts of the body were buried at different places. Bishop Aymer de
Valence, for example, had his heart separately deposited in a shrine in
Winchester in 1261. Often, too, bodies were 'boned'. The flesh was boiled
off the bones and buried in one place, while the skeleton was entombed
elsewhere, a practice much favoured by warriors who died abroad and
wished to be buried at home. The cadaver under Bishop Beckington's tomb
at Wells is particularly grisly, while at Tewkesbury, the corpse of John
Wakeman is shown being devoured by a mouse, serpents, worms, and snails.

These *memento mori* monuments are called the *gisant* type of sepulchral
art. *Gisant* monuments were intended to have an admonitory effect on the

living. A poet of the period, contrasting the grand tombs and their once-grand occupants with the reality of maggots and decay, could exclaim:

Et dans ces grands tombeaux, où leurs âmes hautaines
Font encore les vaines
Ils sont mangés des vers.

Referencces to the realities of death, when bodies became compost and food for worms, were frequently found in the inscriptions on the *gisant* type of monument, such as:

Nunc putredo terrae et cibus verminorum.

Epitaphs sometimes grimly punned, as on the death of the 'Fair Rosamund':

Hic jacet in tumba Rosa mundi, non Rosa munda;
Non redolet, sed olet, quae redolere solet.[8]

Although the funerary art and architecture of northern Europe was often exquisite, and reached the heights in the cathedrals of England, France, Germany, and the Netherlands, there were often horrific aspects where the realities of decay, and the imagined horrors of Hell, were depicted with macabre relish. Somehow the ghastliness of death was avoided to a great extent by Italian architects and artists, so that funerary sculpture and architecture in Italy tend to a serenity that is often lacking in the north. In Italy, funerary architecture was handled with a clarity, a logic, and a sense of tact that transcended the melodramatic art of the *gisant* type. Elements such as effigies, sarcophagi, canopies, and heraldic devices were often handled with a sure touch that created serene and noble architecture. Something of this sense of clarity and simplicity can be seen in the mortuary chapel of Richard Beauchamp, Earl of Warwick, in the Church of S. Mary in Warwick. This family sepulchre is unquestionably the best preserved of English mortuary chapels, and it contains a wealth of late-mediaeval funerary art. The Earl's effigy, in a magnificent suit of armour, lies on a great alabaster tomb-chest enriched by canopied niches containing weepers of latten. The hands of the effigy seem to be embracing the image of Our Blessed Lady as Queen of Heaven, depicted in the vaulting above. The tomb-chest still has the original herse of latten over which the pall was placed (Pl. 29). The figure was made by William Austen, and designed by John Massingham. The reredos of the chapel contained sculpture of the Annunciation, where angels and saints enriched the detail. On the west wall John Brentwood painted the Last Judgement which was re-done rather poorly in 1678. The present reredos is largely eighteenth-century Gothick. The tomb of the Earl was made between 1453 and 1456. Other later monuments in the chapel give an excellent idea of the changes in funerary art from the Renaissance until the end of the seventeenth century.

The building of chantry-chapels enriched cathedrals and churches

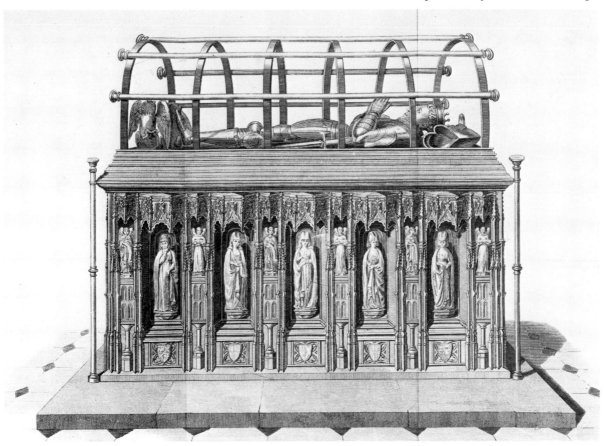

Plate 29 Tomb of Richard
Beauchamp, Earl of Warwick,
in S Mary's, Warwick, drawn
by Carter and engraved by
Basire (*Author's Collection*)

throughout the fifteenth century. The chapel of S. Saviour (1424) in Wells
Cathedral, known as the chantry-chapel of Bishop Nicholas Bubwith, is
another example where delicate open screens of tracery cling to the arcade of
the Early-English nave. This is a fine example of Perpendicular masonry. The
chantry-chapel in Exeter of Precentor William Sylke, however, of the early-
sixteenth century, shows four-centred arches in the screen, while the tomb
itself is incorporated in the screen. The tomb remains an altar-tomb
essentially, but quatrefoils have replaced niches and weepers, and the effigy
itself has become a cadaver. The warning on the cornice above the tomb
itself reads:

Sum quod eris, fueramque quod es, pro me, precor, ora Will Sylke (Pl. 30).

This was again a common admonition, and is even found in S. Maria Novella
in Florence, in Italian.[9][10]

This was a far cry indeed from the simple ogee arches with crockets,
cuspings, and finials, that once sheltered effigies either in the walls of the
church, or as free-standing objects. The Middle Ages had almost passed
away, and indeed the building in 1518 of Henry VII's tomb in Westminster
by the Italian master, Pietro Torrigiani, brought Renaissance ideas and a
new classical manner to tomb design. The immediate effects of Italian
Renaissance designs can be detected in Sir Anthony Browne's tomb of 1540
at Battle, where shell-motifs are used and *putti* appear instead of weepers

Plate 30 Chantry-chapel of Precentor William Sylke, in Exeter Cathedral (*The Author*)

(Pl. 31). The beautiful Howard tombs at Framlingham in Suffolk also have Renaissance motifs. One of the loveliest of late-Gothic tombs is that of Henry II and Kunigunde, in Bamberg Cathedral. It was carved by Tilman Riemenschneider between 1499 and 1513. The effigies of the Emperor and Empress lie on a sarcophagus, the sides of which are carved in high relief showing events in their lives. The tomb of Princess Mary of Burgundy (1495) in the Church of Notre Dame (*Onze lieve Vrouwenkerk*) in Brugge is a refined and serene late-Gothic monument, and consists of a delicately worked recumbent figure in chased and gilded bronze on a sarcophagus of

Plate 31 Monument of Sir Anthony Browne in Battle Church, drawn by Blore and engraved by Le Keux (*Author's Collection*)

Plate 32 Tomb of Charles the Bold (Karel de Stoute) of Burgundy in Onze lieve Vrouwenkerk in Brugge (*Photograph by courtesy of the Courtauld Institute of Art*)

marble. The sides of the sarcophagus are faced with Gothic arches and with niches containing enamelled armorial bearings. This beautiful tomb was created by Pieter de Beckere of Brussels. The adjacent tomb was erected in 1559 by Philip II of Spain, and contains the body of Charles the Bold, Duke of Burgundy, father of Princess Mary. The tomb of Charles the Bold is by Jonghelinck of Antwerp; although superficially similar to that of Princess Mary it is entirely Renaissance in spirit. The two tombs in juxtaposition show how Renaissance art had utterly changed European taste (Pl. 32).

In 1529 an Act of Parliament was passed in England to prohibit any endowments or payments for *Obits*, and chantry funds were confiscated by the Crown in 1547 when the 'vain opinion' of Purgatory was denounced. The wealth tied up in chantries was immense, for no less than ninety collegiate establishments, over a hundred hospitals, and over two thousand guild and individual chantries were dissolved. Some lesser foundations escaped the rapacious Henry VIII, such as Ewelme, where prayers are still said for William de la Pole, the founder of the alms-houses.

The open space round which cloisters were constructed was often used for burial in the mediaeval period; interment took place in the cloister garth or under the flagstones of the cloister itself. The enclosed garth was a peaceful mediaeval graveyard, far removed from the crowded city graveyards. The Gothic cloisters at Sant' Antonio in Padua contain many ancient tombstones. The idea of a cloister as a burial-place was developed to a rational conclusion by the architect Giovanni Pisano, whose Campo Santo in Pisa forms part of the most remarkable group of early-mediaeval ecclesiastical buildings in Europe. It was begun in 1270, consecrated in

1278, and embellished with Gothic tracery in 1463. From the outside, the Campo Santo appears as a simple rectangular building, with a blind arcade of the utmost refinement running all round it. The door in the south side gives access to the cloister. The green garth is surrounded by a spacious cloister with unglazed semicircular-headed openings filled with Gothic tracery. Three chapels adjoin this cloister. The oldest is in the centre of the east side, with a dome of late date. There are frescoes of the Tuscan School of the fourteenth and fifteenth centuries. These include a painting showing three men out hunting finding the three decaying corpses of themselves. The idea of the *Dance of Death* or *Danse Macabre* originated in a thirteenth-century poem, *Le Dit des trois morts and des trois vifs*, and appeared on the cloister-walls of many ecclesiastical establishments throughout Europe. It is also found on the walls of the tiny Oxfordshire church at Widford. Its most celebrated use as a fresco was in the cloisters of the cemetery of the Holy Innocents in Paris, painted in about 1425, above the serried rows of charnel-houses.[10] The Campo Santo contains many sarcophagi and funerary monuments. It must be the most serene and beautiful cemetery in the world, and, architecturally, the finest by far. It is perfection, and a triumph of creation by its architect. The arrangement of vaults in the floor is strictly worked out within the architectural pattern. Bands of black marble in strips follow the rhythms of piers and columns, and define the boundaries of each vault. This is a remarkably ordered pattern, providing a clear and serene solution. Smaller in scale are the cloisters of SS. Annunziata in Florence, decorated with beautiful frescoes, and adorned with funerary monuments (Pl. 34).

In other European countries, Gothic art provided fertile answers to the

Plate 33 The cloisters of the Campo Santo in Pisa (*The Author*)

Plate 34 Cloisters of the
Dead, adjoining the Church
of SS. Annunziata, Florence.
It was built by Simone
Pollajuolo, with frescoes by
Poccetti. There is also a fine
fresco, *La Madonna del
Sacco*, by Andrea del Sarto,
of 1525 (*The Author*)

problems posed by the architecture of death. The Chapel of Santiago (1435)
in the chevet of Toledo Cathedral in Spain is a mortuary chapel of singular
magnificence, octagonal on plan, and richly ornamented with *Flamboyant*
tracery. Spain also can boast one of the oddest mediaeval tombs in Europe,
that of the Royal family at the Carthusian monastery of Miraflores, near
Burgos. The plan is star-shaped, and the detail is exquisite, with angels,
flowers, buttresses, and niches all supporting the recumbent effigies of
John II and his Queen. The designer was Gil de Siloe (Pl. 35). Also at
Miraflores is the magnificent late-Gothic sepulchre of the Infante Don
Alonso, also by Gil de Siloe. Instead of the still calm of a recumbent effigy,
all the figures of this tomb are in some state of movement, and a curiously
unmediaeval note is struck. The heraldic devices, kneeling figures, and
tabernacle work date from 1470 (Pl. 36).

Throughout Europe, the commencement of the sixteenth century saw
increasing evidence of Renaissance influence in funerary design. One of the
last great chantry-chapels built in England is that of Henry VII in
Westminster Abbey. This is set in the Lady Chapel of 1519, which contains
the greatest gallery of figure-sculpture of the period, and which is unusual in
that it has a 'chevet' arrangement of chapels at the east end. In the centre of
the apse is the tomb and chantry-chapel of Henry VII and his Queen,
Elizabeth of York. The altar-tomb is of *touch* (a variety of black marble) and
of white marble with gilt-bronze enrichments. The gilt-bronze pilasters
with Corinthian caps and bases, and the panels with the conventional Italian
embellishments are totally Renaissance in character. The winged *putti*,
heraldic devices, and other ornaments are also uncompromisingly Italian in
manner. The designs of effigies, made in 1512, by Humfry Walker and

Plate 35 Tomb of John II and his Queen at the Carthusian monastery of Miraflores (*Photograph by courtesy of the Courtauld Institute of Art*)

Nicholas Ewen, are by Pietro Torrigiani of Florence, who also designed the whole ensemble of the altar-tomb. The monument itself is a stranger in an environment of Gothic detail. The beautiful bronze screen that surrounds the chantry-chapel is pure Perpendicular Gothic, and hardly prepares the visitor for the logical, humane, classical work that lies at the centre of the chapel (Pl. 37). The contrast is almost unbearable, and the impact of the blinding light of the Renaissance in a world of Gothic mysteries and faith is symbolised most poignantly. A similar contrast is found in the Burgundian tombs in Brugge.

Yet, in northern Europe, the Reformation and other events of the time saw a turning away from the promises of the Renaissance born in Italy. Taste veered towards Flanders, and by the end of the sixteenth century a somewhat coarse style in funerary art prevailed that owed only superficial elements to Italian precedent. The glorious dawn that had been promised in the work of Torrigiani, and indeed in those other works of Italian designers in the thirteenth century at Westminster Abbey, had proved to be false. Perhaps it is true to say that Italian art was not really assimilated by northern

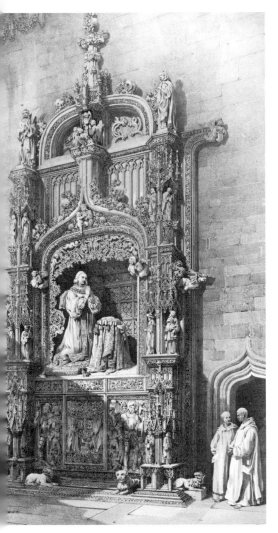

craftsmen, just as Gothic art was never truly assimilated by Italians.[11]

The Reformation caused a denial that the form or situation of a grave had any religious significance. In Protestant countries, therefore, funerary architecture became a purely social manifestation, and design was decided by taste and by individual demand. The change in political power was very considerable, for the position of the Church as an independent organization was weakened. There was no opposition, therefore, when, from the sixteenth century, churches began to be filled with huge funerary monuments. In the British Isles the nobility led the way in this development, while in Sweden the House of Vasa set the fashion. The nobility and the newly enriched demanded huge tombs within the churches. It seemed as though churches would become filled with bulky and incongruous monuments to earthly vanity.[12]

4

The Renaissance and Baroque Periods of Funerary Architecture associated with churches, and their aftermath.

The rise of the individual; Italy; Innsbruck; England; Spain; the Netherlands; Bernini and the Baroque; the influence of Bernini in Europe; Neoclassical funerary art; modern effigial tombs

To subsist in lasting Monuments, to live
in their productions, to exist in their
names, and praedicament of *Chymera*'s,
was large satisfaction unto old expectations,
and made one part of their *Elyziums*.

SIR THOMAS BROWNE (1605–1682): *Hydriotaphia*

The world of the Middle Ages was dominated by faith, perhaps by illusion, and unquestionably by fear. The mists through which we view the mediaeval epoch occasionally part to reveal a man of the period as part of some corporate identity. From the fourteenth century, however, a type of consciousness developed that was hardly mediaeval. The new man was an *individual*, and developed first in Italy, possibly through the struggles between the Hohenstaufen and the Papacy, and later within the many republics and despotisms that flourished in Italy. The glorification of individuals has already been noted in the tombs of the Scaligers at Verona, and in their funerary monuments. The republics and despotisms of late-mediaeval Italy encouraged individual development to the highest levels of *l'uomo universale*. Cosmopolitanism and the rediscovery of the glories of classical culture were part of a movement that produced a Dante, a Petrarch, and the enlightened courts of Ferrara, Padua, and elsewhere. The glorification of celebrities took on a magnificence that had once been given to saints alone. The cult of honouring the birthplaces of famous men was matched by the cult of tombs. It must be remembered that, in northern Europe especially, pilgrimages were made to relics, images, and pictures, rather than to places themselves. The holding of bones or other relics therefore had a value in hard commercial terms.[1]

It is astonishing, given the climate of fourteenth-century Europe generally, to consider how earnestly the Florentines of that era worked to change their cathedral into something approaching a pantheon for their own celebrities. In the following century Lorenzo the Magnificent tried to wheedle the corpse of the painter Fra Filippo Lippi from Spoleto to dignify the cathedral, and Boccaccio tried to obtain the relics of Dante from Ravenna. In the event it was Santa Croce that became the true Florentine pantheon. Naples woke up to the fact that it possessed the tomb of Virgil, and almost every city in Italy eagerly celebrated its artistic and heroic dead.

Savonarola praises secular celebrities as well as saints in *De Laudibus Padavii*, and a tendency to create a pantheon of the famous, in literature at least, was part of a Renaissance movement to elevate those who excelled, rather than the high-born or the holy alone.

Material knowledge of a classical past was not only increased by the study of literature, but by the excavations at Rome and elsewhere. Roman ruins excited scholarly zeal, patriotism, and a kind of melancholy displayed by both Petrarch and Boccaccio. What is more, scholars could study the relics of a pagan past with impunity now that 'true religion' was apparently everywhere triumphant.[2]

In the fifteenth century, Florence developed into the leading city-state of Italy as a centre for banking, commerce, and artistic creation. The Renaissance, as the age of humanism, developed from Florence, and its first, perhaps, greatest, figures were Florentines, including da Vinci, Machiavelli, the Medici, and Michelangelo. The fall of Constantinople to the Turks in 1453 caused a great number of Greek scholars to seek sanctuary in the west, and many settled in Florence under the enlightened rule of the Medici. Platonic ideals were rediscovered, and Florence was in the van of humanist thought, for in a sense Greek learning had come to life again in Florence. Significantly, in the tombs designed by Verocchio for Cosimo, Piero, and Giovanni de'Medici in the Church of San Lorenzo, classical motifs prevail, and no emblems of Christianity disturb the purity of these Renaissance masterpieces. Yet it is the so-called New Sacristy of San Lorenzo that must have pride of place in any mention of early-Renaissance funerary architecture. It was built by Michelangelo for Cardinal Giulio de' Medici (later Pope Clement VII) between 1520 and 1524 as a mausoleum for the house of Medici. It balances the Old Sacristy, built between 1421 and 1428 by Brunelleschi. The building is square on plan and is surmounted by a dome. The monuments are confined to those of Giuliano de' Medici (died 1516) and Lorenzo de' Medici (died 1519). The mausoleum is a work of great beauty, the architectural scheme harmonizing superbly with the sepulchre. The tomb of Giuliano de' Medici represents the Duke as a General of the Church, holding the commander's baton.[3] Below him is the sarcophagus, adorned by the celebrated statues of Day and Night. Opposite is the tomb of Lorenzo de' Medici, who is represented in meditation. The sarcophagus is adorned with statues of Evening and Dawn (Pls. 1, 2). A curious feature of the female figures is the manner in which Michelangelo stylised the breasts and muscles. The breasts look as though they have been applied to male figures, and the female figures are very strange when seen in the context of classical nudes. Truly it might be said by either female figure, as though to admonish us into speaking in whispers:

Grato m' è ' l sonno e più l' esser di sasso,
Mentre che 'l danno e la vergogna dura,
Non veder, non sentir, m'è gran ventura.
Però non mi destar; deh! parla basso!

A corridor leads to the Cappella dei Principi, the mausoleum of the grand

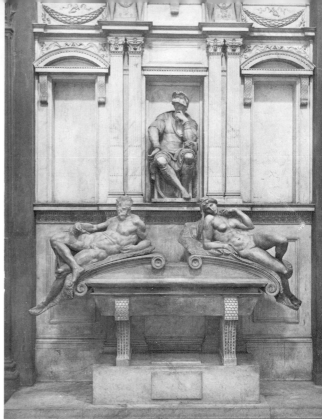

dukes of the Medici family. This huge octagon, decorated with marble and mosaic, was created between 1604 and 1640 to designs of Giovanni de' Medici by Matteo Nigetti. These tombs were quite different in character from those of the Middle Ages. Even the tomb of Henry VII in Westminster was essentially a mediaeval design with Renaissance detail. The Medicis did not look back to the Middle Ages, but rather to the glories of a classical past, for a celebration of the present. In these great Renaissance mausolea, there is no sense of a mysterious after-life; rather there is an eternal present, a *now*, an immense and unmysterious statement of the glory of Renaissance Man. Not for nothing did Lorenzo the Magnificent write:

> *Quant 'è bella giovinezza,*
> *Che si fugge tuttavia.*
> *Chi vuol esser lieto sia;*
> *Di doman' non c'è certezza.*

L. B. Alberti's church of San Francesco at Rimini was a remodelling of an earlier church, to conform to Renaissance tastes. His client was Malatesta, Lord of Rimini, and the casing of the building was begun in 1446. The façade is a re-working of a Roman triumphal arch, but the south side has seven semicircular-headed openings reminiscent of Imperial Roman architecture. Each niche holds a sarcophagus of impeccably classical ancestry, and these are monuments of the worthies of Sigismondo Malatesta's court. It is a commentary on the Renaissance period that Malatesta should have honoured the poets and scholars who brought such

Far left Plate 1 Tomb of Giuliano de'Medici in the New Sacristy of the Church of San Lorenzo in Florence, with the statues of Day and Night (*Mansell/Anderson Collection No. 8450*)

Above Plate 2 Tomb of Lorenzo de'Medici in the New Sacristy of the Church of San Lorenzo in Florence, with the statues of Evening and Dawn (*Mansell/Brogi Collection No. 3102*)

Right Plate 3 Tomb of Costanza Piccolomini in the cloister of Sant'Agostino in Rome (*Author's Collection*)

Far Right Plate 4 Tomb of Cardinal Fortiguerra in the church of Santa Cecilia in Trastevere, Rome (*Author's Collection*)

delight and illumination to his court in this way. The first four sarcophagi contain the remains of Basinio of Parma, Giusto de' Conti, Gennistus Pletho, and Roberto Valturio. Pletho's corpse was brought back to Rimini from Greece, indicating how far the cult of tombs had progressed. No philosopher would have been so honoured in mediaeval times.

The riches of fifteenth-century Italian funerary architecture are immense, and only a flavour of them can be suggested here. The tomb of Costanze Piccolomini in the cloister of the Church of Sant' Agostino in Rome is a full-blown Renaissance monument with a *piano nobile* arrangement of Corinthian pilasters, and a central aedicule (Pl. 3). The date, 1477, is remarkably early for such a tomb, and it must be thought of in terms of what was being built in Northern Europe at the same time. Even earlier is the beautiful Renaissance tomb of Cardinal Fortiguerra, by Mino da Fiesole, in the church of Santa Cecilia in Trastevere. The Cardinal died in 1473, but this fine tomb is almost *Empire* in its form, that of an elegant sarcophagus on a simple podium, with an effigy of the Cardinal on top (Pl. 4). The tomb of the physician Filippo della Valle (died 1494) by Michele Marini in the church of Santa Maria in Aracoeli is yet another variant, for the figure lies on a bed of books in a recess within the podium (Pl. 5). These tombs demonstrate how far Renaissance detail had become assured since the construction of the mausoleum of the Doge Pietro Mocenigo, of 1474–76,

with its curious mixture of Gothic and Renaissance styles. This mausoleum was built to the left of the main entrance of the church of Santi Giovanni e Páolo in Venice, with statuary by Pietro Lombardi (Pl. 6). More assuredly Renaissance in design is the tomb of Bishop Gomiel (died 1514) in the church of Santa Maria del Pòpolo in Rome. The effigy lies on a *quattrocento* sarcophagus within a rich arrangement of double pilasters on high pedestals, with a wide entablature (Pl. 7). The Campo Santo in Pisa contains

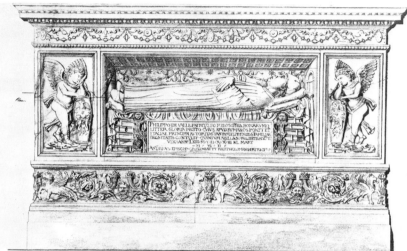

Plate 5 Tomb of Filippo della Valle in the church of Santa Maria in Aracoeli, Rome (*Author's Collection*)

Below left Plate 6 Mausoleum of Doge Pietro Mocenigo in the church of Santi Giovanni e Páolo, Venice (*Author's Collection*)

Right Plate 7 Monument of Giovanni Ortega Gomiel, Bishop of Polenza, in the church of Santa Maria del Pòpolo, Rome (*Author's Collection*)

Plate 8 Tomb of Filippo Decio in the Campo Santo in Pisa (*Author's Collection*)

several magnificent tombs, including many Roman sarcophagi, but one of the finest is that of Filippo Decio (died 1535). The figure is shown reading, reclining on a sarcophagus which is in turn supported by a richly carved entablature set on consoles (Pl. 8).

On the spot where S. Peter is supposed to have suffered martyrdom, in a courtyard beside the church of San Pietro in Montorio in Rome stands one of the most perfect buildings of the Renaissance, the Tempietto, erected between 1499 and 1502 to designs by Bramante. It is a circular building with a peristyle of sixteen Roman Doric columns and a high dome. The decoration is sparse, and the building is tiny, almost a reliquary. The chasm that divides this sophisticated monument of Italian humanism from the northern Gothic art of the same time is immense.

The tomb of Pope Sixtus IV formerly in S. Peter's in Rome is a magnificent work of 1493 by the Florentine artist Antonio Pollaiuolo. The effigy lies on a bronze couch, surrounded by allegories of the disciplines of learning. Other great papal tombs in the churches of Santa Maria Maggiore and San Giovanni in Laterano were powerful influences on funerary design of the period.

The export of such influences from Italy took curious forms in northern Europe, however, for the glories of mediaeval civilization all too often were to give way to a new, rather brash form of Renaissance monument, where the basic form remained mediaeval, yet the detail became influenced by classicism. The clear spirit of Italian humanism was often missing, however, and northern tombs appear for the most part clumsy and bucolic in comparison. Basically mediaeval in form, the tomb of Sir Robert Townshend (died 1581) and his wife in the Church of S. Laurence, Ludlow, in Shropshire, consists of a tomb-chest with fluted Ionic engaged columns

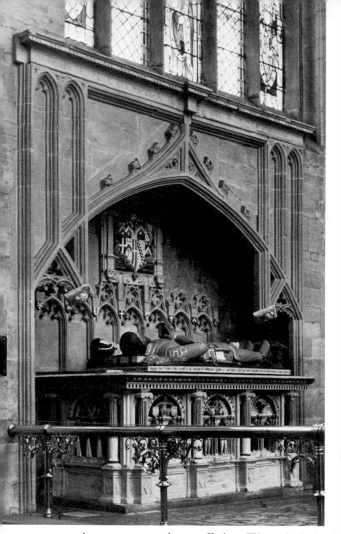

carrying two recumbent effigies. The whole is sheltered within an arched recess. Figures still stand in the niches within the panels between the columns, but the masterly serenity of the Middle Ages has passed (Pl. 9). The earliest indications of Renaissance influence often occur in sepulchral monuments, pulpits, portals, and fittings of existing Gothic buildings. This

Left Plate 9 Tomb of Sir Robert Townshend (*ob.* 1581) and his wife. Church of S. Laurence, Ludlow (*The Author*)

Right Plate 10 Tomb of the Cardinals d'Amboise in Rouen (*Author's Collection*)

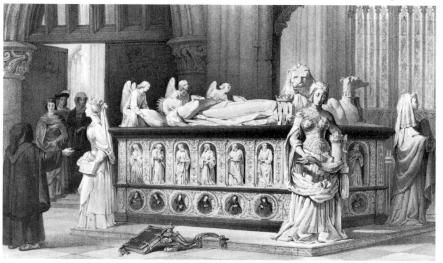

Plate 11 Tomb of François II at Nantes (*Author's Collection*)

is true of England, France, and many European countries. The tomb of Louis XII of 1515 in the Cathedral of S. Denis is an example, while the tomb of the Cardinals d'Amboise in Rouen by Roland Leroux of 1522 retains certain elements of Gothic design, yet Renaissance ornament seems to overwhelm it. Instead of the serenity, balance, and exquisite detail of the Middle Ages, a restless opulence seems to pervade the design (Pl. 10).

Much more mediaeval in spirit, though the detail is Renaissance, is the tomb of François II and his Queen in Nantes. Renaissance pilasters and

Plate 12 Cenotaph of Maximilian in Innsbruck *Left to right*: King Arthur of England, designed by Dürer and cast by Vischer, 1513; Ferdinand of Portugal, ancestor of Maximilian's mother, by Sesselschreiber, cast by P Löffler, 1509; Ernest of Habsburg, grandfather of Maximilian, by Sesselschreiber, cast by him, 1516; Theodoric, King of the Ostrogoths, designed by Dürer and cast by Vischer, 1513 (*Tiroler Volkskunstmuseum, Innsbruck*)

round-headed niches have replaced the canopied niches and tabernacle-work of the past (Pl. 11).

Sepulchral architecture reached new heights, however, in the least likely of places. Innsbruck, the capital of Tirol, was much favoured by the Emperor Maximilian, as it was later by the Empress Maria Theresia. The Hofkirche in Innsbruck owes its origins to the desire of Maximilian to erect a memorial to himself in order to increase the esteem of the House of Habsburg. The original idea for the tomb was a funeral procession of larger-than-life figures of bronze. In addition, there were to be one hundred smaller statues of saints, and some thirty busts of Roman Emperors. By 1502 the painter Gilg Sesselschreiber was appointed to design the large statues, and in 1508 he and the founder Stephan Godl arrived in Innsbruck. The first figures to be cast were the statuettes of the saints, for which the Court painter Jörg Kölderer made the sketches and the sculptor Leonhard Magt made the moulds. The work on the larger statues progressed slowly, but in 1509 Sesselschreiber had designed the first figure, that of Ferdinand of Portugal, and Peter Löffler the founder cast it (Pl. 12).

Work progressed too slowly for Maximilian's tastes, and Peter Vischer, the celebrated bronze-caster of Nürnberg, was brought in, and a foundry was built in Innsbruck. In 1513, the statues of Theodoric the Goth and Arthur, King of England, were cast by Vischer to designs by Albrecht Dürer (Pl. 12). The other statues were cast at Innsbruck. In 1518 Sesselschreiber was dismissed, and Godl was placed in charge. When Maximilian died in 1519, only eleven statues were finished, and Maximilian was buried in Wiener Neustadt. Work on the tomb proceeded, however, under Godl's direction, and in 1550 the last of the twenty-eight large statues was cast, that of the Frankish king, Clovis.

The entire monument became a grandiose cenotaph, and the central empty tomb was designed by Florian Abel of Prague. In 1561 the cenotaph was completed, with reliefs by the Abel brothers and by Alexander Colin of Mechelin. Colin also made the figure of Maximilian himself. The grille surrounding the empty sarcophagus was made by Jörg Schmiedhammer of Prague in 1570 to designs by Paul Trabel of Innsbruck.

In 1553 the foundations of the Hofkirche were laid, which, with the adjoining monastery, was designed by Andrea Crivelli. The vaults were by Marx della Bolla, and the church was consecrated in 1563 in the presence of Ferdinand I. The Hofkirche is really the canopy for Maximilian's superb cenotaph. Here Maximilian, kneeling on his empty tomb, is surrounded by some of the noblest bronze figures ever cast, while statuettes of saints look down from the gallery (Pls. 13, 14).[4]

Maximilian's cenotaph in Innsbruck, the chantry-chapel of Henry VII in Westminster, and the Burgundian tombs in Brugge were perhaps the most successful of early-Renaissance funerary art outside Italy. In northern Europe, the Reformation and the immense social changes that followed the struggles of the period further encouraged the rise of the individual. Merchants, soldiers, landowners, and the newly enriched desired to commemorate themselves in funerary art; churches often became adorned with enormous monuments that were quite out-of-scale and overwhelming in their context. Unfortunately, the desire for display, and the seizing of a new fashion in funerary art and architecture, frequently produced monuments that were vulgar, ostentatious, and artistically shallow. But the beautiful tomb of Henry Fitzroy, Duke of Richmond, in Framlingham in Suffolk, built in 1529 is certainly not vulgar, and is a pleasing interpretation of the Renaissance altar-tomb with pilasters, heraldic devices, and ornament derived from Henry VII's tomb.

The richness of European funerary architecture is hardly appreciated today, despite Mr Crossley's pioneering work, and Mrs K. A. Esdaile's scholarly, entertaining, and informative writings.[5] Initially, the transition from mediaeval to Renaissance design was fairly conventional, the only changes being in the detail. The altar-tomb, the effigy, the canopy, all remained part of the design. The late-Elizabethan tomb of Edmund Walter (died 1592) and his wife in the Church of S. Laurence, Ludlow, shows how Renaissance design had transformed a traditional mediaeval wall-tomb. The tomb-chest, or altar-chest, is subdivided by Tuscan columns between which are the kneeling figures in relief of the children of the Walters. The Walters lie in effigy in contemporary dress, in traditional mediaeval attitudes of supplication, hands pressed together in prayer. The tomb fits within an

Plate 13 View of the Hofkirche, Innsbruck, from the gallery, showing the sarcophagus with kneeling figure of Maximilian, and surrounding bronze figures (*Tiroler Volkskunstmuseum, Innsbruck*)

Plate 14 Sarcophagus and figure of Maximilian. Note the statues of saints in the gallery (*Tiroler Volkskunstmuseum, Innsbruck*)

aediculated opening consisting of a semicircular coffered arch flanked by Corinthian columns that carry the entablature. The spandrels and wall behind the arch are enriched with ribbonwork. The cornice is surmounted by a cartouche set in strapwork, and two obelisks cap the corners in place of finials (Pl. 15).

Much more sophisticated, as befits royal tombs, are the works of the Florentine Domenico Fancelli in the Capilla Real in the cathedral at Granada. The chapel is entered through a magnificent wrought-iron *reja* (Pl. 16). Here lie Ferdinand and Isabella in tombs of white marble, works of the full Renaissance. Near by are Philip of Austria and Joanna in a tomb of equal magnificence by Bartholomé Ordóñez, a Spaniard who knew Italy. The Fancelli tomb of the Infante Don Juan in Santo Tomàs at Avilà is also Renaissance in style. The fine bronze-gilt royal tombs of the Escorial feature kneeling figures above low oratories of black marble. They commemorate Charles V, Isabella, Charles' sisters and daughters, Philip II, three of his wives, and the unfortunate Don Carlos.

The awareness of the individuality of Renaissance man is brought out in

Far left Plate 15 Tomb of Edmund Walter (*ob.* 1592) and his wife, Church of S. Laurence, Ludlow (*The Author*)

Below Plate 16 Capilla Real at Granada, showing the *reja* and tombs (*Author's Collection*)

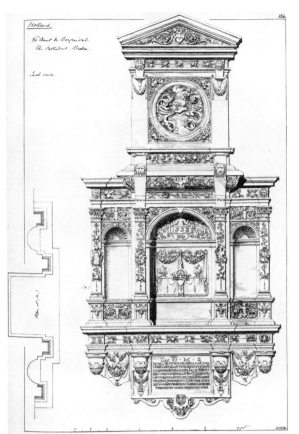

Above Plate 17 Monument to Count Borgnival in Breda (*Author's Collection*)

Far Right Plate 18 The Griffin family tomb, Church of All Saints, Braybrooke, Northamptonshire (*Author's Collection*)

tomb-sculpture. From late-mediaeval times, likenesses of the dead were achieved in effigies. In the Middle Ages as a whole, sculptured effigies tended to be symbolic rather than purely representational, but portraits of the dead became usual with the advent of a Florentine-humanist consciousness.

In Britain, after the initial impact of Florentine sensibility and craftsmanship, Italian influences waned. The Reformation made Papist artists less acceptable, and indeed suspect both politically and artistically. New influences came to Britain, notably from Flanders, whence came refugees from Spanish persecution. Netherlandish funerary monuments had themselves been influenced by the Renaissance. In the Hervormde Kerk in Breda are several fine monuments, which would have been known to many immigrant sculptors. The imposing Renaissance monument to Count Engelbert II, the friend of Charles the Bold, and Stadhouder under Maximilian, was by Tomaso Vincidor of Bologna, who had gone to Holland in 1520 to supervise the making of tapestries from Raphael cartoons. The alabaster figures rest on a sarcophagus, while four kneeling figures carry a slab on which lies the armour of the Count. A similar arrangement is found in the monument of 1609 to Sir Francis Vere in Westminster Abbey, while the Salisbury monument in Hatfield Parish Church by Maximilian Colt has a ledger supported by kneeling figures of the Virtues, with an effigy on the ledger and a skeleton below, yet another variation of the *gisant* monument. Breda also possesses monuments to Count Borgnival (died 1536) (Pl. 17) and Dirck van Assendelfft (died 1553). The Borgnival monument is very much a Flemish adaptation of Italian Renaissance motifs, and it was this adaptation that was to be such a potent model to English architects and sculptors of tombs. The sculptors who came to England (and who would have been influenced by Renaissance development in Italy, in Spain, and by the interpretation of Renaissance themes in the Netherlands), were Protestant, and therefore acceptable. They introduced a new flavour in funerary art, despite the fact that the essentials of English monuments were traditional. The massive Griffin tomb in the church of All Saints, Braybrooke, Northamptonshire (c. 1565) has aspects of its design that are derived from both Italian and Flemish sources. The Braybrooke monument has a base with pedestals, but the *piano nobile* feature has been transformed by the Order of bulging and grotesque Ionic pilasters (Pl. 18). The big wall monument of Sir John Chichester (died 1569) in the Devon church of S. Mary at Pilton has a more conventional Corinthian Order, but the strapwork adds a decidedly Northern European flavour (Pl. 19). Altar-tombs with variants remained valid for grander monuments. The kneeling effigies that came into fashion during the reign of Henry VII became typical in Elizabethan and Jacobean times. The great advantages of such figures were that they could be life-size or in miniature without any loss of character, and could be part of free-standing tombs or wall-monuments (Pl. 19). The mural monument to Thomas Larrance at Chelsea is a case in point. Children could also be portrayed, kneeling with the parents, or replacing the weepers of the past in panels below.

Much less conventional is the series of altar-tombs of the Sylvester family in the chapel of SS. Mary and Anne in the Church of S. John the Baptist in Burford. Five identical tomb-chests were erected between 1568 and 1626 with panelled fronts. Over the tops of each tomb are arms on a medallion,

Plate 19 *Left*: Chichester tomb at Pilton Church, near Barnstaple, Devon *Right*: The mural monument to Thomas Larrance at Chelsea Church (*Author's Collection*)

Plate 20 Tomb of Margaret, sister of Sir Dudley Diggs, at Chilham in Kent (*Author's Collection*)

with bold strapwork scrolls. One of the monuments has, in addition, three tiers of columns carrying a segmental pediment with ball-finials. This curious monument dates from 1654. The Renaissance arrangement of a podium, enriched with heraldic or other devices, that carries a classical Order surmounted by urns, obelisks, or pediments, is found in various permutations and combinations. A fine example is the tomb of Margaret, sister of Sir Dudley Diggs, at Chilham in Kent. The designs on the columns were produced by cutting away the polish (Pl. 20).

117

A variant of these two types is found in the Church of S. Mary, Swinbrook, in Oxfordshire. The north wall of the chancel is filled with grandiose monuments to the Fettiplace family. The earlier tomb of 1613 consists of a large aediculated opening flanked by somewhat coarse fluted Corinthian columns on carved dies. Over is a carved stone entablature, with a semicircular arch over it. The soffite of the arch is decorated with strapwork, and the frieze is enriched with arabesques. The whole composition is crowned by ball-finials, obelisks, and by an angel holding the family crest. Within the aedicules are what can only be described as bunks on which effigies of the Fettiplaces recline on one elbow in a posture of acute discomfort. The carving is primitive, and appears to be of the Burford School. The later aedicule is much more sophisticated, and is a signed work by William Bird of Oxford, built in 1686. It is of marble and alabaster, and the effigies appear altogether more relaxed (Pl. 21). Many of the finest monuments of the seventeenth century were designed by Nicholas Stone who was closely associated with Inigo Jones. The work of Bernard Jansen too is celebrated. During the seventeenth century aediculated wall-monuments became fashionable; derived from Roman sources, they retained all the Jacobean motifs of strapwork, obelisks, panoplies, and heraldry. Within the aedicules were coloured busts. One of the best examples is the monuments of Shakespeare in Stratford-on-Avon (1616).

Where monuments were free-standing, they had canopies, like their mediaeval predecessors. Bloxam, in his work on Monumental Architecture, described the new monuments as:

> altar-tombs with recumbent effigies beneath circular arcades, the soffits of which are richly panelled, surmounted by highly-finished entablatures, which are supported at the angles by columns of the different orders; above these, other arcades and entablatures of smaller dimensions, supported also by columns, often arise; the whole is finished with obelisks and escutcheons, surrounded with scroll work. These stately memorials are composed of various marbles, fancifully decorated with painting, gilding, and sculpture, and present a combination and infinite variety of arches, columns, tablets, pyramids, obelisks, escutcheons, arabesques, and scroll work.

Yet *The Quarterly Review* could describe such tombs as 'architectural solecisms, committed in the attempt to preserve the original Gothic features of the Altar-tomb, with the recumbent figure and canopy, in the altered elements of Grecian or Italian art'. One particularly interesting tomb is that of Lord Chief Justice Tanfield and his family in the north chapel of the Church of S. John the Baptist in Burford, erected in 1628, according to Mrs Esdaile, by the Southwark School of Sculptors. It is probably by Gerard Christmas, and is a richly decorated canopied tomb of alabaster and black marble. Two recumbent figures lie on the table of the altar-tomb. At the head is a kneeling effigy of Elizabeth, daughter of Tanfield, and at the feet is another kneeling effigy of his grandson, Lucius Cary, second Lord Falkland.

Right Plate 21 North wall of the chancel of the Church of S. Mary, Swinbrook, in Oxfordshire. The Fettiplace monuments consist of aediculated openings with effigies on bunk-like shelves. The nearest monument is of 1613, by a sculptor of the Burford School. The farthest monument, signed by William Bird, an Oxford stonemason, was built in 1686 (*The Author*)

Far right Plate 22 Tomb of the Lord Chief Justice Tanfield in the Church of S. John the Baptist in Burford (*The Author*)

Beside the kneeling figure is a demi-figure of Lady Falkland with bared breasts. Under the table of the tomb, on a mat, is a late survival of a Gothic *memento mori*, in an effigy of a hideously decayed corpse. The canopy over the tomb consists of a coffered vault on six black marble columns. The whole composition is surmounted by cartouches and obelisks, and on the corners are elegant figures of the Virtues (Pl. 22).

The tomb of Lewis Stuart, Duke of Lennox and Richmond, in the south chapel of Henry VII's chapel at Westminster, dates from 1623–4. The effigy of Frances Howard, his Duchess, dates from 1639. It is of black marble and bronze, and consists of a double sarcophagus, effigies, and a canopy. The sarcophagus stands on a plinth, and has reeded, shaped and moulded sides, with an inscribed tablet on the north and south sides surmounted by *putti*. The gilt-bronze effigies are recumbent. The Duke is in armour, with the long mantle of the Garter, and the wand of office. The Duchess has a ruff, a stomacher, and a coronet. The canopy is carried by four weeping bronze caryatides, representing Hope, Truth, Charity, and Faith (familiar motifs of the period), with Ionic caps supporting the entablature. Above rises a dome of semi-gilt openwork, with urns at the corners. A statue of Fame blowing a trumpet stands at the summit (Pl. 23).

During the seventeenth century there was mounting criticism of the

Plate 23 Tomb of Lewis Stuart, Duke of Richmond, in Westminster Abbey (*Author's Collection*)

Right Plate 24 Sir Thomas Cholmondley (*ob.* 1864), sculpted by George Frederick Watts, in front of the Norton-Owen monument of the early-seventeenth century in the Church of SS. Mary and Andrew, Condover, Shropshire (*The Author*)

Far right Plate 25 Tomb of Louis de Brèse, Rouen (*Author's Collection*)

funerary monuments that encroached upon the spaces required for worship. In Sweden, the Church Law of 1686 prohibited the erection of tombs that would interfere with worship. From this time, floor-slabs once more became common, and coincided with Netherlandish custom in Britain, although mural tablets often supplemented the information on the vault-covers. These mural monuments became splendid compositions themselves, the simpler giving way to architectural inventions on an enormous scale.

Seventeenth-century wall-monuments are often in the form of aedicules, with an arched niche containing kneeling effigies in an attitude of prayer. Such a type is represented by the tomb of Richard Braybrooke and his wife (1629) in the church of SS. Peter and Paul at Checkendon, in Oxfordshire. Sometimes each kneeling figure is within its own niche, as in the seventeenth-century monument in the church of SS. Mary and Andrew in Condover, Shropshire, before which the eerie figure of Sir Thomas Cholmondeley by George Frederick Watts kneels in prayer, a remarkable example of mid-Victorian monumental art (Pl. 24). The contrast with the grander tombs as found in the monument of Louis de Brèse in Rouen is striking. This colossal monument shows a naked effigy clad only with a shroud, lying on a sarcophagus. The whole tomb, with its caryatides, sumptuous decoration, and ornate friezes is typical of French Renaissance work (Pl. 25).

The lineage of such sumptuous tombs derives from both the Middle Ages and the great Renaissance and Baroque examples in Italy. The supreme creations of Bernini in Rome are spectacular examples of funerary art, and the tombs of the sixteenth- and seventeenth-century Popes are among the greatest of all examples of funerary architecture. Curiously though, Baroque memorials often achieved the greatest refinement in the British Isles rather than in Italy, and the cartouches that grace so many of our churches enrich our heritage considerably.

Baroque architecture frequently included the most bizarre, even horrifying imagery. However, in the hands of Gian Lorenzo Bernini, Baroque funerary art achieved a degree of sophistication that was unmatched in its time. In a sense, he was the logical product of Renaissance man, for he was possibly the first artist who occupied a position almost equal to that of the politicians and nobility of his time. With the election in 1623 of the Barberini Pope, Urban VIII, Bernini's opportunity arrived, for Urban was a builder, and wanted a Michelangelo in his court. When Urban VIII

ascended the Papal Throne S. Peter's had just been completed, but not the decorations. Bernini's *baldacchino* of 1624–33 is perhaps the first great monument of the Baroque, and its success paved the way for his other triumphs, including the design for the gigantic statues of S. Helena, S. Longinus, S. Veronica, and S. Andrew.

With the Tomb of Urban VIII (1628–47), however, Bernini achieved great originality in a monument of supremely Baroque invention, although the immediate precedents of the design dated from 1549. Gugliemo della Porta had designed the superb tomb of Paul III Farnese, and erected it between 1549 and 1575. It is an elegant composition, with reclining figures on scrolls modelled on the general scheme of the Michelangelo tombs in Florence, and a seated figure of the Pope crowning the tomb, forming a pyramidal arrangement (Pl. 26). Alessandro Algardi's tomb of Pope Leo XI Medici, built between 1634 and 1652 (Pl. 27) in S. Peter's consists of a seated figure of the Pope wearing the Papal Crown above a sarcophagus flanked by two standing female figures, the first of a number of tombs influenced by that of Urban VIII. Bernini's design consists of a seated figure in gilt bronze of the crowned Pope giving a benediction. The throne sits on a high podium behind an ornate sarcophagus of bronze and marble. This sarcophagus is flanked by statues of the Virtues with *putti*. Enormous bees, heraldic devices of the Barberini, are found on the sarcophagus and on the podium. A winged skeleton above the sarcophagus inscribes the name of the Pope on a bronze cartouche. The composition is pyramidal, a motif that was to be a powerful and recurring theme in the Baroque period (Pl. 28).

Far left Plate 26 Tomb of Pope Paul III Farnese in S. Peter's, Rome (*Mansell/Brogi Collection No. 12656*)

Below Plate 27 Tomb of Pope Leo XI in S. Peter's in Rome (*Mansell/Anderson Collection No. 207*)

Above Plate 28 Tomb of Pope Urban VIII in S. Peter's in Rome (*Mansell/Anderson Collection No. 215*)

Far right Plate 29 Tomb of Pope Alexander VII in S. Peter's in Rome (*Mansell/Anderson Collection No. 198*)

Bernini's tomb of Pope Alexander VII, erected between 1671 and 1678, is also composed as a pyramid, but this time the effects are sensationally theatrical and full of movement. The Pope is shown praying above his own tomb-chamber with statues of the four Virtues placed below. A shroud of marble partially conceals the door from which springs a skeletal figure of Death holding an hour-glass. The lovely figure of Truth, on the right (somewhat hypocritically and untruthfully clad in later metal drapery to hide unacceptable nakedness), was finished by Cartari, and is an image of almost unbearable sweetness (Pl. 29). Roubiliac's famous animated and skeletal Death striking down Lady Elizabeth Nightingale of 1761 in Westminster Abbey owes not a little to Bernini. This shrouded skeleton, emerging from a vault, thrusts an arrow at the woman, who is vainly shielded by her husband. Apparently the sculptor was suggesting historical fact, for Lady Elizabeth was killed by lightning. The horrible skeleton, rendered even more hideous by its sense of animation and power, is descended from those ancient *larvae* of classical times, as well as from the visions of Death in the Middle Ages (Pl. 30).

The dramatic shock of these Bernini tombs is emphasised further in the statue of the Death of the Blessed Ludovica Albertoni of 1674 in the Altieri Chapel in the Church of San Francesco a Ripa in Rome (Pl. 31). The chapel is domed, and the marble figure of Ludovica lies on a bed, illuminated by hidden windows from the left and right. The vision is theatrical, yet deeply moving; as we draw near we see the face of the woman at the moment of

Plate 30 Tomb of Lady Elizabeth Nightingale in Westminster Abbey (*Warburg Institute, Helmut Gernsheim No. BB 67/7683*) National Monument Record

Below Plate 31 Statue of the Death of the Blessed Ludovica Albertoni in the Altieri Chapel in the Church of San Francesco a Ripa in Rome (*Mansell/Anderson Collection No. 2385*)

death: utterly relaxed, and very feminine. Heads of *putti* float, as if by magic, above.[6]

Perhaps the most beautiful of all Bernini's tombs, and in some ways the most sensational, was the sepulchral chapel of Cardinal Federigo Cornaro in the transept of the Carmelite Church of Santa Maria della Vittoria in Rome. Work began in 1647 and continued through the following decade. In the centre of the composition, within an aedicule over the altar, is the group known as The Ecstasy of S. Teresa. Heavenly light, in the form of golden rods, floods down from behind the swaying, broken pediment. The aedicule is, in effect, a proscenium arch, and to the left and right of it are opera boxes containing sculptured representations of the Cornaro family. The onlooker joins these members of the family, and the theatrical sensations are enhanced by this three-dimensional picture. The dramatic effects of the lighting increase the tension, and we see the Saint and the angel on floating clouds of stucco. S. Teresa in ecstasy is shown being pierced by a spear wielded by a smiling, youthful angel, and her abandoned, voluptuous pose is illuminated by the theatrical lighting. The miracle of the union with Christ becomes almost sexual, the angel becoming the Eros of old. The spear is almost phallic in its reality. The richness, high drama, and sheer

Plate 32 The Ecstasy of S. Teresa in the Cornaro Chapel of the Church of Santa Maria della Vittoria in Rome (*Mansell/Anderson Collection No. 2388*

daring of this work make it perhaps the most interesting and lovely
sepulchral chapel of all time (Pl. 32).

It is perhaps worth noting that English taste, until recently, regarded the
Ecstasy of S. Teresa as gross and offensive, 'The head of S. Teresa is that of a
languishing nymph, the angel a sort of Eros; the whole has been
significantly described as "a parody of Divine Love". The vehicle, white
marble—its place in a christian church—enhance all its vileness. The least
destructive, the least prudish in matters of art, would here willingly throw
the first stone.'[7] The opposing view is, characteristically, French. '*La sainte
Thérèse de Bernin est adorable! couchée, évanouie d'amour, les mains, les pieds
nus pendants, les yeux demi-clos, elle s'est laissée tomber de bonheur et
d'extase.*'[8] (Pl. 33).

This lightness of touch, peculiarly Italian, was not to be found often in
funerary art. The vaults of the Capuchin Church in Vienna contain the
tombs of the Habsburgs (Pl. 34). This vault has an assemblage of funerary
art in such concentrations that the effect is almost overpowering, while the
images of skulls crowned, panoplies of the insignia of power, and massive
sarcophagi contribute to its oppressiveness. The centrepiece of the
collection of tombs is the double sarcophagus of Maria Theresia and her

126

Plate 34 Funeral vault of the Habsburgs in the Church of the Capuchins in Vienna (*Author's Collection*)

consort, designed by Balthasar Moll, and completed in 1754. The royal couple are shown as though on a gigantic bed, dressed in splendid garments, while above them an angel, armed with the *Tuba Mirum*, holds a chaplet over their heads (Pl. 35). These huge tombs in Vienna are impressive, if solemn, heavy and perhaps lacking in grace. The gloom of such places was captured by Hartland in his series of drawings of royal vaults in Europe. The ranks of sarcophagi in Germany, for example, clearly show the smaller urns and caskets containing the hearts, bowels, and other parts of the embalmed bodies. The vaults of the Nieuwkerk in Delft, of Roskilde Cathedral, and of other churches used for the burial of royal and noble persons contain similar arrays of coffins, urns, caskets, and other macabre relics.

The introduction of Italian design and craftsmanship has already been noted in relation to the Cosmati-work of the late-thirteenth century at

Plate 35 Tomb of Maria Theresia and Franz I in the Capuchin Church in Vienna (*Meyer, Kunsthistorisches Museum*)

Westminster Abbey, especially at the shrine of Edward the Confessor and the tomb of Henry III. Italian influences did not appear again until Torrigiani made the tombs of Henry VII and of the Countess of Beaufort. This rational Florentine style was rejected in favour of Germanic types of design imported from Flanders. The architectural emphasis given to chantry-chapels and tombs in the late Middle Ages encouraged a continuation of such emphasis in monuments both free-standing and against walls. As the middle classes came to prominence, they sought burial in churches as a form of status, and were commemorated by mural monuments not directly related to the place of burial. Typical of the

Plate 36 Tomb of William Morgan in Westminster Abbey (*Author's Collection*)

Plate 37 Monument to Thomas Foley by John Michael Rysbrack (1694–1770) in the Church of S. Michael at Great Witley, Worcestershire, of about 1740 (*The Author*)

Baroque wall-memorial is that to Henry Knappe, of 1673, in the church of SS. Peter and Paul in Checkendon, in Oxfordshire. Often, such memorials were in the form of a cartouche, with free, Baroque waving forms, as in the monument to Sir Walter Curl in the Parish Church of Soberton in Hampshire. Often, too, the cartouche type of monument was elaborated and combined with backgrounds of black marble, obelisks, crossettes, and urns, as in the monument to Temple Stanyan of 1751 in the church at Checkendon. Mural monuments, completely surrounded by the surface of the wall on which they were set, are found in great profusion throughout Europe, and are architectural in form. The grander monuments placed against walls, but standing on the floor, are more in the tradition of Gothic and Renaissance designs. A beautiful example of 1683 is the tomb of William Morgan in Westminster Abbey, where the familiar high podium and columnar treatments have become Baroque in detail. The twisted Berniniesque columns, scrolled pediment, *putti* heads and elliptical plaques show how far English designs had progressed after the Restoration (Pl. 36).

The wealth of Baroque monuments in Europe is colossal. One of the largest funerary monuments of the eighteenth century in England is that to Thomas Foley by John Michael Rysbrack, completed in 1740. It is in the church of S. Michael, Great Witley, and consists of a base, a sarcophagus, sculptured figures, a large urn, and a crowning cartouche, the whole being placed against a background of a large obelisk. This is the Flemish influence at work, but the pyramid-form derives from Bernini (Pl. 37). A variation of this type of design is found in the Church of S. Martin in Stamford, to John, fifth Earl of Exeter, who died in 1700. The tomb was designed by Monnot of Rome in 1703 and consists of vigorous, confident sculpture in white marble. The figures recline in decidedly secular fashion on the sarcophagus, flanked by Wisdom and Art. Behind is a great build-up of architectural motifs, including urns, an obelisk, and a cartouche. Similar compositions may be found throughout Europe. While the finest designs are perhaps those in England and in Rome, there are superb versions in the Church of Bon Secours in Nancy. There the tombs of Stanislaus I Leszynski and his consort are fine examples of the pyramidal type of build-up, but veer towards Neoclassicism in style. Yet these pyramidal compositions were censured by J. H. Markland, who credits Bernini with the invention of the pyramid form of tomb. The influence of Bernini was seen by Markland as being responsible for 'the Anglo-Italian style' of funerary monument. The native tomb, 'with the simple effigy, gave place to piles of marble and stone, as offensive to the eye of taste, as the monument of Sir Cloudesley Shovel in later times, on which Addison so justly animadverts.' Markland then went on to describe what he called 'their most striking features' to 'sufficiently explain their deformity.'

The piling-up of sculpture and familiar architectural motifs continued throughout the eighteenth century, with the obelisk a favourite feature, usually combined with a sarcophagus. The tomb of John, Duke of Argyll and Greenwich, is one such example, while that of Lord Chatham is another, the last containing Hellenistic elements (Pl. 38). The Argyll monument (1748–9) is one of the greatest works of Louis François Roubiliac (1705–1762). The high drama of his Nightingale monument may recall Bernini, but the Argyll monument is perhaps supreme. The composition is basically Italian. Eloquence, Liberty, and Minerva are grouped in the triangular form so essential to the Baroque style. On the sarcophagus is a statue of the Duke. Vertue considered this work to show not only the greatness of Roubiliac's 'genius in his invention, design, and execution, in every part equal, if not superior to any others', but also how it outshone 'for nobleness and skill all those before done by the best sculptors this fifty years past'. The Chatham monument is by John Bacon (1740–1799), and is of such a towering size that this type of monument had to be discouraged. It is nevertheless a superb example of Neoclassical sculptural monumental architecture in which Britain excelled. The genius of John Flaxman (1755–1826) entered fully into Greek revival, and his tomb of the Lord Chancellor, Lord Mansfield (1795), expresses a new, thoroughly original type of monument owing little but the basis of its composition to the works of Bernini. The massive dignity of the figure responds to the greatness of the subject (Pl. 39). Neoclassical influences may be found in the royal tombs in Roskilde. The monument of Frederik V of Denmark (1766) is predominantly Neoclassical, while the sarcophagus of Juliana Maria, Queen of Frederik V (1796), is almost *Empire* in style. The tomb of Christian VI can

Right Plate 38 Tomb of John, Duke of Argyll and Greenwich, 1748–9, by Louis François Roubiliac, in Westminster Abbey (*Author's Collection*)

Far right Plate 39 Tomb of Lord Mansfield, of 1795, by John Flaxman, in Westminster Abbey (*Author's Collection*)

even boast supporting sphinxes. The tomb of Frederik V stands in a separate mortuary chapel attached to Roskilde Cathedral. This chapel is probably the purest Neoclassical building in Denmark, and was designed by C.F. Harsdorff.

Such crisp detailing had its counterpart in the mural tablets of the period, when hosts of very simple designs were applied to church walls during the reigns of George III, George IV, William IV, and the early years of Queen Victoria. White marble on black, fine lettering, and ultra-Neoclassical simplicity were keynotes. Occasionally, artificial stones were used, as in the enchanting monument of Coade Stone in the Church of S. John the Baptist in Stamford. This beautiful work shows distinct traces of Neoclassicism, and is exquisitely fashioned.

The huge number of post-Renaissance monuments in British churches demonstrates the fact that burial in churches was still usual until very late, compared with other European countries. Commemorative sculpture also gave scope for certain artistic images denied by Protestantism in other

Plate 40 Monument of
Princess Charlotte in
S. George's Chapel, Windsor,
by M. C. Wyatt (*By
permission of the Dean and
Canons of Windsor*)

forms. Most English cathedrals and parish churches have walls covered with
monuments, mostly of the eighteenth and nineteenth centuries. Great
families built enormous monuments that seriously damaged the spatial
qualities of churches, while those aspiring to respectability covered walls
with mural tablets.

The scope of this book is such that it is impossible to survey the complete
range of funerary monuments of any period, least of all those of the
eighteenth and nineteenth centuries. Monuments of an architectural
character are the subjects under review, and it is important to emphasise the
point.

The difference between the Neoclassical art of Flaxman and Bacon on the
one hand, and the sense of drama and Baroque horror of Bernini and
Roubiliac on the other, will be obvious. The hideous skeletons, vigorous in
their attacks, in the monuments of S. Peter's, Rome, and Westminster
Abbey will not be forgotten, once seen. Jean-Baptiste Pigalle (1714–1785)

worked in the grand manner, although he merged Baroque drama and movement with Neoclassical serenity and detail. His funerary monument of the Comte d'Harcourt in Notre-Dame in Paris, of 1776, is a case in point. The supplication of the widow, the mourning angel with reversed torch, the panoply of arms and flags, the open coffin, the corpse, and the hideous hooded figure of Death create new tensions and modes of expression.

The Romantic decades could indeed combine chaste images with sensational ideas. The monument of Princess Charlotte, who died in 1817, in S. George's Chapel, Windsor, is a supreme example of Neoclassical splendour mixed with Baroque shock. The body of the dead Princess lies covered with a sheet, the lines suggesting voluptuous female flesh. To the left and right are mourning female figures, entirely draped, like the corpse. Above, the Princess ascends to heaven, one breast bared, flanked by angels, one of whom holds the tiny baby, whose stillborn entry into the world caused the Princess's death. This work is perhaps one of the finest of all early-nineteenth-century works of funerary sculpture, and is a work of architecture that enlivens S. George's. The sculptor was Matthew Coates Wyatt (1777–1862), son of the architect James Wyatt (1746–1813) (Pl. 40).

Many works of funerary architecture were erected in the Victorian period. The magnificent canopied tomb of the Duke of Wellington in S. Paul's Cathedral (1858–75) by Alfred Stevens is one of the most impressive. Some of the last distinguished examples of tombs of the altar variety, with effigies, are found in S. George's Chapel at Windsor. The white marble recumbent effigies of Edward VII and Alexandra lie on a sumptuous tomb chest of black and dark green marbles, with gilt-bronze weepers and heraldic devices. This beautiful tomb was designed by Sir Bertram Mackennal, and erected in 1919. Less sumptuous, and lacking the lustrous richness of the tomb of his father, is that of George V and his consort in the nave. This stone sarcophagus with recumbent effigies dates from 1937 and

Plate 41 Tomb of George V
and Queen Mary in
S. George's Chapel, Windsor
*(By permission of the Dean
and Canons of Windsor)*

was designed by Sir Edwin Lutyens. The effigies are by Sir William Reid Dick. The heraldic devices stand proud of the sarcophagus, in the somewhat angular fashion of the period, but the tomb must be one of the last truly serene royal monuments (Pl. 41), although the form of the tomb is a distinct turning back to the past.

Both the previous examples have a setting of splendour in S. George's Chapel. For monuments of such quality, some sort of separate setting provided the most satisfactory solution in design terms, as in the mediaeval chantry-chapels. A charming twentieth-century solution is to be found at Christ Church in Port Sunlight. The architects of the church (1902) were William and Segar Owen of Warrington. They chose an angular Perpendicular style for its design. The richly vaulted narthex at the west end of the church shields the funerary effigies of Lord Leverhulme and Elizabeth Ellen, his wife (1850–1913). These beautiful and noble recumbent bronze figures are by Sir William Goscombe John. The effigies and the figures of the children who crouch at the foot are of bronze, and the tomb itself is of green marble.[9]

Humbler tombs were often of rare interest and beauty. A tomb in the churchyard of Fittleton, Wiltshire, is a particularly fine example of a late-eighteenth- or early-nineteenth-century type of churchyard altar-tomb. The quality of the stone tooling is exquisite.

During the nineteenth century, experiments were made to introduce cast-iron tombs. Some excellent examples survive, especially at Madeley in Shropshire, in the churchyard of S. Michael. The tomb of William Baldwin (died 1822) consists of a pedestal with four fluted columns at the corners supporting an entablature above which is a small sarcophagus. The whole cast-iron monument is surrounded by railings and is painted. Even during the rise of new classes of industrialists, a classical tradition in funerary art survived, and some beautiful designs were produced during Victoria's reign.[10]

The richness of funerary architecture is undeniable. It is all the more depressing to contemplate contemporary funerary design. The uninspired tombstones or memorials erected today have added new terrors to death.

5

The Burial Crisis; overcrowded churchyards; the first fruits of reform; and the first modern cemeteries.

The Europeans in India; Louisiana; Scotland; France and Ireland. The first great cemeteries of modern times, including those of Calcutta, New Orleans, Edinburgh, and Paris

. . . the task be mine
To paint the gloomy horrors of the tomb;
Th' appointed place of rendezvous, where all
These travellers meet.

ROBERT BLAIR: *The Grave*

I have previously noted how Christian practice changed the sensible rules relating to the disposal of the dead in classical times. It is clear that the early Christians, too, regarded dead bodies as unclean, but the fact that the rich and powerful were buried in churches created a demand for similar treatment among lesser mortals. In the Netherlands, especially, the churches became enormous public mausolea, and when Willem the Stadhouder came to Britain to reign with Mary, the customs of Holland became fashionable. Churches became filled with monuments to those lying beneath the floor-slabs. The cult of individual importance undoubtedly encouraged burial within churches from the Reformation. John Evelyn recalled that his father-in-law was disgusted by the 'novel custom of burying everyone within the body of the church and chancel, that being a favour heretofore granted to the martyrs and great persons, the excess of making churches charnel-houses being of ill and irreverent example and prejudicial to the health of the living, besides the continual disturbance of the pavement and seats, and several other indecencies . . .'[1]

Evelyn also describes churchyards in his day as being congested with dead bodies 'one above the other, to the very top of the walls, and some above the walls', so that the churches themselves appeared to be built in pits.[2] This phenomenon is still obvious in City of London churches, and even in country districts, where churchyards often form a raised dyke around the churches. When epidemics, such as those of plague and other diseases occurred, the churchyards could not cope, and often extra land had to be acquired for burial. In the black days of visitation by plague in mediaeval times, the Church ensured that new burial-grounds were suitably enclosed and consecrated according to ecclesiastical custom. Stow related that the deaths from plague and other diseases had increased 'so sore' that extra ground had to be acquired in his day for burial. The epidemic of 1665 created special problems, and considerable organization went into ensuring the dead were suitably buried.

As cities and towns expanded, the old churchyards became over-used. Charnel-houses were built in which the bones of the dead were stacked after they were disinterred to make room for new burials. As Protestantism triumphed, and the cult of the individual grew from Renaissance times, the idea of a communal charnel-house was not favoured, and most ossuaries in Britain were cleared in the sixteenth and seventeenth centuries. A notable exception is the charnel-house at Hythe in Kent. The last significant clearances of bones to new burial-places were made in Victorian times. The new concepts of permanent grave-ownership exacerbated churchyard overcrowding and encouraged abuses.

Men of foresight realised that radical and hygienic methods of disposing of the dead should be adopted. The old churchyards of London and other cities were in a dreadful state in Stuart times. Both John Evelyn and Sir Christopher Wren advised that large cemeteries should be formed outside the City of London after the Great Fire of 1666. Wren visualised cemeteries outside towns where fine monuments could be erected to designs by the best architects and sculptors of the period, subject to certain safeguards as to dimensions and basic form. Wren argued that architects should inspect the designs for individual tombs to ensure a harmonious whole. Evelyn proposed a linear cemetery, about a mile long, to the north of the city, to serve as a universal cemetery for all the London parishes. The cemetery would have been walled, and the walls could be adorned with monuments, inscriptions, and titles. Unfortunately, the visions of these two great men were not realised, probably owing to the opposition from the established Church, which felt obliged to safeguard the income from burial fees.

Plate 1 Octagonal tomb with a surrounding arcade (*India Office Library and Records Office*)

The radical idea of establishing a cemetery, as opposed to a churchyard, in fairly recent times, was realised by Dissenters at Bunhill Fields, near Moorgate. Dissenters did not wish to be buried in the consecrated ground of parish churchyards, and besides could be denied burial by the same Church. A yet more contentious matter was the whole question of payment of burial fees to the established Church. It is said that the name of Bunhill Fields derived from the immense numbers of bones from the City charnel-houses that were buried there in the reign of Elizabeth I. In Maitland's *Survey* it appears that Bunhill Fields was a Dissenter's burial-ground before 1665, in which year it was designated a common cemetery for burial of those struck down by the pestilence. The importance of Bunhill Fields as the 'Dissenters' Westminster Abbey' was recognized in the eighteenth century, for Edmund Curll published his *Inscriptions on the Tombs in The Dissenters' Burial-Place, near Bunhill-Fields* in 1717, and the cemetery was conserved and maintained by the City of London from 1867. There, the seventeenth- and eighteenth-century altar-tombs and memorial stones are among the finest of the period in any burial-ground in Britain.[3]

Necessity created its own solutions, and it is not insignificant that the earliest modern cemeteries were laid out by Europeans in India. The Danish settlement of Tranquebar had tombs of decidedly Baroque form, while pyramid-tombs were not unknown in India in 1680. The English and other

Europeans laid out cemeteries outside Surat in the seventeenth century, and there several enormous mausolea were built. The mausoleum of Christopher and Sir George Oxinden (died 1659 and 1669) owes not a little to the funerary architecture of Islam, of which several supreme examples exist in the sub-continent.

Islamic tombs derive from Persian prototypes, and were usually based on a square or octagonal plan. The tombs were domed, and these compact, very geometrical compositions were to develop into the grander, magnificent buildings of Moghul India. Octagonal tombs were occasionally surrounded by arcades, and several such examples are found in the environs of Delhi (Pl. 1). The simple beauty of these buildings is found in the best of mausolea of all periods and cultures. The formal geometrical arrangements of square, rectangle, octagon, circle, cube, triangle, pyramid, and dome are common to the architecture of death in many lands. The funerary architecture of Islam reached unprecedented heights of beauty, however, and formal geometry was carried to logical developments where buildings, gardens, gates, and canals reached the perfection of architectural symmetry. It was small wonder that the beautiful tombs of India would astonish Europeans, and that they would try to emulate the magnificence of the Islamic mausolea. It must be remembered that free-standing tombs of great size not in churches

137

Plate 2 The Oxinden Brother's mausoleum at Surat. Christopher and Sir George died in 1659 and 1669 respectively. These mausolea emulate the elaborate tombs of India (*Theon Wilkinson, lent by the Brit. Assoc. for Cemeteries in South Asia*)

had been almost unknown in Europe since Roman times, and so the novelty must have been most attractive to men like the Oxindens.

The 'most brotherly of brothers' as the Oxindens were known, share one of the most spectacular of mausolea built for the British in India. The curious opened dome, which appears as though segments have been cut out, is very unusual, and recalls the flying buttress and lantern effects of the crowning of the towers of S. Giles's in Edinburgh and S. Nicholas's, Newcastle-upon-Tyne (Pl. 2). One of the finest of the Surat mausolea is that of Henry Adrian Baron van Reede of 1691 in the Dutch cemetery there (Pl. 3). It consists of a cupola over an octagonal base, and is curiously eclectic in style. The Dutch destroyed the tombs of previous settlers and replaced them with supremely grand mausolea, some of which were constructed by imported builders from the Netherlands to ensure the survival of the monuments until the *laste opstaanding*. The van Reede mausoleum was built to rival that of the Oxindens, and perhaps owes something to earlier octagonal tombs of the fifteenth and sixteenth centuries (Pl. 1), although the mausolea of Theodoric at Ravenna and late-Roman circular examples are also suggested.

The potent example of the Tâj Mahal at Agra (1630–53) was to inspire many Europeans, but it in itself must be one of the most perfect works of funerary architecture in the world. The complex of formally planned gardens and canals, its courts and gates, and the great domed mausoleum itself must be one of the loveliest ensembles ever built. The exquisite nobility

Plate 3 Tomb of Henry Adrian, Baron van Reede (1691) at Surat (*India Office Library and Records Office*)

of the concept and the glorious detail have never been surpassed. The Tomb of Humayun Shah in Old Delhi (1565) is another magnificent domed structure set on an arcaded platform. The plan includes numbers of tomb-chambers for the dynasty, and was the prototype of the Tâj Mahal.[4] Moghul tombs were not only memorials but homes for the dead, and so had to be as delightful as possible. The cool interiors of the Tâj Mahal, the beautiful gardens with canals and fountains, and the serene buildings were to comprise a fit residence for Mumtaz Mahal, the favourite wife of Shah Jehan. Moslem potentates often laid out gardens for mausolea during their lifetimes, and used them for special occasions. Complete royal households were provided to attend to the buildings.

The plan of the Tâj Mahal at Agra is a beautiful example of formal geometry. The gardens are laid out in a square, with canals, kiosks, and pavilion-gateways. The mausoleum itself is fifty-seven metres square in plan, the structure consisting of four octagonal towers linked and carrying a central dome. *Chattris* mark the tops of the corner octagons (Pl. 4). Although the arrangement is similar to that of Humayun's tomb, the proportions and details have reached perfection. The mausoleum in the gardens has a symmetrical beauty that was greatly admired by Europeans. The building with its pavilions and gates can be seen as a whole from across the River Jumna.

It seems that Shah Jehan organized an architectural competition for the great mausoleum, but no reliable account survives. Although the Tâj Mahal

Plate 4 Tomb of Humayun, Delhi (*India Office Library and Record Office*)

derives from a long line of prototypes, its immediate ancestor was Humayun's mausoleum. A comparison of the latter with the octagonal tombs of the Lodi dynasty (Pl. 1) shows how far funerary architecture had advanced. The placing of the mausoleum in a garden was an innovation, while the facing of the building with veneers of marble in patterns, and the inner and outer domes anticipate later examples of the architecture of death.

The tomb of the Great Moghul Akbar at Secundra (Sikandra) was built between 1593 and 1613 and comprises a series of square superimposed terraces much ornamented with pavilions and *chattris*. The form was thus that of a tiered pyramid, and followed the model of ancient Indian monasteries. It was thus Hindu in style, but with Moghul detail. The tomb-chamber was under the central structure, which was surmounted by a copy of the sarcophagus. The mausoleum was designed to stand in a formal garden that was entered through a massive gate not unreminiscent of a triumphal arch.

Such mausolea were potent examples for Europeans, and soon the settlers would build their own cemeteries with magnificent tombs. One of the best-known European cemeteries in India is that at South Park Street, Calcutta,[5] founded in 1767 when the 'sick season' was about to slay large numbers of Europeans. It was founded for hygienic and functional reasons, and pre-dates burial reform in Europe as a whole. South Park Street Cemetery is renowned for the large numbers of stuccoed tombs, many in the form of domed gazebos, and many crowned by obelisks, pyramids, and truncated columns (Pl. 5). It was not only disease that helped to fill the cemeteries: drink and general excess marked much of the late-eighteenth and early-nineteenth-century social life among Europeans. The Honourable Rose Whitworth Aylmer, the beloved of Walter Savage Landor, perished of a surfeit of pineapples in 1800; she is commemorated by a Neoclassical monument of considerable merit.

The building of mausolea in South Park Street appears to have been the work of undertakers who handled all aspects of the funeral trade. A Mr Oldham was one of the most successful, and was responsible for the erection of many tombs. The designs are for the most part excellent, and must have been based on printed sources at some point, notably the visions of Piranesi, whose *Le Antichità Romane* had appeared in 1756. The work of Sir William Chambers is suggested by many of the gazebos and temples, while aspects of French Neoclassicism (derived from Piranesi) may have inspired some of the obelisks and pyramids. Orders for some sculptured monuments were sent to England, so many of the designs may have originated on the drawing boards of distinguished architects.

By 1812 the many acres of South Park Street were 'covered so thick with columns, urns and obelisks that there scarcely seems to be room for another

Plate 5 Tombs in South Park Street Cemetery, Calcutta (*Dr Sten Åke Nilsson*)

Plate 6 Sir William Jones's tomb, South Park Street Cemetery, Calcutta (*Theon Wilkinson, lent by the Brit. Assoc. for Cemeteries in South Asia*)

Plate 7 Neoclassical tomb of Elizabeth Barwell in South Park Street Cemetery, Calcutta (*Theon Wilkinson, lent by the Brit. Assoc. for Cemeteries in South Asia*)

Plate 8 Classical temple-tomb, reminiscent of the work of the Adam Brothers, in South Park Street Cemetery, Calcutta (*Dr Sten Åke Nilsson*)

. . . it is like a city of the dead' (Pl. 6).[6] The largest pyramid commemorates Elizabeth Barwell, and dates from 1779 (Pl. 7). It is proportioned more like the pyramid of Cestius in Rome than the pyramids of Egypt. It stands on a podium, with a pediment on each face, and is thus similar to Hawksmoor's pyramid of 1728 at Castle Howard. The pyramid was entering the architectural vocabulary in Europe, but mostly appears in academic designs of the period rather than in realised schemes. Exceptions are the pyramid-tomb of Olof Adlerberg at Järäfalla in Sweden of 1757, a pyramid in Limehouse churchyard, and other examples. The South Park Street Cemetery also has a number of mausolea in the form of temples (Pl. 8). These are circular, square, and rectangular in plan and are similar to designs for classical temples published in such works as W. Chambers's *A Treatise on Civil Architecture* (London, 1759), and *The Works in Architecture of Robert and James Adam* (London, 1778–1822) (Pls. 9, 10).

Many tombs consist of obelisks set on square podia; often the faces of

these obelisks are carved with symbols to denote the trade or profession of the person commemorated. These Neoclassical designs are usual, and, together with kiosks and temples of the most delightful and respectable classical forms, make the South Park Street Cemetery an outstanding necropolis even by European standards. Rudyard Kipling, in *The City of Dreadful Night*, said of the South Park Street Cemetery that:

Left Plate 9 Design for a tomb by Chambers from *A Treatise on Civil Architecture*, London 1759 (*Dr Sten Åke Nilsson*)

Right Plate 10 Design for a tomb by Chambers from *A Treatise on Civil Architecture*, London 1759 (*Dr Sten Åke Nilsson*)

> the eye is ready to swear that it as old as Herculaneum or Pompeii. The tombs are small houses. It is as though we walked down the streets of a town, so tall are they and so closely do they stand . . . They must have been afraid of their friends rising up before due time that they weighted them down with such cruel mounds of masonry. Strong man, weak woman, or somebody's 'infant son aged 15 months' — it is all the same. For each the squat obelisk, the defaced classic temple, the cellaret of chunam, or the candlestick of brickwork — the heavy slab, the rust-eaten railings, the whopper-jawed cherubs and apoplectic angels. Men were rich in those days and could afford to put a hundred feet of masonry into the grave of even so humble a person as 'Jno Clements Captain of the Country Service, 1820'. When the 'dearly beloved' had held rank answering to that of Commissioner, the efforts were still more sumptuous . . .

Yet Kipling was wrong on several counts. The tombs were not of masonry,

144

Plate 11 Tomb of 'Hindoo'
Stuart in South Park Street
Cemetery, Calcutta (*The
Hon. Lady Betjeman, lent by
the Brit. Assoc. for Cemeteries
in South Asia*)

but of brick coated with stucco and then painted, which is why they are in such a deplorable state today. Men were not excessively rich, but could command labour from the native population at very cheap rates. It is interesting that the British in India trained local people to build in a classical style, while the Dutch imported craftsmen from Holland.

Hindu influences on funerary architecture can be detected in the *chattri*, or umbrella-topped monuments, and in the tombs that resemble Hindu temples, like that of Major-General Charles 'Hindoo' Stuart in the South Park Street Cemetery. Major-General Stuart was an Irishman who became attracted to Hindu custom. When he died in 1828 he was buried beneath a monument that recalls the Knockbreda mausolea in Ulster of the 1790s, but with Hindu motifs substituted for European classicism. This is one of the oddest of marriages of styles (Pl. 11). The Netherlanders built most elaborate mausolea in India, and they seemed to favour an amalgam of European and native Indian architecture. The tomb of Colonel Hessing at Agra of 1803 is a miniature version of the Moghul tombs such as the Tâj Mahal.[7]

Europeans found that the reforms, so necessary at home, were absolutely essential in some of the places they settled. European cemeteries in India were large, set apart from churches, and laid out in a spacious fashion. The French in Louisiana found that the climate and death-rates were so alarming that cemeteries had to be provided.

A plan of New Orleans of 1725 shows a cemetery outside the city, although fashionable burials were within the churches, as in Europe. A flood in 1788, followed by a fire and an epidemic, encouraged the city authorities to establish the St Louis cemetery, and it is this cemetery that contains the first of the famous oven-like tombs. These tombs contained *loculi*, or oven-like recesses, into which the coffins were placed (Pl. 12). After the bodies had decayed, the coffins were removed and burned. The bones were then swept through a hole to fall into a recess or *caveau* below that contained family bones.

New Orleans was predominantly Roman Catholic, and so burial was under the auspices of the ecclesiastical authorities of St Louis. As in Europe, burial was within churches, and in consecrated ground. In 1784, under Spanish rule, church burial was restricted to citizens of distinction, and the events of 1788 put an end to intramural interment.

The first St Louis cemetery is composed mostly of tombs *above ground* so that the flood-waters could not reach the bodies and endanger health. The tombs are built of brick finished with painted stucco; *loculi* are arranged in stacks, the entrance to each space being sealed with memorial tablets (Pls. 13 14). Although there was no local stone available, marbles and other stones were imported to beautify the cemetery from 1820. Costs of stone were high, however, and so stucco-faced brick, wood, and iron were the cheapest materials for tombs, although they did not survive long in a pristine

Right Plate 13 Side vaults, Girod Cemetery (*George Mugnier Collection, Louisiana Division, New Orleans Public Library*)

Plate 12 Oven-tombs of Louisiana. The side vaults, St Roch's Cemetery (*George Mugnier Collection, Louisiana Division, New Orleans Public Library*)

Below Plate 14 Side vaults,
St Louis Cemetery (*George
Mugnier Collection, New
Orleans Public Library*)

state in the swampy cemeteries. Stone was used for sculpture, however, and it is in the cemeteries that the best stonework in New Orleans is found, dating from 1840 to 1875, after which quality declined.

Even grander is the second cemetery of St Louis, for the layout is much more spacious and the tombs are bigger and more sumptuous. The architect

appears to have been Antoine Philippe Le Riche, who was inspector of cemeteries when St Louis II was planned. The cemetery, consecrated in 1824, was established over two kilometres away from the city. By 1820 epidemics of one sort and another had created special problems in New Orleans, and the contamination of water by dead bodies was regarded as a primary source of the problem.[8]

The need to form new, spacious, hygienic cemeteries set apart from churches and from the living was recognized in eighteenth-century Belfast, which at that time was a radical, forward-looking place. It is not insignificant that many of the leaders of the 1798 rebellion were Protestant Irishmen who were steeped in the ideals of the French Revolution, and in Freemasonry. The old Clifton Graveyard in Belfast was established in 1774. In that year the Earl of Donegall gave the ground on which the Charitable Institution was built together with about 7 hectares of land for a 'New Burying Ground' to replace the insanitary and overcrowded churchyard of S. George in the High Street. This new cemetery was enlarged in 1819, and was unattached to a church. It is surrounded by walls, and elaborate tombs are built around the perimeter. The Belfast Charitable Society operated the cemetery which was a fashionable place of burial. The Batts, the McCrackens, Lord Kelvin's father, the whiskey distillers Dunville, and the Lukes were among those buried there. It is in Clifton Graveyard that we find a type of tomb derived from funerary architecture of ancient Rome, with a truncated obelisk surmounting a small rectangular mausoleum. The Luke vault, a distinguished design in sandstone, is one example, although there is a similar building of gault bricks, now much overgrown, in the cemetery. This graveyard also contains the elaborate High-Victorian Gothic mausoleum of the Dunville family[9]

Visitors to Scotland will notice the neat and orderly burial-grounds of that country. Scottish cemeteries do not lurk discreetly, hidden from view, for they are often dominant features of both town and country, often being sited on hilltops or on elevated land. Necropoleis in Scotland are truly cities of the dead, and tend to mirror the scale of the settlements which they serve.

The ancient burial-grounds of Edinburgh are often extremely interesting from an historical point of view, but they are also packed with memorials of considerable sculptural merit. The Grey Friars churchyard, mysteriously hidden behind rows of houses, is an oasis of sculpture and greenery in the grey Old Town, and contains some very fine monuments of the seventeenth century. St Andrews, that still lovely town on the coast of the Kingdom of Fife, has a cemetery that occupies walled enclosures within the precincts of the ruined cathedral. The Romanesque tower of S. Rule still stands, while the ruined east end of the cathedral rises majestically from a city of tombs, many of which, like those in Grey Friars, date from the seventeenth century.

The cemetery on Calton Hill in Edinburgh, however, was laid out in the eighteenth century, and is not associated with a church. It is situated on the western-facing slope of Calton Hill, and so is visible from central Edinburgh. This cemetery was bisected by the new road formed in 1819, and retaining walls relieved with niches and columns were built on either side of the road which is the continuation of Princes Street through

Right Plate 15 Monument to Hume at Calton Hill, Edinburgh, designed by Robert Adam (*The Author*)

Far right Plate 16 Gothic house-tomb at Calton Hill (*The Author*)

Waterloo Place. The cemetery is dominated by the great obelisk of the Martyrs' Monument, erected to those who were tried and banished from Scotland in 1793 for advocating parliamentary reform. The balance of the funds raised to erect this monument was expended on the building of another obelisk in Nunhead Cemetery in London. Near the obelisk is the drum of Hume's grave, designed by Robert Adam in 1778 (Pl. 15), and if both are viewed from within the cemetery, the architectural qualities of the place are immediately apparent. The Tomb of Robert Burn is in a suitably Gothic style made fashionable by the writings of Sir Walter Scott, although the date (1816) is very early for such a monument.

Inside this cemetery the effect is very much that of a series of streets, with single-storey houses on either side. The details of these 'houses' are charming (Pl. 16), and William Raeburn's monument of 1817 incorporates several interesting features. In Scottish cemeteries the custom of inscribing the occupation of the people buried there on the tombs gives an intriguing glimpse of the patrons of cemeteries. In the old Gorbals burial-ground in Glasgow, for example, many stones are decorated with symbols that describe the trade of the person commemorated. Raeburn was a perfumer, and although his grave-enclosure was built in 1785, his death did not occur until 1812, while the Soanesque-like memorial inside the walls was not built until 1817 (Pl. 17).[10]

Even in the north, the influence of classicism remained potent. On the Black Isle in Ross and Cromarty there are several beautiful little cemeteries sited near the sea-shore. The combination of classical tombs, dark evergreen trees, background water, and distant snow-clad mountians creates the images that make one think of the Greek Islands. A small city of the dead, with its own wall, contained, civilized, and urban, in a natural landscape of great beauty and grandeur, is a remarkably architectural statement.[11]

Elsewhere, cemeteries had previously been laid out on much more formal architectural lines, based on the mediaeval cloistered court. The thirteenth-century Campo Santo in Pisa is the most celebrated of all such cloistered cemeteries, but there were others that followed. The Sebastiansfridhof in Salzburg was laid out between 1595 and 1600, and consists of a rectangular space surrounded by arcaded cloisters. Memorials are set against the walls (Pl. 18), the central rectangular space being reserved for earth-burial. In the centre of the cemetery is the Gabrielskapelle, or memorial chapel to Archbishop Wolf Dietrich von Reitenau. The elegant chapel is a masterpiece of the Baroque, with an exquisite interior by Elia Castello (Pl. 19). Though not quite so formal, the cemetery of S. Peter in Salzburg is

left Plate 17 Tomb of William Raeburn (*The Author*)

Right Plate 18 Cloisters of the Sebastiansfriedhof, Salzburg (*The Author*)

Left Plate 19 Interior of the Gabrielskapelle, with decorations by Elia Castello (*The Author*)

Right Plate 20 Arcades in the cemetery of S. Peter, Salzburg (*The Author*)

a model of urbane peace and calm. It nestles against the rocky wall of the Mönchsberg. There are burial-places hollowed out of the rock in the manner of the catacombs, for after all Salzburg is known as the 'German Rome'. It is an ancient cemetery, for the monastery itself was founded in the seventh century, but the beautiful arcades were added in 1627 (Pl. 20). Each arcade contains exquisite wrought-iron work, and the whole is architecturally most satisfying. At S. Peter's cemetery, the arcaded idea taken from the mediaeval cloister and the Italian Campo Santo gains new expression and significance.[12]

In 1783 a second walled cemetery was built at Pisa. This time the style of architecture is grandly Neoclassical, and a robust Doric Propylaeum stands over the entrance. Again, a formal cloistered rectangle has as its centrepiece the chapel, a simple Neoclassical building flanked by cypresses.

Although Europeans abroad had formed hygienic cemeteries, the vast majority of burials in Europe and in Britain took place in churches or in churchyards until the example of France provided a model for all to follow. Yet if France had got the publicity, reforms had already been effected elsewhere. In many European countries burials in churches were discontinued for reasons of hygiene during the eighteenth century. In Sweden, for example, the sale of burial sites within churches was prohibited by Gustavus III in 1783, and that enlightened country also encouraged the formation of new cemeteries beyond the boundaries of towns. Trees were planted in all churchyards in Sweden for reasons of hygiene, and several designs for cemeteries were produced by architects. The project for the New Cemetery in North Stockholm by C. G. Blom-Carlsson dates from 1827, while the charming Neoclassical design of 1829 by Axel Nyström is a splendid scheme with a vast semicircular colonnade of the Greek Doric Order (Pl. 21). An earlier project for a cemetery at Uppsala designed by Gustaf af Sillén in 1801 is also rigorously classical in inspiration (Pl. 22).

Joseph Furtenbach had published a plan for a Protestant town-churchyard in his *Architectura Civilis* in 1628. This consisted of four cloistered courts with family vaults arranged behind the colonnades. The classical arrangements of twenty-six family tombs within a long building where the pilasters replace a colonnade were found in the churchyard of S. Mary in Stockholm, an eighteenth-century development (Pl. 23). This

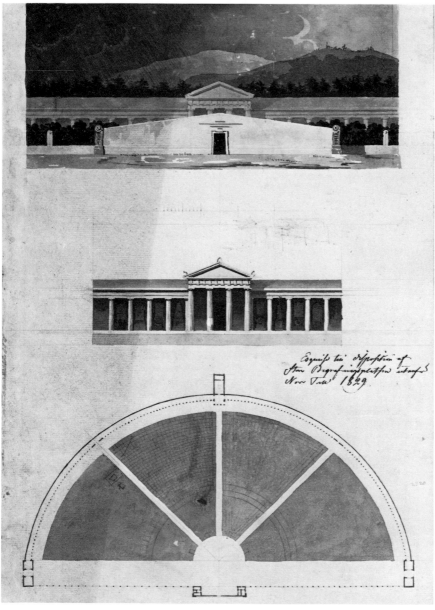

Plate 21 Esquisse by Axel Nyström for the Great Cemetery outside the northern gates of Stockholm (*The Eichhorn Collection, National Museum, Stockholm, lent by Prof. Göran Lindahl*)

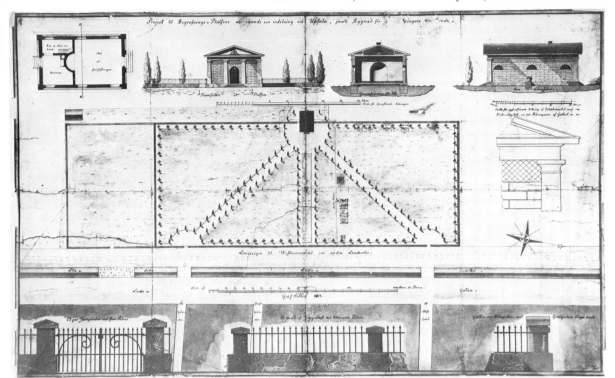

Plate 22 Project by Gustaf af Sillén for the building and layout of the cemetery of Uppsala, with a mortuary chapel (*Landsarkivet, Uppsala, lent by Prof. Göran Lindahl*)

Plate 23 Twenty-six family tombs in a long classical range of blind arcades in the churchyard of S. Mary, Stockholm (*Prof. Göran Lindahl*)

range of family tombs owes much to the Campo-Santo arrangement found in cloistered cemeteries in Italy, Spain, and central Europe.

Opposite Plate 24 View in the Père-Lachaise cemetery, Paris, showing the tombs of Molière and La Fontaine (*Author's Collection*)

The historic cemetery for the east of Paris, called Père-Lachaise, is situated on Mont-Louis and on the surrounding lands of that eminence, covering part of the property formerly owned by the confessor of Louis XIV. Père La Chaise, as the priest was called, ruled over large gardens that became a home for members of the Society of Jesus. As was the case in other cities in eighteenth-century Europe, Parisian churchyards became scandalous, and the reformers demanded new, hygienic cemeteries laid out in the best taste, unattached to churches.

In 1804 Napoleon, then First Consul, decreed that the estate of Baron Desfontaines at Mont-Louis should be a new cemetery for Paris. Nicholas Frochot, prefect, was then entrusted with the negotiations for the sale. In the same year, a decree was issued banning burial within or immediately outside churches, although there had been an investigation into the state of churchyards in 1763. In 1780 a cellar wall adjoining the Cimetière des Innocents gave way, and the ensuing scandal closed the ancient cemetery, which was cleared of bones (following an Order of the Council of State in 1784) between 1786 and 1788. All the bodies were transferred to the catacombs. These were originally subterranean quarries, worked as far back as the Roman period, and yielding a limestone that hardened on exposure. These quarries were converted into an enormous ossuary from 1784 under the direction of the architect Héricast de Thury, and the contents of the mediaeval graveyards were transported and stored there. The catacombs were consecrated by the Archbishop of Paris in 1786.

By 1794, four cemeteries had been proposed for Paris, and plans were advanced by 1800. A decree of Napoleon had also terminated burial in the overcrowded cemeteries of Venice. It was a feature of Napoleonic conquest that reform of the cemeteries followed swiftly. The Cimitero di San Michele was created by joining the islands of San Michele and San Cristofero with fill, and in 1824 Giacomo Massaggia and Bernardo Pasini founded a burial society that was patronised by Venetians. Burial was and is strictly on a leasehold basis, as space is at a premium. In Paris, the architect Brongniart was approached to advise on the general scheme for the proposed cemetery of Père-Lachaise. The beauty of the site, the design of winding paths, and the first monuments erected against a background of foliage, soon attracted customers for these Elysian Fields. The popularity of Père-Lachaise was increased by the translation there of the bodies of Molière, La Fontaine (Pl. 24), Héloïse, and Abélard from older burial-grounds, just as Kensal Green Cemetery was to become fashionable when two members of the royal house were interred there.

There had been grandiose schemes before Père-Lachaise was formed. The architect Gasse had proposed a monumental cemetery, the 'Elisée ou Cimetière Public', in 1799. This huge cemetery was to be approached by enormous ramps, and was grandly formal in plan (Pl. 25). The scheme is influenced by Boullée's designs for a Necropolis, and other Neoclassical plans by Ledoux, Vaudoyer, and other French masters. A comparison with the plans of the great Moghul mausolea in India is also revealing for the

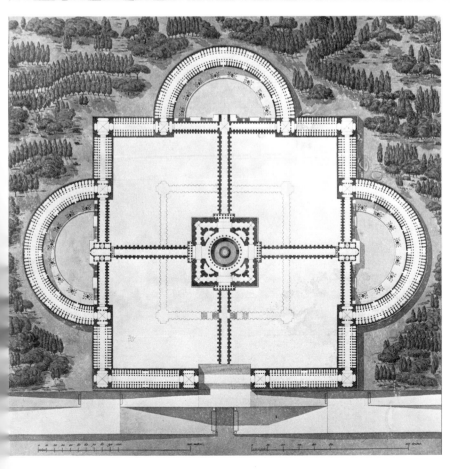

Plate 25 Elisée ou Cimetière Public. A plan for a gigantic formal cemetery, the subject of a competition, by the architect Gasse, of 1799. This formal Neoclassical scheme was greatly influenced by Boullée. Other prize schemes of a similar style exist by Morcau and others (*Author's Collection*)

symmetry, balance, and geometrical formality of the design.

In the last quarter of the eighteenth century, many French architects had produced monumental schemes for cenotaphs, mausolea, tombs, cemeteries, and memorials. The Neoclassical period was particularly fruitful in the development of funerary art, and architects followed French precedent in producing imaginative designs. The megalomaniac scale of much of Boullée's work for civic buildings undoubtedly had an appeal for the French Revolutionaries and for the later Empire. It is no accident that such French Neoclassical schemes had a profound influence on Hitler and Albert Speer when proposals for Berlin were planned.[13]

Much of the grandeur of Père-Lachaise is due in no small part to the architect Godde who embellished the cemetery in the early years of its existence. It was he who designed the main gateway and the chapel, and who advised on the suitability of monuments. The period when Père-Lachaise was founded was a happy one for architectural and sculptural design, and the cemetery contains large numbers of distinguished tombs, cenotaphs, and monuments. Within Père-Lachaise are many examples of the sculptor's art, of the architect's skill in the creation of monumental mausolea, and of the landscape architect's expertise in providing a rich backcloth of planting against which the creations of architect and sculptor can be seen to the best advantage. Here was a truly Arcadian landscape, worthy of the best that Claude might have painted. Again, most happily, the period coincided with Neoclassicism, so Greek and Roman prototypes were reinterpreted in this great French necropolis (Pl. 26).[14] It is hardly surprising, therefore, that the new cemetery proved to be so admired by persons of taste in every European country and in America. The Neoclassical language of the tombs was

Plate 26 Neoclassical tombs in Père-Lachaise, drawn by T. T. Bury, and engraved by Romney (*Author's Collection*)

156

fashionable and evocative and suggested the respectability of the antique.

The principal entry to the cemetery of Père-Lachaise is from the Boulevard de Ménilmontant (Pl. 27). Through severe monumental gates designed by Godde (then architect to the cemetery), an avenue lined with ambitious tombs leads up the hill towards the drama of the Monument aux Morts (1895–99), the chief work of the sculptor A. Bartholemé. This powerful feature shows male and female figures entering a mysterious yet classical door that suggests an awesome and remote world beyond. Other figures representing the souls of the dead rise up above the still, lifeless corpses, while allegories of death, of mourning, of hope, and of resurrection flank the portal (Pl. 28). The inscription is from Isaiah and from Matthew. As with so many rationalist European cemeteries, interment (unless purchased in perpetuity) was for a limited period (*concession temporaire*, or *concession trentenaire*), so ground could be cleared and the bones could be stacked underground. This practice, unfortunately, was not adopted in British cemeteries, so when catacombs or grounds were full, the cemeteries and buildings deteriorated. Bartholemé's great sculpture represents the charnel-house and tomb towards which suffering humanity, filled with hope and fear, proceeds. The angel of immortality holds the door open.

Plate 27 Vue de la Porte d'Entrée du Père Lachaise'. Main entrance from the Boulevard de Ménilmontant designed by Godde, architect to Père-Lachaise. Lithograph by C. Lasalle (*Author's Collection*)

Most burial reformers took Père-Lachaise as their model, and it is no accident that the beautiful cemetery of Mount Jerome, Dublin, founded at the same time as Kensal Green, Glasgow Necropolis, and Norwood, has tombs that recall monuments in Père-Lachaise. The sarcophagus protected by a Tuscan canopy in Mount Jerome is obviously modelled on the Demidoff-Stroganoff tomb in Père-Lachaise (See Ch. IX, Pl. 3). Many mausolea and memorials in Père-Lachaise were illustrated in collections of designs published in Paris in the 1830s and 1840s, and these were copied by the builders of monuments in other European and American cemeteries. The enchanting grounds, planted with great varieties of trees that have now matured, have been developed to take full advantage of the hill of Mont-

Louis. From the principal gate in the Boulevard, grand avenues lead to the chapel that formerly held the eye before Bartholemé's Monument aux Morts was built lower down. The cemetery contains romantic winding paths in the English landscape tradition, and a strongly axial formality that derived from custom in France and Italy but is also known in funerary architecture from a wide range of customs and periods. The classical geometry of Greece and Rome has its parallels in the funerary gardens and mausolea of Islam, where symmetry is carried to perfection.

Plate 29 Plan of Père-Lachaise by Rousseau, of about 1842 (*Author's Collection*)

The plan as reproduced is drawn by the architect Rousseau, and shows

Plate 30 Tomb of Elisabeth, Countess Demidoff, of the family Stroganoff (ob. 1818), designed by Jaunet, Châtillon and Schwind (*The Author*)

the cemetery as it was in the 1840s (Pl. 29). This plan is ingenious, for the routes following the contours produce the most startling effects as, for example, when one comes across the magnificent monument of Elizabeth, Countess Demidoff, of the family Stroganoff. This fine tomb, designed by Jaunet, Châtillon, and Schwind, celebrates the countess, who died in 1818. Dramatic changes of level and heart-stopping vistas are features of Père-Lachaise (Pl. 30).

The cemetery of Père-Lachaise has an urban quality, with paved streets lined with house-tombs. The streets are named and signed, with

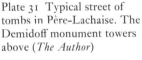

Plate 31 Typical street of tombs in Père-Lachaise. The Demidoff monument towers above (*The Author*)

cast-iron street furniture similar to that of streets in the cities of the living. The urban flavour is enhanced by the detached mausolea, like villas, with their neat front doors. Some tombs are of monumental proportions, and achieve a grandeur that is peculiarly French in quality (Pl. 31). Yet these urban aspects are beautifully complemented by the Arcadian landscapes and by the great variety of the planting (Pl. 32). As one walks in this cemetery, the remarkably peaceful and serene architectural qualities become more apparent. The famous names of the dead occur in such profusion that the visitor becomes almost blasé. The grave of Molière beside that of La Fontaine (Pl. 24) causes no surprise, and familiar names like Rossini (whose body was taken to Florence in 1887), Bizet, Chopin, and Haussmann are seen and accepted as though they had always been there. No strife, no poverties, no contentions nor vices have a place in this enchanted spot. The monumental celebration of Oscar Wilde by Epstein (Pl. 33) is one of the most successful examples of twentieth-century funerary art. Here lie Marshal Ney, with his titles of Duc d'Elchingen and Prince de la Moscowa resounding on his tombstone. Chopin's wistful memorial seems entirely appropriate, while Bellini's *stele*-like stone recalls operatic nights with *Norma*, *La Sonnambula*, and others, although the composer's body now lies

Left Plate 32 Flight of steps, with tombs, in Père-Lachaise (*The Author*)

Plate 33 Oscar Wilde's tomb, by Epstein (*The Author*)

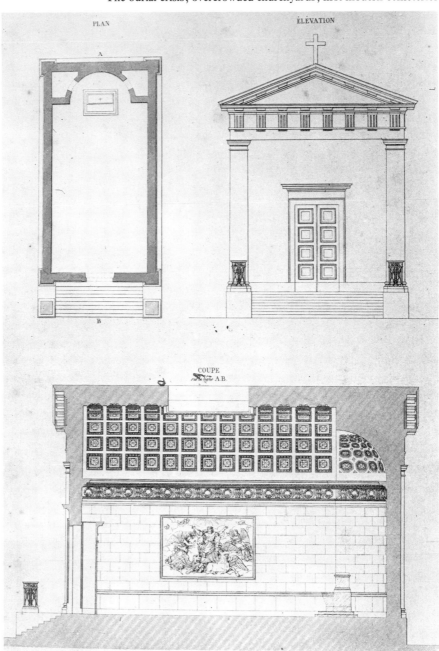

Plate 34 Chapel on the site of the house of the Jesuit La Chaise. It was designed by Godde, architect of the cemetery, and erected in 1821 (*Author's Collection*)

in Catania. One feels one is among old friends in these Elysian Fields where there is nothing to offend either eye or ear.

The main chapel of the cemetery stands on the main axis, high above the Monument aux Morts. It is in the form of a Neoclassical temple, and marks the natural centre and focal point of the cemetery. It was built on the site of the house once owned by Père La Chaise to designs by Godde in 1821 (Pl. 34). Near by are the tombs of Thiers and David.

The cemetery grounds are divided into *Divisions* and *Secteurs*, with each plot identified by a number. The scheme helped to locate plots with ease, and enabled accurate records to be kept. The basic arrangement of divisions and subdivisions proved to be the model for later cemeteries that derived from Père-Lachaise in Europe and America during the last century. In Division 87 is the magnificent crematorium (see Ch. X), surrounded by arcaded cloisters that contain columbaria. Spaces for ashes in the columbarium are let out for a limited period, usually a *concession temporaire*. The Campo-Santo-like calm of this enclosure demonstrates its success, for here is an architecture of death that is as urbane as that of the streets of tombs in the earlier parts of this great Parisian cemetery.

Dr John Strang said much about Père-Lachaise in his *Necropolis Glasguensis*[15] published in Glasgow in 1831. He quoted the cemetery as an example to the Scots to encourage them to form a necropolis in Glasgow. His polemic greatly influenced John Claudius Loudon and other apologists for cemeteries. Strang compared Père-Lachaise with the 'vast fields of rude stones and ruder hillocks' familiar in Scotland, and proposed a 'garden cemetery' which would be a place where 'the widowed heart might occasionally resort to hold spiritual communion' with the dead. The horrific realities 'coupled with a churchyard' would be 'dispelled by the beauty of the garden, the variety of its walks, by the romantic nature of the situation, and, above all, by the commanding view of Paris and its environs which it affords'. In that 'vast grove of the dead', Strang declared, 'each has his own grave, and each his own mausoleum'. In Paris, he had found 'a little flower-garden surrounded by cedar, spruce, cypress, and yewtrees, round which the rose and the honeysuckle are seen entwining'. He noted with approval the 'obelisks, pyramids, temples, and marble sarcophagi', and the 'family

Plate 35 View of Père-Lachaise at the Rond-Point des Peupliers; the tomb of Gaspard Monge is on the left (*Author's Collection*)

sepulchres in some degree similar to those of ancient Rome'. Amid the vast variety of sepulchral ornaments of Père-Lachaise, the 'contemplative mind' was not 'only impressed with sentiments of solemn sublimity and religious awe, but with those of a most tender and heart-affecting melancholy'. In the grounds of Père-Lachaise, the visitor walked 'as in the porch of eternity', and hearts 'at once impressed with a sense of the evanescence and the value of time'. To Strang, a garden cemetery and 'monumental decoration' afforded the 'most convincing tokens of a nation's progress in civilization and in the arts'. He noted with what pains the 'most celebrated nations of which history speaks' had adorned their places of sepulture, and that it is from their 'funereal monuments that we gather much that is known of their civil progress and of their advancement in taste'. The story of Egypt, he said, was written on its pyramids, and the 'chronology of Arabia' was pictured on its tombs. Strang noted that the 'most common burial places, and perhaps the most affecting in this cemetery, consist of a square or parallelogram of ground, of about three or four yards broad, enclosed by a neat little railing of iron or wickerwork. Within this spot, there is always either a sepulchral urn, a small pillar, or a cross, to tell the name and the quality of him who lies below. The remaining portion is filled with flowers and embellished with pots of rare plants. The more ambitious monuments consist of obelisks, pyramids, temples and marble sarcophagi, decorated with figures and *basso relievi*, while a third consist of crypts and family sepulchres in some degree similar to those of ancient Rome'.[15]

John Claudius Loudon, who knew Strang's work, and indeed pillaged it liberally for his own writings, recognized the powerful prototype Père-Lachaise offered to early-nineteenth-century burial reformers. The garden cemetery was not only the 'sworn foe of preternatural fear and superstition', but it offered the solution to the urgent problems of chaos, unsavouriness, and horror associated with the disposal of the dead in the overcrowded graveyards at that time. In an arrangement like that offered by the French model, architects and sculptors such as Rousseau could give free rein to their imaginations. Monuments and nature would combine to create a man-made landscape of sublime beauty.

The early tombs aroused considerable interest throughout Europe, and many examples were illustrated in pattern-books that had a widespread influence. A print of the Rond-Point des Peupliers shows the tomb of Gaspard Monge on the left (Pl. 35). This Neoclassical tomb is explained fully in the plans, elevations, and sections designed by the architect Clochard in 1820. The coffins are placed in recesses within the podium of this fine building which shows considerable Egyptian influence, as did many Neoclassical designs (Pl. 36). Much plainer and more purely classical is Clochard's design for the tomb of Baron Demicoud (Pl. 37). The Arcadian aspects of monuments set among leafy arbours are captured in an enchanting print that shows on the left the tomb of the architect Brongniart designed by Lebas, and on the right the tomb designed by Philippon for Jacques Delille (Pl. 38). Interest was not confined to French engravers, for A. Pugin published a series of prints showing monuments in Père-Lachaise. One of the most interesting of these prints, designed by T. T. Bury, and

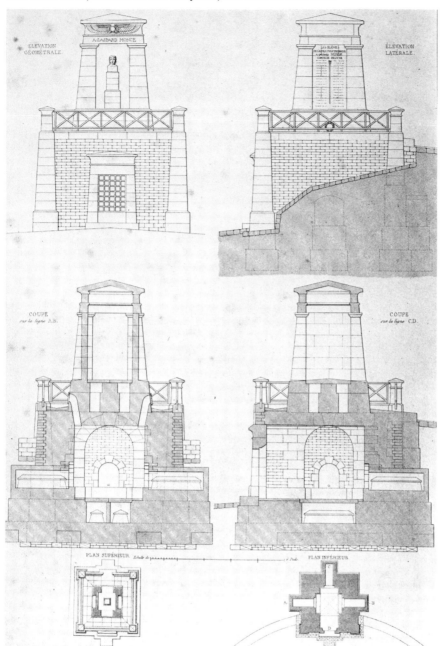

Plate 36 Tomb of Gaspard
Monge (1820), designed by
Clochard (*Author's Collection*)

Opposite above
Plate 37 Tomb of Baron
Demicoud by Pierre
Clochard (*Author's Collection*)

Opposite below Plate 38 View
showing, *left*, the tomb of
Brongniart, by Lebas, and
right, the tomb of Jacques
Delille, by Philippon
(*Author's Collection*)

engraved by Romney, shows a group of magnificent Neoclassical tombs. On
the left is that of L. André Masséna, duc de Rivoli, prince d'Essling,
marshal of France (1758–1817), designed by Vincent Méry. On the right is
the monument to R. Denis, duc Decrès, vice-admiral of France
(1761–1821), designed by Visconti (Pl. 39).

By far the commonest type of mausoleum in Père-Lachaise is the little
house-tomb, of which two sets of designs may be reproduced here: those for
the family Carette, by Visconti; and those for the family Boscary, by
Vincent Méry. The tomb of Baron Haussman, creator of the Paris of

boulevards and grand vistas, is such a type (Pl. 40). Very different, yet not perhaps so divorced from Roman tower-tombs, is the monument of Baron Louis-Félix de Beaujour (1765–1836), designed by Cendrier (Pl. 41).

Today, the cemetery of Père-Lachaise is still one of the finest and most interesting in the world. British and American cemeteries modelled on it were never as splendid, and many have now decayed or become vandalized. The Parisian cemeteries are still impeccably kept, and are even more delightful now than when they were first laid out, for the planting has matured and the monuments have acquired the patina of age. Paris is still a great city: its cemeteries are among its greatest pleasures. The Cimetière du Nord, or Cemetery of Montmartre, and the Cimetière du Sud, or Montparnasse, followed shortly after the foundation of Père-Lachaise, or Cimetière de l'Est. Neither is quite as beautiful as Père-Lachaise, but they have many fine monuments.

In nearly all the propaganda for the establishment of the new cemeteries, Père-Lachaise is quoted as the example that all should follow. The writings of J. C. Loudon, John Strang, G. F. Carden and many others pay tribute to the great Parisian cemetery. The garden cemetery, then, was French in origin, but achieved a peculiarly English interpretation in both England and the United States. By the end of the eighteenth century, therefore, Scots, Frenchmen, and Dissenting Englishmen were arguing for cemeteries, and in some cases getting them. Ulstermen, too, were imbued with ideas of

Plate 39 View, designed by T. T. Bury, and engraved by Romney: on the *left* is the obelisk to L. André Masséna by Vincent Méry, on the *right*, the monument to R. Denis, duc Decrès, by Visconti (*Author's Collection*)

Left Plate 40 Tomb of the Family Carette, by Visconti, and the tomb of the Family Boscary, by Vincent Méry (*Author's Collection*)

Right Plate 41 Monument to Baron Louis-Félix de Beaujour (1765–1836), designed by Cendrier (*Author's Collection*)

radicalism, and Belfast was to get its cemeteries. Bunhill Fields was a seventeenth-century Dissenters' Cemetery in London, and Calton Hill was a product of the Scottish response to the Enlightenment. Père-Lachaise was a synthesis of ideas of Neoclassicism, of radicalism, and of the reforms that had begun in the reign of Louis XVI,[16] probably not uninfluenced by the experiences of the European colonials who had set up cemeteries abroad.[17]

Mausolea and other buildings to celebrate death, from the Renaissance period to the twentieth century.

Sweden; Ireland; India; Italy; England and the United States. French Neoclassical designs by Boullée and others

Monuments are made for victories over strangers:
domestic troubles should be covered with
the veil of sadness.

JULIUS CAESAR: quoted in Plutarch's *Lives*

All mausolea are named after the great tomb built by Queen Artemisia for her husband, Mausolos, at Halicarnassos in the fourth century BC. There have been other great mausolea, such as the imperial tombs of Augustus and Hadrian, and the huge building at Castle Howard in Yorkshire, that are famous throughout the civilized world. A mausoleum is a funerary structure, with the character of a roofed building, set aside for the burial of the dead. Such buildings are objects in space, set immutably in the landscape, silent, and grand. Mausolea and individual tombs had been common in ancient times, but, as we have seen, during the Dark and Middle Ages funerary architecture was almost invariably associated with ecclesiastical buildings. The grander tombs were either extensions to churches, or buildings within churches. During the Renaissance the cult of tombs and the growth of the importance of the individual[1] encouraged individual tombs; the Scaliger tombs at Verona are probably among the first great post-classical mausolea, although primarily Gothic in style. Renaissance and post-Renaissance mausolea are usually buildings in their own right, and while some may be found in churchyards or near churches, many are quite separate, and may even be placed in open parkland.

Burial-chapels or vaults were ways of solving the problem of burying in churches. Chapels were added to churches, and opened into churches, but did not encroach upon space used for worship. These chapels were private property, and were maintained by the owners. Some of the first and finest of seventeenth-century mortuary-chapels are found in Sweden. The burial-chapel of Gustavus II Adolphus in the Riddarholms Church at Stockholm of 1634 was followed by a large number of similar mausolea throughout Scandinavia. They all have two rooms: one under ground for the coffins, and one above for the chapel. Memorials adorned the chapel walls. The Lars Kagg Mausoleum attached to the church at Floda dates from 1666,

Plate 1 Mortuary chapel of Lars Kagg, attached to the church at Floda, Södermanland, Sweden (*Prof. Göran Lindahl*)

Right Plate 2 Interior of the Lars Kagg mortuary chapel (*Prof. Göran Lindahl*)

and was designed by Erik Dahlberg. It is a Greek cross on plan, and has a Giant Tuscan Order of pilasters supporting pediments on three sides. The rich stuccoed interior is by Carlo Carove (Pls. 1, 2). The superb Caroline mausoleum at Riddarholms Church at Stockholm dates from 1671, and was designed by Tessin the Elder.

During the course of the eighteenth century, mortuary-chapels began to be built quite apart from churches, and became enclosed, private places. When they were built in churchyards, they were usually without windows, and emphasized the exclusiveness of the burials they commemorated.

Dr Maurice Craig has pointed out that house-shaped tombs are known in Ireland from early-Christian times, especially those at Banagher, Bovevagh, Corran, Clones, Slane, and elsewhere. 'The house-shaped, temple-shaped, or church-shaped family tomb is familiar to anyone who knows, however superficially, the graveyards of France.'[2] Mausolea are not very common in England, though a few examples exist that are considerable both in size and in architectural merit. As Dr Craig says, at the 'upper end of the scale they shade into the class of the mortuary chapel'. Ulster is peculiarly rich in spectacular mausolea of the eighteenth and early nineteenth centuries, and it is perhaps worth examining a few of the most interesting of those to be found in the province. Most mausolea in Northern Ireland stand in churchyards, although a few exist within the demesnes of country houses. Some funerary buildings stand in cemeteries separated from ecclesiastical buildings. Two mausolea in the grounds of great Irish houses deserve mention here.

The eighteenth century produced many great builders, but in Ireland

Plate 3 Mausoleum at
Downhill, Northern Ireland
(*The Author*)

there were few who could compare with Frederick Hervey, fourth Earl of Bristol and Bishop of Derry (1730–1803). His enormous mansion at Downhill was one of his largest building projects, and was planned for a spectacular site on the noble headlands of North Derry overlooking the sea. Downhill had magnificent grounds, with views of great beauty, and the composition of house, site, prospects, Mussenden Temple, and mausoleum was to the eighteenth-century eye truly sublime. The mausoleum today is a free-standing structure near the ruins of the house, and was erected in memory of the Bishop's brother, the Lord Lieutenant of Ireland. It was commenced in 1779, and was modelled on the Roman mausoleum of the Julii at St Rémy in Provence, a tomb that appealed greatly to connoisseurs of the Enlightenment. The architect Michael Shanahan[3] designed a variation on the Julii tomb which was considered 'a beautifully sublime piece of architecture' at the time. The detailing of Shanahan's building is elegant and refined, although the edifice itself was primarily intended as an eye-catcher in the grounds of the house. The mausoleum consisted of a cubic base on which was an arched opening flanked by an Ionic Order in a Venetian-window type evolved by Wyatt, and so differed in various respects from the Roman original. Above the Ionic entablature was a drum of Corinthian columns that supported a dome on which was an urn. Under this little circular canopy was a marble statue of the Lord Lieutenant carved by John Van Nost (1714–80), the leading Dublin portrait-sculptor of the period. Unfortunately, the statue and cupola were victims of the Great Wind that devastated Ireland in 1839. The inscription by Virgil round the frieze survives:

ILLE MEAS ERRARE BOVES UT CERNIS, ET IPSUM LUDERE
QUAE VELLEM CALAMO PERMISIT AGRESTI

The fragment of this exquisite mausoleum is surrounded today by unsightly fencing, and has overhead power lines sited distressingly near it (Pl. 3).

Even finer in quality, and in a better state of preservation, is the Templeton mausoleum at Castle Upton near Templepatrick in Co. Antrim. It was built in 1789 to designs by Robert Adam at the request of the Hon. Mrs Upton in memory of the Rt. Hon. Arthur Upton. This serene building consists of a plain rectangular roofed structure with one façade treated as a grand arched entrance flanked by niches. Medallions, plaques, urns, sarcophagi, and garlands add to the restrained funereal character of the edifice (Pl. 4).

These two classic mausolea are both associated with great houses, but though fine in themselves they are perhaps eclipsed in interest by the mausolea in the parish churchyard of Knockbreda in Co. Down near Belfast. Four large tombs with architectural pretentions were built in the last two decades of the eighteenth century by various wealthy landowners and merchants of the Belfast area. Some Belfast merchant-families had connections with India, and indeed many Ulster families were associated with the East India Company, a fact not insignificant when considering the

Plate 4 The Templeton mausoleum at Castle Upton, Northern Ireland (*The Author*)

Right Plate 5 The Greg mausoleum at Knockbreda, Northern Ireland (*The Author*)

design of the tombs. The mausolea in Knockbreda churchyard are square on plan, and have most elegant Adamesque arrangements of classical columns, pilasters, and entablatures with almost over-slender proportions. Above the crowning cornices are curious superstructures composed of domes, pyramids, obelisks, and urns. The mausolea at Knockbreda are among the richest and oddest of tombs in Ulster, and indeed cannot be paralleled elsewhere in the British Isles. The most ornate is the Greg family tomb of the last decade of the eighteenth century (Pl. 5), while the contemporary Waddell-Cunningham-Douglas mausoleum, with its crown of urns, pyramids, and other classical elements, is almost as elaborate (Pl. 6). Sumptuous and ostentatious though these tombs are, they have a refinement and delicacy that at once suggests quality. The smaller Rainey tomb, a perfectly proportioned building of the same period, is topped by four pyramids, by an octagonal cap with concave sides, and by a crowning urn (Pl. 7). All these mausolea appear to be by the same designer and form a unique group. Stylistically they are similar to many tombs in the South Park Street Cemetery in Calcutta. Many of the grander tombs in Calcutta pre-date the Knockbreda mausolca, and it is possible that the models for the Knockbreda tombs may have been suggested to Ulstermen returning home

from India who had seen the Calcutta cemeteries. The pyramids, obelisks, and exotic eclecticism in Knockbreda have a certain oriental lushness suggestive of South Park Street Cemetery. Designs by Sir William Chambers and the Adams may also have influenced the creators of the Knockbreda monuments. The case of Knockbreda is interesting in that here a churchyard became a fashionable burial-ground, and so contains a number of ambitious mausolea to commemorate families of substance. The old Clifton graveyard in Belfast contains several less distinguished mausolea, but in this case the site is a cemetery rather than a churchyard. Mention was made of the Clifton graveyard in the previous chapter. Specific note was taken of the Luke vault, and here again the obelisk is reminiscent of motifs in Calcutta. Obelisks and pyramids, as I have noted, were favourite motifs of Neoclassicism. The Neoclassical type of tomb with an obelisk set over a rectangular, somewhat Egyptian chamber, is exemplified by the Luke vault, and by the Greer mausoleum in the tiny historic churchyard at Desertcreat in Co. Tyrone. The Greer tomb dates from about 1830, its battered sides suggesting a pronounced Egyptian influence. The top of the rectangular chamber is crowned by an Egyptian cornice, above which are steps supporting a stumpy obelisk; a small sarcophagus is placed over the entrance.

Neoclassicism found particular favour in Ulster, as it did in Scotland, for

Left Plate 6 The Waddell-Cunningham-Douglas mausoleum at Knockbreda, Northern Ireland (*The Author*)

Plate 7 The Rainey mausoleum at Knockbreda, Northern Ireland (*The Author*)

the Gothic style was associated with Anglicanism or with Roman Catholicism. The rational classical manner savoured of the Enlightenment, while the curious Neoclassical Egyptianizing of Hellenistic ideas may have owed not a little to the strength of Freemasonry in both Ulster and Scotland. The Egyptian elements in Mozart's *Die Zauberflöte* had considerable Masonic significance. Neoclassical forms are found in some profusion associated with funerary architecture in Ulster, France, and Scotland, and indeed with designs for mausolea throughout Europe. Several Neoclassical tombs exist in North Derry, including the Beresford and Conn mausolea of the 1830s in the graveyard of Christ Church, Limavady, and the Cather mausoleum of the same period at Walworth Old Church near Ballykelly. These three tombs are clearly by the same architect, and their details recall those of the gates to Seaforde House. It is possible that the bold acroteria with anthemion motifs, shallow pediments, and other features of the Cather (Pl. 8), Beresford, and Conn mausolea may give a clue to their designer, for we know that John Hargrave was involved in the designs for Drenagh House, near Limavady, and he also seems to have been closely associated with Seaforde. The bold Neoclassical detailing of the gates of Seaforde is too close in style to the decorations of the Cather mausoleum to be accidental.

Despite the long favour that Neoclassicism enjoyed in Ulster, a fact that cannot be entirely explained by the innate conservatism of taste in Ireland nor by the familiar time-lag between fashion in England and in Ireland, Gothic inevitably appeared in Ulster mausolea eventually. One of the best examples is in the Dunville mausoleum at the Clifton graveyard, yet not far

Plate 8 The Cather mausoleum at Walworth Old Church, near Ballykelly, Northern Ireland (*The Author*)

Plate 9 Barrel-vaulted tomb in the Non-Subscribing Presbyterian churchyard, Downpatrick, Northern Ireland (*The Author*)

from the Neoclassical strongholds of Limavady, Downhill, and Walworth, in Tamlaghtfinlagan stands the charming Gothic Gage family vault, a low rectangular building with crocketed finials. This mausoleum appears to date from the 1870s, by which time Gothic was becoming respectable in Ulster. The church at Tamlaghtfinlagan was built by the Bishop of Derry in 1795 to designs attributed to Shanahan, the architect of the Downhill mausoleum.

The churchyard of the Non-Subscribing Presbyterians at Stream Street, Downpatrick, contains several remarkable tombs of a classical flavour. Clearly, the inspirations of the rectangular mausolea with their high concave-sided pyramidal caps were the Kedron Valley tombs near Jerusalem, and certain elements of tomb design in Petra. It is perhaps worth noting that the tomb of Major Hector Munro at Buxar in India is almost identical to the Stream Street mausolea, except that in the Munro tomb the pyramidal cap was elongated to become a concave-sided obelisk, but the type is decidedly odd, and the two sites may be connected through Ulster-Scots families. Other tombs, shaped like wartime Nissen-huts, are found in Downpatrick (Pl. 9), not dissimilar to the vaulted graves in Augerum churchyard in Sweden.

All the Ulster mausolea mentioned so far have had their origins in classical precedent or in Gothic forms. The exotic Stephenson mausoleum in the tiny Presbyterian churchyard of Kilbride in Co. Antrim is quite different, however. It is a miniature Tâj Mahal, complete with dome, pointed arches, and pinnacles. The Stephensons had connections with India,

174

Plate 10 The Stephenson mausoleum, Kilbride, Northern Ireland (*The Author*)

Right Plate 11 The Cleland mausoleum, Dundonald, Northern Ireland (*The Author*)

and this fact is celebrated in the extraordinary tomb on an Ulster hillside (Pl. 10). The recurring themes of Indian or Anglo-Indian funerary architecture in Ulster are too insistent to be mere coincidence. The fact that Ulster Protestants were involved in the East India Company in considerable numbers (Roman Catholics were not permitted to hold high office in the eighteenth and early-nineteenth centuries) gives us the link between mausoleum design in Ulster and in India. Ulstermen who had seen their friends and fellow-countrymen interred in India under monumental tombs were not going to settle for a humble stone when they returned to Ulster. Another Neoclassical design, consisting of a huge podium on which is a peristyle supporting a canopy, stands in the churchyard at Dundonald in Co. Down. It commemorates the Cleland family of Stormount (Pl. 11).

In the Presbyterian churchyard at Duneane, not far from Kilbride in Co. Antrim, is the peculiar tomb designed by John Carey in memory of his father. The extravagant inscriptions celebrate the life and lineage of Carey *père*, who saved the natives of the distant parts of the Empire for Christ and for hygiene. The eclectic base of the monument contains Gothic and classical elements that support a hand with a finger pointing towards celestial headquarters. The cast-iron railings incorporate a disturbingly surrealistic array of interlocking arms and hands.

While the Carey tomb is provincial and coarse, the Murland vault at Clough Presbyterian churchyard in Co. Down is a ripe example of sophisticated Victorian funerary architecture. The Murland tomb has a

Great Order of console brackets, rather than pilasters or columns, supporting the pitched roof. These curiously lugubrious consoles, the massive vermiculated rustication of the entrance, and the eerily shrouded urns convey something of the 'fat atmosphere' of death in the period (Pl. 12). However, not all nineteenth-century mausolea were so confidently designed, as may be demonstrated by the awkardly proportioned tetrastyle temple of the Burges mausoleum in S. Michael's churchyard in Castlecaulfeild. The bucolic interpretation of classical detail is curiously inept for a land where classicism survived until the twentieth century, as tombstones, churches, and halls throughout Ulster demonstrate.

Architectural elements were applied to mausolea in Ulster with wit, style, and fancy. The variety and quality of designs for funerary architecture compare favourably with examples from other areas. Mausolea like those at Castle Upton or Downhill are highly polished monuments by any standards, but the Knockbreda 'family' of mausolea displays an eclectic inventiveness, even a virtuosity, that was later to become a feature of public-house design in Ulster. The smallest churchyards often contain exotic tombs such as the Stephenson mausoleum at Kilbride, one of the oddest of strangers in its setting. The pomp and grandeur of the Murland tomb at Clough belong more to Père-Lachaise or to the United States than to the

Plate 12 The Murland vault at Clough Presbyterian Church, Northern Ireland (*The Author*)

Plate 13 The Schönborn
Kapelle, Würzburg, built to
designs by J. B. Neumann
(*The Author*)

churchyard of a small village in the romantic shadow of the Mountains of
Mourne. Neoclassical designs from France, India, Scotland, and from
other published sources undoubtedly influenced the forms and characters of
mausolea in Ulster; their derivatives can be found incongruously placed in
the most surprising settings. Ulster is a land where magic and the unknown
never seem far away, and the architecture of death found there is among the
most intriguing in Europe. It is an aspect of the Province that is not
sufficiently known, and is certainly not appreciated.[4]

Elsewhere in Europe and America, mausolea took on differing forms and
positions. Adjoining the north transept of the Cathedral of Würzburg is a
mortuary chapel of the grandest style, befitting the burial-places of the
Prince-Bishops of that city. It is the Schönborn Kapelle, a magnificent
structure built between 1721 and 1736 by the celebrated Johann Balthasar
Neumann in the Rococo style. It contains the tombs of J. P. von
Schönborn, Elector of Mainz and Prince-Bishop of Würzburg (died 1673), of
Prince-Bishop F. K. von Schönborn, of J. P. F. and of L. F. von Schönborn,
Elector of Mainz (Pl. 13). The original plan of the chapel had been produced
by Maximilian von Welsch after studies by Georg Bayer and Georg
Hennicke. Neumann revised this plan when he took over in 1722, and further
revisions were made when he visited Boffran in Paris in 1723.[5]

The tomb of Dante in Ravenna is also a structure of undoubted importance as a mausoleum. The poet died at Ravenna, where he enjoyed the protection of Guido da Polenta, on 13 September 1321 at the age of 56, and was temporarily interred in the narthex of the Church of San Francesco. In 1482 Bernado Bembo, the Venetian Governor, caused a mausoleum to be erected from designs by Pietro Lombardi, but this was entirely rebuilt in 1780 by Camillo Morigia. It is a square structure with a dome, embellished with medallions of the poet's teachers and patrons (Virgil, Brunetto Latini, Can Grande della Scala, and Guido da Polenta). Opposite the entrance is a half-length relief of the poet, and above the sarcophagus is an urn containing Dante's bones. The epitaph was composed by Canaccio in 1357:

Plate 14 Tomb of Dante in Ravenna (*The Author*)

Jura Monarchiae, Superos, Phlegethonta lacusque
Lustrando cecini, voluerant fata quousque,
Sed quia pars cessit melioribus hospita castris,
A(u)ctoremaque suum petiit felicior astris,
Hic claudor Dantes, patriis extorris ab oris,
Quem genui pravi Florentia mater amoris   (Pl. 14)

Ravenna, of course, is famed for two other supreme examples of funerary architecture; the mausolea of Galla Placidia and of Theodoric the Goth, discussed in Chapter II.

178

Plate 15 Mausoleum at
Castle Howard in Yorkshire
(*A. F. Kersting, H8911*)

The great mausoleum in the grounds of Castle Howard in Yorkshire is as fine as any comparable building in the world, and must be regarded as one of the greatest of all examples of buildings in this genre, and probably the first great solitary free-standing tomb built in Western Europe since antiquity. It was designed by Nicholas Hawksmoor in 1728–9, and begun in 1731, though not completed until 1742. It is an enormous building of noble proportions, and is an eye-catcher in the park. It has wide-spreading retaining walls, curved, with niches set between square bastions. This base was designed by Daniel Garrett. The whole effect is that of a fortress. On this base, but much smaller, is the square base of the rotunda, consisting of banded rusticated walls accentuated with broad pilasters. Above is the drum of the rotunda, with a peristyle of curiously tall Tuscan columns that carry a Doric entablature. The drum above has square windows and a shallow saucer-dome (Pl. 15). The designs for the mausoleum were passed to Lord Burlington in 1732. The placing of the columns only a diameter-and-a-half apart was, in a circular building of the Doric order, regarded as erroneous. Hawksmoor did battle with the arbiters of taste at Chiswick, and claimed to be the follower of correct classical practice. The building as it stands is undoubtedly Hawksmoorean, and places him firmly in the modern, rather than 'Antient', camp of this day. It is a supreme creation of great splendour, with more than a hint of a later Romantic style about it. The base recalls to mind some elements of the Adam 'Castle' style.[6]

The interior is as noble a space as it is possible to conceive. The crypt is

179

vaulted, with a quatrefoil centre. The main floor is surrounded by a massive Order of Corinthian columns on huge dies, partially set in semicircular recesses. The coffered dome is a masterpiece of English Baroque (Pl. 16).

The great families of Europe often took over side-chapels in churches to serve as family vaults. Occasionally, churches were enlarged to receive yet more monuments, as was the case with the Bridgewater family in Little Gaddesden church in Hertfordshire. Families would thus be together in death, and a social superiority was maintained. Bodies were often brought back from abroad for burial in the family vaults. Frequently, families built mausolea in the grounds of the family seat, to serve as ornamental eye-catchers and as burial-places. The second half of the eighteenth century may be regarded as a new golden age of mausolea, for the architects of the period were obsessed by antique elements and by romantic, semi-gloomy spaces, fired by Piranesian example. James Wyatt's designs (1783) for the mausoleum at Cobham Park in Kent incorporates sarcophagi, a pyramidal roof, segmental openings at attic level, and an austere Roman Doric Order (Pl. 17). The Pelham mausoleum at Brocklesby Park at Great Limber in Lincolnshire is one of the most beautiful of these 'country park' mausolea, circular in plan, and Neoclassical in style. A peristyle of the Roman Doric Order surrounds a drum that is enriched with sarcophagi set in niches. The drum carries a dome. The handsome interior contains Neoclassical

Below left Plate 16 Interior of the Castle Howard mausoleum (*Country Life*)

Below right Plate 17 Mausoleum at Cobham Park, Kent, by James Wyatt (*The Author*)

Far right Plate 18 Mausoleum at Brocklesby Park, Lincolnshire, by James Wyatt (*Country Life*)

Right Plate 19 Interior of the mausoleum at Brocklesby Park (*Country Life*)

monuments arranged round its walls, all incorporating podia, sarcophagi, urns, figures, and pyramidal compositions. The enchanting figure in the centre of the space is by Nollekens. James Wyatt also designed the Pelham mausoleum (1787–94), and demonstrates in these magnificent buildings his mastery of Neoclassical design (Pls. 18, 19).

Very different, but again an object in space, is the work by Ireland's greatest architect, Sir Edward Lovett Pearce (1699–1733). The obelisk at Stillorgan, Dublin, stands on a formally conceived grotto-like base constructed with daring.[7] This huge monument was probably intended as a memorial, and has the character of a funerary structure (Pl. 20).

Mausolea as objects in a landscape were only one aspect of the permutations of architectural ingenuity displayed by eighteenth-century masters. The new Church of S Lawrence, Ayot St Lawrence, Hertfordshire, was itself built in 1778–9 as an eye-catcher, to be seen from Ayot House, to designs by Nicholas Revett. The church is no bigger than, and is similar to, a cemetery chapel of the 1830s. The Greek Revival front is unique, and was certainly a novelty in 1778, for Revett and James Stuart had only published their *Antiquities of Athens* in 1762. The portico, with columns fluted only at the tops and bases, is directly derived from the Temple of Apollo at Delos, but the flanking colonnades and aediculated pavilions as wings are decidedly un-Grecian, and owe more to Palladian influences. Each of these wing-pavilions is, in fact, a mausoleum, with urns on pedestals sheltered by the pavilions. These mausolea commemorate Sir Lionel Lyde and his wife. A drawing of the façade of the church and wings, in Hertfordshire County Council Record Office, shows the pavilions crowned

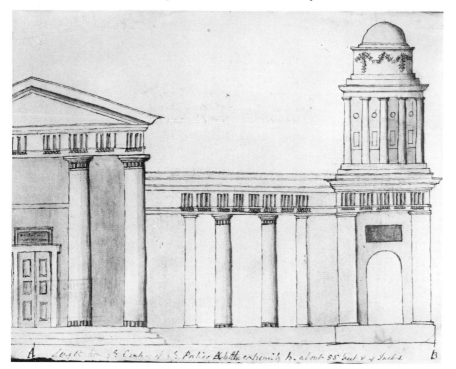

Plate 21 Church of S. Lawrence, Ayot St Lawrence, Hertfordshire. A design, probably by Nicholas Revett, showing the cupola over the mausoleum of the Lydes (*Hertfordshire County Record Office*)

with cupolas of almost Hawksmoorean style (Pl. 21), but these were altered during the last century (Pl. 22).

A building that owes not a little to the Grecian Revival, and a great deal to the Neoclassical movement generally, is the mausoleum at Trentham Park, Staffordshire. Today the building is isolated, cut off from the park of the house by a road. It is so strong in personality that it needs room to be seen, being no longer an object in the wide landscape. It has a battered base,

Plate 22 The church at Ayot St Lawrence after alterations (*The Author*)

Plate 23 Mausoleum at
Trentham Park, Staffordshire
(*The Author*)

square on plan, with strongly battered pilasters, and a stripped-down
Neoclassical entablature. Above the centre is a lantern, again of an utterly
simple Neoclassical style. The mausoleum was built in 1807–8 to designs by
Charles Heathcote Tatham, who had studied in Rome in the 1790s when the
French Academy there was saturated with the ideas of Boulleé, Ledoux, and
Piranesi. The French Neoclassical influence is obvious (Pl. 23).

Basic Neoclassical elements are particularly noticeable in the work of Sir
John Soane, who was a master in the use of funereal motifs, as Sir John
Summerson has described.[8] One of Soane's first contributions to the
architecture of death was his 'Design for a Mausoleum to the Memory of
James King Esq, drowned June 9, 1776'. This consisted of a central domed
structure set on a podium which was joined by diagonal wings to four
pyramid-pavilions. The design could accommodate eighty-four coffins and
twenty-four spaces for ashes (a remarkable feature for the time). The project
was illustrated in Soane's *Designs in Architecture* of 1778. Mausolea were
common subjects for eighteenth-century architects, for the imagination was

183

allowed full rein, and indeed Soane's designs owed not a little to the proposals by Sir William Chambers for a mausoleum in memory of Frederick Prince of Wales in 1751.

Soane travelled in Italy from 1778 to 1780, and absorbed Neoclassical ideas even further, moving away from the Italian models of Chambers into a world where Greek elements became more fully used. He exhibited several designs for mausolea at the Royal Academy in subsequent years in which Greek elements became predominant. His first realized design for a tomb was the sarcophagus memorial for Miss Johnstone of 1784 in the churchyard of S. Mary Abbots in Kensington, but from 1790 sarcophagi, mausolea, and cinerary urns became features of his designs. The vaulted ceilings of his houses at Lincoln's Inn Fields owe much to classical tomb-chambers, while ash-chest lids are used as cappings to piers at the Pitzhanger Manor gates. Soane also used urns and ash-chests to decorate the columbarium-like niches at the front parlour of Pitzhanger.

The beautiful tomb designed by Soane for Samuel Bosanquet was erected in 1806 in S. Mary's Churchyard, Leytonstone, Essex. Many of the elements that Soane later developed are found in this exquisite design. When Soane's wife died on 22 November 1815, she was buried in S. Giles's Burial Ground, adjacent to Old S. Pancras Church. Three months later he designed a remarkable 'monopteral temple' as a family vault. The main feature is a vertical rectangular block of stone under a canopy carried on Ionic columns. A simple pediment surmounts each face. This little canopy is sheltered by a bigger domed canopy carried on square piers. The whole is capped by a pineapple finial. The monolithic cap, with segmental pediments and cylindrical terminal, is based on the lid of a Roman ash-chest. The vault is approached by narrow steps, and the whole mausoleum is surrounded by a balustrade adorned with familiar Soane motifs (Pl. 24). Soane himself was buried here in 1837.

One of the most extraordinary of all mausolea, and indeed of all the designs by Soane, is that of the Dulwich Picture Gallery. Sir John Summerson has told its history. Noel Desanfans, an art collector, had come to England from France with a reputation as a writer. He also collected pictures, and received a commission from King Stanislaus of Poland to form the beginnings of a Polish National Gallery of Art. When Poland was again partitioned in 1795, the King abdicated, and Desanfans was left with the collection. An artist named Peter Francis Bourgeois shared the Desanfans house with the collector and his wife, and had received a Polish knighthood as court painter to King Stanislaus. When Bourgeois became landscape painter to George III, his use of the knighthood was approved, and he became Sir Francis Bourgeois. On the death of Desanfans, Bourgeois and Mrs Desanfans inherited the house, while he himself was left the superb collection of paintings. Under the terms of Desanfans's will, however, a vault was to be built to house his coffin, and Soane was approached to provide a design for a mortuary chapel attached to the house in Hallam (formerly Charlotte) Street. In 1807 Soane's designs were accepted, and a chapel, intended eventually to hold the coffins of Bourgeois and Mrs Desanfans, was completed that year. The mausoleum was in the form of a circular temple with a peristyle of Greek Doric columns carrying a low dome. The burial chamber was a small rectangle off the circular space, and cut into it. This burial chamber was illuminated from above, an almost Berniniesque effect, and one which Soane probably learned when in Italy.

Unfortunately, the house was only leasehold, and Bourgeois attempted to purchase the freehold from the Duke of Portland. When this was refused, he decided to leave the collection to the College of God's Gift at Dulwich. Sir Peter Francis Bourgeois died in 1811, and left all the paintings he had inherited from Desanfans to the Masters, Warden, and Fellows of Dulwich College. As well as this legacy, he left money to build a picture gallery to house the collection, and to erect a mausoleum to hold the bodies of Mr and

Plate 24 Tomb of Sir John Soane in the churchyard of S. Giles-in-the-Fields, adjacent to old S. Pancras' Church, London (*The Author*)

Mrs Desanfans and of himself. By this time, Mrs Desanfans was living in the house with two bodies in the attached mausoleum. She provided £6,000 towards the building of a separate gallery at Dulwich which was to be combined with a mausoleum. Soane was commissioned by the College, and at once got to work, but several sketches were prepared before it was decided to settle for a scheme for a long gallery with a mausoleum projecting from it in the centre of the east front. Between the mausoleum and the wings of the gallery were to be six small almshouses. The materials chosen were stock brick with Portland stone dressings. Building had commenced in 1812 when the College authorities decided that the mausoleum and apartments should lie on the west side, and that the main entrance should be on the east. An early version of the design shows the three burials represented by three Neoclassical sarcophagi on the roof, while the centre of the mausoleum is lit by a lantern with tall semicircular-headed windows. This design is not very satisfactory, however, and it was not long before Soane arrived at the beginnings of the happy solution that was built, and which still delights us today. The lantern is tall and capped by urns, while the three sarcophagi dominate the façades and act almost as pediments. The permutations of the design are interesting, but Soane's obsession with urns, sarcophagi, and the like is demonstrated in this extraordinary building (Pl. 25).

In 1813 Mrs Desanfans made a will, and directed that she should be buried in the Dulwich mausoleum. She died in 1814, by which time the Dulwich buildings were almost completed. The internal arrangements of the mausoleum are repetitions of the original design at Charlotte Street.

Soane's designs for a Sepulchral Chapel are much more ornate. The interior is rich, and owes much to the Greek Revival (Pl. 26). The exterior,

Left Plate 25 Dulwich mausoleum. A sketch (*The Trustees of Sir John Soane's Museum*)

Plate 26 Design for a Sepulchral Chapel by Soane, interior (*The Trustees of Sir John Soane's Museum*)

however, though having rich Doric porticos and pediments, with apsidal portions between the porticos featuring caryatides, is quite astonishing. Huge urns sit round the sides. Each pediment is crowned by a classical sarcophagus. Over the centre of the whole structure is a dome on a drum that recalls Etruscan and Roman Imperial mausolea, surmounted as it is by a statue of heroic proportions. As an essay in the eclectic use of funeral elements, this esquisse could scarcely be surpassed (Pl. 27). It is interesting to note that Soane used sarcophagi motifs as features above the entablatures of buildings in several instances. The best known are the houses for John Robins in Regent Street, London; the Bank of England; and Praed's Bank in Fleet Street, London. The gateway to Pitzhanger Manor in Middlesex and his own house in Lincoln's Inn Fields are not guiltless of funereal motifs.[8]

Neoclassicism, of course, was a movement that drew heavily from funerary sources, including motifs from Egypt. Perhaps the oddest Neoclassical mausoleum is the monument to J. C. J. van Speyk of 1839 by J. D. Zocher. This was a lighthouse on the coast of Egmont, and the massive tower in the form of a column sits on a square Neoclassical base of undoubted funereal character, not unlike the mausoleum at Trentham Park (Pl. 28).

Below left Plate 27 Exterior of Soane's design for a Sepulchral Chapel (*The Trustees of Sir John Soane's Museum*)

Below right
Plate 28 Monument to J. C. J. van Speyk, of 1839, by J. D. Zocher (R.I.B.A. British Architectural Library *Drawings Collection*)

It is fitting that the Neoclassical style should have been used for the Tomb of Napoleon I. The sunken circular crypt was constructed in 1843–53 to designs by Visconti, who was an architect much concerned with funerary monuments, and who designed many tombs in Père-Lachaise. The dome of the Invalides was built by J. H. Mansart in 1693–1706 as the crowning feature of the earlier building by Bruant. Under it, in the centre of the sunken crypt, is the sarcophagus of Siberian porphyry, with a lid with scrolled ends, a motif known from antiquity. The mosaic pavement represents a wreath of laurels, and has the names of the principal battles of Napoleon inscribed. The twelve colossal figures surrounding the crypt are allegories of the main victories, and are by Pradier. The faint, bluish light admitted from above enhances the solemn grandeur of the tomb. The entrance to the crypt is flanked by two bronze statues by Duret. Above the entrance is a quotation from Napoleon's will:

Je désire que mes cendres reposent sur les bords de la Seine,
au milieu de ce peuple français que j'ai tant aimé.

Plate 29 Mausoleum of Napoleon III and his Empress at Farnborough, Hampshire (*The Author*)

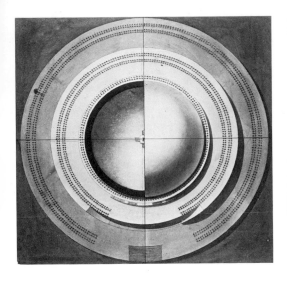

Plate 30 Plan of the proposed cenotaph in memory of Newton (*Bibliothèque Nationale, Paris HA57 No. 5*). *The References HA throughout this chapter are those of the Cabinet des Estampes of the Bibliothèque Nationale in Paris.*

Far right Plate 31 Section through the cenotaph in memory of Newton. Note the rings of cypress trees on the huge base, and the sarcophagus-shaped cenotaph in the centre. The global shape is illuminated to resemble the sky (*Bibliothèque Nationale, Paris HA57 No. 8*)

The crypt has chapels on either side containing monuments of the marshals of Louis XIV, Turenne and Vauban. The chapels at the corners contain the tombs of Joseph Bonaparte, King of Spain; of Jérome Bonaparte, King of Westphalia; and of L'Aiglon. The heart of the Empress also lies here.

The other great Napoleonic mausoleum, oddly enough, is situated in Hampshire. In 1887, the Empress Eugénie built a mausoleum for her husband, her son, and herself in the grounds of her house at Farnborough Hill. This extraordinary building, in the *Flamboyant* Gothic manner, was designed by Destailleur, architect of Waddesdon Manor in Buckinghamshire. The dome, however, despite knobbly crockets, is anything but Gothic, and the whole building is rendered unconvincing by it. Below the dome is a vaulted crypt containing the three huge sarcophagi of Louis Napoleon, Eugénie, and the Prince Imperial who lost his life so senselessly as a British officer during a campaign in Africa (Pl. 29).

Undoubtedly, some of the most exciting schemes for monuments, cemeteries, cenotaphs, and buildings to celebrate death were by Frenchmen. Etienne-Louis Boullée (1728–1799) was a visionary architect and leader of a generation of artists who remained moderates in political terms, while expressing the revolutionary spirit in the arts in pre-revolutionary France.[9] The drawings by Boullée in the Cabinet des Estampes of the Bibliothèque Nationale in Paris are an astonishing array of supremely confident designs, many of which are projects for buildings associated with death. Boullée's designs for cenotaphs and cemeteries show buildings in which Egyptian motifs play no small part. Huge blank walls emphasize the terror and finality of death, and express Boullée's ideas of *architecture parlante*. Cypress trees and sculpture are often used in the designs, recalling the imperial monuments of Rome most vividly.

The celebrated design for a cenotaph of Newton is regarded as one of Boullée's greatest inspirations. The poetry of the imagery is grand in the extreme, while the structure and lighting seem to look forward to our own epoch. The world is expressed as a huge globe that also represents the universe. A Neoclassical cenotaph in the centre of the huge building is the

Plate 32 Section through the cenotaph in memory of Newton. Here the lighting resembles the day, and a blazing globe is set in the centre (*Bibliothèque Nationale, Paris HA57 No. 9*)

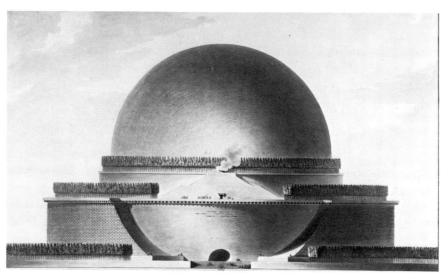

Plate 33 Exterior of Newton's cenotaph. The debt to the imperial mausolea of Rome is clear, although the scale is infinitely greater (*Bibliothèque Nationale, Paris HA57 No. 7*)

Opposite Plate 35 Project by Boullée for a cenotaph to a national military hero. The building is in the shape of a huge sarcophagus. The frieze is a line of figures in the manner of Egyptian statues (*Bibliothèque Nationale, Paris HA57 No. 27*)

focus of attention, set under a sky of infinite vastness. Yet the exterior form owes not a little to the Mausoleum of Augustus in Rome, even to the rows of cypresses (Pls. 30, 31, 32, 33). Boullée visualized funerary monuments as temples of death, designed to chill the heart. He insisted that such buildings should be designed to withstand the ravages of time, while incorporating what he called 'the Poetry of Architecture'.

In general, Boullée's cemeteries are designed to incorporate a surrounding wall with the main monument in the centre (Pl. 34). This enclosing structure is formed of charnel-houses, among which the chapels for funeral services were situated. He sought 'perfect symmetry' and incorporated features such as gigantic Neoclassical sarcophagi, which themselves became huge buildings (Pl. 35), enormous pyramids, and 'funerary triumphant arches' (Pls. 36, 37). By cutting decoration to the

Plate 34 Project by Boullée for a cemetery set in an Arcadian landscape. Note the symmetry and gigantic scale, the blank walls and terraces, and the enormous domed chapel in the centre. Charnel-houses are set in the walls (*Bibliothèque Nationale, Paris HA55 No. 25*)

minimum, Boullée gave his buildings 'a character of immutability'. The cone-shaped cenotaphs incorporate ideas based on both domes and pyramids, with obelisks and cypresses much in evidence (Pls. 38, 39). Boullée could conceive of nothing more appropriate or melancholy than a monument consisting of a flat surface, bare and unadorned, 'absolutely stripped of detail, its decoration consisting of a play of shadows, outlined by still deeper shadows'.[10] 'No gloomier images exist,' he asserted, 'and if we make abstraction of all the beauty of art, it would be impossible not to appreciate in such a construction the mournful effect of the architecture.' Here was the architecture of the sublime indeed!

The essence of these French schemes might be regarded as power. The style was a revolt against the delicate Rococo of the previous generation. Such architectural dreams need not necessarily have any chance of realization, and it was certainly with the sublime designs for buildings associated with death that the French architects achieved their greatest heights. The man who seduced the young architects away from the

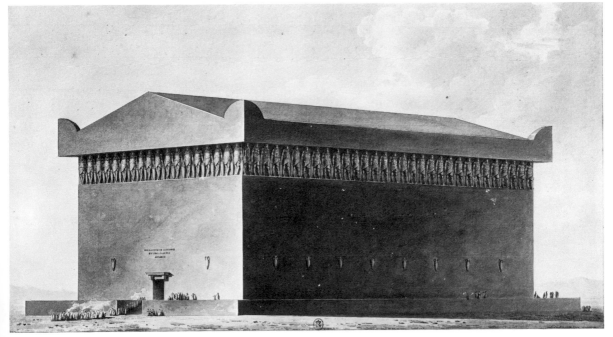

delicacies of the Rococo was G. B. Piranesi, whose etchings of Roman remains were potent images. Piranesi himself probably derived inspiration from J. B. Fischer von Erlach's *Entwurf einer historischen Architektur* (1721). Yet Piranesi exaggerated the scale of the buildings he drew, and so his drawings showed structures beyond anything that Rome had known 'even in the meridian of its splendour', as Horace Walpole remarked. Flaxman, the celebrated sculptor and designer of tombs, found Roman remains less awesome than he had supposed after studying Piranesi. The Venetian engraver was obsessed by pyramids, by Greek Doric columns (especially those at Paestum), and by other elements such as obelisks, ash-chests, urns, and tombs. Piranesian ideas and images became something of a cult among the young French architects at the French Academy in Rome; Peyre's *Oeuvres d'architecture* of 1765 clearly demonstrates Piranesian influences in the overblown scale and megalomaniac repetition of Neoclassical motifs. Jean-Louis Desprez went to Rome in 1777 and produced a number of aquatints of tombs while there. These designs incorporate much Egyptianized ideas, and the sombre funereal character is enhanced by the weight of the masonry above the sarcophagi. Boullée, Ledoux, and their contemporaries were clearly greatly influenced by Peyre, and by Piranesi through Peyre. Both rejected the Rococo and a slavish copying of antiquity. Unlike the Palladians and the Greek Revivalists, the Neoclassicists used antique forms and motifs with eclectic abandon and the greatest freedom. Plain walls, a careful selection of elements, and a daring stripped-down approach to decoration were characteristics of the greatest Neoclassicists, including Boullée and Ledoux in France, Soane in England, and Gilly and Karl Friedrich Schinkel in Prussia.

Plate 36 A design for a cenotaph by Boullée. It is like a gigantic 'funerary triumphant arch', but is a truncated pyramid. Note the huge coffered hemi-dome that forms the entrance; the massive steps up the sides of the pyramid; the obelisks; and the colossal scale (*Bibliothèque Nationale, Paris HA57 No. 13*)

Friedrich Gilly was a considerable influence on Schinkel, and his project for a monument to Frederick the Great of 1797 is a most original design. The triumphal arch appears to be cut from a monolith pierced by coffered vaults at right angles to each other. The monument culminates in a Greek Doric temple set on a gigantic podium. Some of Gilly's other designs for a mausoleum are extraordinary for their date, for mouldings have been stripped away entirely. If Doric was primitive and elemental to the eighteenth-century mind, Gilly's approach to an almost Neolithic form of architecture must have been very disturbing to his contemporaries. Such funerary architecture is similar to the bare essentials of Egyptian mortuary temples such as that of Queen Hatshepsut. Schinkel himself was profoundly indebted to Gilly for his architectural inspiration, and although he also absorbed Piranesian images via the French Academicians, he was also greatly inspired by the Greek temples of Sicily and Paestum, and by Gothic architecture. Schinkel's designs of 1810 for a mausoleum for Queen Louise of Prussia are in the Gothic style, with a pronounced Italian flavour. The ribs of the vaults were enriched with palm-fronds, a curiously Rococo device possibly borrowed from Sans Souci, and intended to create the feeling of a grove of palm-trees. The tomb-chest was to be rose-coloured, and guardian

Plate 37 Another design by Boullée resembling a 'funerary triumphant arch'. The coffered hemi-dome has been raised, becoming the entrance to a mortuary chapel set in the wall of a cemetery. In this design the terror and desolation of death are expressed in the blank walls, devoid of all features save narrow slit windows. The *chapelle des morts* was a chapel where funeral services could be held, and where bones could be stored *Bibliothèque Nationale, Paris HA55 No. 28)*

angels were to surround the effigy of the dead queen. The project was not realized, however, and a Greek Doric building by Gentz was erected instead.

As the engravings of the *Grands Prix*[11] of the French Academy of Architecture show, the Neoclassicists were highly successful in adapting eclectic motifs from antiquity for use in an architecture of death. Fontaine's designs for a cenotaph (1785) are clearly influenced by Boullée, and his use of motifs such as obelisks and pyramids creates a suitably sepulchral image. Boullée's Newton monument was a memorial that would indeed wrap the Newtonian universe in a globular shape, while the sepulchral lamp of old becomes a model of the entire solar system.

The designs of 1788 for the memorial for Lapeyrouse and his sailors is a scheme by Vien for a tomb in a wild landscape on the seashore. The drama of the composition is enhanced by the colouring. Egyptian forms, such as the battered doorway, contrast with the heavy sarcophagus-like form of the tomb itself. The whole composition is essentially pyramidal, however, and enhances the Egyptian element of the design.

The Newton Cenotaph by Deléphine in the *Grands Prix* drawings shows a clear Boullée influence, and indeed a classical Roman influence derived from the mausoleum of Augustus. This was a circular drum with a central hemispherical tomb-chamber. Cypress trees were planted around the hemisphere.

The *Grands Prix* drawings also contain an extraordinary *chapelle sépulchrale* by de la Barre (1764–1833). The central building is clearly based on the Pantheon in Rome, but with four porticos instead of one, and the Order used is Doric, looking forward to a pure Neoclassicism. The Pantheon sits within a huge circular enclosure linking four pyramids. Sphinxes, sarcophagi, and urns complete the familiar vocabulary of an architecture of death. The main influence on de la Barre was Fontaine's magnificent scheme for a cenotaph of 1785. The interest in pyramids and other Egyptian motifs was fostered from 1785 onwards by Quatremère de Quincy in his *De l'architecture Egyptienne*, although Piranesi had been the source of Egyptianizing fashion with his Caffè degli Inglese of 1760 near the Piazza di Spagna in Rome. The decorations for this café were Egyptian, and Piranesi published many Egyptian schemes for decorations in his *Diverse Maniere d'adornare i Cammini* of 1769. The *Cammini* is a primary source of Egyptian Revival, and although Egyptian forms and motifs are treated in the manner of a *Capriccio*, the book offered an enticing array of ideas for architectural invention. The growing interest in the 'primitive' forms of Doric was also responsible for a rediscovery of the possibilities of Egyptian architecture for dramatic effects. The Comte de Caylus published his *Recueil d'antiquités, égyptiennes, étrusques, grecques et romaines* in 1752, and this work included a discussion of aesthetic qualities in Egyptian art and architecture. An interest in Egyptian motifs was not unrelated to the spread of Freemasonry, which was particularly patronized by eighteenth century intellectuals. Mozart, with his Masonic opera *Die Zauberflöte*, is a case in point.[12] It is interesting to recall that Karl Friedrich Schinkel, one of the most successful of Neoclassical architects, influenced by the French designs of the period, designed a superb collection of stage-sets for Mozart's opera in 1815, in which Egyptian elements are used to tremendous effect. Freemasons in Europe were often associated with liberal-humanist ideas, and the Egyptian elements often expressed Masonic sympathies. Certainly, Egyptian motifs had enjoyed a vogue from Renaissance times onwards in order to denote antiquity, and they were often used in arches of a temporary nature, such as for ceremonial occasions. Sphinxes and other Egyptian elements occur in Renaissance funerary architecture, notably in the Tomb of Guillaume du Bellay of 1557 in Le Mans cathedral, and in the tomb of Diane de Poitiers of 1576. Boullée favoured Egyptian elements for cemeteries, cenotaphs, and memorials, since timelessness was suggested by their austerity and by their associations. The pyramid was also used by Ledoux to house furnaces for an iron foundry. The shape was ideal, and allowed for the flues. One revolutionary design of the period shows

Plate 38 A cenotaph consisting of a truncated cone set on a base surrounded by cypresses (*Bibliothèque Nationale, Paris HA57 No. 20*)

pyramids adapted as crematoria furnaces, since cremation appealed to many adherents of the French Revolution as a further method of demonstrating anti-clericalism and radicalism.

Some of the most remarkable royal tombs in Britain are at Windsor. Most royal burials are in the ancient churches with royal associations, such as Westminster Abbey, Winchester Cathedral, and S. George's Chapel, Windsor. The Saxe-Coburg family broke away from the tradition of burial in churches, and began a fashion for erecting mausolea. The first member of the family to build such a tomb was Queen Victoria's uncle, Leopold of Saxe-Coburg, whose wife, the Princess Charlotte, only daughter of the Prince Regent, had died in childbirth in 1817. The Princess was buried in Windsor in the royal vaults, and her monument has already been described. Prince Leopold also built a small Gothic building in her memory in the

Plate 39 Section through a cone-shaped cenotaph (*Bibliothèque Nationale, Paris HA57 No. 14*)

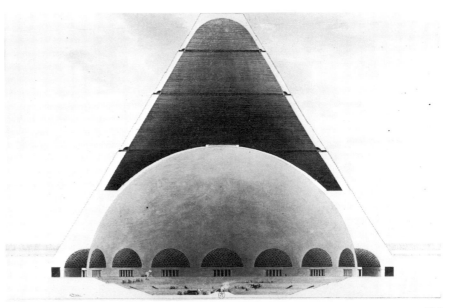

grounds of Claremont, the house in which she died. In 1843 Queen Victoria and Prince Albert visited Claremont and conceived the idea of building a royal mausoleum for themselves at Windsor. In 1844, Duke Ernest I of Saxe-Coburg, Prince Albert's father, died, and the family decided to build a mausoleum at Coburg to designs based on sketches by Prince Albert and his brother, the new Duke. During her visit to Coburg in 1860, Queen Victoria saw this mausoleum, and thought it both beautiful and cheerful.

In 1859 Queen Victoria's mother, the Duchess of Kent, the sister of Duke Ernest, approached the Prince Consort about the possibility of building a mausoleum for herself in the grounds of Frogmore House at Windsor, where she lived. The Prince commissioned Professor Ludwig Grüner, his artistic adviser since 1845, to design the building. The superintending architect was A. Jenkins Humbert, who was later to redesign Sandringham House for the Prince of Wales. The Duchess of Kent's mausoleum was nearly completed in 1861 when she died. It is a domed rotunda, with a massively rusticated sub-structure. The water-colour by W. L. Leitch shows it in its impressive setting (Pl. 40). The sarcophagus itself sits in the

Plate 40 Water-colour by W. L. Leitch of the Duchess of Kent's mausoleum at Frogmore (*By Gracious Permission of Her Majesty The Queen, No. 19741*)

vaulted base and was recorded by W. Corden in a water-colour preserved at Windsor.

Later that year the Prince Consort died, and the widowed Queen chose a site near her mother's mausoleum for a new royal tomb. She determined that the design should resemble the Saxe-Coburg tomb at Coburg. The team responsible for the Duchess of Kent's tomb was chosen, and after consultations with her uncle, Leopold of Saxe-Coburg, then King of the Belgians, the Queen selected a design in the 'Italian' style of the thirteenth century.

The foundations were started in 1862 and consecration took place in the December of that year, although Grüner's sumptuous Raphaelesque internal decorations were not completed until 1871. Externally, the

Plate 41 Plan of the Royal Mausoleum at Frogmore (*By Gracious Permission of Her Majesty The Queen, No. 19736*)

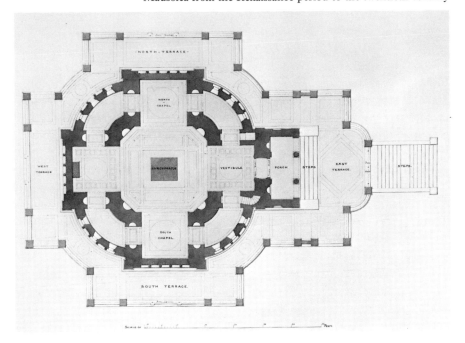

Romanesque style of the building appears unequivocally Germanic, and is more related to a Berlin or Munich *Rundbogenstil* than to Italy. The plan is a Greek cross, with low convex ambulatories in the angles, giving an approximate octagon. Over the crossing is an octagonal dome. The east elevation has an entrance porch with three arches *in antis*. In front of the porch are two fine bronze angels by Georg Howaldt of Brunswick, added in 1878. The outer gates are of bronze, and the inner door is of brass, designed by Grüner and made by Potter & Sons of London (Pls. 41, 42, 43).

Plate 42 Front elevation of the Royal Mausoleum at Frogmore (*By Gracious Permission of Her Majesty The Queen, No. 19738*)

The interior is richly coloured, and is of an Italian High Renaissance style, curiously at odds with the *Rundbogenstil* of the exterior, designed entirely by Grüner. The Raphael cult was a notably German phenomenon, and had been an enthusiasm of the Prince Consort, who planned a work on Raphael with Grüner. In the centre of the mausoleum is an enormous sarcophagus of Aberdeen granite which contains the bodies of the Queen and the Prince. The effigies are of marble. The tomb itself was designed and sculpted by Baron Carlo Marochetti. The four bronze angels, also by Marochetti, were cast by Barbédienne of Paris.

Most of the sculpture was by Germans, usually with Dresden connections, as might be expected since Grüner was from Dresden and had worked with Semper there. The two wings to the north and south contain monuments to Princess Alice, Grand Duchess of Hesse, and one of her children, and to Edward, Duke of Kent. Both monuments are by Boehm. In one of the ambulatories is a supremely noble marble statue of Kaiser Friedrich III of Germany, also by Boehm. Statues of the royal couple in Anglo-Saxon costume, by Theed, form a touching composition. A water-colour by H. W. Brewer captures the sumptuous richness of this beautiful mausoleum (Pl. 43).

One of the oddest results of Queen Victoria's desire to perpetuate the memory of her husband was the transformation of Henry III's chapel at Windsor between 1863 and 1873. The chapel had already been greatly altered during the reign of Henry VII. It was originally intended as the Lady Chapel, and Henry VII determined to set up the Lady Chapel as a chantry-chapel and mausoleum for himself and for Henry VI. The monks of Westminster Abbey, however, claimed the body of the sixth Henry, and so Henry VII built a magnificent Lady Chapel at Westminster as his tomb. The Windsor chapel was left unused.

Wolsey began to construct a tomb for himself in the unfinished Lady Chapel, and in 1524 employed the great Italian Benedetto da Rovezzano to construct a magnificent monument. This was made of black and white marble and stood on a high base. After Wolsey's fall, Henry VIII appropriated the chapel and tomb for himself, and instructed Benedetto to complete the work. The great tomb was not completed, however, and many subsequent monarchs reverted to the idea of building a mausoleum. The Benedetto tomb was eventually set up in a modified form in the crypt of S. Paul's Cathedral, to house the body of Lord Nelson.

In 1863, the transformation began, and the Albert Memorial Chapel, a complete Victorian shrine, took shape. The decorations of marble, alabaster, and mosaics are largely by Baron H. de Trinqueti, and are rich in the extreme. Etched marble and a dado of coloured marbles are oddly classical and curiously un-English. The reredos is by Sir George Gilbert Scott, and the sculpture is by Trinqueti. The cenotaph of Prince Albert, by Trinqueti, is in the form of an altar-tomb, with an effigy of the Prince in armour (Pl. 44).

The chapel is not dominated by the cenotaph of Prince Albert, however, nor by the monument by Boehm to the Duke of Albany. The centre of the space is occupied by the huge monument of Albert Victor Christian

Opposite Plate 43 Interior of the Royal Mausoleum at Frogmore. A water-colour and gouache drawing signed by H. W. Brewer, 1869. Purchased by Queen Victoria, 1869 (*By Gracious Permission of Her Majesty The Queen, Souvenir Album I, p. 15*)

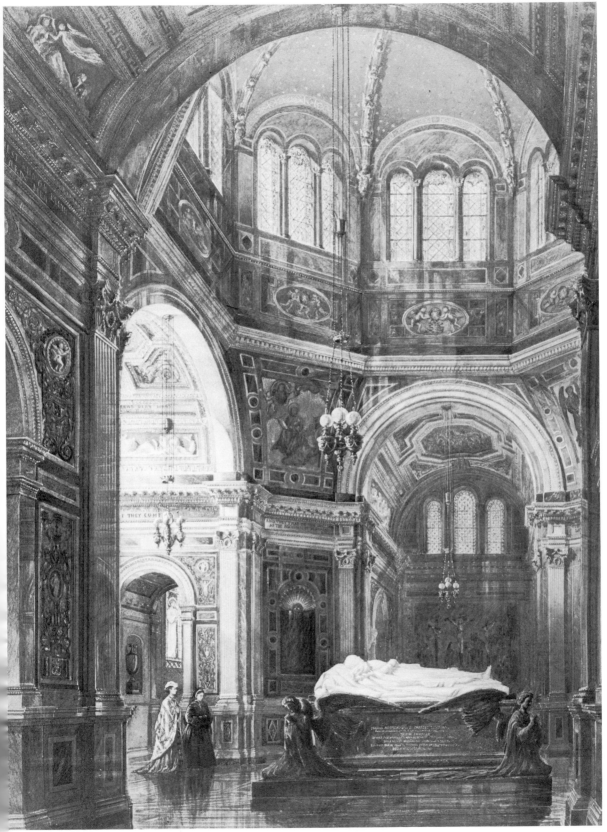

Plate 44 The Albert Memorial Chapel at Windsor, showing the cenotaph of Prince Albert in the foreground, and the tomb of the Duke of Clarence (*By permission of the Dean and Canons of Windsor*)

Edward, Duke of Clarence and Avondale, son of Edward VII and Queen Alexandra, who died in 1892. This sumptuous memorial is by Alfred Gilbert, and is exceedingly daring and novel for its date. The monument was almost finished in 1898, but Gilbert was bankrupted and left the country. He did not return until 1926, after which he made the missing statues. The monument has a recumbent effigy on a large sarcophagus, and this is startling enough in its realism. The grille round the tomb, completed in 1927, is an astonishing example of the Art-Nouveau style, and, like the rest of the Chapel, seems more French or German than English (Pl. 45).[13]

Elaborate tombs built for royalty and for the aristocracy encouraged the middle-classes and those who had acquired wealth to display their respectability in family mausolea of some grandeur. The desire to protect families from the common herd was also a contributory factor in the move to build special tombs where the dead would reside pending a general resurrection. In 1861, Titus Salt, founder of Saltaire in Yorkshire, and later a Member of Parliament, finally returned to Yorkshire disillusioned, and in poor health. He at once commissioned a mausoleum from the firm of Lockwood and Mawson to be attached to his beloved Congregational

Church at Saltaire. This square structure to the south of the church is suitably solid to commemorate its occupant (Pl. 46). A hefty angel, standing between Florentine pilasters, mounts guard above the vault inside the mausoleum.[14]

One of the phenomena of the Victorian Age was its return to eclectic motifs, especially in the designs for monuments. The architect Thomas Willson (born *c*. 1780), had exhibited designs in 1824 for a 'Pyramid Cemetery for the Metropolis', the base of which was to cover eighteen acres 'which being multiplied by the several stages to be erected one above the other will generate nearly 1,000 acres, self-created out of the void space overhead as the building progresses above the earth'.[15] The sixty-eight-year-old Thomas Willson, possibly a son of the progenitor of the 'Pyramid Cemetery', produced a design for 'The Pyramid Mausoleum' in honour of the assassinated President Garfield, in 1882. He submitted the design to the Committee charged with the construction of a proposed monument at the

Plate 45 Effigy of the Duke of Clarence, and the Art-Nouveau grille by Alfred Gilbert (*By permission of the Dean and Canons of Windsor*)

Plate 46 Mausoleum of Sir Titus Salt, attached to the Congregationalist church at Saltaire, Yorkshire (*The Author*)

Lake View Cemetery at Cleveland. The object was 'to give expression (for "all Time") to the profound grief, and indignation excited amongst all classes of the people of England, profound grief for the bereaved widow Lady and her family, and indignation for the dastardly assassin's monstrous and calamitous termination of an illustrious General's life well spent throughout his honourable career in the public service, as a soldier, senator, and President of the United States of America'. The mausoleum comprised a 'noble Pyramid-Mausoleum of unique design', and contained a private chapel with catacombs underneath, 'secure from desecration, when once hermetically-sealed'. The design is extraordinary, and has many eclectic motifs. The pyramid itself is similar in proportions to the Pyramid of Cestius in Rome, and to the elder Willson's designs for a Pyramid Cemetery (see Ch. VII). The main entrances were of the Egyptian style, surmounted by sarcophagi. On top of the whole structure was an obelisk (Pl. 47).

Similar in basic form, but less horrific in detail, is the remarkable design for a mausoleum for the Counts of Henckel-Donnersmarck, of 1897, by Julius and Otto Raschdorff. This is typical of a rather heavy, overblown Renaissance style much favoured in Wilhelmian Germany, and which Raschdorff used for Berlin Cathedral (Pl. 48). The plan is probably based on a pyramid scheme of 1791 by F. Gilly, whose design consisted of a pyramid with a Doric portico on each face.

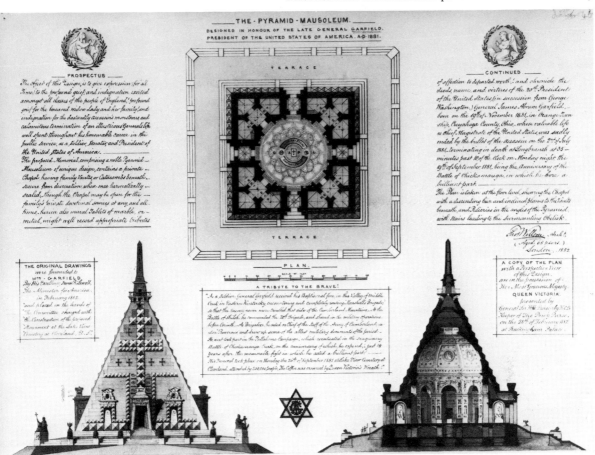

THE · PYRAMID · MAUSOLEUM.
DESIGNED IN HONOUR OF THE LATE GENERAL GARFIELD.
PRESIDENT OF THE UNITED STATES OF AMERICA. A.D. 1881.

Plate 47 Design for a
'Pyramid Mausoleum' for
General Garfield by Thomas
Willson, 1881 (*RIBA British
Architectural Library
Drawings Collection*)

Right Plate 48 Elevation of
the mausoleum for the
Counts of Henckel-
Donnersmarck, by Julius and
Otto Raschdorff, 1897 (*RIBA
British Architectural Library
Drawings Collection*)

The United States of America can boast some of the most interesting mausolea of fairly recent times. The tomb of the Graves family by Lorado Taft (1860–1936) in Graceland Cemetery, Chicago, is particularly eerie, and features a shrouded figure of dramatic menace. Graceland, founded in 1860 by T. H. Bryan, contains one of the architecturally noblest of all mausolea built in the late-nineteenth century. It is by the great architect, Louis Sullivan, and celebrates Elizabeth Getty. It was built in 1890. Frank Lloyd Wright said of this mausoleum that it was 'entirely Sullivan's own, a piece of sculpture, a statue, a great poem'. It is of grey limestone, and is exquisitely decorated. The openings are heroic in scale and recall the grandest architectural statements of Neoclassicism (Pl. 49) transmuted into a totally original idea. Two years later, Sullivan built the Wainwright tomb in Bellefontaine Cemetery, St Louis, to commemorate ·Charlotte Dickson Wainwright, who died in 1891. Her husband, Ellis, who died in 1924, commissioned Sullivan to design this beautiful oriental kiosk, embellished with the finest of lace-like sculpture. The delicacy of the carving and of the metalwork speak of a master's hand (Pl. 50).

There are other celebrated mausolea of recent times. Paul von Hindenburg's mausoleum at Tannenberg was huge, commemorating not only the man, but also the victory; and Lenin's mausoleum in Moscow is well-known. One of the oddest of all mausolea is found at the corner of Paston Place in Brighton. It looks as though, to paraphrase a great wit, Brighton Pavilion had 'pupped', for the style of the architecture is clearly derived from the Pavilion. This was the mausoleum of Sir Albert (*ob.* 1896) and Sir Edward (*ob.* 1912) Sassoon, and it was built in 1892. It is a single-storey square building with a dome over the centre. It is now an extension to a public house, as the Sassoons sold the house to which the mausoleum was attached in 1933 and the bodies were interred elsewhere.[16]

The declining possibilities of acquiring individual wealth, except through dubious means, and a tendency to favour cremation in these secular times, have sadly reduced the possibilities of an architecture of death. The big statement, the public memorial and the grandeur and awesomeness of death have all passed out of fashion. Death is a bad joke, and is best avoided. The dead are got rid of as soon as possible. The realities of death are divorced from so much of contemporary experience. Modern man is born in a hospital, and dies in one, safely out of the way. His progress from the mortuary to the crematorium furnace or the grave is barely recognized by those he leaves behind. Contemporary memorials are usually of a triteness that is a damning condemnation of our society. Contemporary designs for death are banal in the extreme. There will never again be a mausoleum of the stature of Hawksmoor's work at Castle Howard, or Sullivan's designs for wealthy Americans. We no longer are able to celebrate death. An architectural expression of such celebration is today only in the realm of the chimerical.

Opposite Plate 49 Detail from the Getty mausoleum of 1890 in Graceland Cemetery, Chicago, by Louis Sullivan. Note the similarity to some of the Boullée designs (*Mervyn K. Miller*)

Plate 50 Mausoleum of Charlotte Dickson Wainwright (*d.* 1891) and her husband, Ellis (*d.* 1924), by Louis Sullivan, in Bellefontaine Cemetery, St Louis (*Mervyn K. Miller*)

7

The development of cemeteries in Great Britain in the nineteenth century.

Liverpool; Glasgow; The Pyramid Proposal;
Kensal Green, Norwood, Highgate, Nunhead, Abney Park,
Tower Hamlets, and Brompton cemeteries

The cemetery is an open space among the ruins,
covered in winter with violets and daisies. It might make
one in love with death, to think that one should be buried
in so sweet a place

PERCY BYSSHE SHELLEY: from the Preface to *Adonais*

The large cemeteries that were developed in the nineteenth century were the result of a general movement towards the civilizing of urban man. The political and sanitary reforms of the last century have not been neglected by commentators but, curiously, cemeteries have been given scant attention by historians.[1] Many cemeteries are of great architectural and historic importance, yet many are being vandalized or are being deliberately and *officially* destroyed in the interests of administrative convenience and current fashion. The vicar who removes the tombstones from the parish churchyard, and the local authority that levels a cemetery, can both be said to be guilty of vandalism, not only because historical records are thereby destroyed, but a part of the history of taste disappears for ever.

The great influx of people to the towns as a result of the Agrarian and Industrial Revolutions created special problems of hygiene. Sanitation, supply of drinking-water, waste-disposal, and burial of the dead had to be tackled on a scale unknown since Roman times. The mortality rates for the first half of the nineteenth century were enormous. The average age at death of a labourer's family was seventeen, while that of the family of a professional man was only thirty. At the beginning of the nineteenth century there were no towns in England and Wales outside London with a population in excess of 100,000. Ninety-one years later there were twenty-three towns with populations greater than 100,000.[2] The overloading of parish graveyards can be imagined, and it was clear that a radical approach to the burial of the dead would have to be devised. Often, small churchyards had to function as cemeteries for the new towns that had grown up around the village nuclei.

The eighteenth century had tolerated overcrowded burial-grounds and the disgusting conditions of churchyards. The nineteenth century saw a remarkable change, for tender and compassionate feelings towards the weak and the poor were also shown towards the bereaved and the dead. There was a revolt against an age of irreligious clerics, overcrowded and unhygienic churchyards, and godlessness generally. Fear of Jacobinism and a reaction against the excesses of the Regency period encouraged a revival of Christianity as a bulwark against revolution. The existence of the masses was recognized, and new churches were built to bring God to the growing populations in the towns. A more liberal and enlightened attitude began to prevail, and even architecture became a moral issue. The living were to live clean and godly lives; children were to receive the benefits of education; there were to be hospitals and institutions for the sick and the poor; and the dead were to be buried where they would lie undisturbed and where they would not harm the living. Temporary graves in the foul and overcrowded churchyards were to be replaced by the spacious acres of the huge cemeteries. Property became a desirable goal for all men of ambition, and so a family grave became a mark of substance where a family could be re-united after life had run its course. Funerals and monuments became aspects of the establishment of social position, and the rising classes aped the customs of the rich. Secure resting-places for the dead in pleasant Arcadian surroundings became desirable. Corrupt sextons, body-snatchers, re-used graves, and the stench of decay were to be banished.

In the last decades of the eighteenth century, interest in archaeology and in ruins became fashionable, partly, no doubt, because time and decay had given a romantic patina in tune with the times. Even the remains of a Papist past could be studied with a less zealously Protestant eye now that the established Church and Protestantism seemed to be firmly in the ecclesiastical saddle, so to speak. Gothic novels, Fonthill, Strawberry Hill, and a fashion for all things Gothick gave the eighteenth century a new sensation after a diet of classicism amid the groves of Arcadia. Literature, archaeology, and fashion helped to create a new *Zeitgeist* at a time when demographic and social forces were already working to shift the balance of society as a whole. Volumes illustrating ancient sepulchral monuments and journals such as *The Gentleman's Magazine*[3] helped to make Gothic respectable, and to create a new interest in the architecture of death and the design of cemeteries. The Romantic landskips of Shenstone, Repton, and Brown had often provided backgrounds to mausolea, Gothick ruins, and monuments. Society was agreeably diverted by melancholy, and by the vision of a necropolis based on the country park, where tombs and monuments would be set off against the subtle colours and tones of foliage. Art, the Picturesque, and hygienic necessity were to combine in a fortuitous way.

Scotland, Ulster, India, Louisiana, and France had led the field in the establishment of cemeteries based on hygienic principles, but it was not until the barrister George Frederick Carden began his campaign in *The Penny Magazine* for the formation of public cemeteries in 1824 that the idea had any following in England. Carden contrasted the cemeteries of Europe with the 'hideous' burial-grounds of Britain, and agreed that the beautiful new continental cemeteries were often 'favourite places of resort for the neighbouring population.' The sanitary laws of France were greatly approved of by Carden, who noted that the churchyards of Paris had been cleared of bones that were now stacked in the catacombs. Carden said that London was shamed by the example of Paris and even of Liverpool, which was the first English city to establish a cemetery. The large percentage of Dissenters in the population of Liverpool possibly helped in the creation of a climate of opinion favourable to the formation of a cemetery, while the town itself was a leader in urban and sanitary reform. The income from port dues and trade doubtless assisted in municipal enterprises that were to improve the health of the populace.

The Liverpool Necropolis, or Low Hill General Cemetery in West Derby Road, was opened in 1825. It cost £8,000 to lay out, and was only two hectares in extent. An engraving by Robert Wallis after a drawing by Thomas Allom[4] shows the entrance-gates (Pl. 1). Shortly afterwards, Liverpool developed another cemetery in an old stone quarry between 1825 and 1829. This was a much more ambitious project, costing £21,000, and occupying about five hectares in all. Like the Liverpool Necropolis, it was established by a company, but was given added respectability by being known as S. James's Cemetery, in tune with more religious times. This cemetery, opened in June 1829, was designed by the architect John Foster, who created a setting of great magnificence for the interment of the dead by constructing processional ramps in order that funeral-carriages might travel down to the floor of the old quarry. Chambers were cut out of the sides of the quarry to provide catacombs, tunnels being driven through the rock to provide vistas and Piranesian enclosures. The cemetery was landscaped by

Plate 1 Engraving by Robert Wallis after a drawing by Thomas Allom of the entrance to Low Hill General Cemetery, Liverpool (*Author's Collection*)

Plate 2 S. James' Cemetery, Liverpool, showing the ramps, catacombs and mortuary chapel. The circular mausoleum is that of William Huskisson M.P. who was killed while assisting at the inauguration of the Liverpool and Manchester Railway. It has a dome over a drum enriched with fluted engaged Corinthian columns. Designed by Foster, it contained a statue by John Gibson. The temple on the right is the mortuary chapel (*Author's Collection*)

Shepherd, a gardener who had worked with Foster on other projects (Pl. 2). The most architecturally distinguished monument in S. James' Cemetery is the circular mausoleum of William Huskisson M.P., who was killed at the inauguration of the Liverpool and Manchester Railway. The tomb, designed by Foster, consists of a domed drum with a peristyle of engaged Corinthian columns, and it contains a statue of Huskisson by John Gibson. Today, the Anglican Cathedral towers above the cemetery.

It was predictable that the examples of France, of Liverpool, of Edinburgh, and of Belfast would spur Glasgow on to reform. In the early years of the nineteenth century Glasgow was a forward-looking and adventurous city, with men of education and liberal tastes to guide its destinies. The Fir Park, adjacent to the Cathedral of S. Mungo, resembled Mont-Louis in Paris where Père-Lachaise had been laid out. The ground had been in the ownership of the Merchants' House of Glasgow since 1650, and in the second decade of the nineteenth century discussions were being held to examine the possibility of forming a cemetery modelled on Père-Lachaise in Glasgow. The original proposal to form a necropolis on the hill was made by Dean of Guild James Ewing, later Provost and MP,[5] supported by Laurence Hill, the Collector, and by John Strang, the Chamberlain. When Strang published his *Necropolis Glasguensis with Osbervations* (sic) *on Ancient and Modern Tombs and Sepulture* in Glasgow (1831), the only burial-grounds to serve the city were those that had an ancient origin and were associated with churches. The proposed Glasgow Necropolis was to be non-denominational and open to every faith. In 1825 the great monument to John Knox, designed by Thomas Hamilton and William Warren, was erected, and in 1828 the first meeting to form the Necropolis was convened at Ewing's home. It was felt that a cemetery would harmonize beautifully with the adjacent scenery and would constitute a solemn and appropriate appendage to the ancient cathedral. Advertisements were placed in January 1831 for plans, sections, and estimates for the conversion of the park into an

ornamental cemetery in a manner which would best embrace 'economy, security, and picturesque effect'. This was the first really large metropolitan cemetery in Scotland, and in terms of hygiene and sanitation it inaugurated a new era in Glasgow.

When Dr Strang's book was reviewed in the *Edinburgh Observer* it was stated that if the scheme were successful, it would be of enormous benefit. Strang himself was described as a 'brilliant super-orthodox luminary burning in a dense cloud of Scotch prejudice and Glasgow smoke'. The first burial was in 1832, and the cemetery quickly became a success.

There is no cemetery in Britain as spectacular as the Glasgow Necropolis, for it is literally a city of the dead on its site beside the cathedral (Pl. 3). It provides a unique architectural and townscape experience, of almost unparalleled magnificence outside Italy. Both Glasgow and Edinburgh can boast cemeteries of theatrical importance in terms of townscape, but the sheer size and magnificence of the incomparable Necropolis in Glasgow must grant that city the palm for cemetery design in Scotland. The influence of Greece is strong, and the Necropolis is so astonishing that a conscious effort has to be made to realize one is actually in Glasgow when viewing it. Yet Greek Revival is a style found frequently in Scotland, a country, like Prussia, that favoured the mathematical precision of that crisp and rational architecture. Edinburgh possesses many fine buildings in this genre, and Glasgow has its own inimitable work by Alexander 'Greek' Thomson, much influenced by the eclectic work of Karl Friedrich Schinkel. When John Claudius Loudon visited the Necropolis in 1841 his impressions were of a 'grand and melancholy' city on a hill.[6] He was particularly impressed by the 'totally different character' of the 'tombs and gravestones, even at a distance', for there appeared to be 'no mean, trivial, or vulgar form among them'. Loudon also noted that the monuments were all vertical, and that there was nothing of the untidy effect found in English cemeteries. The

Plate 3 View of the Necropolis, Glasgow, from the *Sketches of the History of Glasgow*, by James Pagan. Glasgow, 1847. Drawn and engraved by Allan and Ferguson (*Author's Collection*)

Opposite above
Plate 4 Monument to Buchanan of Dowanhill, in the Glasgow Necropolis. The upper stage of this elegant memorial is based on the Choragic Monument of Lysicrates in Athens. The designer was James Brown, of Brown and Carrick, and the date is 1844 (*The Author*)

Below Plate 5 Glasgow Necropolis, showing the Doric column and monument to John Knox, designed by Thomas Hamilton and William Warren, erected in 1825 (*Francis Frith and Co. by permission of the Rothman Collection*)

designs of the stones were 'of a very superior kind . . . all the monuments in the Glasgow cemetery' conveying the 'dignified idea of being built', 'and had not the mean appearance of being thrust in like slates, or laid down like pavement'.

George Blair, in his *Biographic and Descriptive Sketches of the Glasgow Necropolis*, (1857), regarded the Necropolis as the Westminster Abbey of Glasgow. Nearly every eminent Glaswegian who had died between 1832 and 1867 was either interred within the Necropolis or was represented by a cenotaph. Blair declared that the natural beauty of the rocky eminence 'crowned with its monumental terraces; its claims to distinction as the first ornamental cemetery' in Scotland; 'its close proximity to the old Cathedral, and to other objects of antiquarian interest; the ready access to it from the city, and the noble view which it affords of the surrounding country, render it a favorite resort of our citizens as well as a principal attraction to strangers visiting Glasgow'. This effect, of course, is precisely in accordance with the object and design of the cemetery. 'The elegant and costly monuments' (Pl. 4) with which it is now richly embellished were 'never intended to be hid from view. They resemble a city that is literally "set on a hill"—a silent but significant city of the dead—to draw the attention of the living to the memory and virtues of the departed.' When Queen Victoria and the Prince Consort visited Glasgow in 1849, the beautiful view of the Necropolis was greatly admired, and Prince Albert expressed himself delighted (Pl. 5).

The individual monuments in the Necropolis are often very grand, and most are classical in inspiration, as would be expected in Presbyterian Glasgow. Many are listed as of architectural importance.

The movement to found cemeteries was clearly under way, but London still lagged behind the provinces. In February 1830 Carden convened a meeting to discuss the formation of a cemetery in London. J. C. Loudon published his own ideas in *The Morning Advertiser*[7] later that year, as it was clear that interment in towns would soon be debated in Parliament, and various architects, gardeners, and others wished to be involved in the laying out of cemeteries. Loudon advocated several cemeteries, equidistant from each other, and at a constant radius from the centre of London. They should be regularly laid out and planted with trees and shrubs so that they would function as botanic gardens as well as cemeteries. 'The burial-places for the metropolis', he wrote, 'ought to be made sufficiently large to serve at the same time as breathing places.'

In June 1830 a public meeting was convened to discuss the necessity of forming a general cemetery. Lord Lansdowne said that the modes of interment in London were highly objectionable 'leading to consequences injurious to health and offensive to decency.' He observed that Liverpool possessed 'a large cemetery erected under the care of Mr Foster, a distinguished architect', and that it was 'highly approved of by the people there'.[7] The cemetery was to be owned and managed by The General Cemetery Company, and it was the first such commercial enterprise in London. When it is realized that the population of London increased by a fifth in the 1820s, and that the average number of new burials was two hundred per acre, an idea of the hideous conditions that prevailed in the old burial-grounds may be gained. Between 1832 and 1847 Parliament authorized the establishment of eight commercial cemetery companies in the London area. There was no shortage of people willing to buy shares in the companies, while many architects exhibited designs for cemeteries, no doubt spurred on by the fact that the S. James's Cemetery in Liverpool was paying a dividend of 8% in 1830.

Carden's first proposal for a site for the General Cemetery was Primrose Hill. This stimulated the architect Thomas Willson to exhibit a design for an unusual, even bizarre, cemetery in 1824. In a later published version of this idea entitled *The Pyramid. A General Metropolitan Cemetery to be Erected in the Vicinity of Primrose Hill*,[8] Willson estimated his building could hold five million bodies, as it was 'sufficiently capacious', and stated that considerations of hygiene were most important in his concept. This is a design of truly Utopian grandeur, and an esquisse for a sublime idea. The pyramid was to be built of brick, faced with granite, and would occupy an eighteen-acre site. Willson considered his design to be 'practicable, economical, and remunerative'. The building would be free from vandalism and humidity, and would provide a magnificent ornament to the metropolis. The area was to be 'as large as Russell Square', and the building would 'tower to a height considerably above' that of S. Paul's'. The pyramid would cost £2,583,552, and would contain freehold vaults selling at between £100 and £500 each, while other vaults could be let out to the various parishes. Willson estimated his scheme would bring in a profit of £10,764,800. 'This grand Mausoleum', he wrote, 'will go far towards completing the glory of London'. The structure would contain ninety-four stages of catacombs, and

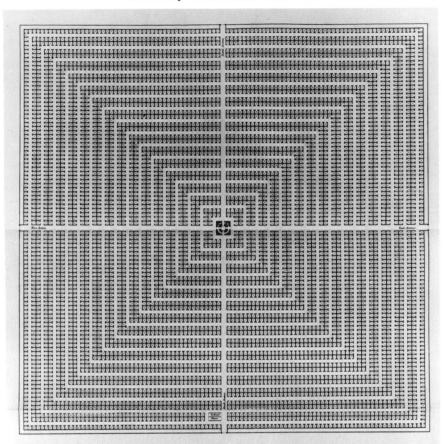

Plate 6 Plan of 'The Pyramid to contain five millions of individuals designed for the centre of the Metropolis' (*Guildhall Library, City of London*)

would be compact, ornamental, and hygienic. At the base Willson proposed a normal cemetery to surround the pyramid. The design recalls the scale of proposals by Boullée and the French Academicians, and it is interesting to note that the proportions of the pyramid resemble those of the pyramid of Cestius rather than Egyptian prototypes. At the top was to be an obelisk on a pedimented podium (Pls. 6–8).

However, Willson's vision did not appeal to the promoters of the General Cemetery Company. A more orthodox scheme influenced by Père-Lachaise was favoured.

In July 1832 the Bill 'for establishing a General Cemetery for the Interment of the Dead in the Neighbourhood of the Metropolis' received the royal assent. The passage of the Bill was no doubt smoothed by the fact that in October 1831 the first cholera epidemic was experienced, and, apart from the chaos caused in the already overcrowded churchyards, an added incentive to form cemeteries was provided by the 'miasmatist' lobby. Several people, including Edwin Chadwick, believed that the epidemics were caused by the evil miasmas that arose from the burial grounds. Unfortunately, Chadwick's belief in miasmas as a cause of cholera led him in 1849 to advocate the flushing of drains, so cholera-infected excrement was washed into the Thames, and increased the epidemic. However, the miasmatists were able to create a climate of opinion in the 1830s that was conducive to the formation of cemeteries, and the Bill incorporated the General Cemetery Company which was authorized to raise £45,000 in shares of £25 each. Some 32 hectares of land were purchased, and chapels were built to designs apparently by John Griffith. The Act of Incorporation provided clauses to ensure that fees were payable to the incumbents of parishes from which corpses buried in the cemetery derived.[9] Many clergymen depended on burial fees as part of their income, so it was essential to silence opposition from churchmen by arranging for burial fees ranging from 1s 6d to 5s to be paid.

Competition to design the buildings for the General Cemetery of All Souls at Kensal Green was keen. Several architects attempted to interest the Company in proposals, including Thomas Willson, but G. F. Carden's opinion that there should be freedom to erect any monument in the cemetery prevailed. The model for Kensal Green was thus based on Père-Lachaise.

The land was conveniently placed in open country adjoining the Harrow Road, and access to the cemetery was provided by road and by the Grand

Plate 7 Sections through Willson's Pyramid Cemetery (*Guildhall Library, City of London*)

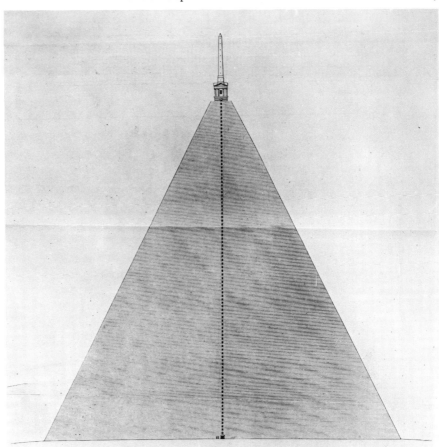

Plate 8 Elevation of Willson's Pyramid Cemetery. Note the gigantic scale (*Guildhall Library, City of London*)

Junction Canal. Some early designs allowed for entrance to the cemetery directly from the canal, as water-borne funerals had a certain attraction. The author of the layout is difficult to establish, but the main ideas for the grounds appear to have come from John Griffith, Sir John Dean Paul (a prominent banker, and chairman of the company), A. C. Pugin, and a Mr Liddell, who had worked in the office of John Nash.

The Company promoted an architectural competition in 1831 to establish the designs of the various buildings. There were no fewer than forty-six entrants, and in March 1832 the premium was awarded to Henry Edward Kendall for his ambitious designs in the Gothic style.[10] Kendall also received the second prize for designs in an Italian manner, but neither of his schemes was ever built. The notice of the competition appeared in the Minutes in 1831. The brief required 'a chapel with ample vaults' to be used for the sole purpose of performing funeral services and to provide a setting for the 'advantageous display of monuments'. Cost was not to exceed £10,000. Other buildings included 'one Principal Entrance Gateway with a Lodge or Lodges' containing at least four rooms. This building was not to exceed a cost of £3,000.

Despite a resolution in March 1832 to accept Kendall's Gothic designs, there was opposition both to the appointment of Kendall as architect and to the choice of the Gothic style from the board of the General Cemetery

Entrance Gateway from the Road to the proposed Cemetery, Kensall Green.

Water Gate from the Grounds of the proposed Cemetery Kensall Green.

Plate 9 'Entrance Gateway from the Road to the proposed Cemetery, Kensall Green' (*top*), and 'Water Gate from the Grounds of the proposed Cemetery, Kensall Green' (*bottom*), by H. E. Kendall. Lithograph by Thomas Allom. Printed by C. Hullmandel (*RIBA British Architectural Library*)

Company. Contemporary journals noted the features of Kendall's scheme with some approval, however, including the delightful water-gate through which funerals could proceed from the canal (Pl. 9). *The Gentleman's Magazine* of 1832[11] carried a review of Kendall's designs. By that time the grounds were 'already laid out in serpentine and other walks, and embellished with a plantation'. The grounds were defined by the Harrow Road and the Paddington Canal, and entrances were to be provided on both sides. In the centre of the cemetery a chapel was to be built (Pls. 10, 11). However, although Kendall was given '100 guineas for the best design' it was not 'settled' if his scheme would be adopted. The 'picturesque effect' of the 'pointed style' was felt to harmonize best with the purposes of the chapel. The propriety of giving the preference to 'native ecclesiastical architectural styles' was unquestioned as 'it is associated in the minds of all' with 'religious feeling' and with sanctity. The style was 'peculiarly suitable to a place designed to be the last home of mortality'. Although the choice of

Plate 10 Proposed interior of the Anglican Chapel at Kensal Green, by H. E. Kendall. Lithograph by Thomas Allom. Printed by C. Hullmandel (*RIBA British Architectural Library*)

Plate 11 'North East View of proposed Cemetery Chapel, Kensal Green', by H. E. Kendall. Lithograph by Thomas Allom. Printed by C. Hullmandel (*RIBA British Architectural Library*)

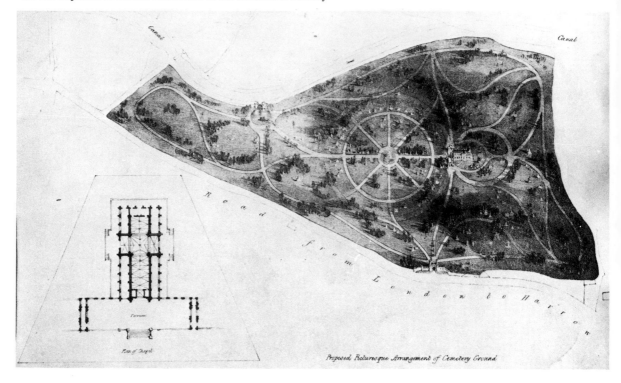

Gothic was felt to be sound, Kendall's interpretation of it was criticized as being 'florid' and 'at variance with the sepulchral character' so necessary in a building with so solemn a purpose. The layout for the grounds could be improved by 'judicious planting, interspersed with tombs', and hopefully the cemetery would, in time, become 'highly picturesque and beautiful'. In any case, the cemetery would be a great improvement on the 'usual depositories of the dead' so familiar at the time (Pl. 12).

Opposition to Kendall hardened, and G. F. Carden, who supported Kendall, was removed from the office of Registrar in June 1833. Nervously, the board of the Company solicited opinions on Kendall's designs from Cockerell, Pennethorne, Smirke, Wyatville, and other eminent architects. It appears that Sir John Dean Paul, chairman of the Company, and a banker, was implacably opposed to Gothic, being a fervent classicist. Having removed the pro-Kendall Carden, and silenced all the Goths in the camp, Paul persuaded the board to instruct John Griffith, Surveyor to the Company, to organize new designs in the Greek Revival style.

John Griffith of Finsbury (1796–1888) was a Fellow of the Royal Institute of British Architects, and later became Chairman of the General Cemetery Company. He must not be confused with John William Griffith (1790–1855) to whom the works at Kensal Green have been erroneously ascribed.

A prospect of the cemetery, dating from 1832 or 1833, shows the canal, the Anglican Chapel in the centre, and the entrance in the foreground. The details of the entrance gates differ from the gate as built, so the drawing clearly dates from the time Kendall's Gothic designs were rejected. The drawing is attributed to Thomas Allom, but may be by Griffith himself

Plate 12 'Proposed Picturesque Arrangement of Cemetery Ground', by H. E. Kendall, Architect, for Kensal Green Cemetery. Lithograph by Thomas Allom. Printed by C. Hullmandel (*RIBA British Architectural Library*)

218

Plate 13 Water-colour, showing a prospect of Kensal Green Cemetery, dating from *c.* 1832 (*London Museum*)

(Pl. 13). It appears that an early layout of the grounds was prepared by a surveyor named Liddell, who had drawn up the scheme 'under the eye of' John Nash.[12] Nevertheless, Griffith's signature appears on the plans deposited with the Commissioners of Sewers in 1832, and it is clear from the Minutes of the Company that Griffith was instructed to furnish plans and sections of the ground as early as 20 September 1831. Griffith's obituary in *The Builder* states specifically that as 'Chairman of the Kensal Green Cemetery Company (*sic*), he was responsible for the laying-out of the grounds'.

The architect of the buildings at the cemetery appears to have been Griffith, although the signature of the builder, William Chadwick, is on the plans still in the possession of the Company. Chadwick built many houses in Kensington, and is also described as an architect. It is just possible that he may have supplied designs for Griffith when tendering for the work. Chadwick had worked with Soane, after all, and indeed Soane was approached by the Company for references concerning Chadwick.[12]

The cemetery buildings consist of two chapels (one for Anglicans and the other for Dissenters), a colonnade above catacombs, and an entrance gateway. As with all the early cemeteries, part of the grounds was consecrated and reserved for use by Anglicans, while the unconsecrated part was used by Dissenters. Both chapels have tetrastyle porticos, and wings. The Anglican chapel has an Order of Greek Doric, and the Dissenters' chapel is Ionic. Both have brick-vaulted catacombs underneath, although the extent of the Anglican catacombs is much greater (Pls. 14, 15). The structure and form of the vaults create their own moving architectural experiences, where coffins lie in *loculi* within the robust framework of brick

The development of British cemeteries in the nineteenth century

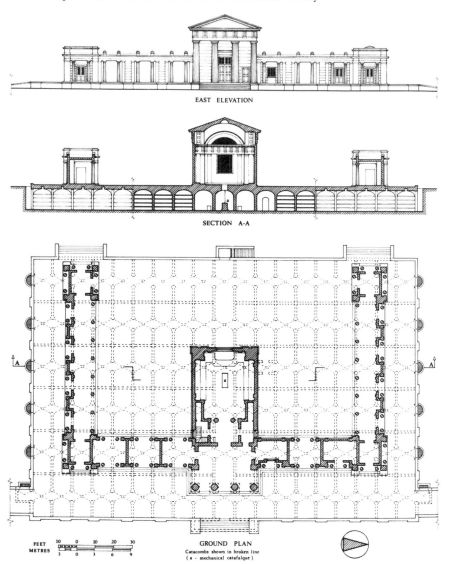

EAST ELEVATION

SECTION A-A

GROUND PLAN
Catacombs shown in broken line
(a - mechanical catafalque)

FEET
METRES

Plate 14 Anglican Chapel, Kensal Green, East Elevation, Section and Plan, showing the chapel and catacombs (*Measured drawing by John J. Sambrook, by permission of the General Editor, the* Survey of London)

Plate 15 Nonconformist Chapel, Kensal Green, Front elevation. Original drawing, signed by William Chadwick. The colonnaded wings have been demolished (1976–7) (*By permission of the General Cemetery Company*)

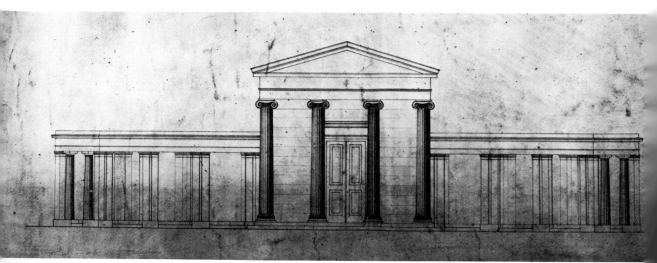

Plate 16 Subsidiary passageway in the catacombs under the Anglican Chapel, Kensal Green, showing individual cells and brick vaulting (*Department of Architecture and Civic Design, G.L.C. Serial No. 70/12199 HB*)

(Pl. 16). The gateway on the Harrow Road includes the lodges and offices, and has a Doric Order applied to a triumphal arch.

From 1831 trees were being planted, and David Ramsay of the Stanhope Nursery, Old Brompton, approached the Company with offers to lay out the ground, but these were turned down. Early in 1832 Griffith opened negotiations with Stephenson, the Surveyor of the London and Birmingham Railway Company, to alleviate the effects of railway construction on the fortunes of the cemetery, and the worst appears to have been avoided.

The Cemetery of All Souls, Kensal Green, was consecrated on 24 January 1833,[13] although the Anglican chapel was not completed until 1837. A novel device was the installation of an hydraulic catafalque so that coffins could be lowered into the catacombs after a service. The buildings were constructed of brick, Portland stone, and Roman Cement.[14] The

ground was mapped and planned so that an accurate record of burials could be made.

The attractive grounds and buildings of Kensal Green Cemetery soon brought custom from London,[15] for it must be remembered that in 1833 the Cemetery lay in rural surroundings. In 1839 the Company was a flourishing concern, and the original shares had doubled in value. A further movement towards fashionable status took place by the choice of the cemetery as a burial-place by Princess Sophia and the Duke of Sussex. Both these children of George III are buried in front of the Anglican chapel. The tomb of Princess Sophia is of distinguished design, and consists of a *quattrocento* sarcophagus set on a high podium. Professor Ludwig Grüner was responsible for the design of the sarcophagus, and Edward Pearce made the podium. The sarcophagus was carved by the Signori Bardi of Carrara. The monument was erected in 1850 by subscription, and Queen Victoria, the King of Hanover, Adolphus Duke of Cambridge, and others contributed (Pl. 17). The famous Duke of Cambridge, Commander-in-Chief of the British Army, also lies in Kensal Green.

The cemetery became one of the sights of London soon after it was opened. Splendid monuments[16] were built among the leafy arbours, and many received the approval of the arbiters of taste.[17] Ducrow's pretty Egyptian mausoleum of 1837, designed by Dawson, recalls the architecture of Highgate Cemetery, but it was denounced in the pages of *The Builder* as an example of 'ponderous coxcombry'[18] (Pl. 18). Knight observed that size of memorials was not a guarantee of grandeur, and criticized 'endless repetitions' of certain motifs.[19] Virtually the whole range of Victorian taste

Plate 17 *Quattrocento* sarcophagus, designed by Ludwig Grüner, and carved by the Signori Bardi. It stands on a podium made by Edward Pearce, and marks the grave of Princess Sophia. In the background is the portico of the Anglican Chapel, Kensal Green (*The Author*)

The development of British cemeteries in the nineteenth century is displayed in this cemetery, from the simplest classical monument to the most grandiose of memorials. Gibson's High Victorian Gothic octagon to the Molyneux family is one of the more ambitious sepulchres (Pl. 19).

By 1835 cemetery companies had become respectable, and John William Griffith's son, William Pettit Griffith, was anxious to establish himself as an expert in the design of necropoleis. Many other professionals attempted to scramble on to the cemetery bandwagon. Some succeeded but many others failed. The success of Kensal Green encouraged the formation of other cemeteries that followed in rapid succession from 1836.

The first of these successors to Kensal Green was the South Metropolitan Cemetery at Norwood, which was consecrated by the Bishop of Winchester in 1837. The architect was Sir William Tite, who designed both the layout and the chapels. The style chosen for the buildings was Tudor Gothic, and the chapels were constructed of stock bricks with stone dressings. As at Kensal Green, the chapels had catacombs underneath, and one building was for Anglicans, the other for Dissenters. The landscape was basically in an English picturesque style, with wide spacious lawns leading up to the buildings. A print of the 1840s shows Norwood as originally laid out, and demonstrates that it was a very splendid composition. It is of some interest to consider J. C. Loudon's criticisms, for he proposed a greater variety of planting, with more evergreens (Ch. VIII, Pls. 10, 11).

Under the original Act of Parliament[20] the South Metropolitan Cemetery Company was empowered to open a cemetery of up to 32 hectares within ten miles of London, to build chapels and to raise capital. Only about 16 hectares were purchased, and enclosed by a boundary wall.[21]

Following bomb-damage and years of neglect, little remains of Tite's

Below left Plate 18 'The General Cemetery, Kensal Green', published in *The Mirror of Literature, Amusement, and Instruction* No. 890, 28 April 1838. In the foreground is the Egyptian tomb of Ducrow, and on the right the tomb of St John Long by Sievier (*Local History Collection, Kensington and Chelsea Central Library*)

Right Plate 19 Mausoleum of the Molyneux family by John Gibson, a High Victorian Gothic octagon in the Italian Gothic style fashionable in the 1860s. The spire has since been demolished (*RIBA British Architectural Library*)

design. Prints advertising the cemetery in the 1840s show the layout before it was cluttered with tombstones. There are several fine Victorian monuments still standing, however, and the cemetery of the Greek Community is packed with splendid mausolea including the Ralli tomb designed by John Oldrid Scott in the Greek Doric style. Since 1966 the cemetery at Norwood has been in the hands of the London Borough of Lambeth.[22]

Within a month of the founding of Norwood Cemetery, another Bill was passed by Parliament that became 'An Act for establishing Cemeteries for the Interment of the Dead, Northward, Southward, and Eastward of the Metropolis, by a Company to be called the *London* Cemetery Company', dated 17 August 1836.[23] The need for such an Act was made clear in the preamble, for 'the Cemeteries or Burial Grounds within the Cities of *London* and *Westminster* and the immediate Suburbs thereof' were of limited extent, and many of them had long been in use. They were 'so occupied and filled with Graves and Vaults as to be altogether insufficient for the increased and increasing Population in the Neighbourhood thereof, and not equal to afford those Facilities for the Interment of Bodies which is necessary and essential to the Convenience of the present and increasing Population', thus the Act argued the case for setting up large cemeteries, well-regulated and maintained.

The Company was empowered to establish and maintain three cemeteries in Surrey, Kent, and Middlesex. They were to be laid out and planted, and the cemeteries were to be 'enclosed by proper walls, fences, gates, etc.' Part of the cemeteries was to be set aside and consecrated for the interment of the dead according to the rites and usages of the 'United Church of *England* and *Ireland*', and was to be consecrated by a bishop. Other parts were to be used for the burial of Dissenters, and so separate chapels for Anglicans and Dissenters were necessary. Catacombs and other structures were also allowed by the Act.[24] The Company was obliged by law to 'keep the said Cemeteries respectively and the said Chapel or Chapels respectively, and the several Buildings thereon and therein, and the external Walls and Fences thereof, and all other parts of the same, in thorough and complete Repair'. Plans were to be kept, with full records of burials and all other transactions. Fees were to be paid to the incumbents of parishes from which corpses derived, an important aspect of early burial reform.

The London Cemetery Company established offices at 29 New Bridge Street, EC, and laid out the Cemetery of S. James at Highgate, which was consecrated on 20 May 1839. It is odd that the name of Stephen Geary is not mentioned in the list of proprietors, for he was described as 'Architect and Founder' of Highgate Cemetery on his tombstone.[25] Geary is also described as the 'Founder of the Cemeteries of Highgate, Nunhead, Peckham, Westminster, Gravesend, Brighton, etc.' on the title-page of a book of *Cemetery Designs for Tombs and Cenotaphs* (1840),[16] engraved by B. Winkles. These designs, by Geary, offer no clue to the authorship of the designs for the chapels at Highgate. Geary's exact part in the design of the cemeteries is difficult to establish, for only his work for the West of London and Westminster Cemetery Company is known from documentary

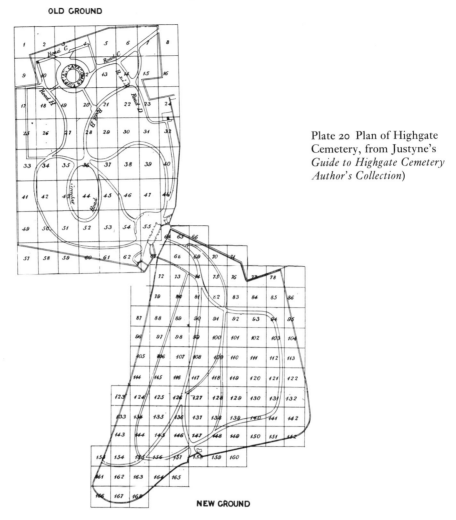

OLD GROUND

NEW GROUND

Plate 20 Plan of Highgate Cemetery, from Justyne's *Guide to Highgate Cemetery Author's Collection*)

evidence.[26] The Gothic catacombs at Highgate are arranged in a similar fashion to a range of Gothic vaults in the extension to the old Parish Churchyard in Brighton, however, and this may indicate that Geary was responsible for both ranges.

Geary was an architect and civil engineer, inventor, and specialist in gin-palace design. He vies with J. B. Papworth for the credit as architect of the Original Gin Palace in the 1820s, but he subsequently disowned his part in the development of an urban pub style, and became a teetotaller. He died on 28 August 1854, aged 56, of cholera. It is interesting to note that nearly all references to Geary are incorrect, and seem to stem from Frederick Teague Cansick's *A Collection of Curious and Interesting Epitaphs, copied from the existing monuments of Distinguished and Noted Characters in the Cemeteries and Churchyards of Saint Pancras, Middlesex*, published in London in 1872. Cansick reproduces Geary's inscription on his tombstone in Highgate Cemetery, and describes him as 'Architect and Founder of this Cemetery'. Unfortunately, Cansick, or his printer, transposed a 5 and a 7, for his text tells us that Geary 'departed this life in the 75th year of his age'. The error is repeated in Frederic Boase's *Modern English Biography*, and I repeated it in

my own *The Victorian Celebration of Death*. Geary died in the fifty-seventh year of his age, that is, at the age of fifty-six. His tombstone has now been found, and verifies this. The cemetery records also confirm his age as fifty-six, so the facts are now established beyond all doubt.

It would appear, however, that Geary acted as architect to the company in its early days, and carried out initial surveys. He was probably responsible for the appointment of David Ramsay as landscape gardener to the Company. Ramsay was a nurseryman at Brompton who subsequently became a speculative builder. Geary was succeeded as architect by James Bunstone Bunning in about 1839.

The twenty hectares of Highgate Cemetery, described as the 'most picturesque cemetery of the north of London' were divided into two sections by Swain's Lane[27] (Pl. 20). The eight hectares of the older part on the southern slope of the hill was landscaped by David Ramsay. The serpentine walks, and the contours of the grounds, create an illusion of great size.[28] The chapel combines both the Anglican and Dissenters' chapels within one buildings, described by Lloyd as 'Undertakers' Gothic'.[27]

The most interesting buildings in the cemetery are the catacombs. An arch flanked by engaged Egyptian columns and obelisks (Pl. 21) gives access

Plate 22 The Egyptian Avenue, Highgate Cemetery, leading to the Cedar of Lebanon catacombs (*The Author*)

Right Plate 23 Julius Beer's mausoleum at Highgate by John Oldrid Scott, 1877–8 (*The Author*)

to the Egyptian Avenue which has tombs on either side (Pl. 22). At the end of the Avenue, under a bridge, is the Cedar of Lebanon range of catacombs (Pl. 22). Steps lead up from this sunken circus to the high ground where there is a range of Gothic catacombs and the great mausoleum of Julius Beer, designed by John Oldrid Scott (Pl. 23). The Cedar of Lebanon stood on the site before the cemetery was constructed. The Cedar of Lebanon Catacombs were built in a ring around the tree, and a sloping area was provided on the other side of the promenade, so that there was a wide ditch around the 'circus' of tombs. Geary probably designed this. The catacombs in the Egyptian Avenue appear to have been built next, and they, together with the arch, were probably designed by James Bunstone Bunning between 1839 and 1842. The circle of catacombs that formed the outer side of the 'street' around the original Cedar of Lebanon catacombs was known as the 'New Catacombs' and was not designed by either Geary or Bunning. The New Catacombs are predominantly classical, with little trace of Egyptian ornament, and they were constructed in 1877[29] (Pl. 24).

The initial success of Highgate Cemetery as a fashionable burial-ground encouraged the London Cemetery Company to procced with the formation of a second cemetery. The desirability of the new cemeteries was further

Plate 24 The Lebanon Cedar. Note the Egyptian Revival detail (*The Author*)

helped by the cholera epidemics and by the pioneering polemics of George Alfred Walker, whose *Gatherings from Grave-yards* had been published in 1839. Walker, a surgeon, also described the sickening goings-on at Spa Fields burial ground in Clerkenwell in a later pamphlet entitled *The Last Fire at the Bone House* published in 1845.

Opinion was not only formed by writers such as Carden and Walker, but by the success of the other commercial cemeteries. Markland, in his influential *Remarks on English Churches, and on the Expediency of Rendering Sepulchral Memorials subservient to Pious and Christian Uses* of 1843, helped the cemeteries further by arguing against burial in churches and in overcrowded graveyards. The beautiful grounds of Highgate, with their great variety of planting, were a serene contrast to the hideous churchyards of the past (Pl. 25).[30] A growth of population, the experiences of epidemics, and, above all, the dividends being paid by other joint-stock companies encouraged the London Cemetery Company to establish the Cemetery of All Saints at Nunhead in order to cater for the burial of London's dead south of the Thames. Once more, a site on a hill was chosen, and part of the twenty-one hectares was consecrated by the Bishop of Winchester on 29 July 1840, with a section reserved for Dissenters.

Plate 25 The strange, Italianate landscaping of Highgate Cemetery (*The Author*)

Nunhead Cemetery is the best-known landscape layout of James Bunstone Bunning (Pl. 26). A formal drive approaches the Anglican chapel through noble cast-iron entrance gates and classical piers of Portland stone designed by Bunning. This axial approach is further emphasized by the rows of trees that flank the drive and draw the eye to the tower of the Anglican chapel. Just inside the entrance gates in Linden Grove are two small symmetrically balanced lodges of exquisite Neoclassical design worthy of the work of Karl Friedrich Schinkel in Berlin, or that of Alexander

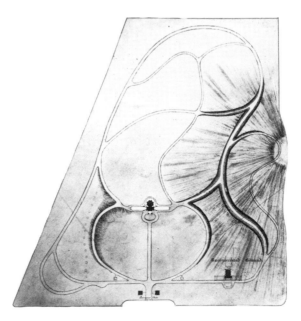

Plate 26 'Nunhead Cemetery. Plan shewing the Proposed Sites of Chapels in accordance with the designs submitted by Mr Thomas Little, Archt.'. This plan clearly shows the strong main axis of the entrance gates and lodges, avenue, and Anglican Chapel in the centre. The Dissenter's Chapel is to the right. The serpentine walks and the hilly nature of the ground are also clearly shown. The drawing also confirms, in a note, that the ground was 'laid out by J. B. Bunning', and that the Chapels were erected to designs by Thomas Little in 1844 (*RIBA British Architectural Library Drawings Collection*)

'Greek' Thomson in Glasgow (Pl. 27). They are indicative of how inventive Bunning could actually be. Subsidiary entrances and the boundary walls (of stock brick with stone dressings) are in a stripped-down classical manner. The plan of the grounds has only the main drive as a concession to classicism. A road at right angles to the main drive led to the Dissenters' Chapel and to the outer paths of the cemetery. Elsewhere, throughout the grounds, the drives and paths are circuitous and winding, somewhat reminiscent of the layout at Highgate; they may have owed something to the designs of Stephen Geary and to the 'serpentine' paths of Père-Lachaise and Kensal Green.

The monuments of Nunhead Cemetery are not as distinguished as those in earlier London cemeteries, perhaps reflecting the less socially élite classes of those buried there. Among the most impressive memorials is the high granite obelisk to commemorate the Scots Martyrs to the cause of Parliamentary Reform. This was erected in 1851 from funds collected by

Plate 27 One of the remarkably fine lodges by J. B. Bunning of 1840. The assured Neoclassical hand of Bunning is evident. The building is of yellow stock bricks with stone dressings. The design of the chimneys resembles classical mausolea (*The Author*)

Joseph Hume, MP, and celebrates the memories of those Scots who were sentenced to transportation for advocating a representative democratic system. A similar obelisk, of Craigleith stone, had been erected in the Calton Hill Cemetery, in Edinburgh, in 1846, and it was the remainder of the fund that was expended on the memorial at Nunhead.

As with other early cemetery promotions an architectural competition was organized for the designs of the proposed cemetery buildings, and the first premium was awarded to the architect Thomas Little in 1844. Little's proposals for the two chapels were in the Decorated Gothic style, and the materials chosen were Kentish ragstone with freestone dressings (Pls. 28–31). Little was also to design one of the first of the later non-commercial cemeteries for the Parish of Paddington in Willesden Lane. His complete drawings for the Nunhead chapels survive in the Drawings Collection of the Royal Institute of British Architects.

When J. C. Loudon published his work on cemeteries in 1843, Nunhead

Plate 28 Thomas Little's contract drawing of the Plan of the Vaults of the 'No. 1' or Anglican Chapel, signed and dated April 1844 (*RIBA British Architectural Library Drawings Collection*)

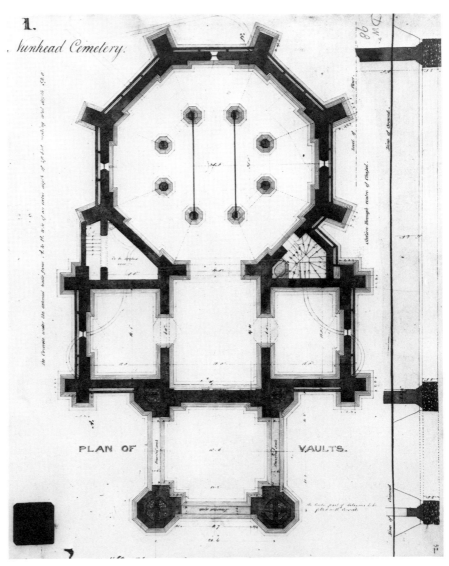

Plate 29 Front elevation of the Anglican Chapel at Nunhead Cemetery showing the dramatic Decorated façade with the tower and *porte-cochère*. A Contract Drawing by Thomas Little (*RIBA British Architectural Library Drawings Collection*)

Opposite Plate 31 Thomas Little's Elevations of the 'Chapel for Unconsecrated Ground'. It had a crypt, chapel and gallery; also a robing-room and store for tools. There were 28 seats in the stalls, room for 28 more in the body of the chapel, and an extra 46 seats in the gallery (*RIBA British Architectural Library Drawings Collection*)

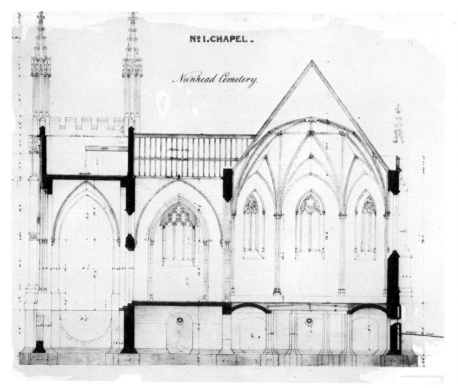

Plate 30 Section through the Anglican Chapel, showing the *porte-cochère*, octagonal chapel and crypt. A Contract Drawing by Thomas Little, dated 1844 (*RIBA British Architectural Library Drawings Collection*)

Opposite Plate 32 Romantic view of Nunhead Cemetery, showing the hilly nature of the site and the marvellous views over London. The dome of St Paul's Cathedral may be seen on the left. This view must have been published shortly after the cemetery opened, for it shows J. B. Bunning's two gate lodges and the entrance gates. The boundary walls, consisting of brick piers with iron railings in between, are also shown. The date must be about 1843, for buildings that are clearly temporary chapels are indicated (*Southwark Library Services*)

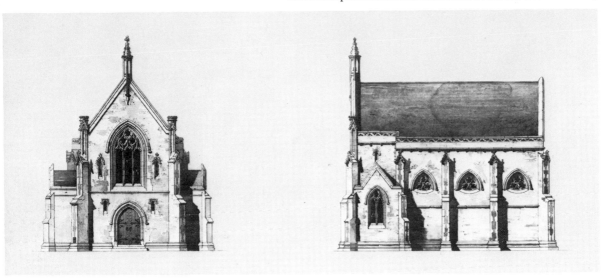

was well established. Some early prints (doubtless produced to attract customers and capital) are indicative of the semi–rural charm of the site (Pl. 32). Nunhead was almost a garden-cemetery, and, with its monuments, could only be beneficial to public morals and manners. The cemetery occupied a site of which Loudon approved, for he is known to have considered that the chapels should be placed in a central and conspicuous position so that they could be seen from all the prominent points on the roads and paths. However, Loudon was less happy about Bunning's

Plate 33 'All Saints Cemetery, Nunhead, Peckham Rye': the print shows the main gates in Linden Grove, the two lodges by J. B. Bunning, and the vista towards Thomas Little's Gothic Anglican Chapel. The print must date from the late 1840s or 1850s, for the main avenue's trees do not appear to have reached any size (*Southwark Library Services*)

lodges, for he felt they were unrelated to the gates and walls and would have been better as one building (Pl. 33).

Loudon specifically mentions Mr E. Buxton, the first superintendent of Nunhead, and appears to have been impressed by Buxton's inventive brain. Indeed, Buxton's designs for grave-shuttering are reproduced by Loudon, who loved practical gadgets and ideas. Shuttering was necessary in the thick clay, especially when deep common graves were to be sunk. According to the approving Loudon, Buxton took 'a deep interest in the Nunhead Cemetery, and in the subject of cemeteries generally'. This is an understatement, as we shall see.[31]

Although the Act of Parliament that enabled the cemeteries of Highgate and Nunhead to be set up specifically demanded that the Company should hold meetings twice a year, annual meetings were usual.[32] The presentation of accounts was therefore also yearly, and financial progress appeared to be satisfactory. Edward Buxton's zeal at Nunhead, and Loudon's approval of him, encouraged the directors to appoint him Secretary to the London Cemetery Company on 19 January 1847, a post he held for eighteen years.[33] 'By his apparent regularity and strict attention to the business of his office, he gained the entire confidence of the Board and Proprietors.' In 1865, however, Buxton died, and the subsequent horrific discoveries nearly ended the fortunes of the Company, for the Secretary had been practising an ingenious system of fraud and forgery over a number of years. Fictional bankers' pass-books had been shown at board meetings, and the correct statements had been concealed. The frauds perpetrated by Buxton were not petty, however, for it was found that he had tampered with shares, and had created 'shares' by the issue of forged certificates and fraudulent transfers with forged names, bogus sellers, and non-existent witnesses. Several shareholders therefore had fewer shares than they appeared to hold, while others appeared to hold shares that were never properly assigned. False dividends were drawn up, and a book purporting to show a deposit of £7,500 at the bank was false, no money whatever having been deposited.

Buxton's will of 1836 left all his property to his wife and child. On his death, his Estate was found to be 'considerable', but all assets had to be accounted for through the Court of Chancery. The unfortunate Mrs Buxton was prevailed upon to renounce her claims to Buxton's 'Estate' in consideration of payment of one pound per week for ten years from the Company.

All certificates of shares were then called in to be authenticated, and a new register of shareholders was prepared. In 1866 a statement of the amount of Buxton's cash frauds and of the extent of the issue of false shares by him was made. The Company resolved to accept the liability on account of the 'spurious shares surreptitiously issued by the late E. Buxton', and these shares were added to the capital. The holders of the Buxton 'shares' were therefore admitted as part-proprietors. Dividends were restored to twelve shillings a share in 1866, when a profit of nearly five thousand pounds was announced. Unfortunately, the 'accounts' left by Buxton showed a deficiency of £18,179 3s 2d, a colossal sum for those days, and a fortune if translated into today's values. Buxton had fraudulently issued 2,434 shares up to 1 March 1865, and a further 230 up to 5 July. He paid 'dividends' from cheques fraudulently obtained, or from his own funds. The directors were empowered to compromise with Buxton's creditors to the sum of fifteen shillings in the pound.

However, the Buxton scandals were still in the future when *The Builder*, *Household Words*, and many other publications took up the cudgels on behalf of the new, hygienic cemeteries. Some eight years after the publication of Walker's *Gatherings*, a Burial Authority was constituted to close churchyards, lay out new cemeteries, and take over others. The directors of the private cemeteries anxiously watched the chain of events that led up to the passing of the Metropolitan Interments Acts. In 1850, the General Board of Health was granted powers to purchase the commercial cemeteries already established. In fact, only one, Brompton, was acquired, but the threat of what was virtually nationalization hit the joint-stock companies very hard, including the London Cemetery Company, for Nunhead had been mentioned in regard to a possible takeover. Repeal of the Act did little to improve matters for the companies, because the public cemeteries formed by the burial boards were set up in direct opposition to those established by the joint-stock companies. Thus, by 1867, when public cemeteries in South London were in operation, the London Cemetery Company had to try to attract custom to Nunhead Cemetery by improving the buildings and the grounds.

In 1868 there was a disastrous economic recession which discouraged people from purchasing the more expensive graves. Oddly, there was also a low rate of mortality that year owing to the 'sanitary improvements working out their beneficial results which must be gratifying to all'. The directors noted, however, that this improvement in health could only affect the income of the Company in a temporary manner, as 'the average thus thrown out of course from a particular course must in time revert to its former result'.

That winter must have been particularly lethal, for the minutes of 1869 mention an increase in profits that was 'the best for many years'. Just as gratifying was the observation that 'the grounds, both at Highgate and Nunhead, were in a most satisfactory condition both as to ornamental and substantial repair'. It was reported that the 'better classes of Vaults and Graves' (brick-lined graves, brick vaults, and catacombs) were the most profitable, and at 'the same time consistent with the character of the cemeteries'. By 1876 nearly all the Lebanon Catacombs at Highgate had been sold, so the erection of some additional catacomb chambers was thought to be necessary. Brick graves of the 'most select character' were also advised. The proposal to build yet more catacombs at Highgate as late as 1876 is curious, for by that time public opinion had turned away from catacombs as a mode of interment as concern with hygiene increased. While there were catacombs under both chapels at Nunhead, there were also underground rectangular catacombs and one cylindrical shaft-catacomb at that cemetery, despite the fact that the catchment area was for a less salubrious cross-section of the population than was the case at Highgate. In 1877, the 'New Catacombs' at Highgate were completed, and were 'much admired'. They form wings on either side of the 'magnificent Mausoleum in course of construction by Julius Beer, Esq.,' and in fact are the outer crescents around the Egyptian-style Cedar of Lebanon Catacombs.

In 1880 the Burial Laws Amendment Act was passed, enabling Dissenters to be buried in consecrated ground, a major change since 1830, when the Joint-Stock cemeteries were being set up. By 1888 business was on the mend, but the use of brick graves had declined. These 'pestilential vaults' had long been denounced by reformers, but vanity and caste encouraged the construction of expensive vaults. It looked as though the Company had backed the wrong horse in building yet more catacombs. The first major change in the Company since its foundation took place in 1911. This was in a Bill to rearrange, reduce, and fix the capital of the London Cemetery Company, and to extend the power of the Company to acquire and hold land. Cremation was being actively discussed, and sites for a crematorium were considered at Nunhead. It was decided in 1913 that the cost of a crematorium should not exceed £4,000. The First World War caused great difficulties, although dividends were still being paid at 6% per annum. 1919 saw big increases in wages, and the necessity to repair all roads, paths, and buildings. In the same year the London Cemetery Company became a Limited Liability Company. In following years, the capital of the Company was reduced, and the dividend dropped to 5% per annum less income tax. War-damage in 1941 did not help Nunhead, and 1942 was a very difficult year, for the decision by the government to remove the iron railings in 1943 left the cemetery wide open to vandalism and misuse at a time when the records and head office were moved to the lodges at Nunhead. The end of the Second World War caused the Company increasing difficulties with rising costs. By 1948 stocks were being sold to pay dividends, and increasing wage-demands obviously brought the Company increasingly to its knees. In 1951 the issued capital was reduced to £16,596. Thefts of lead were reported from all chapels and even vaults in 1952, and in 1954 the issued capital was reduced to £4,149.

The following years were a time of rapid decline. Throughout the 1950s, assets were being sold, and monies in the Perpetuity Account (cash paid by owners of graves and vaults to ensure the fabric would be kept in good order) were used for acquiring freehold ground rents. It was revealed that a new director (who had family interests in a property company) had bought controlling shares *en bloc* by 1950, and in 1957 he became Chairman. The Secretary also became a director. Two other directors at once resigned as a result of the proposed future financial policies of the Company under the new régime. By 1958 only the Chairman and Secretary were usually present at meetings of the Board, and it was decided to extend the Company's scope of activities in the property market. In the 1950s, the Company was still taking on perpetuity undertakings, and in 1958 it acquired all the issued share capital of Raybar Properties Ltd for £28,000. The Chairman visited Edinburgh, and saw the possibility of taking over other cemeteries. An offer was made to purchase the Metropolitan Cemetery Co. Ltd of Edinburgh, and 1,940 shares in the Edinburgh Cemetery Co. Ltd were acquired. Six hundred shares were acquired in the Edinburgh Western Cemetery Co. Ltd, and a controlling interest in several Edinburgh cemeteries was established, although shares were later sold and many non-cemetery shares were purchased. The ground and buildings of the Rosebank Cemetery of Edinburgh were transferred to the Company by the Edinburgh and Leith Cemetery Co. Ltd at a book value of one pound. By 13 January 1960, Nunhead, Highgate and Rosebank, Edinburgh, were incorporated as United Cemeteries Ltd, which became a subsidiary of the Raybourne Group Ltd in 1967; in 1969 Nunhead was closed. In the early 1970s the cemetery at Nunhead, like that of Highgate, had become a scandal. Vandalism was widespread, brick vaults and catacombs were broken into and ransacked, and monuments were desecrated. The plight of both Highgate and Nunhead received local and national publicity.

In 1974 the London Borough of Southwark, in whose territory Nunhead lies, decided to attempt to purchase and manage the cemetery. In view of the heavy cost of restoration, the Council had delayed taking action because it was felt that every effort should be made to require the owners to fulfil their statutory obligation to keep the cemetery in repair, or, alternatively, that the Council should obtain financial assistance from central government. One of the difficulties of acquiring the cemetery was that the original Act of 1836 prohibited the sale of land used for burial. To overcome this problem, another Act of Parliament was needed which the Council decided to promote by means of the Greater London Council (General Powers) Bill, 1974–75, which became law in August 1975. Part IV of that Act empowered the Council to purchase Nunhead Cemetery compulsorily. Part of Nunhead is to be administered as a cemetery, under normal cemetery laws, but the rest will be freed from the effects of consecration, and will not be used for burial. Use of land for a nature reserve, for an open space, or for any purposes under the Physical Training and Recreation Act 1937, will now be possible, and the local authority may level or raise the surface of the land on the open space, and cover, remove, or dispose of any memorial, subject to safeguards to record inscriptions. Similarly, the Council may demolish, seal up, or fill in any buildings in the open-space lands. Areas where the

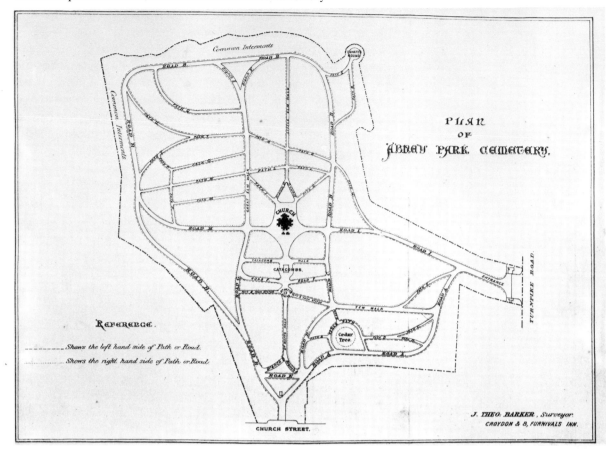

Plate 34 Plan of Abney Park Cemetery by J. Theo Barker, Surveyor, of Croydon, and 8 Furnivals Inn (*Author's Collection*)

Commonwealth War Graves Commission have been granted exclusive rights are protected. The Act of 1836 under which Nunhead Cemetery was established has now ceased to apply, and Southwark took possession in 1976.

A scheme was prepared providing for some nine hectares to be retained as a cemetery, of which some five hectares will be converted to a lawn cemetery, and the remainder, densely wooded, left as it is to become a public open space and nature reserve. The Anglican chapel has been burned down, but the tower should be retained as an eye-catcher (Pl. 33). The Borough Council formally took over Nunhead Cemetery on 24 November 1976 on payment of a purchase price of £1, and the freehold interest passed from United Cemeteries Ltd. The area to be retained for burial will be known as Nunhead Cemetery, but the spaces to be used as a park and nature reserve will be called Waverley Park, something the Scots Martyrs would no doubt applaud.

So ended the fortunes of one of the great commercial cemetery companies of London. Perhaps the London Borough of Southwark will give Nunhead a new lease of life as a cemetery, but the formal avenues, noble buildings, and grand memorials set in a romantic landscape will not be the same. This great Victorian cemetery has been so badly vandalized and neglected that it is difficult to assess just how much of the original conception by Bunning and Little will survive.

The story of the London Cemetery Company, though unusually hair-raising, highlights the difficulties the joint-stock companies faced. Catacombs became wasting assets, and more expensive to maintain. Graves sold in perpetuity became neglected by owners, and perpetuity undertakings became impossible to honour with the rise in inflation.

Elsewhere in London cemetery promotions continued. Abney Park Cemetery at Stoke Newington was opened by the Lord Mayor of London on 20 May 1840. The architect was Professor William Hosking, who provided gates in the Egyptian manner, and a curiously folly-like chapel in the Gothick style. The cemetery was celebrated for its magnificent planting which was varied and carefully chosen (Pl. 34). Trees and shrubs were labelled for educational purposes, and the cemetery was a true aboretum. The tombs are undistinguished in design, but there is a fine statue of Dr Isaac Watts by the sculptor Baily[34] (Pl. 35). This cemetery is very overgrown and neglected today.

To the east of London the dead were to be accommodated by the Tower Hamlets Cemetery, established by the City of London and Tower Hamlets Cemetery Company. The cemetery was consecrated in 1841, and was designed by Wyatt and Brandon. The chapels were destroyed during the Second World War, and it is difficult to visualize what the cemetery was like in its heyday, although a pretty print by G. Moore shows an alluring prospect from above Mile End Road (Pl. 36). The two delightful Gothic chapels are clearly shown, with an elegant gateway and lodge. In the distance are Shooter's Hill and Greenwich Hill. The planting shows little of

Plate 35 Statue of Isaac Watts and the chapel at Abney Park (*Author's Collection*)

Loudon's influence. The cemetery was taken over by the Greater London Council in 1966.

The last of the joint-stock cemeteries in London to be discussed in this study is the West of London and Westminster Cemetery at Brompton, consecrated on 15 June 1840.[35] Stephen Geary was appointed architect to the Company in 1837, and was involved in the early works. In 1838 it was decided to offer premiums by advertisement for designs for the buildings, including walls, chapels, catacombs, and the lodges.

The cemetery was slow to develop, for the Bill of Incorporation[36] was introduced to the House of Commons in 1837, but initially very few subscriptions were received. The clergy wished to protect themselves against the loss of burial fees following their experiences at Kensal Green. One guinea per interment was paid to the parish from which the corpse came by the South Metropolitan Cemetery, but Brompton Cemetery's Bill proposed a fee of ten shillings.

David Ramsay was appointed landscape gardener in 1837, and in the same year Carden, smarting after his experiences at Kensal Green, approached the Company with offers of advice; but he was politely refused, probably because Pleydell Bouverie, the Chairman (and another banker), was a friend of Sir John Dean Paul.

In September 1838 the designs for the cemetery buildings were examined, and the first premium was awarded to Benjamin Baud. H. E. Kendall and Thomas Allom won the second premium. Geary resigned as architect in January 1839, and brought an action against the Company for the payment of fees and compensation as the 'projector' of the cemetery.[37]

Unlike Kendall, Baud was successful in getting his designs adopted, but he probably regretted his involvement in later years. Baud's design was

Plate 36 'View of the City of London and Tower Hamlets Cemetery, Mile End Road'. This delightful lithograph shows Wyatt and Brandon's design, with the Thames, Shooter's Hill, and Greenwich Hill in the distance (*Guildhall Library, City of London*)

Opposite Plate 37 Anglican Chapel and catacomb arcades at Brompton Cemetery (*Kensington and Chelsea Public Libraries*)

formal and symmetrical. An axial road was driven from the Old Brompton Road to the Fulham Road, marked at the northern end by an arched entrance gate with lodges. On this axis Baud planned a domed chapel for Anglicans, to the north of which was to be a Great Circle of colonnades over catacombs. On either side of the Great Circle were to be chapels for Roman Catholics and Dissenters. More colonnades over catacombs were to stretch along the main avenue towards the Old Brompton Road, enlivened with cupolas over the entrances (Pl. 37). The bird's-eye lithograph of Baud's design shows the grandeur of his scheme in its entirety, before the Great Circle became cluttered up with densely packed marble tombstones. To the west was to be a long range of catacombs (Pl. 38).

It should have been obvious to the board that Baud's design, though magnificent and impressive, was bound to be a disaster financially. The enormous amount of catacombs would be expensive to construct, and, once taken, would be wasting assets, needing upkeep in perpetuity. Worse still, the *loculi* in the catacombs allowed for coffins to lie parallel to the walls, so space was used up quickly. Capital was eaten into, and soon the Company was in difficulties.[38] Even in 1840 more capital had to be raised by borrowing, and progress was very slow. In addition, faulty workmanship meant that expensive repairs had to be carried out to the ranges of catacombs, and relations between Baud and the Company soon deteriorated. Furthermore the protracted building works did not encourage 'patronage', and income was minimal. At one stage, the staff was being 'paid' in shares, and Baud himself was owed £1,436. By 1844 Baud was no longer working on the designs and he was removed from the office of architect to the Company. He tried to recover his fees in an action in 1846, and lost. He specialized in painting and drawing thereafter, and seems to have built some houses for private clients.[39]

In 1851 further problems reared their heads, owing to the passing of the Metropolitan Interments Act through Parliament. Until 1850, the establishment of commercial cemeteries was favoured, and in 1847 the Cemetery Clauses Act was passed to provide general guidelines applicable to all public companies that might establish future cemeteries.[40] Shortly

afterwards, thanks to agitation which will be described later, there was a change of outlook. A parliamentary report observed that burial of the dead was a most unfit subject for commercial speculation, and in 1850 an Act of Parliament[41] constituted a Metropolitan Burial District and granted powers to the General Board of Health to provide burial-grounds and to purchase the joint-stock companies that had already been established. In fact only Brompton was acquired, and the Act was repealed in 1852, when the vestries were empowered to form Burial Boards.[42]

The Directors of Brompton Cemetery could not petition against the principle of the Bill, which was intended to alleviate the problems of intramural interment, but they were more successful in increasing the compensation payable to people who had invested in cemeteries. In 1851 Brompton Cemetery was valued by the General Board of Health, and £43,836 was offered to the Company which had expended £147,685 7s 2d on laying out the cemetery. After prolonged negotiations, £74,921 14s 0d was offered, but the Board tried to abandon the purchase as it was clear the Act would be repealed. The Company decided to demand the award should be enforced. Unfortunately for the General Board of Health there were clauses that safeguarded the Company's legal right to have the purchase completed. In 1854 the Company was wound up. The cemetery is now administered by the Department of the Environment as successors to the Commissioners of H.M. Works and Public Buildings, the body that effectively took over the cemetery.

Brompton Cemetery has a number of tombs of interest. The charming tomb of Leyland, patron of Whistler, is a sarcophagus on colonnettes, made of stone inlaid with bronze. The monument of Coombes, the champion sculler, was castigated by *The Builder* which described it as 'bad and vulgar, so ugly as a whole, so execrable in the details'.[43] A fine tomb by Ashpitel was approved of by *The Builder*,[44] but, taken as a whole, the tombs of Brompton are not nearly as distinguished as those of Kensal Green, Norwood, or Highgate.

Soon after Brompton Cemetery was completed, William Cowen made an indigo wash drawing of it from the canal-bank. The rural setting shows the cemetery as it was intended, literally a walled necropolis set in open country. Today, even the canal has vanished, for its bed is the track of the District Line railway (Pl. 39).

Many cemeteries were founded at the same time as the London cemeteries, and, although the stories of Nunhead and Brompton are particularly fraught, generally followed patterns similar to the building of Kensal Green, Highgate, and Abney Park.

These early cemeteries have all suffered with time. Vandalism, neglect, the machinations of the property market, wage increases, taxation, and changes of taste have all contributed to their decline. The history of the early joint-stock cemetery companies represents part of the story of an extraordinary movement in taste and in the civilizing of urban man.

Plate 38 'West of London and Westminster Cemetery, Earl's Court, Old Brompton'. A lithograph by Hawkins, showing Baud's axial design (*Kensington and Chelsea Public Libraries*)

Opposite Plate 39 Indigo wash drawing by William Cowen showing Brompton Cemetery and the old Kensington Canal (*Kensington and Chelsea Public Libraries*)

John Claudius Loudon and the Garden Cemetery Movement.

The influence of the prolific and indefatigable Scot on the design of cemeteries.

'A garden cemetery, and monumental decoration afford the most convincing token of a nation's progress in civilization and the arts, which are its result.'

'A garden cemetery is the sworn foe to preternatural fear and superstition.'

'A garden cemetery and monumental decoration, are not only beneficial to public morals, to the improvement of manners, but are likewise calculated to extend virtuous and generous feelings.'

JOHN STRANG: *Necropolis Glasguensis: with Osbervations* (sic) *on Ancient and Modern Tombs and Sepulture* Glasgow, 1831

'Churchyards and cemeteries are scenes not only calculated to improve the morals and the taste, and by their botanical riches to cultivate the intellect, but they serve as *historical records.*'

JOHN CLAUDIUS LOUDON: 'Principles of Landscape-Gardening applied to Public Cemeteries' *The Gardener's Magazine* 1843

John Claudius Loudon (1783–1843) was an industrious Caledonian who, in the words of John Gloag, 'lived a full, varied, and occasionally adventurous life, unencumbered by any misgivings about his personal abilities'. He was 'sustained through many misfortunes and disappointments by the blissful self-confidence and iron certitudes of the well-educated Scot'.[1] Indeed, there can be no Scot who has exercised a greater influence on landscape, popular architecture, and gardening than Loudon. His *Encyclopaedia of Cottage, Farm and Villa Architecture and Furniture*, published in 1833, had an enormous effect on taste, and helped to change the appearance of English houses and landscape from the first half of the nineteenth century.

Loudon embraced many innovations with enthusiasm, and the new cemeteries generally met with his approval. 'Cemeteries', he wrote, 'are increasing throughout the country; and, though many of these are not laid out in the manner which we think they ought to be, yet, as they multiply, they will excite the attention and criticism of thinking persons which will in the end lead to the adoption of a better taste.'[2]

From the beginnings of the cemetery movement, Loudon tried to influence developments, and his writings are full of references to cemeteries. In 1842 he wrote approvingly of the 'New Calton Burying-Ground' in Edinburgh. Here, 'scientific skill and good taste have contributed much to heighten the beauty of the place. The walks are neatly formed of gravel, tastefully edged with grass, kept smooth and firm by rolling, and frequently mown to keep it short. A circular-built watch-house, commanding a full view of the whole cemetery, which at night is lighted with gas, and the many ornamental tombstones, with the nicely planted roots and flowers showing the affectionate regards of surviving friends, fill the visitor with a pleasing and tender melancholy.'³ Yet what appealed to the practical Loudon most of all was 'Lamb's Receiving-Box', seven feet long, four feet broad, and thirty-two inches deep, in which earth from the grave was placed. The sides of the box were removable, so that when the coffin was placed in the grave, a side could be removed so that the earth ran freely into the grave. The tidiness of this invention ensured that there was no mess of soil around the new grave.

Loudon collated his notes, and in 1843 *The Gardener's Magazine* carried a series of articles on 'The Principles of Landscape-Gardening and of Landscape-Architecture applied to the Laying out of Public Cemeteries and the Improvement of Churchyards; including Observations on the Working and General Management of Cemeteries and Burial-Grounds'. This series was later published as a book.⁴

The stimulus for the work on cemeteries appears to have been a commission from the directors of a cemetery company at Cambridge to form a plan for the arrangement of the grounds. The main object of a burial-ground is, of course, 'the disposal of the remains of the dead in such a manner that their decomposition and return to the earth shall not prove injurious to the living, either by affecting health or by shocking feelings, opinions, or prejudices'. To Loudon a secondary object was 'the improvement of the moral sentiments and general taste of all classes and more especially of the great masses of society'.⁵

Decomposition was best achieved by interring a body in a wooden coffin in the free soil, in a grave five or six feet deep. This grave should be rendered secure from violation, and no body should have been placed in it previously. Loudon deplored the practice of burying several bodies in the same grave, and poured scorn on the modes of sepulture by which decomposition of a body or its union with the earth were prevented. He abhorred the use of leaden or iron coffins, and the practice of 'burying' in catacombs, vaults, and mausolea. 'We are of the opinion', he wrote, 'that the modes of burial which prevent the body mixing with the soil, which, for the sake of distinction, we shall call the sepulchral modes, cannot, on account of the danger to the living, be continued much longer in a highly civilized country, yet, in considering the conditions requisite for a complete cemetery suited to the present time, the various modes of sepulchral burial at present in use must be kept in view.'⁶

Loudon objected strongly to the re-use of graves after a limited time, which is surprising. He quoted Jewish, Quaker, and Moravian custom with approval, where single burial was usual, with no subsequent disturbance. He was more scathing about the practice of depositing bodies in leaden coffins in catacombs, owing to the dangers of putrefaction, and the tendency of gases to accumulate in lead coffins. 'Even in some of the public catacombs of the new London cemeteries explosions have been known to take place, and the undertaker obliged to be sent in order to resolder the coffin; which shows the disgusting nature of this mode of interment, and its danger to the living.'[7]

The security of graves was very important, until it became possible for surgeons to obtain cadavers legally. In some cases, security was effected by surrounding a graveyard with walls or railings; sometimes it was achieved by constructing watch-houses (Pl. 1); occasionally bodies were buried in walled graves covered with an iron grating or mort-safe over them (Pl. 2); sometimes great iron cases were erected over the grave; and occasionally iron boxes were dropped over the coffin until sufficient time had passed to render the body useless to the 'Resurrection Men'. In Scotland, where the medical schools had a voracious appetite for corpses, watchmen were employed to guard the burial-grounds. The entrance-gates to the churchyard of S. Michael, Dumfries, are flanked by gigantic gate-posts which are hollow to accommodate the watchmen (Pl. 3).

'The secondary object of cemeteries, that of *improving the moral feelings*',

Plate 1 Watch-house in the old graveyard of Cathcart, Glasgow (*The Author*)

Plate 2 Mort-safe in the old graveyard of Cathcart, Glasgow (*The Author*)

was of great concern to Loudon, 'for it must be obvious that the first step to rendering a churchyard a source of amelioration or instruction is to render it attractive'.[8] In Loudon's day, churchyards were often covered with a 'black unearthly-looking surface, so frequently disturbed by interments', that no grass would grow on it.[9] In the crowded cities, churchyards were often further disgraced by the emptying of chamber-pots out of adjoining houses. It was little wonder that Blair would state that his task was to 'paint the gloomy horrors of the tomb'.[10] He described the grave as a 'dread thing'. Of it, he wrote:

Men shiver when thou'rt nam'd: Nature appall'd,
Shakes off her wonted firmness. Ah! how dark
Thy long-extended realms, and rueful wastes!
Where nought but silence reigns, and night, dark night,
Dark as was chaos, ere the infant sun
Was roll'd together, or had try'd his beams
Athwart the gloom profound! The sickly taper,
By glimm'ring through thy low-brow'd misty vaults,
(Furr'd round with mouldy damps, and ropy slime)
Lets fall a supernumerary horror,
And only serves to make thy night more irksome.

It was the revolting horrors of the unsavoury vault and parish graveyard that Loudon sought to dispel. Washington Irving could ask why death should be clothed with unnecessary terrors, and why horrors should be spread around the tombs of those we love. According to him, the 'grave should be surrounded by every thing that might inspire tenderness and veneration for the dead, or that might win the living to virtue. It is the place, not of disgust and dismay, but of sorrow and meditation'. Coleridge, too, compared the 'unsightly manner in which our monuments are crowded together in the busy, noisy, unclean, and almost grassless churchyard of a large town' with the 'still seclusion of a Turkish cemetery'. Picton warned against a tendency 'in our anxiety to escape from gloom and horror', to 'run into the opposite extreme of meretricious gaudiness', a warning that might be heeded by the perpetrators of tombstone design today. 'Death and the grave are solemn and awful realities; they speak with a powerful and intelligible voice to the heart of every spectator, as being the common lot of all. Our cemeteries, then, should bear a solemn and soothing character, equally remote from fanatical gloom and conceited affectation.'[11]

It is clear that Loudon and most contemporary opinion approved of the cemetery of Père-Lachaise in Paris as a model, although Loudon noted that

Plate 3 Hollow gate-posts at the entrance to the churchyard of S. Michael, Dumfries, gave shelter to night-watchmen (*The Author*)

a report to the French Government of 1842 stated that much ground had been lost in consequence of the cemetery's not having been originally laid out on a rigid systematic plan, and the want of walks, of roads, and of drainage was noted, as was the dilapidated state of some of the monuments. These faults were shortly to be remedied.

Loudon quoted extensively from, indeed shamelessly plagiarized, *Necropolis Glasguensis*, a seminal work by his fellow-Scot, John Strang.[12] This book obviously provided Loudon with much of his material, even his inspiration, and Strang's insistence on the moral, improving, and educational aspects of cemeteries struck a chord in Loudon. Strang's prolix and lugubrious tome was really a tract to persuade public opinion of the wisdom of forming a large commercial cemetery on a hill adjacent to S. Mungo's Cathedral in Glasgow. Loudon acknowledged that churchyards had had little influence (up to that time) in 'improving the taste'. Yet a 'general cemetery in the neighbourhood of a town, properly designed, laid out, ornamented with tombs, planted with trees, shrubs, and herbaceous plants, all named, and the whole properly kept, might become a school of instruction in architecture, sculpture, landscape-gardening, arboriculture, botany, and in those important parts of general gardening, neatness, order, and high keeping'.[13] Indeed, some of the new London cemeteries at that time might be referred to as answering 'in some degree these various purposes, and more particularly the Abney Park Cemetery'. The latter contained 'a grand entrance in Egyptian Architecture; a handsome Gothic chapel; a number, daily increasing, of sculptural monuments; and one of the most complete arboretums in the neighbourhood of London, all the trees and shrubs being named'.[14] Thus instruction and education, so important in Strang's reasoning, became part of the general cemetery movement. Strang himself declared that the 'tomb has, in fact, been the great chronicler of taste throughout the world'.[15]

While Loudon's moral and educational arguments have a certain period charm, his practical views on the layout of cemeteries are of considerable interest, for he influenced the design of cemeteries and was responsible for laying out a few in his time. He also designed a curious monument to his father in the churchyard at Pinner that consists of an obelisk with a sarcophagus projecting from it.

Cemeteries, according to Loudon, should be at a distance from human dwellings, and should be situated 'in an elevated and airy' place, with a southern aspect, so that the surface should be dried by the sun. He considered subsoils to be of great importance, for cemeteries draining into public wells were a menace to health. He favoured a chalky or gravelly soil, where decomposition would be rapid. The London clays, with their moisture content, preserved bodies rather than allowed their rapid dissolution. All cemeteries should be secured by boundary walls or fences, ten or twelve feet high, 'to give the wall an architectural character'. Walls and piers would also carry the numbers and letters used as indexes to lines for the identification of plots. There ought to be one main entrance and one subsidiary gate.

In the laying out of the grounds the position of chapels, the road plan, and the accessibility to the whole of the cemetery were important. No part of the cemetery should be remote, either from the point of view of upkeep or of the desirability of graves. Good drainage was essential, and Loudon deplored the sodden parts of Kensal Green in winter. All cemeteries should be divided into sectors that could be easily identified, and these should in turn be subdivided into plots. Loudon emphasized the necessity of a coherent system of marking plots (sector A, plot 3, etc.), not only for ease of management, but for the keeping of records. He advocated a layout of 'double beds with green paths between', to facilitate ease of access to each grave, and to help the problem of surface drainage.

Chapels should be in conspicuous positions, as focal points. He was highly critical of Norwood Cemetery because both chapels were 'placed equally near the eye'. Lodges were important, for here there could be the residence of the superintendent and the records office. One lodge should be enough, and Loudon was critical of the two lodges at Nunhead Cemetery. He seems to have approved of the lodges at Abney Park, at Tower Hamlets, at Kensal Green, and at Brompton.

Trees and shrubs were important, but they should not 'impede the free circulation of the air and the drying effect of the sun'. Loudon advocated the planting of trees with 'conical shapes, like the cypress . . . associated with places of burial from time immemorial'. He favoured evergreens because the 'variety produced by deciduous and flowering trees is not favourable to the expression either of solemnity or grandeur'.[16] Deciduous trees also created problems in autumn, when the leaves had to be cleared. Loudon suggested that pines and firs, cypress, Irish yew, Swedish juniper, and other species would be most appropriate. Only evergreens with 'naturally dark foliage and narrow conical heads, or which admit of being pruned with little difficulty' should be planted.

Loudon disapproved of the planting in most cemeteries as being too much like 'pleasure-grounds'. He advocated the planting of 'no flowers at all' because he abhorred any ground that 'had the appearance of being dug or moved for the purpose of cultivation'. A state of quiet repose was essential.

He then turned his attention to the buildings of a cemetery. Chapels were important because the burial service was often read under cover, and thus bad weather could be avoided. It was necessary to have a bier in the chapel that could be fitted with rollers so that a coffin could be rotated after the ceremony. In Kensal Green Loudon described the catafalque there that could be turned round or lowered, depending on whether the coffin was to descend to the vaults or be carried outside. This machine was built by 'Mr Smith, Engineer, Princes Street, Leicester Square'.[17] In Norwood Cemetery, the catafalque was controlled, not by a screw mechanism, but by 'Bramah's hydraulic press', manufactured by Bramah, Prestage, and Ball, of 124 Piccadilly.

On gate-lodges, Loudon was adamant. 'The *entrance lodge* to a cemetery ought to comprise a room to serve as an office to contain the cemetery books, or, at least, the order book and register, and the map book, where, from the system of squares being employed, such a book is rendered necessary.' He was particularly impressed by the lodge at Tower Hamlets Cemetery, designed by Wyatt and Brandon, which he thought very convenient. The most appropriate cemetery lodge, according to Loudon, was that at Newcastle by 'Mr Dobson'. This lodge could 'never be mistaken either for an entrance to a public park or to a country residence'.[18]

Loudon then discussed other buildings. Vaults, he said, should be constructed in the face of a steep rock, where no drainage would be required, as at S. James's Cemetery in Liverpool. Catacombs above ground, as in Brompton or Kensal Green, were in 'bad taste'. When vaults were constructed with subdivisions into cells 'like bins in a wine-cellar', Loudon describes the cells as 'catacombs', though that term is also given to vaults or crypts not subdivided into cells. Each cell, once a coffin had been inserted, was sealed with brickwork or by a tablet on which there would be an inscription. Loudon noted with disapproval that in many new London cemeteries the cells or catacombs were often only closed with an open iron grating, the ends of the coffins being exposed to view. In the Brompton Cemetery, the whole of the side of the coffin was so exposed, as the cells were literally shelves. Loudon felt these modes of 'interment' were fraught with danger to the living.

He tells us much about the methods of construction of individual buildings within cemeteries. Private vaults, for example, could have steps leading down to the floor. The stair-well was covered with a flat stone, level, or slightly above the surface. In some cases, where the steps were under a path, the stone was concealed under this. Over the vault itself was a monument, most commonly a square tomb, or an altar-tomb. It is particularly interesting that Loudon should advocate such a big foundation for the headstone. He admired the regular verticality of headstones in Scotland and suggested good foundations for headstones in England.

A brick-lined grave is a substitute for a vault, but unlike the latter it differs from an ordinary grave in having the sides and ends constructed of brickwork or masonry, and in being covered by a large flat stone, technically called a ledger-stone. Brick-lined graves can be sufficiently wide for two coffins, but are generally only wide enough for one, and vary in depth from ten to twenty feet or more. The side walls have to be constructed as arches to take the strain of the soil outside, and engineering bricks are often used, as they are impervious to damp. When an interment takes place, the stone is loosened by levers, and removed on rollers. The coffin is then let down as in common graves. The sides of many brick graves have ledges that project from each side for retaining a flag-stone or slate between each coffin; in most cases there are no projections, but one coffin is prevented from resting on another by the insertion of two bars of iron in the side walls to support each coffin. Needless to say, time and rust have played havoc with most graves of this type. Loudon disapproved of this method, too, for hygienic reasons. He illustrated a typical brick grave, with openings in the side walls 'to permit the lateral diffusion of moisture and mephitic vapour'. Adjacent is a normal grave, so that the headstone would suffice for both graves, being inscribed on each side.

In respect of sepulchral monuments, Loudon was most particular. They ought, he wrote, 'whether mausoleums (which is a term only applied to the most sumptuous description of tombs), square tombs, ledger-stones with inscriptions, sarcophagi, pedestals, vases, urns, columns, obelisks, pillars, crosses, &c., to have the appearance of security and permanence, to exhibit two features: they ought to be perfectly erect or perpendicular, and they ought to rise from an architectural base'.[19] Such a foundation would have to be as deep as the adjoining grave or graves. In the case of vaults and brick graves, this foundation was supplied by the structure itself, but in most cemeteries, 'even in Père-Lachaise and Kensal Green', the greater part of the monuments had no other foundation than the moved soil. The consequence of this was, of course, that monuments started to lean, and gave any impression but that of permanence. Loudon recommended two brick or stone piers at the head of each grave, carried up from the bottom, and from twenty centimetres to over half a metre square, according to the depth. The lintel capping these piers would be the foundation of the headstone. Where a pedestal ornament of any kind was to be erected, one foundation-pier eighteen inches square should suffice, or, where there was no danger of the ground being moved, a nine-inch square pier would stop the memorial sinking. Loudon recommended a space half a metre wide between each double row of graves. When a suggestion was made to have a double line of brick graves, or to fill up a cemetery regularly, without allowing choice, then Loudon recommended a foundation-wall two feet in width, regularly carried up along the middle space, from one end of the line to the other, to support head-stones.

Loudon suggested that memorial-tablets, busts, reliefs, and other sculptures could serve to beautify chapels, boundary walls, and colonnades. All boundary walls should have letters and numbers set into them to identify the runs of graves and to facilitate plot identification. Drainage of cemeteries was most important to make grave-digging easier and to avoid the scandal of water-filled graves or vaults. Loudon advised cesspools under gratings for retaining sand and gravel, so that these could be cleaned each year. He discussed everything, from tools to grave-boards, and no aspect of cemetery design and management escaped his eagle eye. Grave-boards were necessary where a grave was to be dug more than five or six feet deep, to prevent the sides from caving in. The grave-boards, designed by 'Mr Northern, superintendent of the Tower Hamlets Cemetery', were illustrated by Loudon. The sides were hinged, so as to form a concave side to resist the lateral pressure of the earth in the manner of an arch. The boards and end-pieces were joined together, and let down from the top, one above the other, as in well-sinking. The shuttering was then removed as the grave was filled in. One side was hinged, and the other was retained in its angular position by strong iron plates. Both boards were fastened to the ends by iron pins which dropped into eyes at the angles.

Loudon's concern with detail is astonishing, and his practical mind approved of all sorts of gadgets invented to ease the running of cemeteries. He advocated no burials in land that had been used for interment before, unless two metres of soil lay between the first burial and the second. This obsession with hygiene led him to suggest filling brick graves with earth in exactly the same manner, although he grudgingly admitted that if each coffin were hermetically sealed in compartments, separated from its neighbours by flagstones or slate panels set in cement, then a great many coffins might be got into one grave. However, with characteristic foresight, he said 'there is always the possibility of desecration at some future period', and advocated earth burial only. He was right, as any visitor to the London cemeteries in the 1960s and 1970s can testify. Loudon would 'allow of few or no catacombs or vaults in buildings, and certainly none in or under churches, or other places where assemblies of human beings were held'. Indeed, he felt that the boxing up of dead bodies 'as if in defiance to the law of nature' was 'disgusting and in bad taste'. He advocated a heavy tax on this mode of interment, and that all bodies then in vaults or catacombs should be taken out and buried in the free soil. Loudon felt he would 'encourage the erection of handsome monuments, and the inscription on them of moral sentiments, the former to improve the taste, and the latter to cultivate the heart and affections'. Cemeteries should at all times be kept in the best possible order. The grass should be kept short and smooth by regular mowing, and all paths, drains, buildings, and planting should be kept in thorough repair. In order to ensure the keeping of monuments in good condition, Loudon advocated the payment of a sum to the cemetery companies for upkeep in perpetuity. Currency in Victorian England was stable.

Loudon was confident that, if his ideas were implemented, all cemeteries would be as healthy as gardens or pleasure-grounds, and indeed would form the most interesting of all places for 'contemplative recreation'. Cemeteries could be 'rendered inviting' by being ornamental and 'highly kept', and it would be desirable to 'have a considerable display of monuments on the borders of roads and main walks, and along the boundary wall'. To Loudon, the finest of ancient monuments in the churchyards of Scotland were the sepulchral structures projecting from the walls of Greyfriars churchyard in Edinburgh, and in the cathedral graveyard in Glasgow. Yet these themselves celebrated interments in the free soil, and were 'superb architectural and sculptural compositions'. He contrasted these splendid Jacobean memorials with the monuments over brick vaults in the London cemeteries. Loudon felt it should be a general rule that handsome monuments should be placed at particular points of view, such as at angles formed by the junction of roads, as eye-catchers.

The need for the keeping of orderly records is stressed in Loudon's work. The 'curator' of a cemetery 'ought to be a man of intelligence, and of cultivated feelings, with a taste for and some knowledge of gardening'; for all which reasons Loudon thought 'the situation one well adapted for a middle-aged gardener'.[20] Loudon was practical about cemeteries, for he wrote that 'the greater the number of present cemeteries, the greater the number of future public gardens'. All cemeteries, once filled, should be closed as burial grounds, and in a few years opened as public walks or gardens, *but all gravestones and all architectural or sculpural monuments should be retained and kept in repair at public expense.* He was therefore mindful of the future need to conserve cemeteries.

No human dwellings should be built within cemeteries, except the entrance lodge. Once again, Loudon argued vehemently against the building of vaults and catacombs, not only for reasons of expense, where such burial modes were seen as being 'high–class', but from the point of view of hygiene. The inevitability of eventual desecration is stressed, and the examples of the crypts of London churches adds weight to Loudon's arguments.

Loudon was much concerned with the burial of the poor; on health grounds he was opposed to common graves being sunk in the London clay. He advocated the burial of London's poor outside London, as the price of land within ten miles of London was much too high to allow their burial in the London cemeteries. With remarkable foresight he suggested the purchase of eight hundred hectares of poor land at Woking, where the gravelly soil was ideal, and would enable yews, junipers, pines, and firs to grow. This idea was obviously the beginning of Brookwood Cemetery, near Woking. As an alternative, he suggested 'temporary cemeteries' for paupers that, once filled, could revert to agriculture, subject to safeguards concerning the future use of the land. Such cemeteries would preferably, or even essentially, be on a railway line, so that large numbers of bodies could be moved at any one time. Loudon could see no reason why this concept of funerals by train could not be an encouragement to companies to set up large monumental cemeteries, as well as temporary ones, on poor soils at great distances from London, along the railway lines. Union workhouses could have portions of their gardens used for burial, to be restored to cultivation eventually. Loudon also suggested that landowners should be encouraged to bury on their own grounds in the free soil, provided proper records were kept.

The cemeteries of Frankfurt-am-Main and Munich were observed to 'add greatly to the convenience, economy, and salubrity of persons having only small dwelling-houses, and moderate incomes'. In Frankfurt the cemetery was entered through an open propylaeum between two wings. In one wing was the residence of the overseer and his assistants, while in the other were ten cells in which coffined bodies were deposited for some days before interment. As a precaution against premature inhumation, cords communicating with bells were fixed to fingers of the dead, so that the least movement would be detected. In Munich, the *Leichenhaus* held the dead in open coffins for forty-eight hours before interment.

After this examination of Loudon's opinions on cemeteries, it is all the more interesting to turn to his design for a cemetery at Cambridge, based on his report to the directors of the cemetery company. The ground, just over one hectare in extent, was inspected by Loudon in November 1842. The site was flat and well drained, the soil being a blue clay. The object of the cemetery company was to form a cemetery for the middle classes at a cost, including the purchase price, of £2,000. Loudon proposed a scheme, the most important part of which was that no part of a coffin or its contents should ever be exposed to view after burial. Since the cemetery was intended for all sects, Loudon opposed consecration by any one party. He proposed a lodge, a shed, a yard, and a chapel as essential. He further suggested that the frontage, and a portion of the land along the Histon Road, should not be included in the plan in the first instance, in case the cemetery should fail commercially, but that the frontage should be added later. Since the site was rectangular, he proposed an orderly rectilinear arrangement of paths and plots with trees planted around the perimeter and along the main walks. Trees with narrow conical shapes, such as cypress, were preferable, and indeed all varieties should be evergreen, to avoid maintenance problems and so that light and air could get to the surface of the ground. Loudon reluctantly allowed for ample space for vaults, but recommended against the construction of any catacombs above ground.

The designs, estimates, and plans of the lodges and chapel were by E. Buckton Lamb, architect, and Loudon's collaborator, who estimated the costs of buildings at £1,000. The 'proposed general arrangement of the grounds' (Pl. 4) shows the entire site surrounded by a holly hedge. The main entrance is at the west end, opening into the Histon Road, and a secondary entrance is shown on the New Huntingdon Road. On either side of the main entrance is a garden for the cultivation of flowers for sale. The chapel is in the centre, and turning space for hearses is provided. The ground at the top left-hand corner is reserved for superfluous earth, and for the storage of bricks and other materials. Borders were formed, six metres wide, planted with trees at regular distances. Spaces in the borders could be let as the most desirable plots for burial. Between every two trees there could be one burial-space, rendered ornamental by monuments. This space is divided into beds six metres wide, with paths between them just over a metre wide, and a space under a metre wide, raised about eight centimetres, is shown in the middle of each bed, on which space all headstones could be erected on a foundation of brickwork carried up from the bottom of each grave. Thus the verticality of monuments was assured, and each monument would stand independent of each grave. The paths between the beds are connected with a common path of under two metres' width which surrounds the beds and communicates with the main or central road. A funeral could thus be performed at any point without once deviating from the path or treading on the graves.

The planting consists of Taurian pines along the main avenue. This species was chosen because of its dark and solemn air, and the tree could easily be trimmed to form a conical shape. The trees at the corners of the space around the chapel are Cedars of Lebanon, the trees bordering the terrace walk being Irish yews. Around the ground at the top are Taurian or black Austrian pines. Should catacombs be demanded later, Loudon suggested that a range of these could be substituted for the curved walk, thus forming a 'handsome arcade with vaults behind and underneath'.

The designs for the entrance lodge and chapel were provided by Lamb 'both in the Gothic and Italian styles'. The directors chose Gothic, but Loudon preferred to illustrate the Italian design. The entrance gates and lodge contained a porch, an office, a living-room, kitchen, and an open court and shed. The first floor contained three bedrooms and closets (Pl. 5). The chapel itself was to be a pretty little building, to be constructed of stone, with dressed quoins, plinth, entablature, and aedicules, but with rubble walls (Pl. 6).

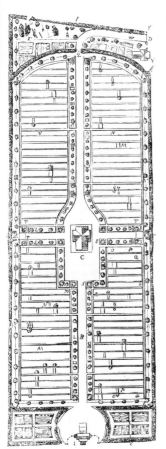

Plate 4 Plan of Loudon's design for the Cambridge Cemetery (*Author's Collection*)

Plate 5 Entrance lodge in the Italian style, designed by E. B. Lamb for the Cambridge Cemetery (*Author's Collection*)

Loudon envisaged deep graves, some eight metres deep, to allow for two metres of earth over each coffin, and thus he calculated the cemetery would be full in sixty years. It is clear that his preoccupation with hygiene was not likely to provide a good economic basis, and the directors do not appear to have adhered to his recommendations in this respect.

After Cambridge, Loudon designed a cemetery on hilly ground, but with grave layouts based on the same principles as those he had adopted at Cambridge. The great extent of the borders in this cemetery rendered it 'particularly eligible for being planted as an arboretum' (Pl. 7).

From a consideration of his own designs, it was logical that he should turn his attention to a criticism of the eight cemeteries that had so far been laid out in London. He reiterated his objection to catacombs, and to all interments therein. In the cemeteries of London, he declared, 'so great an expense has been incurred in the catacomb department, that it must operate as a serious drawback to the profits of the shareholders'. This was wisdom indeed, as all catacombs are wasting assets that are expensive to maintain. Loudon also criticized the laying bare of coffins in new interments, and emphasized the offensiveness and dangers of disturbing the earth less than two metres above a recent burial. Loudon suggested that graves should be as deep as wells to ensure that layers of soil between coffins were adequate.

He objected to the system of laying out cemeteries in imaginary squares, for it did not allow of an obvious order and arrangement of graves, and made mapping and registration difficult. Frequently graves could only be found with the assistance of a member of the cemetery staff. All the London cemeteries appeared confused in their layout; most, being on clay, were inadequately drained, and Loudon advocated a clear, logical system of layout, where drains would be placed under paths.

Plate 6 Chapel in the Italian style, designed by E. B. Lamb for the Cambridge Cemetery (*Author's Collection*)

Plate 7 Design for Laying
Out and Planting a Cemetery
in Hilly Ground (*Author's
Collection*)

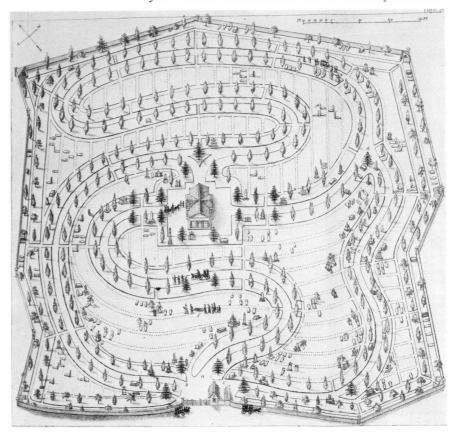

The planting of all the cemeteries was 'highly objectionable' to Loudon, as being 'too much in the style of a common pleasure-ground, both in regard to the disposition of trees and shrubs, and the kinds planted'. Clumps of trees should be avoided, he declared, as it was impracticable to form graves in clumps and belts of trees. The South Metropolitan Cemetery at Norwood was advertised in an engraving, of which Loudon made a copy (Pl. 8),

Plate 8 South Metropolitan
Cemetery, Norwood, planted
in the Pleasure-Ground Style
(*Author's Collection*)

Plate 9 The South Metropolitan Cemetery, Norwood, planted in the Cemetery Style, as proposed by Loudon (*Author's Collection*)

showing the cemetery 'Planted in the Pleasure-Ground style'. Loudon published his own version of this view 'Planted in the Cemetery Style', showing his ideals of evergreen trees that were more like continental and eastern cemetery designs (Pl. 9). The cemetery at Eyub, near Constantinople, had planting of cypress-like trees. Turkish cemeteries were generally places of public resort, and the chief promenade in the evenings for the inhabitants of Pera was the cemetery, 'planted with noble cypresses', and 'thickly set in many places with Turkish monuments'. Opulent Turks had their graves railed in, and often a building over them, in some of which lights were kept constantly burning. Turkish cemeteries were generally out of cities, on rising ground, planted with cedars, cypresses, and odoriferous shrubs. Graves of males were usually adorned with turbans at the heads of the flat tombstones, and nearly all had plants growing from the centres of the stones.

Persia was celebrated for its mausolea, but Loudon found the cemetery of Hafiz particularly pleasing. This was square and spacious, shaded by poplars (a rare tree in Persia) and surrounded by a brick wall. Individual tombs covered the ground. In China, the high lands where rice could not be cultivated were set aside for burial, and Loudon illustrated two examples of Chinese cemeteries. From these examples he felt he could further justify his advocacy of evergreen trees in cemeteries on historical precedent.

From cemeteries he turned his attention to churchyards. 'The intellectual and moral influence which churchyards are calculated to have on the rural population', he felt, would not be disputed. Loudon deplored the unkempt condition of churchyards in his own day, and observed that the cause of their untidiness was that they had never been laid out to a systematic plan. He demonstrated how paths could be laid in a churchyard without removing any headstones or other monuments. Disused churchyards could be planted as a cemetery garden, and new grounds could be added for burial (Pl. 10).

Plate 10 Churchyard no longer used for burial, planted as a cemetery garden, with a new piece of ground added and laid out (*Author's Collection*)

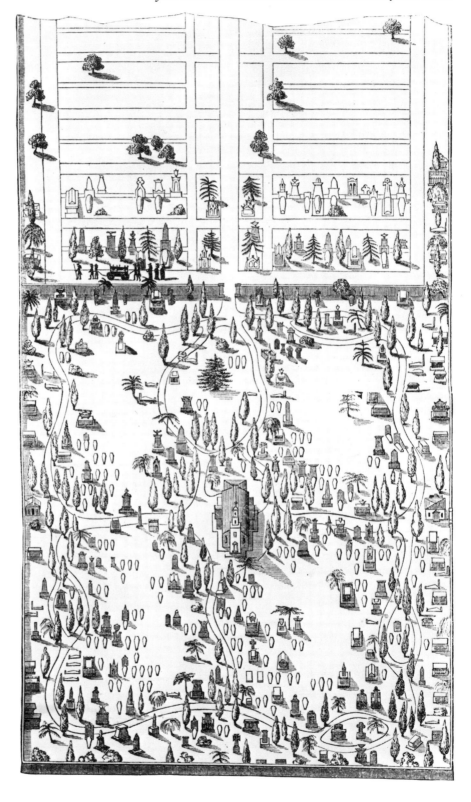

Adequate drainage, records, foundations, and upkeep were advised, much on the lines of his cemetery recommendations.

Loudon designed a churchyard 'adapted for an agricultural Parish'. He illustrated the ground plan of this, which shows an 'isometrical' view (Pl. 11). A wall protects the enclosure, and there is only one entrance. The trees are Cedar of Lebanon, yews, thorns, and cypresses. Irish yew, Irish juniper, Swedish juniper, and other varieties were recommended. Burials without memorials were to be encouraged in the borders. In all this Loudon's sense of order and symmetry is displayed.

Throughout his writings, Loudon's sense of practicality is emphasized. Styles, and arguments about styles, were of little importance to him, except in that they could have an educational purpose. As education improved and became available to everyone, Loudon felt that styles as such would cease to be of any relevance. In any case, fitness for function was infinitely more important to Loudon than style, as the illustrations to his copious works should demonstrate. The great nineteenth-century cemeteries were laid out to satisfy a need, and though the first cemeteries were highly ornamental and picturesque, their style was soon superseded by the huge, almost rural, cemeteries of Brookwood and Little Ilford. Brookwood might be seen as the final realization of Loudon's philosophy, for this huge cemetery is on its own in country surroundings, and is planted in line with Loudon's theories. The fact that Brookwood was designed to be served by railway would have appealed to the practical Scot. Only twenty-five years lie between the founding of Kensal Green and the laying out of Brookwood, yet the differences in scale and in style are immense.

Loudon's ideas were strongly moral. He had faith in education and in liberal–humanitarian ideas of progress, social reform, education, and moral improvement. Like Archibald Alison, he had a firm belief in the value of common sense, and in the ability of the ordinary man to discern beauty. Education could give all men limitless associations: the function of the artist was to awaken responses to those associations. The cult of the associations of a place with a person, so much a concern of the Italian Renaissance, was important to Alison and to Loudon. The association of a house with the place of residence of a person 'whose memory we admire' would start a sequence of improving thoughts. 'The delight with which we recollect the traces of their lives, blends itself insensibly with the emotions which the scenery excites; and the admiration which these recollections afford, seems to give a *kind of sanctity* [my italics] to the place where they dwelt, and converts everything into beauty which appears to have been connected with them.'[21]

The idea of associations with the dead, and with worthy memories, was central to much of the thinking behind nineteenth-century cemetery design. Loudon believed that architecture, beauty, scale, and style were not concerned with aesthetics, but with fitness for function.

Some twenty pages of Loudon's tome on cemeteries were devoted to lists of plants that he felt were appropriate for use in burial-grounds. It is also interesting to note that he considered the lodge to the cemetery at Newcastle-upon-Tyne as 'peculiarly appropriate for a cemetery, on account

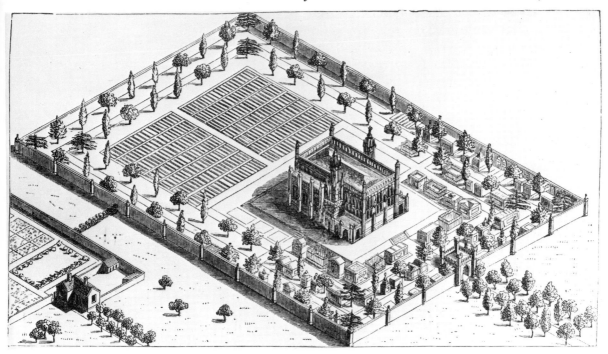

Plate 11 'Isometrical' view of a churchyard adapted for an agricultural parish (*Author's Collection*)

of its church-like towers'. The design was by John Dobson, who contributed to Loudon's *Encyclopaedia of Cottage Architecture*.

Loudon greatly admired the urban effect of the Glasgow Necropolis, and particularly the verticality of the monuments. He recognized that adequate foundations were necessary, and found Scotland greatly superior to England in this respect. He drew attention to Edinburgh, Glasgow, and Dumfries as examples where fine monuments had an added dignity by remaining sound and upright. The great Parisian cemetery of Père-Lachaise had been an influential example to the founders of the British cemeteries, and John Strang was a fervent admirer of this magnificent necropolis, but Loudon was critical of the haphazard way in which graves were laid out and sold, and felt the cemetery would be difficult to maintain.

In 1843 Loudon was employed by the Town Council of Southampton to make a plan for a general cemetery.[22] For this he devised a plan to provide for the superfluous earth dug out of graves. The pile of superfluous earth at Kensal Green was 'enormous', and could not be sold, as it was consecrated ground. Loudon devised a system where alternate beds were to be used first, the soil being spread over the cemetery so that levels were everywhere adjusted and raised to the heights of the beds already used. Eventually the surfaces of the compartments would be raised above the natural surface, and ramps would be provided. Of course, individual headstones would have to be raised continually 'at a moderate expense' as the ground level was raised.

Loudon's commission to prepare plans for Southampton Cemetery was his only one for a public cemetery. It will be recalled that he had submitted plans and a report for the new Cambridge Cemetery, a private concern, and months before his death he was to design a cemetery for the Rector of Bath

Abbey. These three cemeteries, one public, one private and speculative, and one ecclesiastical, constitute Loudon's *oeuvre* in cemetery design, excluding those cemeteries on which he advised, and those where his ideas were influential. The Bath Abbey Cemetery is by far the most beautiful of the three, owing to its planting and to the idyllic views from it. The Cambridge Cemetery is recognizable from the original designs, with some changes to the planting and considerable demolition. The Southampton Cemetery, however, is scarcely identifiable from Loudon's Report to the Committee of 31 August 1843.[23] As Miss Melanie Simo has pointed out, the history of the planning and development of the cemetery stresses the wide gap between Loudon's ideas about cemeteries and those of contemporary received opinion. Loudon's arguments and designs were difficult to accept for two reasons: they were not conducive to the picturesque, and they were not based on 'Christian' premises. His approach was hygienic and essentially utilitarian.

The Corporation of Southampton submitted a petition for a municipal cemetery which received the Royal Assent on 6 July 1843.[24] Only a week later Mr Doswell, Surveyor, was instructed to identify some six hectares in the south-west corner of Southampton Common, and on 24 July Loudon explained his ideas before the Committee. He was then instructed to proceed with the plans. Drainage was Loudon's first concern, and he based his scheme on Captain James Vetch's reply to Edwin Chadwick.[25] The layout of the cemetery differed only slightly from his earlier design for the smaller Cambridge cemetery. However, the central avenue would be intersected by several cross-walks rather than two, as at Cambridge. The site for the chapels was about a third of the distance from the main entrance lodge on the south, as opposed to the centrally sited Cambridge chapel (now demolished). With economy in mind, Loudon had planned the Southampton chapels in one block, orientated east-west, with an arcaded gallery around the building to house the memorials. Areas for vaults were planned along the east and west boundaries of the cemetery, facing the respective Anglican and Nonconformist chapels, and Loudon suggested that if catacombs were to be provided under the chapels, they should only be used for the temporary storage of coffins.

The character of the cemetery was to be like that of a solemn garden. The ground was to be sown with rye-grass and with white clover. Trees, hollies, and thorns existing on the site were to be conserved. The borders of the main walks were to be planted with cypresses or with Irish yews.

Loudon was paid £34 3s 4d for his travel expenses, Report, and Plans. He did not live to see his designs realized, however. The committee members seem to have had a good opinion of Loudon, but they did not adopt his advice unreservedly. In February 1844 they considered alternative plans for the cemetery by W. Page and by W. H. Rogers. They accepted Rogers's plan on 27 February with some reservations. However, the original conception by Loudon, and Rogers's amendments, were arbitrarily altered by the committee. In addition, the Bishop of Winchester ordered the chapels to be built separately on sites completely surrounded by their respective consecrated and unconsecrated portions. Indeed, the cemetery today hardly fits the description given in a local paper two days after it had been consecrated:

> No site ever selected for a Cemetery has been so favourably situated as this, being backed by a dense mass of wood, having in front some of the finest park scenery in England, and disclosing in all directions, save the Hill Lane side, a variety of views, yet in quietness of tone, which harmonises most agreeably with the associations belonging to the place . . .
> Mr W. H. Rogers has contrived to unite all the requirements of a cemetery, as regards plotting out of the ground, giving easy access by paths to every part, and yet has deprived it of all formal character, and contrived to retain the fine trees which were already on the land.[26]

Loudon's design was too rigidly planned, and perhaps too urban in character for contemporary taste. His cemetery was intended for use by the living as well as a depository for the dead. Fairly big, open areas, devoid of memorials and tall plants, would allow the ground to dry easily, and so aid decomposition of the interred corpses. The cypresses and yews, that were intended to flank the perimeter and the smaller walks, would not impede the free passage of air, while the borders that were to be laid out with varieties of plants would become a veritable arboretum. Here, the committee appears to have shared Loudon's enthusiasm for trees. In May 1846 *The Hampshire Advertiser* waxed almost lyrical on the planting of the cemetery:

> Here are to be seen, for instance, the largest oak, thorn and holly on the Common. The shrubs are so disposed as to form vistas, and each plot or subdivision is an arboretum in itself, consisting of hundreds of varieties, among which are to be found some of the handsomest of the Coniferae tribe, as Pinus Cambra, Excelsa Douglasii, Cephalonia, Norinda, Cedar of Lebanon, and Laricis. Here are all the weeping trees of the lime, willow, birch, Chinese ash, elm, poplar, and oak, also the Irish junipers, arbor vitae, new hollies, the elegant juniperus, repandus, ditto chinense, cyprus, laburnums (six varieties), flowering acacias, almonds, thorns, many sorts of arbutus, scarlet and yellow chestnuts, hemlock spruce, hybrid rhododendrons and magnolias and others. These are all planted twenty feet apart along the borders of the walks, and when they have grown to a proper size will have a most beautiful effect.

Loudon would no doubt have objected to the weeping willows. These lugubrious trees were associated with water, and so were inappropriate for a cemetery that was supposed to be properly drained. He would have approved of the arboretum, however, especially since it was to be maintained by the municipality 'at the expense of all, for the benefit of all'.

In his description of his works at Southampton we find a startling side to Loudon, for he refers to the suffering of 'bodies to be decomposed in the soil' giving way to the 'practice of burning'. Loudon was convinced that cremation would be adopted for the disposal of 'the great mass of the dead

... much sooner than even the most enlightened people' of his time could imagine. 'Every large town will have a funeral pile, constructed on scientific principles, instead of a cemetery; and the ashes may be preserved in urns, or applied to the roots of a favourite plant.'[27]

Loudon was not to see his prophecy fulfilled, for he died on 14 December 1843, shortly after completing his book on cemeteries, and was buried in the General Cemetery of All Souls, Kensal Green. His work on cemeteries had enormous and lasting influence, however, not only in respect of the mode of layout of grave-plots, but especially in relation to the planting of evergreens. His advocacy of cemeteries outside London to be reached by train eventually gave rise to Brookwood Cemetery and to the Great Northern Cemetery. His amazing far-sightedness has been proved right in regard to cremation too, although what he would have said about the design of contemporary crematoria remains a matter for agreeable speculation.

9

Other great nineteenth-century cemeteries in America and Europe.

*Dublin; the United States of America; Italy;
further problems and reforms; funerals by
train; Australia*

There is a certain frame of mind to which a cemetery is, if not an antidote, at least an allcviation. If you are in a fit of the blues, go nowhere else.
ROBERT LOUIS STEVENSON: *Immortelles*

John Strang, in his lugubrious tome *Necropolis Glasguensis*,[1] observed that 'amid the green glades and gloomy cypresses which surround and overshadow the vast variety of sepulchral ornaments of *Père La Chaise*, the contemplative mind' would be suitably impressed by sights and by emotions.

Many cities in Europe and America experienced problems of a similar nature to those in Britain. Necropoleis had to be built and laid out to accommodate the dead.[2] In most towns legislation was enacted to prohibit or drastically reduce intramural and churchyard interment. The great cemetery of Père-Lachaise influenced design in the British Isles and in America. French cemeteries as a whole tend to be much more formal in layout than those in Britain or America. Père-Lachaise appealed to reformers because it combined decency, hygiene, and the picturesque with a romantic English landscape style. The urban character of many French cemeteries is also found in Louisiana, in Scotland, and in Italy. Provincial France has cemeteries containing tombs of iron and glass that give a curious atmosphere of macabre allotments, although the cemetery chapels are often in an austere, no-nonsense Neoclassical style (Pl. 1).

The English landscape tradition proved a potent model for cemetery designers, except in Southern Europe, where the *Campo-Santo* type of walled and cloistered cemetery had long been established, and gave rise to the urban cemetery that was truly a necropolis. The high density of burial in Italian cemeteries, and the custom of letting *loculi* in vaults ensured that buildings rather than landscape predominated. Jewish cemeteries are not normally planted with trees because of the possibility of roots disturbing the bodies. The picturesque qualities of the Old Jewish Cemetery in Prague derive from the walled fifteenth-century enclosure with the myriad tombstones, often Baroque in style, and the fact that older graves were

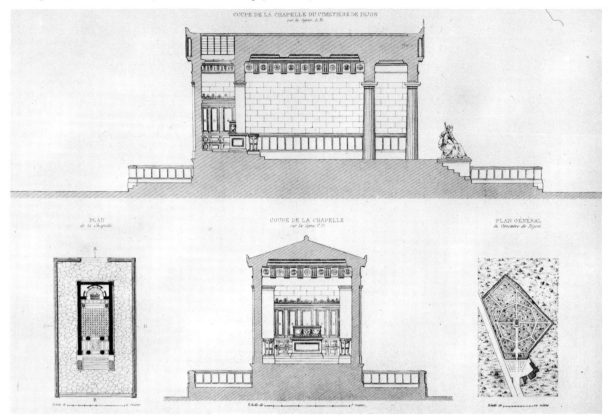

covered with soil to accommodate later burials. The trees that shade the tombstones today have seeded themselves.

Liverpool, Glasgow, and London developed their cemeteries at almost the same time. During the period 1820–1840 many cemeteries were formed throughout Europe and America, and this chapter will describe some of the most important layouts and buildings. Père-Lachaise was never far away from the minds of the designers of these pioneer cemeteries, as we shall see.

Mount Jerome in Dublin, for example, is perhaps more like Père-Lachaise in character than any other cemetery more consciously modelled on it. Certainly, the grandeur and bare urban quality of the Glasgow Necropolis are peculiarly Scottish, and owe little to French precedent, despite Strang's polemic. Dublin at the time was the second city of the Empire, and experienced the familiar overcrowding of graveyards, especially when the cholera epidemics struck. The promotions in Glasgow, Liverpool, and London were known, and influenced the formation of the first cemeteries in Dublin apart from the old churchyards. Ireland had a rich heritage of monumental sculpture erected by the Anglo-Irish in the cathedrals and parish churches.[3] The first private-enterprise cemeteries in Dublin were founded by Protestants. Perhaps the finest of these is Mount Jerome Cemetery, one of the most lovely of all the cemeteries in the British Isles. Founded by a joint-stock company, it is beautifully and serenely planted, setting off the classical tombs to great effect. There are considerable ranges of catacombs that give an urban quality to the cemetery (Pl. 2). The

Plate 1 Cemetery chapel at Dijon, designed by Saintpère (*Author's Collection*)

266

Plate 2 A range of vaults in
Mount Jerome Cemetery,
Dublin (*The Author*)

Plate 3 Neoclassical tombs
(derived from French designs
in Père-Lachaise) in Mount
Jerome Cemetery, Dublin
(*Dr Maurice Craig*)

Plate 4 Round tower over the tomb of Daniel O'Connell in Glasnevin Cemetery, Dublin (*The Author*)

Neoclassical tombs are very French in inspiration, like the beautiful sarcophagus on a podium in memory of Thomas Drummond, whose last words were:

> Bury me in Ireland, the land of my Adoption,
> I have loved her well, and served her faithfully.

Other classical tombs might well have been transported from Italy or Greece via Père-Lachaise to this peaceful Irish cemetery (Pl. 3). Neoclassicism, especially of the French variety, appealed to the architects and sculptors who embellished Mount Jerome, and a strongly vermiculated rustication serves as a base to the monuments.

Contemporary with Mount Jerome, which was essentially for Protestants, is Glasnevin Cemetery, Dublin, also founded in 1832, largely through the demands of Daniel O'Connell. His monument, a replica of a round tower, stands sentinel over his grave (Pl. 4). The tower was begun in 1847 as part of a project for a group of buildings suggested by George Petrie, but only the tower was completed. Glasnevin also has considerable and extensive ranges of catacombs, or individual mausolea, partially underground, but it differs from Mount Jerome in favouring Celtic crosses, the Romanesque style of architecture, and a very open, spacious layout, much more of a garden cemetery than the urbane classical peace of Mount Jerome. The entrances, offices, and chapel were completed in 1878 to designs by J. J. McCarthy. The chapel is Irish Romanesque in style, and is constructed of granite and limestone.[4] Near the chapel are two distinguished monuments in the Romanesque style, including the tomb of Archibishop McCabe by G. C. Ashlin, erected in 1887 (Pl. 5). Glasnevin is more akin to Green-Wood, to the City of London Cemetery, and to North American cemeteries than to its direct ancestor, Père-Lachaise.

It is interesting to compare the British attitudes of the 1850s with those of the United States of America in the late 1830s. The early settlers in the American colonies had no problems with burial until the development of towns. Traditional European attitudes prevailed, and interment took place in churches or in churchyards. A familiar pattern followed when the towns expanded, and the original churchyards proved too small for burials. Scandalous, unhealthy, and horrific conditions were common, and it became necessary to build cemeteries outside the towns. The French settlers in Louisiana had formed cemeteries outside the towns from necessity, but rational solutions were not to develop in the rest of the United States until almost exactly the same time as the joint-stock companies were laying out cemeteries in Britain.

Mount Auburn Cemetery near Cambridge, Massachusetts, was one of the first cemeteries to be established in the States. It was the first *landscaped* cemetery in America, as opposed to the more urban cemeteries of Louisiana,

Plate 5 Romanesque architecture in Glasnevin Cemetery, Dublin. *Right J. J. McCarthy's chapel. The tombs are those of Roman Catholic Archibishops. In the background is Archibishop McCabe's tomb by G. C. Ashlin, erected in 1887 (The Author)*

Plate 6 Egyptian Revival entrance to Mount Auburn Cemetery (*Author's Collection*)

and was directly inspired by Père-Lachaise. It dates from 1831, and was conceived by Jacob Bigelow, a botanist and poet, author of *American Medical Botany*. True to the ideals of J. C. Loudon, Mount Auburn was backed by the Massachusetts Horticultural Society for the purpose of creating 'a rural cemetery and experimental garden'.[5] The site was some forty metres above the Charles River, and had a fine view of Boston. Wealthy Bostonians subscribed to this cemetery, and Bigelow designed the Egyptian Revival gates, described in an 1846 guide-book as 'in imitation essentially of some of the gateways of Thebes and Denderah'. (Pl. 6).

Plate 7 Chapel and Hall of Fame at Mount Auburn Cemetery (*Author's Collection*)

Plate 8 'Proposed Entrance to the Ground of the General Cemetery Company by B. Ferrey' (*Author's Collection*)

The Chapel and Hall of Fame was built *c.* 1838, and is in a curious style of Dissenters' Perpendicular Gothic (Pl. 7). Many of the mouldings are oddly Egyptian, however, and several American cemeteries favoured Egyptian Revival as a style, though Pugin had lampooned this mode. The Grove Street Cemetery gates at New Haven, Connecticut, for example, were erected between 1845 and 1848 to designs by Henry Austin in a robust Egyptian manner. Egyptian Revival had been out of favour in England at least a decade before, but the style lingered on in the United States, especially in relation to funerary architecture. A 'Proposed entrance to the Ground of the General Cemetery Compy. by B. Ferrey' of approximately contemporary date shows an essay in the Early English style of architecture. England was thus Gothic-minded at an earlier stage (Pl. 8). Yet Mount

271

Auburn and Green-Wood had parts that were astonishingly reminiscent of Père-Lachaise in the 1830s and 1840s. An engraving from N. Cleaveland's and Cornelia Walter's *Green-Wood and Mount Auburn*, published in New York in 1847, shows the Arcadian landscape to perfection.

Philadelphia and Green-Wood in Brooklyn, New York, soon followed. When the proposals to form a cemetery at Green-Wood were first made, the intention was to set up a joint-stock company modelled on British lines, and shares were to be of $100 each. The total capital needed was over $250,000, and discussions concerning finance were protracted and heated. The puritan consicence was strong, however, and the whole conception of forming a company was denounced as unsavoury. Eventually trustees were appointed by the Legislature of the State of New York to a body corporate. The charter was granted by an Act of the Legislature dated 18 April 1838. The niceties of raising capital are interesting, for funds were derived from the giving of bonds and by pledging the proceeds as payment. No profits would be amassed by any individual, and all thoughts of speculative developments or gain from death were banished.

The hilly site of Green-Wood Cemetery was not dissimilar to that of Père-Lachaise, for it was well wooded and beautiful, as well as being large. The spacious grounds and dominance of nature were important assets, and the men behind the cemetery promotion were determined to enhance these to attract New Yorkers to bury their dead among trees and shrubs rather than in the unsavoury graveyards of the city. Before the establishment of Green-Wood, New Yorkers experienced similar horrors to those familiar to Londoners, Glaswegians, and Parisians. Outbreaks of cholera and other diseases took a fearful toll in early-nineteenth-century New York, and an intolerable amount of overloading was experienced in city churchyards. It must not be forgotten that in 1839 New York had a population of well over 250,000, and at times of crisis and epidemics was often forced to bury its dead in its cemeteries at Mount Auburn or Laurel Hill. The latter was one of the most beautiful of early American cemeteries, and was incorporated in 1836 as a result of an Act of the Pennsylvania Legislature. The cemetery contains many distinguished monuments.

Green-Wood Cemetery was carefully surveyed and divided into small lots, with a margin between each lot. These lots were sold, and so the capital was recouped. The man behind the planning of Green-Wood was Henry Pierrepoint who was appointed in 1835 to be chairman of a commission to lay out the streets of the city. He reserved land for a cemetery, and this eventually became Green-Wood. Pierrepoint took as his inspiration the great cemetery of Père-Lachaise, but more immediately his model was Mount Auburn which he had visited in 1832, where he had been very impressed by the site and by the views.[6] The superb landscapes, hills, lakes, drives, and woods of Green-Wood were planned by Pierrepoint who worked closely with David B. Douglass, an army engineer.

The site afforded spectacular views of Brooklyn and of New York. It was one of the largest landscaped cemeteries in the nineteenth-century world (Pl. 9). Richard Upjohn was the architect who designed most of the original classical buildings for Green-Wood, and with his son designed the

Opposite Plate 9 Plan of Green-Wood Cemetery with vignettes. *Top left*, monument to William A. Lawrence; *top right*, Receiving Tomb, Arbor Water; *bottom left*, Lawn Girt Hill; *bottom right*, Ocean Hill (*Author's Collection*)

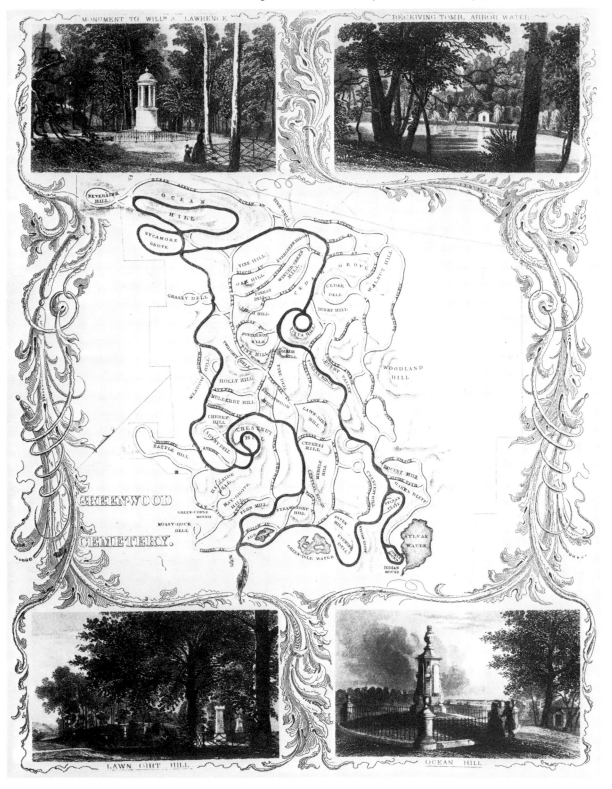

MONUMENT TO WILL^M A. LAWRENCE

RECEIVING TOMB, ARBOR WATER

GREENWOOD CEMETERY.

LAWN GIRT HILL.

OCEAN HILL.

Receiving Vaults which could hold 1,400 bodies.

Green-Wood became one of the most fashionable of American cemeteries. It is described in an *Exposition of the Plan and Objects of the Green-Wood Cemetery, an Incorporated Trust Chartered by the Legislature of the State of New York*, published in New York in 1839. A prospect of the cemetery shows it in relation to New York Bay. The northern entrance, a fanciful composition with eclectic use of Decorated motifs, was constructed in the second half of the nineteenth century to designs by Richard Mitchell Upjohn.

It is worth noting that the Egyptian Revival style was thought to be particularly suitable for cemetery gates, as eternity was evoked by the massive forms, an idea not far in spirit from the theories of Boullée. In the United States the first Egyptian cemetery gates are those at Mount Auburn of 1831, followed by Mount Hope at Rochester in 1838, and by Laurel Hill in Philadelphia in the same year. Grove Street Cemetery gates at New Haven, Connecticut, were perhaps the most celebrated, designed in 1845 by Austin. Abney Park Cemetery at Stoke Newington has fine Egyptian gates by Professor William Hosking. In his *Apology for the Revival of Christian Architecture*, of 1843, Pugin denounced the use of Egyptian Revival for cemetery gates, and included an illustration of an entrance to a 'New General Cemetery for All Denominations', drawn with particular venom.

Albany Rural Cemetery was established nine years after Mount Auburn. A group of Albany citizens met in 1840 'to take into consideration the propriety of and importance of purchasing a plot of ground for a new public cemetery, on a plan similar to the cemetery at Mount Auburn'. The Cemetery Association was incorporated in 1841, and two tracts of land were purchased. Today, the area is about 194 hectares. The planning of the cemetery was by Major David B. Douglass, who had played such an important part in the planning of Green-Wood, although John Hillhouse also contributed to the design of Albany Rural Cemetery. This fine cemetery contains many elaborate tombs, and has survived on the segment of land on the west bank of the Hudson, very much as its designers intended. The plan is ingenious, as an engraving by John E. Gavit of 1871 shows (Pl. 10). The paths meander, and there is a considerable area of water, for this was an 'English landscape' carried to its ultimate Romantic conclusion. There was an enormous Receiving Vault reminiscent of the designs of the French Neoclassicists, with a mighty rusticated and battered façade. The Albany Rural Cemetery was much improved under the surveyorship of J. P. Thomas, and a new, more open style of landscape emerged.[7]

These three American cemeteries were founded in an atmosphere of civic improvement, rather than commercial speculation. In England, however, private companies with shareholders continued to be formed even where the local authorities were entering the field of cemetery design.

By 1849, St Louis was a thriving city, and several older graveyards stood in the way of development. Prominent bankers and lawyers led the movement to found a new cemetery, and nearly 56 hectares were purchased for Bellefontaine Cemetery. An epidemic that began in New Orleans killed a tenth of the population of St Louis in 1849, and it was clear that

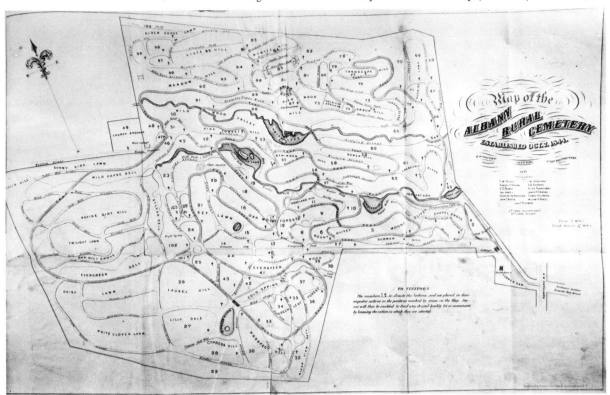

Plate 10 Plan of 1871 shows
Albany Rural Cemetery.
Engraving by John E. Gavit
(*Author's Collection*)

Bellefontaine had not been established one minute too soon. Almerin
Hotchkiss, who had previously been associated with Green-Wood
Cemetery, was the architect, and held the post of superintendent for forty-
six years. Bellefontaine has winding paths and rich planting derived from
the English landscape tradition via Green-Wood. It contains the celebrated
tomb of the Wainwrights by Louis Sullivan.[8]

The most famous cemetery in the United States today is undoubtedly
Forest Lawn Memorial-Park, and it is agreeable to consider it in the light of
Loudon's ideas. Perhaps it is the twentieth-century answer to Loudon, and
there can be no doubt that he would have approved. Most cemeteries in the
United States had followed similar developments to those in Europe, and
the best American cemeteries were based on Père-Lachaise and on English
landscape-design.

Just as cemeteries replaced the churchyards and church vaults in the
nineteenth century, so the Memorial-Parks appear to be ousting cemeteries
in America. They are all based upon the Forest Lawn Memorial-Park,
immortalized by Evelyn Waugh and Jessica Mitford.[9] Forest Lawn has
concert halls, chapels, a cinema, and many other facilities. It was founded by
Hubert Eaton at the end of World War I, and was originally an older
cemetery of 1906 that had gone to seed. Eaton made it respectable and
created a tourist attraction into the bargain.[10] Dr Eaton, known as 'The
Builder', conceived of the cemetery as a 'sacred, protected, permanent
resting place for the departed, but also as a place of service to the living'.
Forest Lawn was to be a 'safe repository' for the dead, and a place for the

'sacred enjoyment of the living'. Dr Eaton's ideas as expressed sound remarkably similar to the aims of Strang, Loudon, and others in the nineteenth century. Indeed, the language of Eaton's writings irresistibly remind the reader of Strang and of other prolix nineteenth-century cemetery enthusiasts. Today, there are four 'Memorial-Parks', totalling some 480 hectares. There are mausolea, columbaria, cenotaphs, and buildings of decidedly eclectic architecture. Compton Wynyates, Stoke Poges Parish Church, the Kirk at Glencairn, and other buildings have been erected in replica. Weddings often take place in the cemetery chapels, an unusual departure, although many ecclesiastics hold that a good funeral is always more cheerful and agreeable than a wedding. The concept of sculpture in the landscape at Forest Lawn is pure Loudon, although Dr Eaton's eclectic tastes ranged to lengths of which even Loudon might have disapproved, despite the example of E. Buckton Lamb, whose architectural looting often reached bizarre heights. The Great Mausoleum is 'inspired' by the Staglieno at Genoa, but scarcely does justice to the original. Forest Lawn is thus an enormous transmogrification and extension of nineteenth-century ideas.

European ideas first helped to create the great nineteenth-century cemeteries in the United States, which often outdid European cemeteries in splendour. In the present century the new ideas are coming from America, and certain aspects of the memorial parks are finding acceptance in Europe. Costs of labour and of maintenance have encouraged cemetery superin-tendents to abolish grave-kerbs, and even headstones. An absence of tall memorials appeals to the tidy-minded as well as to the egalitarians, and there are certainly many who argue for the removal of all memorials in graveyards and cemeteries.

Arlington National Cemetery, the Valhalla of the United States, is some 166 hectares in area, and is situated in Virginia, on the banks of the River Potomac, opposite Washington D.C. It was founded in 1864 when the grounds of the Custis Lee mansion became a military cemetery by order of the Secretary of War following the Government's taking possession of the land under the 'Act for the Collection of Direct Taxes in the Insurrectionary Districts within the United States'. The United States Government obtained a clear title to the site in 1883, by the payment of $150,000 to George Washington Custis Lee following a suit brought by Custis Lee who claimed the Government was a trespasser. The cemetery is spacious and beautiful, chastely classical in its monuments, the finest of which is probably the arcaded amphitheatre that surrounds the Tomb of the Unknown Soldier. Many cemeteries founded after the Civil War were beautiful and serene places that commenced a tradition of war cemeteries in which the United States was later to excel.

Other cities developed cemeteries in conformity with the ideas of the times and for reasons that were universal. Venice had its Cimitero at San Michele since Napoleonic times. Vienna formed the Zentralfriedhof in 1873 to be one of Europe's largest and grandest cemeteries, and the bodies of many celebrated people, including Beethoven and Schubert, were transferred there. As in Père-Lachaise, distinguished dead are grouped by

profession in certain quarters of the cemetery. The Novo-Devichy cemetery in Moscow is well-wooded and crammed with memorials, while the great cemeteries of Berlin and other European capitals have their qualities. German cemeteries are particularly attractive, being planted with a wide variety of trees and shrubs.

It is in Italy, however, that we find the most consciously architectural and urban cemeteries. Rome built its huge Campo Verano by the church of San Lorenzo fuori le mura in 1837, but it is not distinguished architecturally. Milan has its formal and symmetrical Cimitero Monumentale, designed by C. Macciachini, complete with cloistered arcades and Neoclassical crematorium, and this cemetery is truly magnificent. However, even finer is the grand cemetery at Genoa, which is based on the same principles as those of Pisa, Milan, and the Sebastiansfriedhof in Salzburg.

Developed as one of the most important ports of the Mediterranean, Genoa is sited on the sides of the steep hills that surround the harbour. The riches of its treasures and its magnificent setting earned it the title La Superba in the days of its greatest glory. As with other nineteenth-century cities it became necessary to establish a new cemetery to serve the needs of Genoa's large population. Italian cemeteries are usually dramatic and often urban in character. The Pisan Campo Santo, perhaps the most serene and dignified cemetery in the world, is in the form of a large rectangular cloister enclosing an open garth. The Cimitero di Staglieno in Genoa is a development of this enclosed type of graveyard, designed on a monumental scale as a series of arcaded sculpture-galleries. If Père-Lachaise is the most Arcadian cemetery in Europe, then the Staglieno, with its classical architecture, dramatic site, and essential urbaneness, is unquestionably the grandest of all the cemeteries in Europe. Many connoisseurs consider it to be

left Plate 12 A Gallery in the Staglieno (*The Author*)

Plate 13 A Gallery in the Staglieno (*The Author*)

the most splendid cemetery in the world because of the excellence and quality of sculpture in its galleries. Within the precincts of the Cimetero di Staglieno the eye is feasted with a wealth of detail.

The cemetery was formed between 1844 and 1851 on the north bank of the River Bisagno, and is an axially planned work of Neoclassical splendour that hugs the lower slopes of the Appennines[11] (Pl. 11). It consists of walled cloistered spaces with splendid stairs and great broad ramps leading to the upper galleries that flank the dominant central building known as the Rotunda. Behind the Rotunda the paths are laid out along and across the contours, and are lined with individual tombs set among the trees. To the north-east of the main rectangular Campo Santo are curved sweeps of more cloisters with flanking ramps, catacombs, and *loculi* for coffins. The rising ground is enlivened with ostentatious mausolea placed among the cypresses.

This great necropolis was designed by the architect G. B. Resasco for the Comune di Genova, although the first designs were prepared by C. F. Barabino who died before work could be commenced. Other architects have since been responsible for further additions. The Comune di Genova was determined not to be outdone by other European cities that had laid out cemeteries in the course of the first half of the nineteenth century. In the event, it created one of the most beautiful necropoleis ever built.

Plate 14 Rotunda and statue
of Faith (*The Author*)

The cemetery is entered via three arched openings set under a pediment
in the centre of a long wall that is enlivened with blind arcades. This
entrance, almost a triumphal arch, is vaulted; on either side are double
galleries that comprise the cloisters within the walls. These galleries contain
loculi for coffins over and under the paved floors, and are crammed with a
magnificent array of sculptured memorials, all in the classical style
(Pls. 12, 13). On the main axis that runs through the centre of the principal
gate stands the noble statue by Santo Varni that represents Faith. This
statue is in the middle of the primary rectangular cloistered space, and
behind it, dominating the whole composition, is the Pantheon or Rotunda
which is approached by a majestic stair with flanking ramps (Pl. 14). This
Rotunda, or Cappella dei Suffragi, consists of a circular domed structure
carried on sixteen monolithic columns of Varenna marble in front of which
is a marble hexastyle portico of the Doric order. It was designed by the
celebrated Neoclassical architect C. F. Barabino, to contain the tombs and
memorials of successful Genoese. Barabino's original design for the
Rotunda incorporated a Doric portico, a circular Pantheon-type body, and a
crowning pyramid, in a curious example of mixed motifs. On each side of
this Pantheon are further colonnaded galleries with an applied Doric Order
engaged. These galleries are the setting for many sculptured memorials, and

Plate 15 Grander tombs among the cypresses (*The Author*)

have projecting wings like end-pavilions to a Palladian composition, centred on the dome and portico of the Rotunda.

Paths and ramps bordered by cypresses and by sweet-smelling bushes lead to groups of individual free-standing mausolea (Pl. 15) set on the terraces that lie with the contours above the Rotunda. These elevated terraces, where verdant foliage and scented flowers abound, offer magnificent views of the cemetery below. Every possible space is used for entombment. Bodies are even sealed in above lintels, in attics over cornices, and in every corner imaginable (Pl. 16). Sculptured figures people the silent galleries, and effigies stand by graves, memorials, and mausolea.

A huge set of colonnaded galleries, semicircular on plan, lies at the north-eastern end of the Staglieno. In the centre is a portico that gives access to the Cremation Temple (see Ch. X). Great curved ramps rise from the Temple to the levels of the Rotunda and its wings.

The visitor to the Staglieno will not fail to notice that many 'burials' consist of the entombment of bodies in *loculi*, sealed in, either in vaults

Plate 16 A corner of the
Staglieno (*The Author*)

under the gallery floors, or in the galleries themselves. The dead are
celebrated by sculptured memorials in great variety. Sentimentality, horror,
nobility, grandeur, pomposity, and even greatness are expressed. Terrify-
ingly realistic skeletons embracing naked damsels, frock-coated city
worthies, weeping widows in drawing-room dress, biblical figures, and
children in fancy dress people the galleries in a profusion of curious, even
bizarre, expressions of death. The traditions established by Bernini and by
Canova were very much alive when the Staglieno was embellished. Further
enrichment of memorials is given by the lamps that are fixed to each tomb.
These are responsible for warm, even comforting, light in the darkness of
some of the galleries.

It is clear that the adornment of the Staglieno was an aspiration of
Genoese society. Position in society could be suggested by the commission-
ing of large and costly monuments from fashionable sculptors such as
Saccomanno, Scanzi, Varni, and others. Social and financial status could be
demonstrated by conspicuous yet tasteful monuments. A magnificent

281

family grave could ensure respect in society for its builder. Even the poor desired a worthy tomb in the Staglieno, and in some cases fine monuments commemorate the poorest of individuals. Such a demand for sculptured memorials encouraged a school of ingenious Genoese sculptors to develop. Masterpieces of funerary art were commissioned to embellish the severe Neoclassical architecture of the galleries. A vigorous tradition of Italian sculpture ensured that monuments were rarely dull; vivid portrayal, high drama, and Baroque movement were present in quantities unrivalled elsewhere. No cemetery in the world can boast such treasures of the sculptor's art.

In 1867 Mark Twain visited the Staglieno, and described it in his incomparably entertaining *The Innocents Abroad*. He gave the cemetery high praise, and said he would always remember it. It was certainly much more interesting than the famous palaces he had visited. He described it as:

> a vast marble colonnaded corridor extending around a great unoccupied square of ground; its broad floor is marble, and on every slab is an inscription—for every slab covers a corpse. On either side, as one walks down the middle of the passage, are monuments, tombs, and sculptured figures that are exquisitely wrought and full of grace and beauty. They are new and snowy; every outline is perfect, every feature guiltless of mutilation, flaw or blemish; and therefore to us these far-reaching ranks of bewitching forms are a hundredfold more lovely than the damaged and dingy statuary they have saved from the wreck of ancient art, and set up in the galleries of Paris for the worship of the world.

Opposite Plate 17 Tomb of E. Piaggio, by Giovanni Scanzi (*The Author*)

Far right Plate 18 Lavarello monument, by Saccomanno (*The Author*)

A perambulation through the long, silent galleries is one of the most interesting and rewarding of experiences. The monumental designs are vigorous in the way that only Italian sculpture can be, and the full-size figures by tombs have a dramatic and macabre effect. The Piaggio monument, for example, consists of a life-size statue of a woman outside the door of the tomb (Pl. 17). Giovanni Scanzi was the sculptor of this beautiful memorial which symbolizes remembrance, but the realistic figure dressed in the high fashion of the last century can catch the visitor unawares, and cause the sculptured figure to be confused with a living person, if even for a moment. The seated female figure on the Lavarello monument, carved in 1890 by Saccomanno, is also faintly alarming, for it is in a shaded part of the Rotunda galleries, and is disturbingly realistic in the dim light (Pl. 18). This serene and lovely figure is an allegory of the peace of the grave, and of eternal repose.

The Staglieno is one of the greatest examples of nineteenth-century architecture, and is in many ways the ideal necropolis for burial on traditional Christian lines, with its serene classicism and suggestions of the catacombs in its *loculi*. The architecture and sculpture haunt the memory, and the 'inscape' (as Hopkins would have said) of the place draws one back to see it in the mind's eye. Mark Twain was quite correct, for its personality and image are so strong that they are burned into the consciousness.

This cemetery by the Bisagno is one of the fairest of all cities of the dead, and has an air of unruffled serenity within the enclosures of its high wall. It is a supreme essay in Neoclassical architecture, and is set with flowering plants and with the comeliest of cypresses. Italian cemeteries have a distinctive character; they are bold statements on the landscapes, with their cloistered galleries set off by darkly towering trees. The Staglieno, with its rational colonnades, its myrtles and cypresses, its flowers and mausolea, is an Elysium indeed, and offers coolness and quietude in contrast to the din and brightness outside. Italian cemeteries are not gloomy places, but are architectural statements, reposing with order, grace, tranquillity, and dignity in their appointed places in the landscape. Within the walls of the Staglieno one walks over ground *dove ogni passo è una memoria*, and the memories always return, so remarkable is this city of the dead, and so great is its conception and execution.

Many of the cemeteries in Europe and America have immense riches in terms of architecture, landscaping, planting, sculpture, and atmosphere.

One of the most extraordinary of the late-nineteenth-century mortuary chapels, very far removed from the chaste Neoclassicism of Père-Lachaise or Kensal Green, or the Gothic of Nunhead, is that at Arbroath, in Scotland. It is a strange phantasy of superb workmanship, designed by Patrick Allan-Frazer, the painter, who married Miss Frazer of Hospitalfield, and who remodelled that house and built a new Blackcraig in Strathardle (Pl. 19).[12] Although begun in 1875 the exquisite carving was carried out over a number of years. It must be one of the finest chapels in the British Isles for such a late date, and can hold its own with any later examples. For pure invention, it is unusually fine.

Apart from the cemeteries in Italy, most examples after 1875 tend to be increasingly less architectural, and much more open in character. The grandeur of the heroic periods of cemetery design was replaced by a growing timidity. Grass and flowers replaced trees, mausolea, catacombs, and grand architectural effects. The dead were no longer to be given resting-places the living could enjoy.[13]

The private-enterprise cemeteries formed in Britain in the 1830s and 1840s were the first phase in the development of reform in modes of disposal of the dead, and are characterized by a mixture of grandeur and Romanticism in their treatment. Their celebrity was short-lived, for more agitation, together with financial difficulties, contributed to their decline. It is to the new phase, following the growing awareness of the difficulties private cemeteries were bound to face, that I now turn.

The main problems of the commercial cemeteries derived from the initial capital expenditure on buildings (especially catacombs), drainage, and layout. The income from burial was often insufficient to repay the capital, let alone to ensure dividends to shareholders. In addition, the costliness of interment in these cemeteries prevented the evils of intramural burial from being alleviated, for the great mass of the population could not afford to pay for graves. Shortly after the commercial cemeteries had been formed, opinion began to be revolted by the idea of establishing cemeteries on a profit-making basis, and the acquisition of Brompton Cemetery was a short-lived attempt to nationalize all the private cemeteries, although it is perhaps significant that only Brompton, which was in dire financial trouble, actually was acquired. In any case, as the fabric of cities expanded, cemeteries which only a few years earlier had been in open country were engulfed, so the fears of disease from graveyards continued.

Following G. F. Carden's success in creating a climate of opinion by which the commercial cemeteries were formed, further propaganda was published attacking the existing churchyards, crypts, and burial-grounds in cities and towns. Between 1835 and 1855 the Press and Parliament were concerned to draw attention to the continuing horrific state of city graveyards. The resulting agitation was to end intramural interment and to place the onus of laying out and managing cemeteries firmly in the hands of public authorities as opposed to commercial interests.

In 1842 an investigating committee of the House of Commons reported on the terrible conditions regarding burial of the dead that prevailed in London. At that time there were over 80 hectares of burial grounds in

Plate 19 Mortuary Chapel at Arbroath, by Patrick Allan-Frazer, of 1875 (*The Author*)

London, and nearly 50,000 bodies were crammed into them each year.[14] The publication of George Alfred Walker's *Gatherings from Graveyards, particularly those of London; with a concise History of the Modes of Interment among different Nations, from the earliest Periods; and a Detail of dangerous and fatal results produced by the unwise and revolting Custom of inhuming the Dead in the midst of the Living* was widely publicized, and was reviewed in *The Gardener's Magazine* by J. C. Loudon.[15] Again, architects and landscape-gardeners saw the possibilities of developing cemeteries on an enormous scale, and *The Builder*, with other journals, joined in the universal chorus of denunciation of churchyards.[16] Members of Parliament drew the attention of the House of Commons to the necessity of improving the health of towns by the prevention of burial of the dead within built-up areas.[17] Walker described Spa Fields Burial Ground and the 'tremendous stench' caused by the practice of burning coffins and even human remains there. In order to make room for further burials in this notorious burial-ground, it appears to have been the practice to resort to several dubious means. Walker said that sparks and smoke were often seen to come from the charnel-house, and human flesh quarried from the open graves had been consumed in the furnaces. Two deaths had been reported from 'putrid fever'.[18] Charles Knight said that although Spa Fields was full, it was always possible to get a grave there, and indeed an 'age of miracles' had revived with regard to many of the burial-grounds.[19] Yet even the affair of Spa Fields was overshadowed by the scandals of Enon and Elim Chapels, both Dissenters' establishments. The chapels were erected as speculative enterprises. The upper part of Enon Chapel, in Clement's Lane, The Strand, was opened for worship in 1823, and the lower part was used as a vault for coffins. According to Knight, the crypt was about 400 cubic metres in capacity, and yet there had been 12,000 bodies 'interred' under the chapel.[20] Space was created by destroying the coffins or by selling them back to undertakers, and bodies were hacked to pieces and burned. The vault of Enon Chapel was divided from the space for worship by a wooden floor that was not even tongued and grooved. Prosecutions over Spa Fields commenced, and the Enon Chapel affair was investigated.

Dubious chapels were not the only sources for disquiet and scandal. The old churches often had vaults and they and the graveyards were filled to capacity. The raising of the ground above its natural level often meant that accommodation for the living was separated from masses of decomposing corpses by damp and crumbling walls, as a horrifying cross-section of a typical London church and graveyard demonstrates (Pl. 20).

The House of Commons decided that the practices of burial in towns was 'injurious to health', a conclusion that the city fathers of Rome had arrived at two millennia previously. Yet despite the efforts of Carden, Walker, and others there was considerable opposition to ending these unhygienic and disgusting practices. Dissenting ministers were loath to abandon lucrative sources of income; clergymen of the Established Church did not wish to lose burial fees; sextons and gravediggers who made handsome livings from selling coffins and coffin-furniture back to undertakers did not want to live on wages alone; and the poor did not wish to spend more money than was necessary to dispose of their dead. Better ventilation and the drainage in large towns were being accomplished, and these were felt to be 'but trifles in comparison' with the proposed burial reforms.[21]

There was a danger that the ferocity of the debate would tend to polarize the various opinions. Radical rational persons identified the clergy with reactionary and harmful practices, while supporters of cemeteries were regarded as dangerous revolutionaries in certain quarters. Walker began a series of public lectures on the condition of the graveyards of London, and there were even letters in *The Lancet* and other medical journals concerning the 'mephitic' gases from churchyards and the effects on those who breathed them.[22]

One of the supporters of burial reform, the Member of Parliament Mackinnon, introduced a Public Cemeteries Bill in 1846 which he withdrew

Plate 20 Intramural Burials. A horrifying cross-section of a typical city burial-ground in the mid-nineteenth century, showing the insanitary conditions caused by overcrowded churchyards (*Author's Collection*)

on the understanding that its principles would be adopted by the Government as soon as possible.[23] A Cemetery Clauses Bill was brought in to prevent burial under any cemetery chapel, and to lay down regulations for burial in brick graves or catacombs. Density of burial was also subject to legislation, all doubtless due, as we have seen, to J. C. Loudon's pioneering work and his exhaustive treatise, which had appeared three years earlier.

Polemics were published for and against the proposed reforms. In 1848 *The Cemetery. A brief appeal to the feelings of Society on Behalf of Extra Mural Burial* painted a colourful picture of the terrible overcrowded graveyards, where 'in livid heaps the quarried flesh' endangered life and health.[24] The new cemeteries, 'where dissolution's aspect' was repose, and where beauty and ingenuity would 'domesticate the dead', were enthusiastically advocated. The opposition published vicious attacks on the evidence produced by Walker and others, but the main bone of contention seems to have been the fee payable to the incumbent of the parish from which any corpse derived.[25] The fee of ten shillings payable when a body was buried in Brompton Cemetery was bad enough, but the sum of one pound as was the case in Norwood was 'monstrous beyond credibility.' One of the chief objections to the legislation regarding cemeteries was the payment of money to the Established Church. This payment was intended to compensate clergy for the loss of burial fees, but the intention stirred up a hornet's nest of Dissenting opinion, since some of the worst burial-grounds were run by nonconformists. It would therefore be clear that the problems of the burial of the dead and their reformation were almost entirely financial in origin.

Arguments might have continued indefinitely had not sheer necessity forced the Government to act. The first cholera epidemics had been highly unpleasant, like that of 1831–2 which had helped the legislation regarding commercial cemeteries. However, at the height of the debate on intramural interment, a cholera epidemic of singular ferocity occurred in 1848–9, reaching a total of 53,293 dead. There were other outbreaks in 1853, 1854, 1865, and 1866. Stephen Geary, the architect and specialist in cemeteries, was himself a victim. The ignorance of the public in the face of these epidemics was appalling, as many contemporary pamphlets made clear; unlikely causes were blamed, including cucumbers, 'feverish vapours', and the air that lay above churchyards.[26]

Some eight years after the publication of Walker's *Gatherings* and in spite of a Select Committee's inquiries into 'Intra-Mural Sepulture and the Effect of Interment of Bodies on the Health of Towns' reform still seemed elusive. When the cholera epidemics put an intolerable demand for space on the already crammed graveyards panic ensued, and official action at last indicated that Parliament considered interment of the dead too important to leave to private enterprise. As we have already seen, an Act of Parliament was passed to enable public intervention in the burial of the dead to take place, and to grant the General Board of Health compulsory powers to purchase the existing commercial cemeteries.[27]

The Board of Health proposed to make Kensal Green Cemetery the nucleus of a Great Western Cemetery, and to form a huge Great Eastern Cemetery at Erith. Transport by boat down river was essential to such a scheme, so 'receiving-houses' were proposed at points along the banks of the Thames. The Treasury was not particularly forthcoming in regard to the provision of a distant 'Metropolitan Cemetery, or rather Necropolis, upon a grand and comprehensive scale',[28] and it was unhappy about the proposed closure of so many of the existing cemeteries that had only been established for fifteen years or so. The problem was that the Board considered these cemeteries unsuitable for burial because of the nature of the subsoil (usually a stiff clay). Besides, the layouts designed in the 1830s incorporated many features of landscape and building denounced by Loudon, whose views had become posthumously accepted as dogma. The phenomenal growth of London also meant that established cemeteries were too near the living, and so the proposed cemeteries would have to be formed at a very great distance from central London.

It is one of the ironies of history that the Board of Health Plan (which had the backing of Chadwick and others) was dropped, for the Woking Necropolis Plan[29] appeared at the same time and proposed the setting up of one enormous cemetery for the whole of the country. This huge necropolis was to be run by the State, and linked to all the towns of the kingdom by water and by rail. The pusillanimous attitude of the politicians and the lack of nerve on the part of the Treasury prevented these imaginative schemes from being realized, partly, no doubt, as politicians and civil servants were lulled into a false sense of complacency as the 1849 cholera epidemic abated. The irony stems from the fact that a cemetery of enormous size was actually laid out near Woking, but not by the State. The political climate was not amenable at the time to State enterprise, so the London Necropolis and National Mausoleum Company was incorporated in 1852, and purchased some 830 hectares at Brookwood in Surrey. A novel feature of this venture was that the directors of the Company came to an arrangement with the London and South Western Railway for the conveyance of bodies to the

Plate 21 Tomb of the Drake Family at Brookwood Cemetery (*The Author*)

cemetery by train. The Company also had close ties with the parochial authorities of Shoreditch, Bloomsbury, Westminster, Southwark, Wapping, Whitechapel, and Deptford to ensure that there would be no dearth of corpses. All denominations were to be catered for. Only the very poor could not be accommodated, and the problem of burial of the poor was not truly solved until the formation of public cemeteries.

The Company first laid out some 200 hectares of its land as a cemetery to plans by Sir William Tite, who had designed the South Metropolitan Cemetery at Norwood some time before. The gravelly soil was easy to drain, and Tite planted a great variety of trees and shrubs, including redwoods and rhododendrons to give a special quality to the grounds much influenced by Loudon's writings. Hygiene was the most important aspect of Brookwood, the largest of all the London cemeteries. The railway terminus of the London Necropolis Company was in Westminster Bridge Road, and contained waiting-rooms and a chapel in which bodies lay before being carried to Brookwood.

Opinion against intramural interment was so strong in the 1850s that many city graveyards and crypts were cleared and the remains re-interred in Brookwood and in other cemeteries. Monuments stand over the mass-graves of those who were once buried in the city, though there are few tombs of architectural distinction at Brookwood. One of the finest is that of Sir William Drake and his family, erected in the 1880s in an Italian manner (Pl. 21). Part of the cemetery near the railway line is reserved for the dead of

Islam and of the Parsee communities. Tombs of the latter, not so far distant in style from those in the ancient Roman cemeteries, are among the most interesting mausolea at Brookwood (Pl. 22).

Plate 22 Mausolea in the Parsee section of Brookwood Cemetery (*The Author*)

Another private company formed the Great Northern Cemetery near Friern Barnet in North London that was also served by rail from King's Cross. The concentric avenues around the Gothic chapel were planted in a Loudonesque manner, the designs for the cemetery being prepared by Alexander Spurr. This cemetery also acquired the contents of various crypts and graveyards, including aristocratice bones from the Savoy Chapel.

Plate 23 Lithograph by J. and E. Harwood showing the cemetery at Sheffield (*Author's Collection*)

By 1850 every town and city in Britain had acquired a cemetery of some sort or another from sheer necessity. Many were established by private

enterprise, and often the architecture and layout prove to be of high quality. Sheffield, for example, favoured a robust classicism in keeping with an architecture of banks and offices (Pl. 23), but such enchanting designs were not usual. When Gothic became the only acceptable style for ecclesiastical architecture, cemetery chapels were built in that style, and all too often were mean and unconvincing in their detail.

The experience in Britain encouraged similar developments in the colonies. The growing city of Sydney in Australia developed large cemeteries not unlike the British models. One of the most interesting Australian cemeteries is called Rookwood and was, like Brookwood, served by rail. The railway stations at Rookwood are of some considerable interest, and an original water-colour perspective drawing of the cemetery station survives in the RIBA British Architectural Library Drawings Collection (Pl. 24), where it has been incorrectly attributed to Sidney Smirke. The building was erected in 1868 as the 'Receiving House', to designs by James J. Barnet, 'a native of Arbroath, NB, Colonial Architect from 1865 to 1890' (Pl. 25), who died on 16 December 1904. He was also responsible for the

Plate 24 James J. Barnet's drawing of the Receiving House, Haslam's Creek, Rookwood Cemetery, Australia (*RIBA British Architectural Library Drawings Collection*)

Plate 25 Receiving House,
Rookwood Cemetery, 1868
(*Public Transport Commission,
N.S. Wales*)

'Despatching Station' (otherwise known as Redfern Station) in Regent's
Street, Sydney, from which funerals left for the Receiving House (Pl. 26).
Thus Rookwood Cemetery of the 1860s is based upon the philosophy
behind the foundation of Brookwood Cemetery, Surrey, in the 1850s, and
the Great Northern Cemetery near London, in the 1860s. The 'Receiving
House' at Rookwood was also known as the 'number one mortuary station',
and received the trains that carried the dead of Sydney as they were taken to
their final resting place at Rookwood Cemetery.

Barnet, the architect, was born in Arbroath in 1827 and studied with C. J.
Richardson. He emigrated to Australia in 1854 and must have known about
the Brookwood Cemetery promotions in England at that time. He published
a paper in 1899 describing the mortuary railway stations at Sydney and the
cemetery at Rookwood to demonstrate the application of Gothic
architecture to a 'novel purpose'. Originally, the building was known as the
'Receiving House, Haslam's Creek'. It was built for £4,407 by a Mr
A. Loveridge. With the advent of motor transport, the branch line fell into
disuse in 1939, and the Receiving House became redundant. It was put up
for sale in 1952 and the stonework was purchased by All Saint's Church in
Canberra in 1957. In May 1958 the entire station was transported to
Canberra and rebuilt as a church: it is a most interesting survival of a great
Victorian cemetery.[30]

Barnet's designs are quite extraordinary. Like the works of Enoch Bassett
Keeling, whose 'acrobatic Gothic' excited the anathema of the Ecclesiologists, Barnet's buildings might be said to be 'Continental Gothic, freely
treated'. Indeed, Barnet's work has something of that barbaric, rasping
spikiness, so characteristic of Keeling's work during the 1860s. One can only
speculate as to whether Barnet had seen Keeling's designs in the
architectural journals of the day. Certainly his own association with C. J.

Plate 26 Despatching
Station, Redfern Station,
Regent's Street, Sydney,
Australia, 1868 (*Public
Transport Commission, N.S.
Wales*)

Richardson may have taught him many things, but hardly an impeccably
correct adherence to stylistic niceties. The juxtaposition of the clumsy little
bellcote and the great arch of the station (adorned with angels trumpeting)
recalls Keeling at his most ham-fisted. Even the stumpy columns of Barnet's
station suggest the nave arcades of Keeling's London churches, while the
jagged, notchy, biting trusses could almost be by Keeling himself. Keeling
came from a Dissenting background, and was born in Sunderland in 1837.
He was thus ten years younger than Barnet, who outlived him by eighteen
years, but Keeling was attracting the attention of the professional journals in
the mid-1860s, so Barnet may have known of his work.

In Britain, public cemeteries were established from the 1850s by burial
boards set up by the vestries. Thomas Little was still actively engaged in
cemetery design at this time, for he designed Paddington Cemetery in 1855,
using the Gothic style for the buildings. The two chapels are linked to a
belfry by *portes-cochères* in the centres (Pl. 27).

The City of London Cemetery at Little Ilford is probaby the finest of the
first public cemeteries in Britain. It was opened in 1856 as a direct result of
the pressures caused by the closing of the churchyards in the City of
London, and by an Act of Parliament that enabled an eastern cemetery to be
formed.[31] It was laid out by the Commissioners of Sewers of the City to
designs by William Haywood.[32] The gravelly soil was ideal for burial, and
the grounds, comprising nearly thirty-seven hectares, were allocated in
parcels to Anglicans and Dissenters, with some nine hectares un-
appropriated.[33] The cemetery has since been extended by another eighteen
hectares. The grounds are beautifully planted, while the rhododendrons,
azaleas, and the many trees suggest the influence of Loudon and the
Arboretum approach at Abney Park. The ingenious plan, with its *rond-
points*, vistas, and winding avenues is a fine example of cemetery planning

293

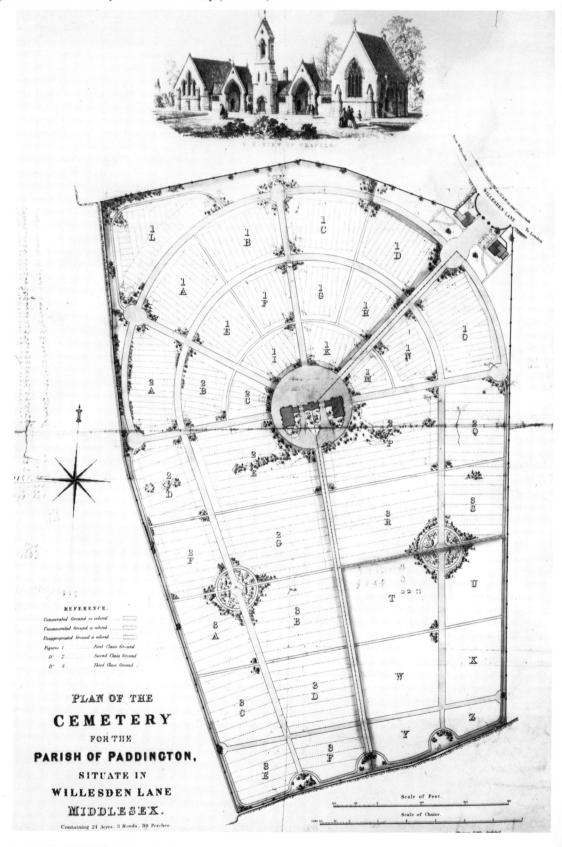

PLAN OF THE
CEMETERY
FOR THE
PARISH OF PADDINGTON,
SITUATE IN
WILLESDEN LANE
MIDDLESEX.

Containing 24 Acres, 3 Roods, 39 Perches.

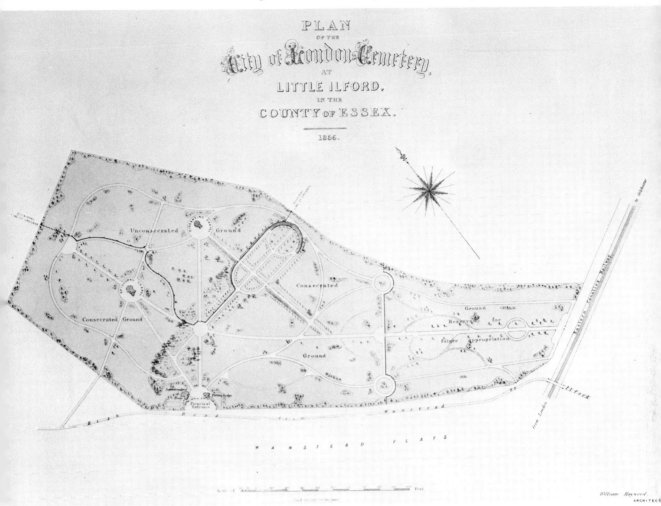

PLAN

OF THE

City of London Cemetery,

AT

LITTLE ILFORD,

IN THE

COUNTY OF ESSEX.

1856.

Plate 28 Plan of the City of London Cemetery at Little Ilford in the County of Essex, 1856, by William Haywood, Architect, dated 1856 (*Guildhall Library, City of London*)

Plate 27 *Opposite* Plan of the cemetery for the Parish of Paddington, 1855, with a vignette of the chapels, by Thomas Little (*RIBA British Architectural Library Drawings Collection*)

(Pl. 28). The 'Catacomb Valley', artificially formed in the shape of a Roman circus, is superbly planted. At the eastern end is the long, low semicircle of Gothic catacombs, while the main gates, house, and lodge are picturesque compositions in the French Gothic style (Pl. 29). Like several others of the period, the Little Ilford cemetery contains the burial-places of remains cleared from the crypts and churchyards of the City (Pl. 30).

The chapels are in the Continental Gothic style (Pl. 31), and the old crematorium, dating from 1902, is also Gothic, built to designs by D. J. Ross. A new crematorium, designed by the City Architect, has been erected in the Catacomb Valley. The cemetery also contains the Gothic mausoleum of Haywood, designed by him and erected in 1889, although both the architect and his wife were cremated at Woking.

Following the various enactments relating to burial reform, over 500 consecrated graveyards were closed in 1854–5. From 1860 most cemeteries in Britain were established by public authorities, and were utilitarian, hygienic, and for the most part uninteresting. The public-health enthusiasts could regard the reforms of thirty years or so as a victory of some magnitude, and it has even proposed to continue the fight against intramural interment so that the royal vaults at Windsor would be closed, if not cleared. There were still scandals, but not on anything like the scale previously described. As the century grew older, many more graveyards were closed by Orders in Council and by other means, including the Disused Burial Grounds Act of 1884,[34] the Metropolitan Board of Works (Various Powers) Act of 1885,[35] and the Open Spaces Act of 1887 which allowed for the conversion of graveyards into public parks.[36]

Plate 29 Catacombs (*top*) and entrance gateway, superintendent's house, and porter's lodge (*bottom*) at the City of London Cemetery, Little Ilford, by William Haywood, dated 1856 (*Guildhall Library, City of London*)

Opposite above
Plate 30 Monument erected in the City of London Cemetery at Little Ilford in 1871 over the human remains removed from the churchyards of S. Andrew, Holborn, and S. Sepulchre, as a result of the Holborn Viaduct construction works, designed by William Haywood, 1872 (*Guildhall Library, City of London*)

Opposite below Plate 31 The Anglican (*left*) and Dissenters' (*right*) Chapels in the City of London Cemetery at Little Ilford, both designed by William Haywood (*Guildhall Library, City of London*)

Episcopal Chapel.

Dissenting Chapel.

Regrettably, although hygienic and rational considerations had triumphed (a fact that would have pleased Loudon) aesthetic aspects declined, and cemeteries in Britain and America became mostly dull, and often vulgar in the trivial designs of memorials and landscapes. The concern with public health and with hygiene brought new problems, while the desire to provide permanent graves that would be sold in perpetuity created inevitable difficulties once the cemeteries had filled. European practices, involving the leasing of a grave or a *loculus*, or even a space in a columbarium, for a limited period, have proved to be far more sensible.

10 The problems of disposal in ever-increasing centres of population

The development of cremation and of buildings associated with the burning of the dead

How the bulk of a man should sink
into so few pounds of bones and ashes,
may seem strange unto any who considers
not its constitution, and how slender
a masse will remain upon an open and urging
fire of the carnall composition.

SIR THOMAS BROWNE: *Hydriotaphia*

By the 1870s most of the problems associated with the disposal of the dead had been dealt with on the lines suggested by some reformers. Yet it had become apparent to many people that the new hygienic cemeteries were bound to cause great difficulties themselves as they too filled with bodies. There were worries about pollution of rivers, while the sheer bulk of human remains caused great concern. Commentators on taste were bothered by the rapid decline in tombstone sculpture, for they considered that landscapes were being blighted by hideous memorials.

The very regulations that controlled exhumations and the management of cemeteries caused the burial-lands to fill rapidly, so they became larger, utilitarian, and ugly. Francis Seymour Haden proposed a solution to the problem, pointing out that burial customs from the Reformation and subsequent attitudes to the ownership of graves caused the difficulties. In particular, the protection of the dead from the natural processes of dissolution simply took up space, for bodies that were sealed in leaden or other air-tight coffins reached a stage of advanced but unprogressive decay. Haden proposed to remedy this by ensuring that bodies came into contact with the earth as soon as possible in order that they would break down quickly. His solution was to provide coffins of paper, wicker, or other substances that would not hinder decay, or that the tops and sides of coffins would be removed after the body had been committed to the grave. Another novel suggestion was that bodies would be embedded in charcoal in crypts in which there was excellent ventilation, so that after an appropriate period the bones would be stored in catacombs or buried. Using his ideas, Haden reckoned that 800 hectares would bury the dead of England for ever, as the ground would be continuously re-used.

Haden's ideas were partially developed by the London Necropolis Company, which provided 'earth-to-earth' coffins that quickly disintegrated in the gravelly soil of Brookwood. Unfortunately the sensible theories of Haden and others were not adopted on any scale, probably because the undertaking trade had too much to lose. In addition, there began a shift of sympathy away from interment altogether, as the hygiene fanatics moved one step further towards complete destruction of human bodies by burning. The cremationists were to be more successful in promoting their point of view than were the 'earth-to-earth' enthusiasts.

As the nineteenth century grew older, the moral arguments for cemeteries dwindled. Utilitarian notions came to the fore, and there was less talk of cemeteries as open-air galleries or botanic gardens. However, William Robinson, clearly a devotee of Loudon, was arguing for landscaped 'garden-cemeteries' in 1883, and observed that the burial of ashes in urns or caskets need not prevent good landscape design.[1]

The Victorians were becoming less interested in art and more expert in efficiency. The disposal of the dead was now being argued more and more from a functional point of view, and the various options and possibilities were debated at length.[2] Bodies could be processed, broken down for use as fertiliser or for food, interred, exposed to the air, burned, preserved, frozen, artificially and speedily decomposed, sunk at sea, eaten by wild animals or birds, eaten in token or completely by humans, ground up and spread, or mixed with water and treated as sewage, all of which were the subject of examination by commentators of the day. It is interesting to note that many people who had served in India were cremationists, but many others were impressed by the customs of the Parsees, who adopted the approach of giving back the dead to Nature. This was accomplished by building circular platforms with concentric depressions to hold dead bodies (Pl. 1). Corpses were taken to these 'towers of silence' and laid in a vacant 'tray'. Vultures and other carrion-birds devoured the flesh, and the body fluids were drained into a central well. Supplies of water ensured that the towers were cleansed regularly, and that all particles were washed away in the connecting channels by rain and by water from the wells. Similar beliefs about giving all dead flesh to birds and animals were found in Persia (where Zoroastrian ideas originated) and in the Himalayas. In central Himalayan customs, the bones were ground to pieces so that even the skeletons were devoured by scavengers, and no part of the body remained.

The fear of decay, pollution, and contamination encouraged the ideas of destroying bodies by fire, and indeed early posters of the Cremation Society, founded in 1874 by Sir Henry Thompson, emphasize the hygienic aspects of cremation. The vast cemeteries that were being laid out in the nineteenth century as populations increased aroused fear and revulsion in many people. These emotions were not merely because of fear of infection, but were associated with contamination of the air, of the soil, and of drinking water. Such fears had been voiced ever since 'miasmas' were blamed for 'feverish vapours', for 'mephitic poisonings', for the cholera, and even for sudden unexplained deaths. There is no doubt that crowded churchyards were often malodorous, unpleasant, and attended with occasional horrors, but the fears surrounding death and graveyards owed more to ignorance, to Gothick novels, to Romantic and moral verse such as Blair's *The Grave*, and to the

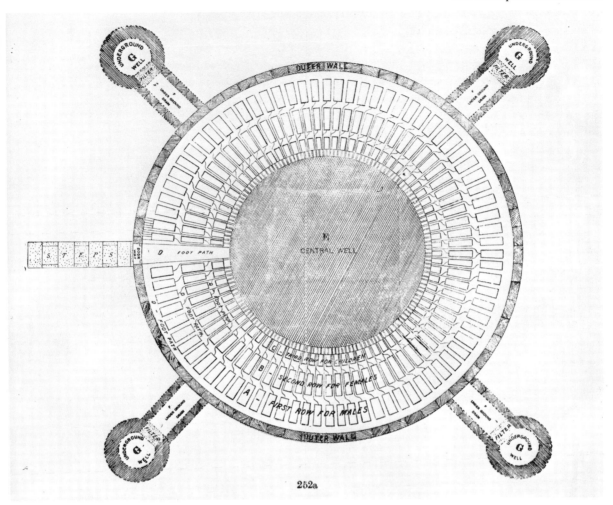

252a

fecund imaginations of the burial reformers than to reality. Myth and beliefs are often more significant than facts or sober historical truth in human affairs however, so the large cemeteries were feared because their miasmas and sheer bulk of bodies were so much greater than those of the graveyards. As late as 1888, one fearful commentator computed that there were one hundred thousand bodies in Highgate Cemetery, so the future of the cemetery was 'a matter of serious consideration for the neighbourhood, the earth becoming yearly more densely charged with the most poisonous matter.'[3] Lloyd said that churchyards, disgusting though they might be, were at least of limited size, but that metropolitan cemeteries could be a great menace in the future. Similar fears were voiced in Europe and in America. Cremation had been respectable in classical times, and Sir Thomas Browne's *Hydriotaphia, or Urne Burial*[4] had attracted devotees since the seventeenth century by the beauty of the prose and the wealth of knowledge contained. Burning of bodies had been known in Biblical times when pestilence struck, or when it was necessary to prevent bodies being taken by enemies, so various divines could argue that there was a precedent of sorts for cremation.[5] The general reaction to cremation in the nineteenth century could be roughly divided among the orthodox Christians, who were against the burning of bodies, and radicals, who supported cremation.

In 1769 the body of a lady who gloried in the name of Honoretta Pratt was cremated, and this fact was recorded in the churchyard of S. George, Hanover Square. The worthy woman believed that 'the vapours arising from the graves in the churchyards' of populous cities could be harmful to the living, and so ordered that her own corpse should be destroyed by fire 'in the hope that others would follow her example'. The affair caused a scandal, for the Christian attitude to cremation was historically one of opposition. It made matters worse for supporters of cremation when that mode of disposal became associated with French radical thought, with Godlessness, and later, with Jacobinism. Cremation appears to have been introduced into France in 1797, when a Jesuit priest declared himself in favour of cremation, and there were several architectural schemes promoted in competitions for crematoria and columbaria. The designs for these schemes were staunchly Neoclassical in style, in the manner of the French architectural academicians of the time. Cremation as a rational method of disposal of the dead always appealed to anti-clericals, revolutionaries, and radicals. From the beginnings of Christianity, burial in the Jewish fashion had been usual among the followers of the new creed, and the testimony of the catacombs tells us much of the modes of Christian sepulture. Indeed, the early Christians had strongly objected to the practice of cremation, as it savoured of paganism and rival religions, and also destroyed the body that in the new religion had taken on a new significance. The example of Christ's entombment was followed as precedent, and a new reverence for the dead, and especially for the relics of martyrs, encouraged the protection and preservation of bodies in catacombs and *loculi* in tombs. The enormous imperial funerals disgusted Christians by their ostentation and prodigal waste, while rich Roman pagan funerals had a certain vulgar extravagance that savoured of luxury, sin, and general excess. '*Execrantur rogos, et damnant ignium sepulturam*' could sum up the Christian attitude to cremation. The pagan funeral was anathema to the Christians, who viewed with horror what appeared to be extravagance, falsehood, and emphasis on worldly success. Sir Thomas Browne tells us that pagans 'with rich flames, and hired tears', solemnized their obsequies.[6]

The favouring of cremation by anti-clericals has been a consistent factor in recent history. The theories of French Revolutionary cremationists found enthusiastic adherents in the South American revolutionary leaders, and the cremation movement achieved further notoriety in more orthodox circles when the bodies of the drowned Williams and Shelley were burned on an Italian beach. There was nothing of the defiant gesture, and even less of the Romantic in that affair, for the authorities insisted that decomposed matter that was washed up should be burned to prevent pollution and infection. The cremation, under a military guard, was witnessed by Lord Byron and by Leigh Hunt, who were both revolted by the sight and by the smell. Shelley's heart was plucked from the flames and later interred in the exquisite Protestant cemetery in Rome.

One of the first influential papers on cremation in the nineteenth century was published in Edinburgh in 1817.[7] This was a scholarly and historical work that recorded the facts concerning cremation. Unquestionably the most amazing statement on cremation in the first half of the nineteenth century was that of J. C. Loudon, who was convinced that cremation would become universal in Britain, in Europe, and in America.[8] Articles on cremation were published in the 1854 *Encyclopaedia Britannica*, and various publications on cremation appeared during the 1850s.[9] The British in India were familiar with Hindu practice, and many advocated cremation themselves. Army officers took an interest in the development of crematoria in India to replace the inefficient and malodorous pyres that disfigured many river banks.[10] The 1870s saw the beginning of pro-cremation propaganda on a big scale, with some ominous suggestions of compulsion.[11] Dr A. E. Parkes wrote a paper on the 'Disposal of the Dead'[12] that was influential, but *The Contemporary Review* contained the most persuasive of the papers, and a spate of publications followed.[13]

G. A. Walker had gone so far as to advocate cremation in 1842, but it is likely that his views caused as much horror as did his *Gatherings from Graveyards*. Although J. C. Loudon had said that cremation in Britain was inevitable, most of contemporary opinion felt that cremation was 'repugnant' to Christians. Ecclesiologists objected to cremation, and to symbols of cremation such as urns, ash-chests, and torches. The agonizing that went on in Victorian times was largely concerned with Christian belief, but the advances in hygiene together with the inroads of scientific thought undermined objections to cremation. Sir Henry Thompson, the Queen's Surgeon, was eminently respectable, and his views for cremation attracted the support of Millais, Trollope, Voysey, Tenniel, and others. Thus in England cremation was becoming associated with the Establishment. Sir Henry Thompson was to argue in favour of cremation as 'a necessary sanitary precaution against the propagation of disease among a population daily growing larger in relation to the area it occupied'. Although his case was largely based on sanitary considerations, it also included arguments that cremation would prevent premature burial (although he failed to note that premature cremation would be just as horrific), reduce the expense of funerals, shelter mourners during inclement weather, and enable ashes to be stored securely.

At the same time, Christians were concerned about the problems posed by cremation. Various tomes were written to argue the Christian position, and many more were produced to point out that Christians could be cremated without any problems of re-assembly should there be an eventual need to join in a general resurrection. Similar difficulties regarding Christians who had been devoured by wild animals or burned were debated in the Middle Ages in *La Lumière as Lais*. Scientific argument was used to demonstrate that dissolution by fire posed no more insuperable task of reconstruction for the Almighty than decay in the earth.[14] With the obstacles of religious objection in Protestant countries being overcome, the cremationists felt they could now develop and experiment. Roman Catholicism was opposed to the burning of bodies on religious and historical grounds, but this encouraged radicals in Roman Catholic countries to advance the cause of cremation.

The development of cremation

In 1872 an experiment in cremation was carried out by Gorini and Polli, and by Professor Brunetti of Padua, who exhibited his results at the Vienna Exhibition in 1873. Brunetti's first demonstration of cremation was in 1869, and was performed in an out-of-door furnace. In 1874 there was an experiment in Breslau, and shortly afterwards the body of an Englishwoman was cremated in the Siemens apparatus at Dresden, where a congress was held two years later. At the congress various designs for crematoria were exhibited, including a magnificent building by Pieper and Lilienthal that was to incorporate the Siemens Regenerative Process. Earlier cremations had not placed the bodies in closed receptacles, and the Siemens process was an attempt to introduce high technical performance into cremation practice. It was essential that cremation should be as quick as possible, and should be

Plate 2 Siemens' Cremation Apparatus. Note the cast-iron cover, and the mourners placed as though round a grave. From Tegg, William *The Last Act* London 1876 (*Author's Collection*)

Plate 3 Façade of the Milan Crematorium, with wings containing columbaria (*Author's Collection*)

free from smoke and from odours. The Siemens furnace was gas-fired, air being introduced by a valve system to make the furnace as hot as possible, including the fire-brick lining which became white-hot. The cast-iron cover of the cremating furnace was lifted, using a counter-balance, to allow the coffin to be lowered. Once the coffin was in position the cover was replaced, and cremation proceeded. Committal, which could have been highly dangerous, according to the picture (Pl. 2), was similar to interment.[15]

Following the Dresden experiment, the first cremation in a closed receptacle in Italy took place in Milan in 1876, using gas for fuel. This cremation was that of Alberto Keller, and was described in a work published to promote Keller's enthusiasm for cremation.[16] The original crematory was Neoclassical in form, shaped like a sarcophagus, with an urn on top from which a flame of gas burned. This sarcophagus stood in an open temple.

This early crematorium was altered in 1880 to incorporate modern equipment, and wings were added following its presentation to the city of Milan by the Keller family. It is situated in the Campo Santo, or Cimitero Monumentale, which was designed by C. Macciachini. The 'Tempio Crematorio' is built in a prominent position on the cemetery's main axis. A formal composition, the crematory is centred and flanked by columbaria. The style of architecture is a severe Greek Doric, an Order much favoured in Italian funerary architecture. The material used is white marble, and the whole structure has a serene nobility appropriate to its purpose (Pl. 3). The

Plate 4 Tempio Crematorio in
the Staglieno in Genoa (*The
Author*)

Tempio Crematorio in Turin was also built in the Doric style, to designs by
Marini, in 1887. The entrance to the incinerating chamber was of noble
Neoclassical design with a pyramid motif. It is interesting to note that
Roman Catholic Italy led Britain in experiment, as cremation was
considered radical, and therefore popular in cities like Milan, Turin, and
Genoa, where it symbolized anti-clerical protests. The Neoclassical
Tempio Crematorio in Genoa is situated in the Cimitero di Staglieno, and is
distinguished by a drum above the roof that supports a flaming urn of
stucco. In the Staglieno there is a large columbarium associated with the
Temple (Pl. 4). The Società Genovese di Cremazione was active in
propaganda in the last century, and a similar society was formed in Milan.
The northern Italians had long professed a tradition of radicalism and anti-
clericalism, so cremation was a means of expressing such aspirations. For
Roman Catholic Italy, a surprising number of the *loculi* in both the
Staglieno and in Milan are occupied by cremated remains. The Roman
Catholic Church forbade cremation until 1963, although 'when it is evident
that cremation has been decided upon as a denial of Christian teaching,
either for propaganda purposes, or out of hatred for the Catholic Church
and the Faith' the provision of Canon Law will still apply.

Cremation was first introduced in Germany in the 1870s, and the first
official crematorium was built at Gotha in 1879, on principles established
following the Dresden experiments and the practice of cremation as
developed in Italy. One of the finest of early German crematoria was that at
Heidelberg, erected to designs by Thomas in the Roman Doric style. The
Deutsche Feuerbestattungstasse *Flamme* developed branches throughout
the Reich, while the Volks-Feuerbestattungs Verein also played a prominent
part, despite the fact that cremation was forbidden in Prussia, Saxony,
Bavaria, and Württemberg.

After the establishment of the Empire in France and the restoration of the
monarchy, the subject was not broached again until the 1870s, when a
republic was once more the mode of government. In 1885 the Minister of
the Interior gave permission to establish a crematorium to dispose of débris
from dissecting-rooms, and in 1887 the law was changed to enable any
person to have his or her body disposed of by either burial or burning.
Perhaps the finest group of crematorium buildings in France is at Père-
Lachaise, designed by Formigé, chief architect of the city of Paris. In its
original form it had three halls, each filled with a furnace in the shape of a
sarcophagus. It is surrounded by arcaded columbaria. Cremation was
practised at Père-Lachaise from 1889, and the whole group of buildings,
including the columbaria, is of immense distinction (Pls. 5, 6, 7).

The idea of cremation was promoted in the United States in 1873 but it
was only in 1876 that positive moves were made. Dr F. Julius Le Moyne of
Washington, Pennsylvania, built a small furnace for the eventual cremation
of his own body, and occasionally sanctioned other cremations to promote
the movement. In 1877 Dr Charles H. Winslow was cremated at Salt Lake
City. In 1881 the New York Cremation Society and the United States
Cremation Company were formed. Among the first crematoria were the
Earl Crematorium at Troy, New York; the Cincinatti Crematorium (1888);

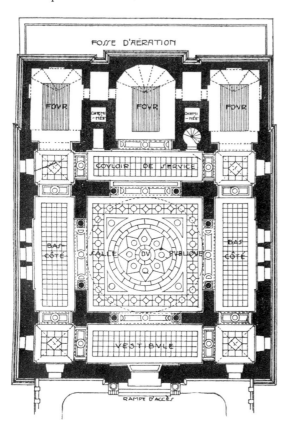

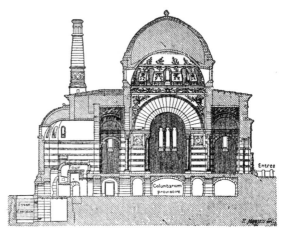

and that at St Louis (1888). The Odd Fellows' Cemetery in San Francisco established an early crematorium, and a large columbarium was also erected in 1895 with provision for nearly 2,000 niches. The building was constructed of mass-concrete, and is a remarkable example of funerary architecture. Buffalo Crematorium was erected to the designs of Green and Wicks, and was among the first in the United States. The Crematorium at Graceland, Chicago, was erected in 1893 to designs by Holabird and Roche.

Following the articles in *The Contemporary Review* of 1874, Sir Henry Thompson's championing of cremation bore fruit. The Cremation Society of England was formed in 1874, in which year experiments were made. The Council of the Society determined to establish a crematorium in 1875, and in 1878 a suitable site was obtained at Woking. A utilitarian crematorium

was erected in the following year, with a furnace designed by Gorini. The crematorium was not used for several years, however, as the Home Office would not authorize cremation, but in 1882 the Society was approached by a Captain Hanham to perform the burning of a member of his family who had expressly desired to be cremated. Unwilling to risk a showdown with officialdom, the Society declined, and Hanham built a furnace himself in the grounds of his house. The next year, Hanham's body was cremated in the same furnace. There was no reaction from the Home Office. In the same year, however, following the cremation of a child in Wales in defiance of the coroner's authority, legal proceedings were taken against the child's father, the disputatious and radical Dr Price. In 1884 Mr Justice Stephen, deciding the case, declared that cremation was not an offence provided no nuisance was caused, and in the following year the first legal cremation was performed at Woking. In 1889 a more fitting building was erected at Woking to designs by E. F. Clarke. A columbarium was also added.

Once the legal possibilities had been clarified, several crematoria were established in Great Britain. The first after Woking was Manchester (1892), designed by A. E. Steinthal in a subdued and appropriate Romanesque style. After Manchester, Glasgow (1895), Liverpool (1896), Hull (1901), Darlington (1901), Leicester (1902), and Golders Green (1902) followed. The latter is one of the most architecturally successful of all crematoria in Britain, and is in an Italian Romanesque style, built of a warm red brick, to designs by Sir Ernest George and Alfred B. Yeates. The simplicity of the materials and the composition of the arcaded cloisters, chapels, columbarium, and towers make this building one of the most appropriate to its purpose. Most crematoria in Britain, however, are distressingly banal and poorly designed, and are composed of disparate elements that are uncomfortably unresolved. Many early crematoria were disguised to look like churches, with the flues installed in the 'bell-towers'. The louvres that should have emitted joyful peals often belched smoke. Inside these vaguely ecclesiastical buildings there were often two foci: the catafalque, and the place where the catafalque *ought* to have been. All too often the coffin was placed to one side, so that there was no sense of direction or of attention. Nearly all British crematoria suffer from philosophical confusion in their layout, their functional bases not having been thought out. It is time they were, for the vast majority of crematoria in Britain do not provide surroundings, atmosphere, or architecture appropriate to the solemnity of their purpose.

William Eassie's *Cremation of the Dead* was published in 1875, and it is interesting to note that, as Secretary of the Cremation Society, he argued that burning the dead would once more enable remains to be placed in churches. To this end he advocated that urns should be styled to conform to Christian taste. William Robinson's *God's Acre Beautiful, or the Cemeteries of the Future* appeared in 1880 as a polemic in favour of garden cemeteries. Robinson, like many other people of the period, was concerned about the metropolitan cemeteries becoming sources of infection; he advocated cremation as the bodies of the poor in common graves were often burned anyway, after only a few years in the earth. Robinson advocated urn-burial which would save land, be hygienic, and offer no offence to the living. He observed that urn-burial would not mean the end of tombs as such, for the Romans and Greeks had built superb tombs to house ashes. Money otherwise wasted on elaborate funerals could be spent on beautiful urns and tombs set in an Arcadian landscape. While trees and shrubs would create glades within the cemetery, the perimeter of the grounds could have arcaded columbaria to resemble the cloistered cemeteries of Italy. Robinson's ideas might have created some beautiful cemeteries, with landscapes reminiscent of those of Claude.

The French, the Germans, and especially the Italians have approached crematoria design with *panache*. Crematoria are accepted for what they are. They are places where bodies are consumed by fire, where bones are ground up in pulverisers, and where the resultant ash is stored before being scattered, placed in an urn, buried, or transported. They have other functions that are associated with the primary function, for there may be religious services, or some other ritualistic or symbolic farewell involving friends or relations.

The whole modern cremation movement was historically secular, functional, hygienic, and even anti-clerical. Religious aspects have been applied to cremation ceremonies, as will be apparent from the Siemens Apparatus picture, where the image of a grave is foremost (Pl. 2). The uncomfortable designs of so many British crematoria seem to owe their origins to woolly thinking, to misplaced sentiment, and to a suffocating attempt to pretend that everything is not what it seems. The depressing gentility of crematoria becomes staggeringly banal when attempts are made to brighten up chapels with light woods, plastic seats, and pastel colours.

Man has disposed of his dead with ceremonial grace throughout his history. The rites of disposal have involved a framework within which deep emotions can be expressed. The design of crematoria does not evolve from any liturgical requirement, since there was no rite in modern times for cremation in a European tradition. The usual form of rite at a British crematorium is the burial service, adapted indifferently, and embarrassingly used. A crematorium should deal with the emotional needs of the bereaved as well as with the industrial process of disposal of the dead, but the usual building either offends feelings or lets the mourner down badly by not satisfying a basic human need. Mourners arrive at the crematorium and enter the chapel. There may even be a waiting period if the chapel is being used, and so emotional discomfort is experienced at the beginning. The coffin may be on the catafalque (usually placed off-centre) or it may be carried into the chapel. The service will be perfunctory, and at the words of committal the coffin disappears by being screened, by being lowered through the floor, or by being trundled horizontally through a door. Whatever the method used (and the movement by remote control simply adds to the sense of unreality and even of offence) the service has ended, the coffin has vanished, but there has been no sight of the obvious ending, as there is when a coffin drops into a grave, or a body is buried at sea. The significance of seeing a body buried in the earth or at sea is profoundly moving, and those who have experienced such committals have an emotional response that becomes part of life, enriching, and teaching. In crematoria, the coffin has been transferred mechanically to a chamber, where it is placed on a trolley to await the entry to the furnace. Thus any committal that is spoken has not been a committal, and yet a committal at the time of the saying of the words should be the climax of the ceremony, and the point where the emotional realities should be experienced. These realities involve a sense of severance from the ties with the dead person, and a consummation of the ceremony. There should therefore be a true and direct committal to the flames when the words are spoken. Only then can the profound emotional experience of an ending and a farewell be felt. The failure to see what happens to the coffin merely leaves mourners uncertain, with a sense of having left the dead in the lurch.

Mr Peter Bernard Bond[17] has suggested that the problems of unresolved design and unsatisfactory function seem to stem from the use of an intermediate chamber to which the coffins go to await transfer to the furnaces. These 'committal chambers' appear to be so placed because it is thought to be more fitting to prevent the mourners seeing the entrance to the furnace, and also because cremation of a body takes over an hour, while a service may only last fifteen minutes. The committal chamber may therefore have several coffins awaiting their turn. Mr Bond suggests that the committal chamber should be done away with and that at least three furnaces should be installed. The chapel would then become a place of prayer or of meditation, and the 'absence of the device used for removing the coffin' obviates the distraction normally created by having two foci. Mr Bond suggests that after the service the coffin, minister, and mourners should then leave the chapel and proceed together to the places of committal which would be in the form of cloistered courts with pools in the centres. 'By passing out of the chapel into the open air there is an environmental change which can provide a certain relief, and this is enhanced by the small level of background noise from beyond the boundaries of the site together with the presence of trees, plants and perhaps running water in pools within the courts themselves.' However, it is off these courts that the entrances to the cremators would be situated. The actual committal would thus 'no longer be carried out by municipal operatives but by the minister himself. The committal is thus direct and true to the words of the service, with nothing coming between the ceremony and its fulfilment.' As Mr. Bond points out, however, views 'differ violently on whether or not mourners should see the coffin entering the interior of the cremator'. He suggests a 'baffle chamber' which would permit the doors of the aperture in the court to close before those into the cremator open. 'If desired both can open simultaneously, and so permit a view of the coffin entering the flames. Thus the differing wishes of different people are catered for, and provision is made for any future change of attitude that may take place in relation to this all-important question, for there is no escaping the fact that the committal of the body to the flames is the real conclusion to the ceremony and, being real, it may be valuable, however painful, that it should be faced.' The committal could become an act of great dignity in which the mourners would participate more fully.

Plate 8 Crematorium
designed by Gunnar
Asplund, built between
1935–40 (*Photograph by C. G.
Rosenberg, lent by Sveriges
Arkitekturmuseum, Stockholm*)

The disposal of ashes has encouraged various solutions, including scattering, burial, or storage in columbaria. Many nineteenth-century solutions[18] proposed large columbaria or landscaped areas where ashes could be built into walls specially constructed to take memorial-bricks or tablets. Most columbaria were operated on the principle that niches could be purchased for a few years, or in perpetuity. Ideas for columbaria were probably the last instances where buildings associated with death in Britain had dignity, although there is still an honourable tradition of funerary architecture in Europe and in America. In the 1870s Willson's ideas for a pyramid were revived, this time to accept urns and caskets. They were not to be realized, however.[19] The cremation movement, being largely the work of nineteenth-century committees, is particularly well documented. Exhaustive and exhausting accounts are given in many publications.[20]

In Sweden, one of the first crematoria was erected in 1889 in the Eastern Cemetery in Gothenburg, to designs by Hans Hedlund. In this crematorium, as with many of the early examples, the body was placed directly in the furnace without any intermediate chamber. Committal really was committal, and mourners witnessed the coffin going into the fire.

The Svenska Eldbegangelse-foreningen helped to create a climate of opinion that established cremation near centres of population. Scandinavia has been in the van of good modern design, but Sweden has particularly distinguished herself in the design of cemeteries and of crematoria. The beautiful cemeteries, with headstones and other memorials subtly related to each other and to their setting in forest glades, will be unforgettable images to those who have experienced them. The rolling landscapes, trees, shrubs, walls, and buildings of Swedish cemeteries are intensely moving, and very appropriate. Crematoria need settings of landscaped parkland, or even of woods, as they should be remote, quiet places. There are certain symbolic and emotional reasons why they should be near water or should have artificial lakes or pools formed near them. Fire and water, as opposites, should be found together to create a balance. The beautiful crematorium and cemetery outside Stockholm, by Gunnar Asplund, of 1935–40, comprise a work of great serenity where there is nothing of the commonplace (Pl. 8). Perhaps for the first time in modern architecture, buildings and landscape have been successfully blended in this unique work by a Swedish master. The classical serenity of the great portico to the crematorium gives a sense of repose to the building. The cross, as a Christian symbol, may reassure, but it is the classical balance and calm of the structure in relation to the landscape that induce an easing quietude in the beholder. Asplund had a classicist's sense of reticence and order, but his detailing was superbly refined as well, so the whole cemetery with its buildings is perhaps one of the greatest works of twentieth-century funerary architecture.

War cemeteries and memorials

Pugna suum finem, cum jacet hostis, habet.

OVID *Tristia*, book iii, Eleg. 5, line 34

There are few die well that die in a battle.

SHAKESPEARE: *Henry V*, Act IV, Sc. 1, line 148

Permanent memorials to the dead have been desired by generations of people in Western European culture. The wish to make a structure that will withstand the worst that time and the elements can do has existed since the beginning of history. This wish is connected with a need for a permanent record as well as with the need to make some visible symbol to express what society feels it should remember. Death, sacrifice, gratitude, remembrance, sorrow, loss, victory, effort, waste, and heroism can be commemorated by a monument; at times of great loss or disaster the need for a memorial asserts itself. Since the Great War of 1914–18, many consider that national memorials should take some utilitarian form. This tendency reflects the materialistic attitudes of the puritan forces in our midst, and was mentioned by Adshead during the 1914–18 War when he noted that credit should be given to the 'utilitarian patriots of the last century' for the discovery 'that a memorial could take the form of a hospital or similar institution'. One Urban Council, according to Adshead, commemorated the Jubilee of Queen Victoria by constructing a new public sewer.[1] One shudders to think what European civilization would be like if the Greeks, the Romans, and the great monumental builders down the centuries had set their sights on purely utilitarian values. All vivid expression and all the poetry of art and sculpture would have been denied, had a utilitarian attitude to commemorative works prevailed. There is a tendency today to pay lip-service to social causes, forgetting that all great art can uplift and express deep emotions without having any intrinsic 'use', or social purpose. A great war memorial, like Sir Robert Lorimer's Scottish National Memorial in Edinburgh, is far removed from a hospital, from a municipal hall, or from a new sewer: it is rather a work of a sublime and uplifting quality, and cannot be measured in utilitarian terms. As such, it is equivalent to the very greatest memorials that European civilization has produced.

Certainly, in 1945, the philistines were in full cry, demanding memorials that were not 'lifeless stone', but of some 'social purpose'. Lord Winster spoke against them in the House of Lords, and expressed his concern that 'war memorials' should be 'used as a means of raising money in order to carry out somebody's pet scheme or further somebody's pet hobby'.[2] In the same debate, Lord Chatfield observed that a war memorial 'is not a means of relieving the State of its reponsibilities to our fighting men and women' after the war; nor should it be 'something which would in any case be provided by the State or by a local authority'.[3]

A memorial is a memorial, not a social service. If the two functions are combined, the fact that a building or a fund may be a memorial will quickly be forgotten. Even a celebrated memorial, such as the Shaftesbury Memorial Fountain in Piccadilly Circus, by Alfred Gilbert, is hardly remembered as such. It is simply Eros in Piccadilly. Very different is the Albert Memorial in Kensington, for the shrine-like qualities of this noble, glowing work of Italian Gothic render it unmistakable. Memorials, to be successful, must have a spiritual and poetic content. The Cenotaph in Whitehall, the great memorials to Lincoln and Jefferson, the war cemeteries in Flanders and The Somme, and the imperial tombs of Rome, all express something beyond pure function. The attempt to combine commemoration with practical use causes problems. Use may be an attribute that disqualifies a memorial from success, for the confusion of the concept clouds the purpose and obscures its impact. A true memorial should simply *be*, and not be confused with good works. Its purpose is to cause people to remember, and to provide a reminder. Its *raison d'être* is to keep before the beholder what or who is being commemorated. Eros, on his marvellous *Art-Nouveau* base, is a fine piece of civic art, but as a memorial, he fails.

The huge losses of human life in the war of 1914–18 defy comprehension. The British dead of two World Wars lie in 23,527 cemeteries that contain 1,135,645 burials, including 204,206 unidentified bodies. The latter are included in the staggering total of 764,344 names inscribed on memorials as 'missing'; and so half a million British soldiers have simply disappeared, drowned in the mud of Flanders, or blown to smithereens.[4] The statistics of the First World War are truly terrible, and the need to provide burial grounds and memorials for the dead was profoundly necessary to a nation that had lost so much. That need was equally necessary to the French, to the Germans, to the Italians, and to all the countries that had shared in the destruction and the carnage. In France and Belgium the cemeteries of war are among the most disturbing of the monuments of man. There is perhaps no other experience that has moved me as much as the visits to the ossuaries, memorials, and cemeteries of Flanders Field. The idiocy of war, the suicide of European manhood, and the immense and overwhelming waste, are hammered home when we survey these bitter reminders of that brutal foolishness of mankind.

Yet it is a measure of the greatness of the architects, like Blomfield, Lutyens, and others, that their designs for the memorials and cemeteries of the vast armies of the British Empire can move the beholder so deeply by the consistency of their reiterated themes. The Stone of Remembrance of Lutyens and Blomfield's Cross of Sacrifice are constant motifs that transcend banality and sentimentality by their quiet, classical beauty. The sight of Blomfield's cross above a low wall in a field of corn, or standing high on a hill backed by woods brings comfort, a lump to the throat, and a sense of timeless and universal eloquence.

The vast numbers of dead and the ghastly mess of the battlefields, demanded that bodies should be recovered, identified where possible, and buried in an orderly fashion. After 1918, this enormous task was commenced, and the grisly business moved apace. There were pressing reasons why the dead had to be honoured. In Britain, as in other countries, the propaganda of hatred and of joys to come had been immensely successful. The stark realities of the aftermath of war, including unemployment, inflation, and the fact that the nation was practically bankrupted, began to stir elements within the populace. Germany was ruined, and France had lost nearly one in every twenty-eight of her population. Revolution had come to Russia, to Austria-Hungary, to Germany, and to other countries. Starvation had weakened the European peoples, so that the Spanish Influenza epidemic was able to claim victims on a scale worthy of modern warfare. Moreover, there was trouble in Ireland, and troops were sent to Glasgow. The sacrifice had to be *seen* to provoke a response, and so war memorials to honour the vanished armies had to be created. The bereaved had to be reassured that their losses were appreciated. The dead of perhaps the greatest catastrophe the nation had ever experienced had to be commemorated. In short, war memorials were seen as necessary by the existing powers.

Designers had the awe-inspiring task of creating in three-dimensional form something that would symbolize the greatness of the sacrifice. It is no accident that the architects who were commissioned by the Imperial War Graves Commission rose to the challenge by using the language of classicism, as the only vocabulary that could adequately express the magnitude of the disaster. Some later memorials in a so-called 'modern' idiom have only demonstrated its inadequacy. A movement without a grammar or a vocabulary will be hard pressed to produce satisfactory monuments.

The architects who designed the memorials and cemeteries did not make monuments to celebrate victory or to praise war. There was nothing of the bombast of imperial Roman monuments, of Napoleonic triumphal arches, or of Prussian victory columns. The Menin Gate at Ypres is a profoundly moving gate to a city, stark in its simple classicism. Even more bare is the gigantic memorial to the missing at Thiepval, which is stripped almost entirely of its classical elements, leaving only the form and bones of a last memory of classicism.[5]

The dead of battle were tipped into mass-graves in the past, while even in the nineteenth century the practice of antiquity was usual after battles. The tumulus of Marathon is both the grave and the memorial of those who perished in the battle. Later tumuli were carefully shaped and surmounted by sculpture, as at Waterloo. Yet the battles of the past, however bloody, were tiny affairs compared with the monstrous slaughter of 1914–18, and still the Imperial War Graves Commission provided individual graves in the cemeteries. In the course of Victorian times, respect for the dead, like compassion for the underdog, became usual, and demanded that all the dead in battle should be decently buried and properly commemorated. The American Civil War was the first war of modern times in which proper

cemeteries for all ranks were laid out, and the Franco-Prussian War of 1870–1 produced a similar concern for the dead on both sides. Soldiers were no longer 'professionals', in the sense that armies became huge, and were largely composed of conscripts; therefore national interest in the burial-places of individuals also increased. During 1914–18 whole populations were flung into the deadly struggle, and so each death had to be commemorated, since every individual now counted, although it would not seem so from the casualty figures or from the profligate manner in which soldiers were sent to die.

In 1919 architects in Britain were steeped in a classicism derived from the seventeenth century and from a European tradition. Albert Richardson, one of the best classicists of his generation, had produced a book on monumental classical architecture in 1914, and had also written articles on monumental architecture in which he showed sympathy for Neoclassical French examples and distaste for the later monuments of the Second Reich. Laurence Weaver's influential work also set a certain tone by which a classical language was established as a natural mode for monumental art.[6]

The ideas for setting up machinery for registering graves of soldiers came from Fabian Ware, who began to realize the necessity of the task during his work for the Red Cross. The War Office recognized Ware's work in 1915, and the Graves Registration Commission was transferred to the Army. Land was granted in perpetuity by the Belgian and French Governments, and in 1917 the Imperial War Graves Commission was established to care for all the graves of soldiers of the Empire. Ware approached Lutyens and Herbert Baker to advise on the cemeteries to be established, and Lutyens produced a memorandum in 1917 in which he recommended each cemetery would have 'a great stone' of 'fair proportions' raised on steps. Later recommendations advised that all headstones should be uniform, that each cemetery should have a chapel, and that landscape advice should be sought.

The Government decided in 1916 that families would not be allowed to reclaim bodies for burial at home, something that caused much debate and distress at the time. Instead, uniform headstones inscribed with the name, rank, and regimental badge of the dead were to be erected.

Much of the classical language used for the cemeteries was criticized for being pagan, but Blomfield's Cross of Sacrifice was to provide a Christian symbol to stand sentinel over the cemeteries. Lutyens was anxious to give these places 'repose and dignity', while Baker emphasized the 'sense of reverence and peace' that was so desirable.

In 1918, Baker, Lutyens, and Blomfield were appointed principal architects for the cemeteries in France, and Holden was appointed in 1920. There was a team of assistants set up in France, and these architects designed the mass of detail in hundreds of cemeteries, using the main elements designed by the masters. Blomfield tended towards a classicism derived from Wren. Lutyens created an individual monumentality that owed much to classicism, but was stripped, transmogrified, and changed to something deeply personal and very moving. Baker's work leans more heavily on heraldry, and perhaps betrays a hint of the sentimental at times. Holden's classicism is even more stripped than that of Lutyens, and was sometimes criticized for its severity.

The architects were anxious to avoid sculpture as much as possible, so that the ghastly angels and sentimental figures of French memorials could be eschewed. Architectural elements were of paramount importance, and include sarcophagi, huge blocks of stone, strips, arches, colonnades, stone flags, and stone wreaths. Some excellent sculpture was nevertheless executed by leading artists of the period.

Sir Robert Lorimer designed many fine cemeteries in Northern Italy and in Greece, in country that appealed to this great Scots architect. Another Scot, Sir John Burnet, contributed many moving designs in Palestine.

There were special problems associated with the memorials to the missing, for almost half the casualties had no known graves. It was not practicable to put up memorials with the names of the missing at the places where they were assumed to have died, and so it was determined to erect such memorials in association with the battle monuments. The first of these was planned at Ypres by Sir Reginald Blomfield, who produced sketches for a memorial gateway to the ruined city in 1919.

The triumphal arch, familiar from Roman examples like the Arch of Titus, the Arch of Septimius Severus, and the Arch of Constantine, have had their progeny. The Arc de Triomphe de l' Etoile in Paris is an obvious example, but less well known and certainly as significant, are the All India National Memorial, the Somme Memorial, and the Menin Gate. One of the

Plate 2 The Menin Gate, Ypres (*The Author*)

problems of a triumphal arch is that it is only successful as an object from the front or the rear. The Paris arch was widened to have arches in the sides, and so it is more three-dimensional in character. It was begun in 1806 to commemorate the Battle of Austerlitz, and was designed by Chalgrin. The All India National Memorial in Delhi was completed in 1930 to designs by Sir Edwin Lutyens, and this, too, has arches in the sides, to increase the three-dimensional effect. Lutyens was to achieve the complete metamorphosis of the triumphal arch so that the subordinate sides became triumphal arches in themselves in his Somme memorial at Thiepval (Pl. 1). While here, pile upon pile of monumental masonry and brickwork achieves a sublime effect expressing the stupefying losses in war, it is arguable that one of the most serene and moving memorials on the triumphal-arch theme is the Menin Gate at Ypres. This is essentially a long, arched gate to the city, situated on the ramparts. The triumphal arches are façades, and are of the Roman Doric Order. On either side of the tunnel is a colonnade of six columns. One triumphal arch is surmounted by a lion, carved by Sir William Reid Dick, while the other is capped by a draped sarcophagus. The walls of the coffered vault are covered with the names of the British killed in the battles of the Ypres Salient, who have no known graves (Pls. 2, 3).

Unfortunately, even the huge expanses of stonework at the Menin Gate were insufficient for the recording of the 'intolerably nameless names', so Herbert Baker had to provide a great curved wall at Tyne Cot cemetery at Passchendaele to enable a permanent record to be created.

Competitions were arranged for further memorials, but the French

Plate 3 Interior of the Menin Gate, Ypres (*The Author*)

government became concerned at the number and size of British memorials, so many cemeteries were enlarged to include memorials. H. Charlton Bradshaw's designs for Ploegsteert was one such enlargement, and is very successful, in the form of a circular colonnade that encloses an open space. Sculptured lions by Gilbert Ledward guard this memorial to the missing (Pl. 4).

The Loos memorial by Baker is combined with the Dud Corner cemetery, and consists of a colonnade at one side of the walled cemetery. In the centre of the colonnade is the Cross of Sacrifice on a series of steps. The colonnade itself has pavilions capped by domes (Pl. 5). W. H. Cowlinshaw used a much more severe and unrelieved colonnade of Tuscan columns at Pozières on the Somme. The only point of focus is the Cross of Sacrifice (Pl. 6). H. Charlton Bradshaw also designed the memorial to the missing of Cambrai in the Louveral military cemetery. It consists of a triumphal arch before a semicircular colonnaded cloister that embraces the Stone of Remembrance of Lutyens. The sculptured panels are by Charles Sargeant Jagger (Pl. 7). Perhaps the finest of all colonnades is that at the Faubourg

Plate 4 Memorial to the missing in the Berks cemetery extension, Ploegsteert (*Commonwealth War Graves Commission*)

Plate 5 The Loos memorial to the missing at Dud Corner cemetery (*Commonwealth War Graves Commission*)

Opposite above
Plate 6 Pozières on the Somme, memorial to the missing (*Commonwealth War Graves Commission*)

Below Plate 7 Cambrai memorial in the Louveral military cemetery (*Commonwealth War Graves Commission*)

d'Amiens cemetery at Arras, by Lutyens (Pl. 8). The G. H. Goldsmith design for the missing of the Marne at La Ferté-sous-Jouarre consists of a blocky podium (flanked by pedestals on which are urns) and surmounted by a sarcophagus. The composition is noble in its classical severity (Pl. 9).

Plate 8 Arras memorial at the Faubourg d'Amiens cemetery, near Arras (*Commonwealth War Graves Commission*)

The national and battle memorials of the Great War are often of superlative quality. They show how an interpretation of classical elements could produce monuments that truly functioned as such. Even the Ossuary at Douaumont has an essentially severe, classical form and general arrangement. British and American war cemeteries are generally of a very high standard of design. The Loos memorial at Dud Corner Military Cemetery by Sir Herbert Baker; the Ploegsteert Memorial, by H. Charlton Bradshaw; the Canadian National Memorial at Vimy Ridge, by W. S. Allward; the Etaples Military Cemetery by Sir Edwin Lutyens; the Meuse-Argonne American Military Cemetery, by York and Sawyer; the St Mihiel American Military Cemetery, by Thomas Harlan Ellott; the Aisne-Marne American Memorial at Château-Thierry, by Paul P. Cret; the American Memorial of Saint-Mihiel at Montsec, by Egerton Swartwout; and many others in Flanders and on the Somme, are supreme expressions of the architecture of death.[7]

The Meuse-Argonne American Cemetery is formally laid out on a slope not far from Verdun. The memorial buildings themselves are at the top of the hill, and are Romanesque in style, with a chapel and flanking wings. Greek Doric was preferred for the buildings at Saint-Mihiel which consist

Plate 9 The Marne memorial at La Ferté-sous-Jouarre (*Commonwealth War Graves Commission*)

of an open colonnade attached to a chapel and a museum. The dignified American cemeteries are superbly maintained, nobly conceived, and usually classical in inspiration. The war cemeteries of the Second World War are also fine, but the classical influence is less strong. The central building of the Ardennes American cemetery consists of a large rectangular block on a podium, reminiscent of a gigantic mausoleum. The American cemeteries at Florence and Nettuno are perhaps the most successful, owing to their landscaping and siting.

The national battle memorials of India and Canada are perhaps among the best of the national memorials. The India memorial is by Sir Herbert Baker. The Stone of Remembrance is in the centre of a circular space enclosed by a wall. One half of the wall is formed of Sanchi rails not unlike those around Buddhist shrines. On a pedestal is an Indian column flanked by tigers, in a composition reminiscent of the Lion Gate at Mycenae. On either side are domed pavilions (Pl. 10). The celebrated Canadian Memorial at Vimy Ridge designed by W. S. Allward reaches heights of originality. It consists of two vertical shafts that stand on a platform, the shafts being carved with figures that seem to grow from the stone (Pl. 11).

The Military Cemetery at Etaples by Sir Edwin Lutyens has a particularly fine setting for the Stone of Remembrance and the Cross of Sacrifice. Both are in the centre of a long podium with a screen wall at the rear. On either side of the podium are pavilions consisting of miniature triumphal arches surmounted by catafalques and sarcophagi (Pl. 12).

Plate 10 Indian Army memorial in Neuve Chapelle (*Commonwealth War Graves Commission*)

Plate 11 Canadian Memorial at Vimy Ridge (*Commonwealth War Graves Commission*)

Plate 12 Pavilions in the
cemetery at Etaples (*Country
Life*)

There can be few memorials as moving and as saddening as those in the
vicinity of Verdun in France. This fortress town was battered by huge
German armies in 1914–18, and France was nearly bled white, such was the
steady flow of young men along the Voie Sacrée. To lose Verdun would have
been a disaster in terms of national morale, and the government would not
have survived. As it was, holding on to Verdun was also a disaster, for the
toll in lives was colossal, and the effect on France was of long duration. Here,
there was no poetry, only the horror of mechanized war. The famous
rallying-cry of '*Ils ne passeront pas*' was effective, and the Germans did not
pass, although they captured Fort Douaumont at one stage, almost by
accident.

At the head of a mighty flight of steps in the town ramparts is a huge
battered pedestal on which stands a Frankish warrior looking out over the
battlefield. The architect was Chesnay, and the sculptor was Jean Boucher.
This monument, expressing the vigilance of France, was erected between
1920 and 1929 (Pl. 13). Across the river is a wall, with sculptured figures of
five soldiers of different armies forming a wall against the enemy. This is the
town memorial of Verdun, designed by Forest and carved by Grange
(Pl. 14).

The long and violent fighting, the very high casualties, and the huge proportion of unidentifiable bodies created special problems at Verdun. From August 1914 until the Armistice there was not a single day without a bombardment. By 1918 the ground around Verdun had become a desert, stripped of all vegetation, and covered only by fragments of corpses, bones, and the deathly jetsam of war. Only 120,000 bodies of French soldiers could be identified, approximately one third of the total killed. The identified dead

Plate 13 Monument on the walls of Verdun (*The Author*)

Plate 14 *Ils ne passeront pas* (*The Author*)

Plate 15 Ossuary at Douaumont (*The Author*)

were buried in the French national war cemeteries, except for about one tenth claimed by families.

In order to answer the demands of bereaved families, a committee was formed by Monsignor Ginisty, Bishop of Verdun, for the erection of a monument in the centre of the immense battlefield near Fort Douaumont. The unidentified bodies were moved to a temporary mortuary in 1919, where the remains were sorted and laid in coffins bearing the names of the battle sectors where they had been found. These names were later engraved on the sarcophagi in the Ossuary.

The subscription appeal was launched throughout all French territories, and a foundation-stone for the great Ossuary of Douaumont was laid on 22 August 1920. In March 1923 the committee selected a design by the architects Azéma, Hardy, and Edrei, and in September 1927 work was advanced enough to allow for the transfer of the bones to the sepulchral vaults of the monument. The Ossuary was officially inaugurated by the President of the Republic on 7 April 1932. His Excellency, Monsignor Petit, President of the Ossuary Committee, observed that:

> '*Douaumont, rempart contre l'envahisseur, est devenu le rempart contre l'oubli.*'

The Ossuary is a gigantic barrel-vaulted structure, about 140 m. long. In the centre is a huge tower, bearing a cross on each face. This tower is both belfry and beacon, and commands views over the whole battlefield. In front of the Ossuary is a large esplanade, bordered by twelve bollards linked by chains (Pl. 15). The largest national military cemetery in the area lies before the Ossuary.

Inside the barrel-vaulted Ossuary are eighteen alcoves with two sarcophagi in each. At each end are further sarcophagi. The graves underneath each have a capacity of about fifty-five cubic metres. Two other immense sepulchral vaults, completely filled with bones, lie under the granite shields at each end of the building (Pl. 16). The sarcophagi are of Breton granite. The inlaid floors represent the military orders. The names of the dead are inscribed on the walls of the Ossuary. On axis, behind the main entrance, is a chapel.

This astonishing, horrifying, and melodramatic building is one of the most anguished celebrations of death it is possible to conceive. The immensity of the slaughter is reflected in the memorial, and the jagged, rasping qualities of this extraordinary work of architecture abide with the visitor. It is a calamitous and agonizing experience to go to Douaumont. The Memorial is a private institution, but is recognized by the State as being of public interest. It is administered by a Committee presided over by the Bishop of Verdun.[8]

Very different is the Scottish National War Memorial in Edinburgh, designed by one of the greatest of all British architects of this century, Sir Robert Lorimer, who worked with his partner, John F. Matthew, on the realization of the project. Laurence Weaver compared the Cenotaph in Whitehall with Lorimer's masterpiece, and said that while 'England has made an ethereal monument of her inarticulateness, Scotland has seized the occasion to mobilise all the resources of her national art into a visible monument with form and colour'.[9] The memorial at Edinburgh Castle consists of a long gallery of honour, with wings, and an apse for the shrine opening from the centre. The styles chosen are curiously original. The shrine, in the form of a Gothic vaulted apse, contrasts with the gallery which owes not a little to classicism. The building attempts to record what the forces of Scotland did during the war, and has an atmosphere of repose and remembrance that is of the essence of poetry.

The Memorial was opened in 1927. The exterior is based on sixteenth-century Scottish Gothic to harmonize with the buildings of Edinburgh Castle. The walls are massive and bare, save for aedicules containing badges and statuary. The apsidal shrine is buttressed and though massive in itself, seems more decorated and lighter in character when seen against the stark stonework of the walls (Pl. 17). The exterior scarcely prepares the visitor for the richness and rare beauty of the interior. Opposite the entrance is the lofty arch of the shrine containing the Roll of Honour within a steel casket (Pl. 18).

Individual war memorials throughout Europe and America will be familiar to many. Several memorials in Britain consist only of Blomfield's Cross of Sacrifice, on its base, in combination with screen walls, altars, and inscriptions. Many larger cities chose a Cenotaph type of memorial, including Glasgow, Liverpool, Manchester, and Belfast, although the latter

Plate 17 Exterior of the Scottish National War Memorial at Edinburgh Castle, showing the apsidal shrine (*Wilson S. Groat, supplied by the Memorial and Records Office of the Scottish National War Memorial*)

has its Cenotaph backed by a beautiful semicircular screen of Greek Corinthian columns.

Memorials of extremely high quality include that of the Royal Artillery at Hyde Park Corner by Adams, Holden, and Pearson, with splendid sculpture by Charles Sargeant Jagger. The magnificent granite and bronze war memorial in Port Sunlight, Merseyside, marking the centrepiece of the cruciform pattern of boulevards, was designed by Sir William Goscombe John (1860–1952), and was erected in 1921.[10]

British war-memorial architecture was generally of the highest order, and those of the United States were also impressive, in the manner of the classical *Beaux-Arts* tradition so pre-eminent in the America of the time. Germany was not permitted to build large memorials in France or in

Plate 18 View into the apsidal shrine of the Scottish National War Memorial (*Wilson S. Groat, supplied by the Memorial and Records Office of the Scottish National War Memorial*)

Plate 19 Steps of the hundred-thousand dead at the Sacrario of Redipuglia (*Commissariato Generale Onoranze Caduti in Guerra*)

Belgium, but her cemeteries have a moving quality, with buildings generally in a German Arts-and-Crafts style, and crosses of black iron or granite. The memorials within Germany itself are often craggy and monolithic. The tomb of her Unknown Soldier was fashioned by Tessenow within the Neoclassical Neue Wache by Schinkel.

The finest and most impressive of German memorials were the Reichsehrenmal at Tannenberg, a massive work that commemorated the great victory over the Russians in 1914. The memorial was destroyed in 1945, and the body of von Hindenberg was removed from the mausoleum there to avoid its falling into the hands of Soviet forces. There is a curious Expressionist monument at Laboe, near Kiel, that also merits mention, and a delightfully whimsical 1870–1 *Jugendstil* memorial at Nördlingen.

Plate 20 Sarcophagus of the Duke of Aosta at Redipuglia (*Commissariato Generale Onoranze Caduti in Guerra*)

The Italians built their memorials with an imagination and sense of the theatrical that was perhaps avoided by the British and Germans. The great verve of the Italian approach is best expressed in the Redipuglia memorial where the ranks, each answering to the word '*Presente*', lie on the terraced slopes of a hill (Pl. 19). This magnificent memorial, near Udine–

Monfalcone, was designed by Giovanni Greppi, with sculpture by Giannino Castiglioni. The great steps with the '*Presente*' inscriptions are known as the stairs of the hundred-thousand dead. At the base of the steps is the great sarcophagus of the Duke of Aosta (Pl. 20). This noble memorial dates from 1938. The huge flight of steps at Redipuglia leads as though to the sky, for the only visible 'stop' consists of three slim crosses, as though on Calvary. The Italian landscape, with its many hills, suggested similar architectural solutions for other war cemeteries, including Monte Lungo and Monte Grappa. The latter is a vast circular tiered podium with a crowning chapel, also designed by Giovanni Greppi with sculpture by Giannino Castiglioni. The faces of the huge steps are pierced by tiers of semicircular-headed *loculi* containing the remains of the dead. Several sealed *loculi* are simply inscribed with the laconic inscription '*cento militi*

Plate 23 Ossuary at Castel
Dante di Rovereto
(*Commissariato Generale
Onoranze Caduti in Guerra*)

Plate 24 Sacrario Militare di
Asiago of 1936
(*Commissariato Generale
Onoranze Caduti in Guerra*)

ignoti'. Austro-Hungarian dead are also entombed in this enormous work dating from 1935 (Pl. 21).

The extraordinary *panache* of the designers of Italian memorials during the Fascist régime owed much to classicism, to monumentality, and to the dramatic possibilities of the sites. The enormous ossuary and memorial at Montello, designed by Felice Nori of Rome, was completed in 1935. It consists of a square podium approached by a monumental flight of steps. The main entrance is set beneath a ferociously simplified Greek Doric engaged portico. On the battered plinth is a large battered cubic form of masonry. Inside, *loculi* contain the remains of the dead (Pl. 22).

The great circular mausoleum-ossuary of Castel Dante di Rovereto dates from 1936 and was designed by Fernando Biscaccianti. It consists of a drum set on a podium composed of two vast steps. This monument recalls Hawksmoor's mausoleum at Castle Howard, but is in the undecorated, unenriched classical manner favoured by architects of the Fascist period (Pl. 23).

Mention should also be made of an Italian response to the triumphal-arch theme, so successfully exploited by Lutyens at Thiepval. The vast Sacrario Militare di Asiago of 1936 was designed by Professor Orfeo Rossato of Venice. It consists of a huge square podium on which is set a gigantic triumphal arch, square on plan, and with an arch on each face, a supremely successful solution to the problem of triumphal arches as a whole. The base contains the crypt, with the inevitable *loculi*, while the arch itself is a ciborium for a symbolic votive altar (Pl. 24). It contrasts with the ossuary of Pasubio, inaugurated in 1926, consisting of a battered tower on a podium that contains the ossuary. It is built on a commanding site which ensures that its unredeemed coarseness is visible for miles. The architect was Chemello of Vicenza.

Plate 25 *Sacrario Militare di El Alamein (Commissariato Generale Onoranze Caduti in Guerra)*

One of the last truly monumental war cemeteries is the Sacrario Militare di El Alamein designed by Paolo Caccia Dominioni and built in the 1950s. It consists of a battered octagonal tower on a long low podium, and is a noble and restrained monument in the impressive desert setting (Pl. 25). The plain masonry walls and the lack of decoration create a monolithic effect. Inside, the usual arrangement of *loculi* for the bodies is evident.

The sensitive designs of Eric Gill and others who worked on a revival of the best qualities of memorial art between the wars seem today to be largely forgotten; so, too, are the great celebrations of death found in war memorials, in individual monuments, and all aspects of such memorial sculpture and architecture. An entire language of how to celebrate death in some tangible memorial has been squandered. Death, sacrifice, even life itself, are now of little consequence. The banality of contemporary memorials reflects how society as a whole views the entire matter. Any memorial erected today for a statesman, for a cause, for an army, or even for one individual in a cemetery, graveyard, or crematorium will cause even the strongest to quail at the triviality of its mediocre language. It is perhaps significant that the most successful memorials and cemeteries of the post-1945 period are those designed by the Italians. A natural result of possessing the classical architecture of Greece and Rome as an architectural vernacular style has been the creation of some truly magnificent memorials by Italian architects and sculptors. The El Alamein Sacrario is one example, but just as moving are the smaller Sacrari, like that of the Fosse Ardeatine, a *tour de force* of monumental design worthy of the eighteenth century at its most inventive. Inspiration has failed the Anglo-Saxons, however.

A supreme sacrific, a great life, a national disaster, even an uneventful existence, deserve better memorials than the contemporary celebration of death can offer. The terrors of death are made more terrible by the insults of present-day designs for funerary memorials, especially in Britain. A language of expression has been lost. Nothing has replaced it.[11]

12

Some grander buildings to celebrate individuals and national events.

National Pantheons; Walhalla; Edinburgh; Obelisks; Cenotaphs and Shrines

In the afternoon of time
A strenuous family dusted from its hands
The sand of granite, and beholding far
Along the sounding coast its pyramids
And tall memorials catch the dying sun,
Smiled with content, and to this childish task
Around the fire addressed its evening hours.

R. L. STEVENSON: *Underwoods*

Great buildings to celebrate individuals and heroes, families, and victories were known in ancient times. The monuments of Greece and Rome were often associated with national events, as the grandeur of processional ways, triumphal arches, columns, and statuary makes clear. The classical language of architecture was always eminently successful in expressing solemn and important occasions. The cenotaphs and memorials of Greek culture were noble and moving works of art, while the power of Rome was often suggested by the mighty monuments of her triumphs, victories, and memorials.

Equestrian statues, busts, full-length figures, reliefs, and inscriptions can serve as memorials to eminent persons. Equestrian statues, from the time of the noblest of them all (that of Marcus Aurelius in Rome), have given the world grand civic ornaments that also function as memorials. Donatello's statue of General Gatamelata in Padua (1450) and Verrocchio's figure of Colleoni in Venice (1481) are good examples. The fine statue of Charles I by Le Sueur is somewhat lost among the mess of traffic in Trafalgar Square today, but is still a supremely successful memorial work of civic sculpture.

Other memorials may express religious belief, and often take the form of an altar, religious symbols such as the cross being much in evidence. Many Greek temples were war memorials, which also expressed thanks to the gods for deliverance or for victory. The Parthenon itself was an expression of thanks to Athene for the great victory over Persia. The huge public altars, like that at Pergamon, were altars of thanksgiving for victory.

Triumph and victory are often expressed by winged female figures, based on Greek statues of Nike, while horsemen or charioteers riding over the vanquished have a similar classical origin. The familiar statues of S. George and the Dragon on war memorials continue this theme into our era. Michael the Archangel slaying the dragon is a variation of the same idea, and columns and triumphal arches are recurring themes.

To the mediaeval mind monuments to events were unthinkable. Funerary architecture, as we have seen, was confined to the enrichment of churches. In some cases, chantry-chapels were added to churches. Tombs of the great were within churches, and were enriched architecturally within the all-embracing canopy of ecclesiastical buildings, with certain exceptions, like the Scaliger tombs, built at a time when the individual was already rising. The monumental crosses erected to mark the places where the bier of Queen Eleanor rested were unusual, for they were free-standing commemorative crosses to an individual.

The Renaissance in Italy encouraged the celebration of the individual.[1] The thirteenth-century political phenomena of tyrants and despots flourished following the transformation of the Empire under Frederick II, and later despotisms in which great individuals were raised to glorious heights saw a development of memorials and of funerary architecture. I have noted the tombs of the Scaligers in Verona. Though Gothic in form, they were free-standing works of architecture in their own right, and so were new and unmediaeval in spirit. During Renaissance times tombs of poets, philosophers, and artists achieved prominence. Dante's mausoleum is one example, and the unedifying squabbles over the poet's remains show a new emphasis.[2] Relics of saints had been important in the Middle Ages for commercial and religious reasons, but from Renaissance times bodies of the eminent in many fields achieved a new value of their own.

The development of the individual was matched by a corresponding desire for outward show, even for glory. Fame, like victory, was to demand its own memorial.[3] Certain poets were even offered processions, music, and clouds of incense such as had only been offered to saints in the past. Both Petrarch and Dante succumbed to the attractions of fame, but having tasted it they observed that it was foolish and brought its own problems. I have noted that the cult of preserving birthplaces and tombs of celebrated men grew from Renaissance times. Florence tried to make her great cathedral (and later the church of Santa Croce) a Pantheon, and efforts were made to retrieve the corpse of Dante from Ravenna, as well as Fra Filippo Lippi's from Spoleto. That these efforts were repulsed demonstrates how much the cult of secular tombs had moved. The Florentines had to be content to erect cenotaphs in several instances. Many Italian cities began to celebrate long-dead citizens with memorials. Renaissance topography demanded that no local celebrities would be forgotten, and thus the shift of importance away from churches was significantly advanced. Classical poets, historians, and other celebrities joined the saints as star attractions in city after city.

An impetus to the relishing of ancient art was given by the discovery, under Pope Julius II, of the Laocoön, of the Vatican Venus, and of other great classical sculptures. Raphael, outraged by the destruction of so much of ancient Rome, proposed that full surveys should be made of all remaining ancient buildings. Marble columns, once looted by the score to build Christian churches, were now falling victim by the hundred to builders who burnt the columns for quicklime. The ruins of a classical past and the tombs that lined the Appian Way gave incentives to archaeological zeal and to an expression of elegiac melancholy.

The great funerary architecture of the Renaissance and Baroque periods was usually associated with churches, and it was only with the eighteenth century that mausolea, free-standing and set apart from churches, became once more fashionable. A return to classical antiquity in the design of tombs as buildings in their own right did not occur until very late. The Hawksmoor mausoleum at Castle Howard, as we have seen, is one of the earliest.

Yet commemorative and monumental buildings, where the dead were *not* buried, had also been known in classical antiquity. Not Italy but France was to be the breeding-ground for a development of monumental architecture. Designs for buildings became profoundly changed in eighteenth-century France. Pierre Patte in his *Monumens érigés en France à la gloire de Louis XV* praises scientific and cultural achievements, emphasizes the need to reject superfluous ornament, and suggests that architecture would benefit all classes of society. Edmund Burke's influential *A Philosophical Enquiry into the Origins of our Ideas of the Sublime and Beautiful* had come out in 1757; it suggested that huge dimensions help us to experience the sublime, while the effects of darkness and shadow enhance this experience. Burke unquestionably influenced the French architects of the latter half of the eighteenth century, notably Boullée, who probably read Burke in Des François's translation of 1765. Ideas on aesthetics were propounded in the *Encyclopédie*, and a simplified style of Neoclassicism developed.[4]

Patte's book, published in 1765, proposed a number of *places* for his reconstruction of Paris, and motifs such as triumphal arches, statues, columns, and other civic ornaments point the way to a severe architecture that owed not a little to Burke. French architects and writers proposed radical approaches to town planning, involving ordered, classical layouts that were formal in the extreme.

Planning was also concerned with the dead and there was a growth of interest in the design of cemeteries, tombs, and cenotaphs. Boullée and his circle, as I have demonstrated, produced some astounding designs which show an optimism and understanding of the fullness of life. Diderot suggested that the respect of posterity could become a future catalyst for cultural revival, and would thus replace belief in the survival of individual souls. Monuments, cenotaphs, pantheons, and cemeteries were thus aspects of an expansion of ideas of rationality, secularism, and French philosophical development. William Godwin, the anarchist, published an *Essay on Sepulchres* in 1809, and his ideas are similar to Diderot's. Taste at the time favoured a monumental approach, as will have been demonstrated by Boullée's work. Godwin wrote that monuments to the dead were as important to a nation as were libraries.

Some of the most ambitious memorials were conceived when Neoclassicism flourished. The Panthéon in Paris on the Mont de Paris occupies the site of the tomb of S. Geneviève (422–512), the patron saint of Paris. The chapel erected over her tomb was replaced by a church. The present building, designed by Soufflot, was erected between 1764 and 1790 as a church dedicated to S. Geneviève. In 1791 it was decreed that it should be converted into a national memorial temple to be called the *Panthéon*, dedicated with the words *Aux grands hommes la patrie reconnaissante.*

Plate 1 The Panthéon, Paris
(*The Author*)

Mirabeau was interred there on 15 April 1791, and on 10 July the remains of Voltaire were also placed within the noble pile. Two further attempts were made to restore its use as a church in 1806 and 1851, but it was secularized in 1885 for the obsequies of Victor Hugo. Also buried in the Panthéon are Rousseau, Soufflot, Carnot, La Tour d'Auverge, and Bougainville. The Plan of the Panthéon is that of a Greek cross. The building is surmounted by a dome on a drum with a peristyle of Corinthian columns. A huge portico, based on that of the Pantheon in Rome, forms the entrance to this austere building (Pl. 1).

Neoclassical architecture, as suggested by Boullée, was ideally suited to the architecture of death. The blank walls of the Panthéon inspire awe, and the building has a curious serenity and stillness, giving it the air of timeless quality, an object in space. It is aloof, static, and far removed from the vulgar.

The influential designs by Percier and Fontaine for the Champs Elysées, Rue de Rivoli, and the Arc de Triomphe revived the Roman ideas of processional ways, triumphal arches, and great vistas, but on a much greater scale. The Arc de Triomphe is vast, its scale enhanced by the stripping of most of its decoration. That this is truly an heroic arch there can be no doubt in the beholder.

The Madeleine in Paris (1806–42) was intended as a Temple of Glory by Napoleon I. It was designed by P. Vignon in the manner of an octastyle peripteral Roman temple, and was completed in 1842 to designs by Huvé, though not as a Temple. Louis XVIII wished to make it an expiatory church with memorials to Louis XVI and his Queen, but a separate Chapelle

Expiatoire was erected elsewhere. The Madeleine became a Christian church, although its form betrays its original symbolism.

It is not surprising that two of the most successful practitioners of Neoclassicism, schooled in the formal eclecticism of Boullée and the Academy, Percier and Fontaine, chose that style for their Chapelle Expiatoire. The first stone was laid in 1815, and the building was completed in 1826. It was erected to the memories of Louis XVI and Marie Antionette, on the site of the old cemetery of the Madeleine, where the royal corpses lay from 1793 to 1815, when they were translated to the royal vaults at Saint-Denis. Louis XVIII took a personal interest in the erection of this extraordinary building, as well he might, and the construction was supervised by the architect Lebas.

The design for the Chapelle Expiatoire consists of a rectangular elevated courtyard surrounded by severe masonry. This courtyard is approached through a doorway set in a blank wall. Steps give access to the raised court. The temple itself is a square domed compartment with three *exedrae* and a tetrastyle portico of the Roman Doric Order (Pls. 2, 3, 4).

Also in Neoclassical style, but of a much more severely strict Greek Revival, is the Walhalla, near Regensburg, situated on a hill above the Danube. A broad flight of steps, divided into terraces, ascends to the building from the river-side. The site is beautifully chosen, and is surrounded by the woodlands of the high Breuberg. The views from the Walhalla are spectacular.

During the Napoleonic Wars in 1807, the young Crown Prince Ludwig of Bavaria (1786–1868) determined to build a temple to honour great Germans. He began collecting busts and statues of the heroes of the fatherland, including the painters Schadow, Rauch, Tieck, Dannecker, and Kauffmann; the regal figures of Heinrich I, Otto the Great, Konrad II, Frederick the Great, and Maria Theresia; the poets Albrecht von Haller, Klopstock, Lessing, Wieland, Winckelmann, Schiller, and Goethe; the musicians Haydn and Gluck; and the philosophers Leibniz and Kant. About sixty busts were assembled when Ludwig ascended the throne of Bavaria in 1825. The good monarch was not exactly narrowly nationalistic in his selection of those to be honoured, for in the teeth of criticism he began to include Swiss, Netherlanders, Anglo-Saxons, and Austrians for his pantheon.

In 1814 the Crown Prince had organized a competition among German architects for the building of his 'Ehrentempel'. In 1821 Leo von Klenze (1784–1864), one of Germany's greatest architects of the Neoclassical period, put plans before Ludwig. Leo von Klenze was involved in a number of royal building projects in Munich at the time, and in 1827 the ground for the Ehrentempel was selected in the Weinbergparzellen of the Breuberg. The idea of a Greek Doric temple on a massive podium of titanic size seems to derive from designs by Gilly for a monument to Frederick the Great, although this was never built. Gilly also used triumphal arches and obelisks to heighten the ornamental effects of his design. Sketches of a Walhalla had been made about 1815 by Karl Freiherr Haller von Hallerstein (a pupil of Gilly), and his ideas clearly inspired the built version.

Right Plate 2 Plan of the Chapelle Expiatoire in Paris (*Author's Collection*)

Far Right Plate 3 *Top*: elevation of the Chapelle Expiatoire *Bottom*: section through the court, showing the portico and dome of the Chapelle Expiatoire (*Author's Collection*)

Plate 4 Longitudinal section through the Chapelle Expiatoire (*Author's Collection*)

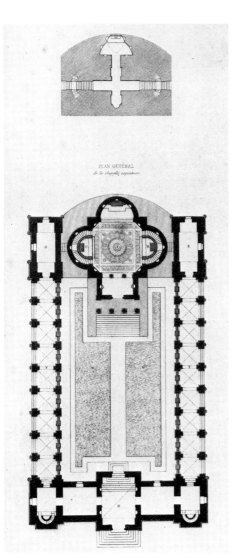

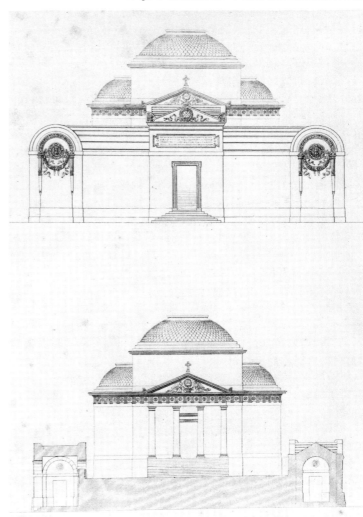

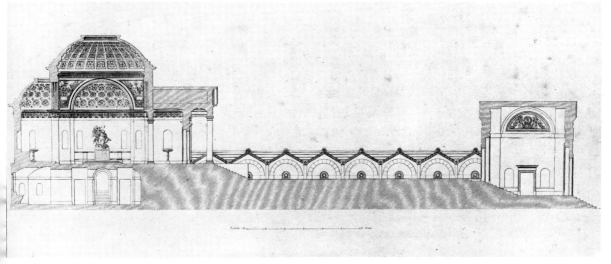

Ludwig I of Bavaria laid the foundation stone for the Walhalla on 18 October 1830, and the building was opened on 18 October 1842. The exterior is essentially modelled on the Parthenon (although the base derives from Gilly), and is a Greek Doric temple with a peristyle of fifty-two columns (Pl. 5). It is constructed of unpolished grey-white marble. Each pediment contains vigorous marble sculpture in the tympanum: that to the south is an allegory of the German states regaining their liberty after the Battle of Leipzig; while that to the north celebrates the victory of Arminius over the Romans in the Teutoburger Wald in AD 9. Both groups were sculpted by Ludwig Schwanthaler (1802–1848).

The interior, of the Ionic Order, is a work of supreme achievement. It consists of a nobly proportioned hall, with a coffered ceiling illuminated by three roof-lights. The main entablature is enriched by a marble frieze by Johann Martin Wagner (1777–1858) that represents the history of the Germans from the dim past to the arrival of Christianity. The attic stage is carried by caryatides, carved by Schwanthaler. This stage is embellished with tablets recording the names of famous Germans of whom no portrait survives. Marble busts line the walls, and this pantheon is still being added to by the Bavarian authorities.

A seated statue by F. von Miller of Ludwig I, clad in Roman toga, presides over the hall. The King had to relinquish his throne during the disturbances of 1848, when the righteous revolutionaries objected to his liaison with the dancer 'Lola Montez'. The rich, glowing colours of the interior, consisting of dark reds, greens, and whites, with gilding, contribute to a most satisfying architectural experience. Marbles from the Danube, from Rosenheim, from Carrara, from Schlanders, from Weltenburg, and from Tirol were selected by von Klenze to heighten the effects he sought.[5] (Von Klenze was also responsible for the Doric *Ruhmeshalle* in Munich of 1843–53 which contains busts and monuments of eminent Bavarians.)

Not far from the Walhalla is the Befreiungs-Halle on the Michaelsberg near Kelheim. It is a rotunda designed by Gärtner and von Klenze in the Greek Revival style, freely adapted. It was founded by Ludwig I in 1842 and was inaugurated in 1863. The exterior is embellished with eighteen figures representing the German provinces, and above the colonnade of seventy-two Doric columns are eighteen trophies. The interior contains allegories of victories by Schwanthaler, and the rich marble is further decorated with the names of German generals, captured fortresses, and celebrated German victories. The 'Hall of Liberation' is a national monument to celebrate the victories of the German States over the French.

Thomas Harrison's visionary and unexecuted schemes for a national British Valhalla are also firmly rooted in the Greek Revival, although he combined severe Doric Orders with central rotundas modelled on the sublime Pantheon dome in the Eternal City. Harrison's designs dated from 1814–15, and recall Barabino's schemes for the Staglieno in Genoa.

Thomas Hamilton and W. H. Playfair almost succeeded in converting part of Edinburgh into a Neoclassical masterpiece of monumental architecture. These two architects can be compared with von Klenze and Schinkel, for they raised the style of Greek Revival far above that practised

Plate 5 The Walhalla and
podium seen from the
Danube (*The Author*)

by Smirke and Wilkins. Hamilton's Edinburgh High School is perhaps the
most grand of all buildings of the Greek Revival in the Scottish capital,
while his Burns monument near by of 1830–32 combines ideas derived from
the Choragic monument of Lysicrates with details drawn from the temple of
the Sibyls at Tivoli. Playfair was more of a compromiser than the rigorous
Hamilton, yet his monument to Dugald Stewart of 1831–2 is firmly derived
from the Lysicrates prototype. The National Monument on Calton Hill in
Edinburgh was conceived in 1817 as a memorial to Scots killed during the
Napoleonic Wars, but it was also intended as a national Valhalla. It was
derived from the Athenian Parthenon, and it would have rivalled von
Klenze's Walhalla near Regensburg or his great Ruhmeshalle in Munich. It
was designed by C. R. Cockerell and W. H. Playfair, but only twelve
columns were erected, and it became known as 'Scotland's Disgrace', a
symbol of what Playfair called 'the pride and poverty of Scotland'.

The pantheon-type of hall of honour tends to express a certain national
pride, and may celebrate distinguished persons of all walks of life. It is far
removed from other memorials that express sorrow, death, or resignation,
such as in the memorials of ancient Greece and Rome, and in the monuments
of the Renaissance, classical, and Victorian periods. Mourning female figures
are found in classical designs, and often family groups may be found. Symbols
such as the inverted torch, the skull, the hourglass, and the scythe, all express
death, and have been familiar motifs since Renaissance times. Cenotaphs, or
memorials erected when the body was placed elsewhere, were found in the
classical period and were frequently employed as memorials to the fallen of the
Great War of 1914–18. The national Cenotaph in Whitehall, designed by Sir
Edwin Lutyens, is a fine example of this type.

Often great events or individuals have been celebrated by the erection of columns. Such memorials were known in ancient Greece, but reached a new popularity in Rome, for the statue could be raised above those of lesser men. Trajan's column in Rome has a spiral band of sculptured reliefs that celebrate the victories of the Emperor. Nelson's columns in Dublin and London, the Duke of York's column at Carlton House Terrace, and the many columns in country estates and provincial towns in Britain will be familiar. The great French celebration columns, such as the Colonne Vendôme, give focus to the townscape in Paris. A variation of the classical column with a statue on top is the variety of elongated pedestal, capped by a figure, found at the Lever Memorial at Port Sunlight, erected in 1930, and designed by Sir William Reid Dick.

Perhaps even more potent an image than the column is that other Neoclassical device, the obelisk. The grandest of all such memorials is undoubtedly the Wellington Testimonial in Phoenix Park, Dublin, by Sir Robert Smirke. It is one of the biggest obelisks in the world (the Washington monument of 1877–84 by Robert Mills is even bigger). On the massive base are bronzes celebrating events of the Duke of Wellington's life, three of which are by J. R. Kirk; the fourth (the Waterloo panel) is by Farrell. Subscriptions were collected from 1817, but the monument was not completed until 1861 (Pl. 6).

A memorial can serve as a reminder of sacrifices, and why such sacrifices were made, besides expressing mourning and a hope for the future. The Lincoln Memorial in Washington by C. F. McKim, executed by Henry Bacon, was built between 1915 and 1923; it is an eminently serene example of a memorial where a monument has been combined with a wider sense of remembrance. This cool Doric temple is in the line of a tradition of Neoclassical memorials. The Jefferson Memorial in Washington, completed in 1943, was designed by John Russell Pope, with Otto Eggers and Daniel Paul Higgins, and is an Ionic version of the Pantheon in Rome, but with a peristyle as well as a portico. Both memorial 'temples' enshrine huge statues of the men commemorated, and texts from their writings are inscribed on the walls.[6]

The cult of memorials achieved great impetus in the nineteenth century, and every new war brought forth patriotic memorials. Nationalism therefore was a most important factor in the development of memorials. Allegorical figures in profusion began to grace monuments. Where once the simple column or obelisk had been considered a powerful enough motif, now elaborate memorials were created on an unprecedented scale.

Significantly, generals, politicians, and rulers were the most frequently honoured during the nineteenth century. The enormous number of statues to celebrate the heroes of long-forgotten skirmishes bear witness to a glorification of arms and a new overweening national pride.

There are exceptions, of course. The death of the Prince Consort in 1861 brought forth a number of memorials, the finest of which is that in Kensington Gardens. The Albert Memorial was the subject of study by no less than nine architects who submitted proposals in 1863. P. C. Hardwick produced an uncovered equestrian statue, but all the other eight designs

Plate 6 Wellington Testimonial, Dublin (*The Author*)

were elaborate, consisting of a protective architectural scheme for statuary. Charles Barry proposed that 'the new metal, aluminium' should be used for the Prince's statue. G. Gilbert Scott, the architect whose design was finally selected, had been engaged by the Queen to convert the 'Wolsey Chapel' at Windsor to the Albert Memorial Chapel, and in 1862 he had ventured to suggest to the Queen that a proposal for an obelisk memorial would be unsuitable. Scott was the only Gothicist among the architects involved, and he clearly felt isolated. In his submission, he indicated that the inspirations for his design were the Eleanor Crosses. The canopy was 'to protect and overshadow the Statue of the Prince'. This idea is the keynote of his design, and Scott was anxious to suggest a 'vast shrine' enriched with 'all the arts by which the character of *preciousness* can be imparted'. Scott's scheme was for a colossal statue of the Prince placed 'beneath a vast and magnificent shrine or tabernacle, and surrounded by works of sculpture illustrating those arts and sciences' which Albert had fostered. The architect saw his design as a ciborium, like the canopy over an altar in an 'ancient Basilica'. The Albert Memorial is based upon canopied shrines of the Middle Ages. It consists of a statue of the seated Prince, by Foley, set on a great stepped base and podium. Over the statue is a magnificent canopy in the Italian Gothic style of the thirteenth century, lavishly decorated with mosaics. The marble reliefs around the base show celebrated people from every age, while allegorical groups flank the steps. The design of the canopy is clearly derived from the Scaliger tombs at Verona, and from other canopied features of Italian Gothic art, especially the reliquaries (Pl. 7). Time and pollution have started to cause the marble statuary groups and reliefs to deteriorate to a considerable degree. The proposal by Sir Henry Cole to enclose the memorial within a glass conservatory or 'winter garden' similar to the Crystal Palace in detail might well appear far less extravagant today in view of the havoc caused by acidic deposits.

The equestrian statues that adorned European cities were all inspired by Roman precedent, and many fine adornments to cities resulted. Statues of persons not on horseback also became common. George Square in Glasgow is positively crammed with statues. All these monuments obeyed the same rule: a base of granite or other enduring stone was built and inscribed, on which stood a statue, usually of bronze. Early nineteenth-century statesmen are often shown robed like Roman Senators, but contemporary dress was usual during the Victorian period. The most gigantic of all statues of a Neoclassical type is the figure of Liberty in New York by Frédéric-Auguste Bartholdi, but even Liberty stands on a huge podium, obeying the basic classical formula. Allegorical figures adorned monuments to celebrate national pride, or victory. The Victory Column of 1873 in Berlin by Strack, for example, has a podium of impeccable Neoclassical type, not unlike that of the Wellington Testimonial in Dublin. Above is a fluted column with its base surrounded by a Tuscan peristyle. The winged female figure by Drake that crowns the column wears a helmet adorned with the German eagle and carries a crown of victory. The great bronze reliefs were by Calandrelli, Schulz, Keil, and Wolff. The colonnade surrounded a drum of mosaics designed by von Werner and executed by Salviati of Venice. Even more grandiose was the design by Karl Weisbach for the Niederwald monument of 1877. German victory-memorials tended to be somewhat overblown and excessively decorated, while their scale was often huge.

For all the over-elaboration of many late-nineteenth century monuments, the language of classical architecture was the vocabulary most widely used to express commemoration. Boullée wrote that if we desire to pay homage to great men, the simplest of effects should be employed to emphasise the play of light and shade, and of form against form. By means of triumphal arches, obelisks, pyramids, sarcophagi, and blank walls, the glory of a dead hero can be expressed. Boullée considered that such monuments expressed the grief of the nation and the desire to perpetuate memory. The use of simple geometrical forms, arranged within a formal layout based on classical principles, achieved new heights in monumental design in the hands of Boullée and his contemporaries. William Wood, in *An Essay on National and Sepulchral Memorials*, published in 1808, also suggested the use of

Plate 7 Albert Memorial in Kensington (*G.L.C. Department of Architecture and Civic Design*)

antique forms, such as the pyramid, combined with Neoclassical cornerpieces not unlike the tomb at Walworth Old Church. Boullée, in his design for Newton's cenotaph, used the globe as his primary architectural element. The classical tradition in funerary architecture was emphasized by J-N-L. Durand in his *Recueil*, where there is a survey of cenotaphs, fully illustrated. Yet Boullée observed that in architecture the word colossal is often confused with what artists term grandiose. To Boullée a colossal monument should excite admiration, and it should overwhelm all that surrounds it. He admired Trajan's column in Rome, because its proportions are 'extraordinary, its concept astounding', and the whole is satisfying. He contrasted this column with the interior of S. Peter's in Rome which does not overwhelm, because we 'do not experience any sensation that corresponds to its size'. The wonder that the visitor experiences inside the Pantheon in Rome, however, is undeniable. Boullée emphasized that size itself could defeat its purpose by destroying the sense of proportion in the beholder. To many of the French architects of the period, the sense of the sublime could invoke the infinite.

Lutyens was undoubtedly successful in creating a sublime monument at Thiepval, and the scale of this colossal arch would doubtless have appealed to Boullée and his associates. No monument of modern times conveys so much of the disasters of the First World War, or is as successful in suggesting the infinite through its sublime proportions. Lutyens, a master of classical form, used the supreme language of classical architecture to commemorate a catastrophe. The monument, in its silence, is more eloquent than words.

It is all the more painful, therefore, to turn to the latter-day disasters of contemporary history. The horrific genocide of the Hitler period left problems of mind-boggling proportion. The evil and the terror of such unbearable wickedness should have produced an architectural response worthy of the ideas of Boullée. The slaughter of the Somme had been nobly commemorated at Thiepval, and the French had built an Ossuary of sublime terror at Douaumont. Yet the infamous events that occurred in Dachau, Bergen-Belsen, Auschwitz, and the other camps, have scarcely been commemorated architecturally. Any attempts to build memorials have produced solutions of staggering understatement and bathos.

The rejection of classicism as a language was already being expressed after 1918. Furthermore, the rejection of monumental memorials in Britain after the Second World War coincided with a political shift of emphasis that encouraged a utilitarian attitude towards memorials. Hospital wards, halls, funds, clinics, were proposed as 'useful' ways in which memorials could be functional. Yet, as I have demonstrated, such 'useful' memorials too often become forgotten as memorials, so their function fails.

Memorials were built after the Second World War. Those of Russia and East Europe tend to be conventionally classical in style, with heroic statuary and stripped-down classicism. In Britain, France, and Germany, names were often added to memorials of the First World War. American memorials of the Second World War still owed much to classicism, but were often simplified down to bare essentials.

Where problems of peculiar difficulty arose, such as the planning of the memorial at Auschwitz, a classical language was abandoned. At Auschwitz, Giorgio Simoncini created a platform on which is sculpture.[7] Lines of trees, fragments of buildings, the line of the Birkenau sidings (where prisoners arrived), and other features, were retained. The bleakness and the failure to create a modern statement as powerful as those of Lutyens or of Boullée are perhaps indications of how limited is the language of a modern art that is divorced from nearly all precedent. Without an adequate vocabulary it cannot tell a story. Another scene of horror, Dachau, is commemorated in a scheme by Josef Wiedmann, R. Ehrmann, and O. Peithner. A Carmelite convent was added to the former camp, and certain features, such as the gas-chambers, were retained.[8] The formal layout with a circular central chapel owes a great deal to classicism although the architecture is perhaps much too low in key to be successful.

Georges-Henri Pingusson was the architect for the memorial situated at the tip of the Île de la Cité in Paris. This was completed in 1962, and commemorates the French who died in National Socialist murder camps.[9] Little of the structure is visible above ground, and the memorial is in the form of a crypt reached from the gardens at the east end of Notre Dame. The interior contains cell-like compartments arranged symmetrically, and urns containing ashes from several camps are built into the walls. The entire structure is of concrete, heavily textured. Spiky iron grilles and gates suggest the cruelty of torture or of barbed wire. The impact of this memorial derives partly from its setting, which is spectacularly beautiful, and partly from the association of ideas. The lettering on the walls is angular and spiky, like the ironwork, yet the overall effect is nevertheless one of great refinement and delicacy. M. Pingusson has told me that 'the difficulty to express the feelings and the meaning of the memorial lies in the fact that on the spot you are *in* the space, surrounded by space, involved in the whole' and no one photograph can do his work justice. The fact that the crypt '*est dédiée au souvenir des Deux Cents Mille Français sombrés dans la nuit et le brouillard exterminés dans les camps nazis le 1940 a 1945*' is enough to create difficulties of scale and of imagination. The ossuaries of Douaumont, Asiago, Montello, and Castel Dante di Rovereto are grandiose statements that try to express the huge loss of life involved in modern war. M. Pingusson's design suggests, by infinite subtlety and understatement, the enormity of a terrible event. Only gradually does the overwhelming beauty of this masterpiece of modern design begin to convey, by the most civilized of means, the actuality of what is commemorated. The spaces, the myriad points of light suggesting each ended life, the lettering, and the whole marvellous concept leave one free to examine the spaces objectively yet become emotionally involved. Consciences are stirred, and gradually the textures, contrasts, symbols, and allegories become terribly hard to bear, so painful and so intensely personal is this great memorial. M. Pingusson has created a vocabulary that is civilized enough to express the deepest feelings. The retreat from classicism has created special problems for designers. M. Pingusson's invention is a triumph (Pl. 8), for the very plan-form he adopted is in the tradition of the best of funerary architecture from the

Plate 8 'Cette Crypte n'est pas faite pour des spectaculaires manifestations. Elle exige de pieux pèlerinages. La méditation, le silence, appellent la solitude' (Y. Duprat, lent by M. G.-H. Pingusson)

earliest of times, and is formally symmetrical (Fig. 1).

The memorials to the victims of the National Socialist terror are selfconsciously understated, and may fail, for the most part, as memorials. The 1959 design by Gino Valle for a monument to the Resistance at Udine, is interesting because it comprises a terraced circular depression set in the centre of the main square of the town. Over this is a massive square concrete slab supported on four huge bastions, giving a sense of overpowering oppressiveness not unlike French Neoclassical cenotaphs, for a cenotaph the Udine memorial undoubtedly is. The success of the design stems from the use of the geometrical forms of square and circle, with the suggestion of a mighty sarcophagus lid in the great slab. The origins of Valle's design are rooted in an architectural vocabulary of respectable antiquity.[10]

Perhaps even more moving is the monument to the heroes of the 1916 Easter Rising in Dublin. This is placed in a churchyard, and consists of a simple curved stone wall with the proclamation of the Republic inscribed in

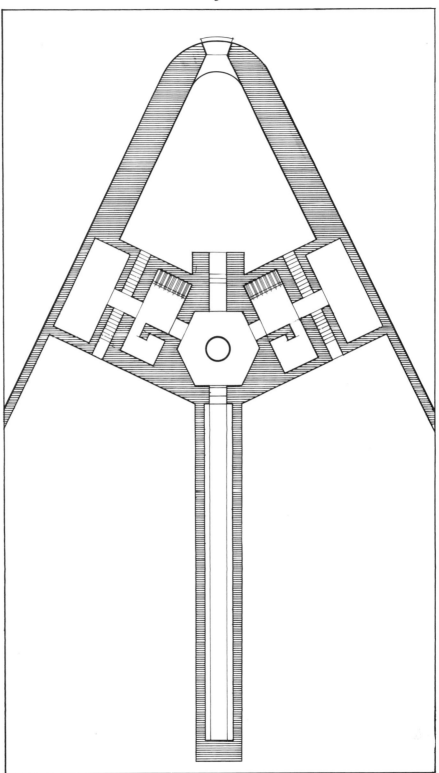

Fig. 1 Plan of the Mémorial
des Martyrs de la
Déportation, Paris (*G.-H.
Pingusson*, redrawn by The
Author)

Irish and English. The beauty of the language, and the quality of the carving are contributory factors to the success of this fine work (Pl. 9).

Monolithic forms have always been successful in memorials. The Sacrario delle Fosse Ardeatine consists of a huge slab placed over the sarcophagi of the victims of a massacre by Nazis in March 1944. The architects were Giuseppe Perugini, Nello Aprile, and Mario Fiorentini, while the sculptors were Mirko Basaldella and Francesco Coccia. The overwhelmingly oppressive weight of the mighty monolith over the tomb suggests entombment itself as well as tyranny (Pl. 10).

The French architects who designed memorials to heroes of the Napoleonic wars understood the great variety and the dignity that classicism could bring. The design by Godde for a monument in Père-Lachaise to commemorate the victims of June 1832 is severely Neoclassical and successful. Memorials to commemorate huge numbers of people that actually express something of the scale of the disaster have been built. The monuments at Thiepval, Douaumont, and Ypres are all superlative examples of their kind. A fear of using the language of classicism for memorials after 1945 may have been due in no small measure to the desire to get as far away as possible from the architecture of the Third Reich. The Neoclassicism of von Klenze and Schinkel had been well established in Germany. The proposals by Speer for a new Berlin owe not a little to Boullée, and it is clear that the French architects of the eighteenth century were a profound influence on Speer. The designs for official buildings in Berlin and for the great monuments of National Socialism had an unmistakable Neoclassical pedigree as did those of Fascist Italy. Unfortunately, classicism as a whole, Neoclassicism in particular, and monumental Neoclassicism most of all, became identified with Fascism and therefore fell rapidly from favour. Memorial and monumental architecture therefore had no place in the post-war world.

Attempts to create a civic art that owed nothing to the past have resulted in ungainly and unbalanced statuary, banal monuments, and memorials that express nothing but a paucity of modes of expression. The statues of Churchill and Smuts in Parliament Square will indicate how unfortunate is any attempt to stray from a serene and well-tried classical idiom. The statue of George VI in Carlton House Terrace appears not only weak, but far too small in scale, and lacks conviction in its attempted classicism. On the other hand, the vigour and imagination displayed in the Royal Artillery Memorial at Hyde Park Corner show how an assured development of classical ideas can succeed.

Schemes for grandiose buildings to celebrate death are still being produced in some countries, however. In Italy, where cemeteries and memorials are so much more monumental than in other European countries, Castiglioni and Fontana produced a design in the 1960s for a spiral cemetery in the form of a huge concrete structure which would store coffins and urns in *loculi*.[11] Willson's pyramid comes to mind as a precursor of this idea. Nanda Vigo and Cesare Tacchio designed a cemetery in the form of four twenty-storey tower-blocks (not a bad idea when we consider how inappropriate are tower-blocks as dwellings for the living). In Latin

Plate 9 Monument to the leaders of the Easter Rising in Dublin (*The Author*)

Plate 10 Monumental Sacrario delle Fosse Ardeatine (*Commissariato Generale Onoranze Caduti in Guerra*)

America schemes for cemeteries involving modern developments of the Campo-Santo type of cemetery enclosure have been built, notably Nelson Boyardo's massive columbaria in Uruguay.

One of the most successful examples of funerary architecture of the present century is the mausoleum of the Račić family at Cavtat built between 1920 and 1923. The architect and sculptor was Ivan Mestrovič. It consists of an octagonal domed chapel with a portico carried by two

caryatides *in antis*. Sculpture and architecture are beautifully fused in this distinguished design which owes not a little to classical example.

    The most astonishing of all grandiose schemes to celebrate death was not produced by the French, the Bavarians, or even the Italians, however. The reticent British for once won the palm for sheer daring, though, alas, the proposal was never implemented. The Monumental Halls designed by L. Harvey and J. P. Seddon constituted one of several schemes considered by a Royal Commission in 1890. The fact that Westminster Abbey was rapidly becoming filled as a place of burial of the eminent suggested that a new Campo Santo should be created to commemorate the worthy dead of the Empire. The gigantic pantheon and burial place was to stand in Abingdon Street, and would have cost £200,000. A prospect of the huge tower, which was to be part of a complex of buildings around the Chapter House of Westminster Abbey, shows that this example of the architecture of death would have dwarfed the Palace of Westminster and the Abbey, yet its elegance and beauty would have shamed later gigantic towers erected in London in the last two decades (Pl. 11). One can only regret that this *tour de force* of the Gothic imagination was never realized.

Plate 11 Monumental Halls, Westminster, designed by L. Harvey and J. P. Seddon (*RIBA British Architectural Library*)

Epilogue

A Monument is a Thing erected, made or
written for a Memorial of some Remarkable Action,
yet to be transferred to future Posterities.

JOHN WEEVER, 1631

'The treasures of time lie high, in Urnes, Coynes, and Monuments, scarce below the roots of some vegetables.' So Sir Thomas Browne, in his celebrated *Hydriotaphia*, emphasized the truth of how important are the funeral customs of the ages in telling us of the peoples of the past.

Death is the lot of every person born. The earliest civilizations built tombs and monuments to house and to honour the dead. Grand mausolea were built, because the dead would be longer in the tomb than in any dwelling during life, so the tomb had to be of some splendour. The dead had to be protected, made comfortable and commemorated, but they also had to be provided with an attractive home so that they would not return to bother the living. Egyptian funerary architecture reached heights unsurpassed and much of the economy was geared to providing tombs for the dead that were decorated, furnished, and secure.

The Greeks and the Romans built monuments, tombs, cemeteries, cenotaphs, memorials, and mausolea. Many Greek tombs were magnificent and among the finest of classical buildings. The Mausoleum at Halicarnassos was one of the most celebrated tombs of the ancient world. The best of ancient tombs were separate buildings, complete in their perfection. The Romans adopted aspects of Greek funerary architecture, but developed their own huge columbaria and catacombs. The great mausolea of imperial times were among the most spectacular tombs of all time, and smaller circular tombs, following the drum-like forms, became fashionable. Rock-cut tombs with elaborate façades were known throughout Asia Minor, and burial in larger hypogea was also common at one time.

The Christian Church gradually assumed responsibility for burial, and hygienic laws relating to disposal of the dead were relaxed as the population of Rome declined. Burial within churches began, as demand for secure burial in consecrated ground increased. Funerary architecture became associated with churches as free-standing mausolea were discouraged. Tombs within churches used pre-Christian motifs such as sarcophagi, canopies, and arcades. Gothic funerary art developed from Early Christian and Romanesque examples, the finest designs being found in shrines and reliquaries. Royal tombs of England, France, and Spain reached splendours in the Gothic period, and often Italian craftsmen were responsible for enriching tombs in the west. The *Cosmati*-work at Westminster is a case in point.

The development of chantries ensured that ambitious chantry-chapels, almost churches within churches, were built. The finest of these chapels are the tombs of the Bishops of Winchester, and the royal chantries at Westminster Abbey. Richer families often added chantry-chapels to existing churches, or took over parts of churches as their own chantry-chapels. The coming of the Renaissance changed the character of funerary architecture, and in Italy the first tombs were built unattached to churches. The Reformation ended chantries, but not the erection of grand monuments. The cult of the individual and the encouragement of the glory of heroes, of great men, and even of families, established a fashion for erecting enormous tombs in churches that quite dwarfed their surroundings. Great families took over parts of churches as private burial-places, and segregated even their dead from the dead of the common man.

At times of crisis, during epidemics, churchyards became filled to capacity, so extra ground had to be acquired. In the Middle Ages burial in churchyards was usually for a limited period. Bones were dug up and stored in charnel-houses, so that the ground could be re-used. The Reformation and the Renaissance encouraged a new approach to individualism that insisted on the permanency of a burial-place, and so churches and churchyards became crammed with corpses.

As populations grew and the numbers of corpses to be interred increased, pressures to develop new cemeteries outside towns on the principles of classical times were mounted. Evelyn and Wren demanded new cemeteries for London, but the first cemeteries unattached to churches in modern times were established by Europeans in India and America.

It is worth noting that Vanbrugh was aware of the importance of the cemetery at Surat, for an autograph of his in the Bodleian Library, Oxford,[1] entitled 'Mr Van-Brugg's Proposals about Building ye New Churches' contains a substantial note about burial reform, with a drawing of the Necropolis of Surat. Vanbrugh argued that churches should:

> be free'd from that Inhumane custome of being made Burial Places for the Dead; a Custome in which there is something very barbarous in itself besides the many ill consequences that attend it; that one cannot enough wonder how it ever has prevail'd amongst the civiliz'd part of mankind. But there is now a sort of happy necessity on this Occasion of breaking through it: Since there can be no thought of purchasing ground for Church Yards, where the Churches will probably be plac'd. And since there must therefore be Caemitarys provided in the Skirts of the Towne, if they are ordered with that decency they ought to be, there can be no doubt but the Rich as well as the Poor, will be content to ly there.
>
> If these Caemitarys be consecrated, Handsomely and regularly wall'd in, and planted with trees in such form as to make a Solemn Distinction between one Part and another; there is no doubt, but the Richer sort of People, will think their Friends and Relations more decently interr'd in those distinguish'd Places, than they commonly are in the Ailes and under

Pews in Churches; And will think them more honourably remember'd by Lofty and Noble Mausoleums, erected over them in Freestone (which no doubt will soon come into practice), than by little Tawdry Monuments of Marble, stuck up against Walls and Pillars.

Vanbrugh then sketched the cemetery at Surat, showing a walled enclosure, with a pyramid on a square base at each corner of the cemetery, and a triumphal arch in the centre of the wall. Over the top of the wall can be seen an array of obelisks, pyramids, columns, towers, and circular temple-like mausolea. A note states that this 'manner of Interment has been practic'd by the English at Suratt and is come at last to have this kind of effect'. It is quite clear that the model cemeteries of seventeenth- and eighteenth-century India had a considerable influence on important European architects.

Dissenters also established a cemetery in London, and Belfast had its cemetery in the eighteenth century. Apart from the cemeteries in India and in Louisiana, the first great metropolitan cemetery in Europe to be founded in modern times was that in Paris. Père-Lachaise became the model for all Europe and America to follow, although the Neoclassicism of most of the monuments was detested by the Ecclesiologists. Greek and Egyptian Revival earned the uninhibited scorn of Pugin and others, who did not approve of commercial cemeteries anyway.[2]

The belief that churchyards produced harmful miasmas that caused cholera and other diseases encouraged reformers to press for an end of intramural interment, and of burial in town churchyards. Large cemeteries were established in most European and American cities, and fine tombs and mausolea were erected in them. Individual tombs, unattached to churches, and with architectural pretensions, appeared again in Europe with the Renaissance, but the first great mausolea of post-Roman times were built in Britain in the eighteenth century. These were free-standing, in parks, and were the burial-places of noble families. The segregation from the common herd was thus even more complete.

Cremation appealed to rational reformers who were worried about hygiene and about the amount of land being used for cemeteries. From the last century, cremation has been quickly established as a major mode of disposal. There are indications, however, that cremation has brought its own problems. This mode of disposal is currently very expensive, and likely to become more so with rising costs of fuel. Experiments are being conducted in America to reduce the mass of human bodies without using the crude method of burning. A corpse can be cooled and solidified by using liquid nitrogen, after which it can be pulverized in an automatic crusher so that it is reduced to particles resembling gravel. These particles can be further reduced in size by 'freeze frying' which removes all body fluids. The remains can then be stored in an urn or casket.[3] This method is likely to be expensive, however, and so a rational means of disposal involving burial at sea (which would provide food for fish), or shallow earth-burial might well be sought.

The decline in funerary architecture reflects a turning away from a celebration of death. It suggests a form of emotional anaemia. For the first time in the history of mankind, the disposal of the dead is treated as unceremoniously as possible. The holocausts of two wars and the mass-murder of millions by totalitarian régimes have almost rendered futile the gesture of building memorials at all. The monuments at Thiepval, at Verdun, and at Ypres were among the last great expressions of classicism, while later attempts to build memorials using an under-developed architectural vocabulary have produced buildings of stupefying banality, with a few honourable exceptions.

The fact that cemeteries, memorials, and celebrations of death are now unfashionable in certain countries, including Britain, prompted me to try to record what I could of the architecture of death during the 1960s. In Britain, vandalism, arson, and lack of maintenance have reduced some of the great cemeteries to horrifying wildernesses where graves are desecrated, chapels are burned, and destruction of the most disgusting kind is widespread. I believe that no civilized society desecrates the abodes of its dead, and I see the phenomenon of present times in a most serious light.

The funerary art of the past offers scope for serious study. It is a curious comment on our society that great efforts are still being made to find out more about the tombs of vanished civilizations, while the tombs and monuments of our own eighteenth, nineteenth, and twentieth centuries are being wantonly destroyed. The nineteenth century, with all its immense achievements, was an age when ancient truths were questioned, when faith was replaced by doubt, and when doubters were bombarded by the high moral tone of ferocious and zealous evangelists of every religious persuasion. Darwin had shattered a belief in the literal truth of the Bible, causing havoc in fundamentalist circles. The average nineteenth-century family knew that Death was a frequent visitor and took comfort in religious teaching. The funerary art of the period was reassuring of some future celestial bliss where real angels would people the paradise. The threat to belief must have been traumatic indeed to those families who knew Death only too well.

It is odd to reflect that a nineteenth-century heaven is today beyond belief for most of us, and yet there are many people born into the nineteenth century and its beliefs who are still alive. The awesome funerals of yesteryear have vanished, with the horses, ostrich feathers, and magnificent hearses; so too the funerary art that produced elaborate mourning-cards, mourning-card mounts, mourning-rings and jewellery, mourning-fans, and funerary monuments.

Cemeteries, once regarded as useful for 'instruction in architecture, sculpture, landscape gardening, arboriculture, botany, and in those parts of general gardening, neatness, order, and high keeping', are today a nuisance to most people. The pleasures of the study of funerary art and of cemeteries are unknown to many. Cemeteries and churchyards are in danger, for we no longer understand them. Thousands of churches and churchyards are threatened with redundancy, so the loss of funerary monuments on an unparalleled scale is inevitable. Our great heritage of funerary architecture and its embellishments is very likely to be dissipated together with so much else of artistic worth. A celebration of death has passed into the realms of the fabulous, and, as such, is embarrassing to an increasingly philistine and materialistic society. Monumental art so often has reflected the tastes and aspirations of society. It is therefore an invaluable historical record. Often humour, banality, sentiment, profundity, and even sheer vulgarity, may be found in individual tombs. Yet the very best of art is often displayed in the surviving architecture and sculpture of death.

Redundant churches, unmaintained burial-grounds, and vandalized monuments have created problems. Unfortunately, once a tomb has been damaged, official action moves quickly to 'remove the eyesore' rather than to deter the mindless destroyers. Zealous churchmen often show indecent haste in wishing to remove tombstones from churchyards, and are unfortunately supported by those who ought to know better. It is nonsense to assert that memorials, tombstones, mausolea, and monuments detract from the setting of churches, and it is vandalism to remove memorials from churches or from churchyards because such memorials are records of people, of craftsmanship, and of taste. There is nothing more terrible to the student of monumental design than to see serried ranks of tombstones lined up against the walls of churchyards, three of four deep. This is presumably to prevent anyone from actually seeing the designs or reading the inscriptions. The pretext given for such vandalism is usually that the stones are unsightly or untidy, and that the churchyard is difficult to maintain. I suspect that the real reason is a hatred and fear of the past, and an irrational desire to deny that death and its realities have any place in the modern world. The destruction of funerary architecture and sculpture drives the past further from our own time, and helps to obliterate roots, tribal memories, and records. Death must now, it seems, be kept out of sight and out of mind, and we must pretend it never actually existed. The obsession with tidiness, like some over-anxious mother's reaction to potty-training, refuses to accept that death is not a tidy thing, and must not be placed in a compartment separated from life and from the living.

A celebration of death has proved a rich find for designers, and has left a record of the prevalent taste of society. The current attitudes towards death and graveyards perhaps reflect other aspects of how society sees the old and the infirm. This is an age when youth is worshipped, the cult of youth having almost become a religion itself. Old age, like death or illness, has no place in such a cult, so there will be no architectural expression of death.

Cremation now accounts for the disposal of the majority of the dead in Britain. The amount of energy taken to destroy a human body is very considerable, for it takes about an hour and a quarter in a furnace at high temperatures to do so. It would be much less extravagant in terms of energy, and more ecologically apt, to bury in the mediaeval fashion in shallow graves without coffins, and to re-use the ground after a decent passage of time. Francis Seymour Haden, in his letters to *The Times* in 1875, said that cremation was 'a wild project' and that to 'drive into vapour the bodies of the 3,000 people who die weekly in Greater London alone, at a needless cost', was an 'infinite waste'. Certainly it would seem that he was right, and that a less destructive and more rational return to ecological methods would be more reasonable. The bones could eventually be stored in catacombs. The possibilities for awe-inspiring designs are endless. The catacombs of Paris, and the great charnel-houses of Europe are examples to us, for often the Paris cemeteries have graves for a limited tenure. When the lease is up, the bones are stored in the great underground catacombs and charnel-houses, so the ground is always used. The great galleries of Italian cemeteries would suffer the fate of the catacombs of Brompton and other British cemeteries unless the income for a place of burial were ensured. Italy still builds huge galleries with *loculi* in her cemeteries, and these spaces are leased at realistic figures to make the upkeep of the buildings possible. In Spain and Portugal tombs similar to those in New Orleans are common, arranged in banks or galleries. Even niches in the columbaria at Père-Lachaise are let for very short periods, so that space can always be had there, and prices can be adjusted with rising costs. The system of ensuring that realistic sums are paid to ensure that cemeteries are maintained prevails throughout Europe. The Roman Catholic countries naturally maintain their graveyards, and vandalism in Italy, Spain, and France is practically unknown compared with the state of affairs in Britain. In Scandinavia, Holland, and Germany a less urban type of burial-ground is usual, and planting plays a more important part in the design. Vandalism and maintenance seem to raise fewer problems in those countries either. A sound financial base, and a rational approach to 'ownership' make visits to European cemeteries pleasant experiences. There, like Sir Thomas Browne, we can feel that 'time, which antiquates Antiquities, and hath an art to make dust of all things, hath yet spared these minor monuments'. British cemeteries, originally founded as commercial speculations, and run with ideas of ownership of spaces in catacombs or graves firmly implanted, are wasting assets. Yet British cemeteries could be used in perpetuity if their financial bases were worked out on European models. The concept of the regularly cleared cemetery, with its ranges of charnel-houses and catacombs, would be greatly less wasteful of resources than cremation, which consumes a lot of gas, and which, in days of energy crises, is grossly wasteful. Cemeteries, on the other hand, provide valuable open spaces in or near urban areas, with possibilities for rich planting and the provision of interesting vistas and landscapes enriched with sculptures and buildings. Shallow burial, as in mediaeval times, with only a shroud to cover the body, would ensure quick dissolution so that bones could be disinterred and stored in charnel-houses, as is still common practice in some parts of the world. Resources would not be wasted, and dignity would return to the cemeteries. There would be considerable architectural and landscape possibilities for such ideas. The best cemeteries will need future conservation proposals worked out, as not only do the spaces and landscapes need careful husbandry, but the buildings and memorials must be protected as places for future generations to admire and use. European architecture and sculpture would be the poorer, for example, if Père-Lachaise and the Staglieno were to be destroyed.

The poverty of current designs for death requires explanation and comment. The mawkishness and vulgarity of so much contemporary work since the First World War are the antithesis of the nobility and inventiveness of the past. In the 1840s, Pugin, Strang, Markland, and others denounced 'modern sepulchral monuments' as 'essentially pagan'. Urns,

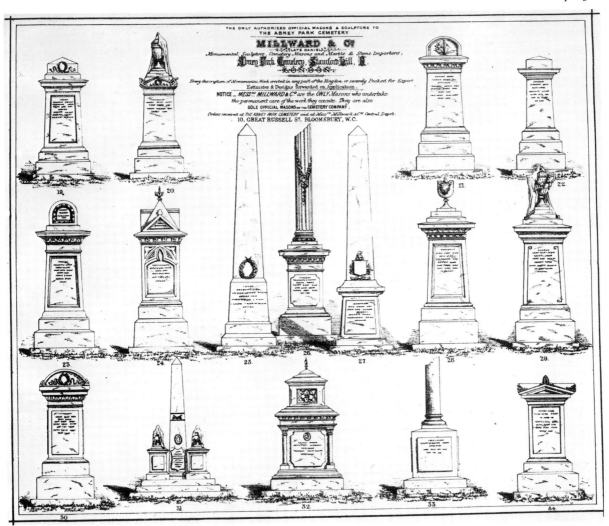

Plate 1 A typical array of Victorian tomb-design by Millward & Co. From Justyne, William *Guide to Highgate Cemetery* (*Author's Collection*)

broken columns, inverted torches, extinguished lamps, and sarcophagi were looked upon as immoral and un-Christian (Pl. 1). The Cross, recumbent effigies, and 'emblems of mercy and redemption' were the only acceptable emblems on tombs. The moralistic fervour of these Goths certainly eliminated 'heathen notions, and all the emblematical devices of despair'[5] in favour of crosses, the 'high coped tomb, or the more sumptuous erection of a Mortuary chapel'.[6] Ecclesiological correctness, moral worth, and Gothic forms were to be triumphant. Funerary design, according to the nineteenth-century reformers, had suffered from a 'degradation' from the Middle Ages, and this decline was associated with the loss of 'true' (i.e. Roman Catholic) religion. The ancient words of prayer were changed, and then the attitudes. Pride of birth, of qualities, or even of a totally baseless nature 'began to raise up the Effigies of the dead'.[7] These effigies lolled on their elbows, 'dressed out in flowing wigs and court suits',[8] while excessively long epitaphs extolled lives that were often worthless. Markland himself complained that for 'more than a century, mural monuments with cherubs, sculls, lamps, and twisted columns, with little variety, were permitted to deform our

363

Churches. In later days, we have had the Urn and the Sarcophagus, strange ornaments in a Christian Temple! or a figure veiled with drapery, sitting under a willow, bending over a tomb, or a boy leaning upon an inverted torch!'[9]

Such designs, and others like them, were 'wearisome and uninteresting from repetition'. Markland denounced the pyramid as having 'originated with Bernini', who was censured by Flaxman for his 'violation of taste and judgement'.

> The representation of a building, intended from its immense size, and its solid base, to last thousands of years, indicated by a little slab of marble, an inch thick, 'to be the back ground of sculpture, belonging to none of the ancient classes, foisted into architecture, with which it has neither connection nor harmony', does appear to be the very climax of absurdity, were it not heightened by making the pyramid rest upon four round balls, or, as we have already seen, upon four skulls.

Markland was particularly concerned with the damage done to ancient fabric by the erection of such grandiose monuments. 'Low, indeed, must the piety and the taste of an age have fallen, when anachronisms and mythology' were 'obtruded into the holiest of buildings'. The tombs of Westminster Abbey were criticized, for when

> a Christian nation could find no better mode of commemorating the dead than by re-erecting images of Neptune, and Mars, and Fame, and Victory, mixed up with dragoons and drummers, catapults and cannons, men without clothes in a field of battle, or English generals in Roman togas, and all the trash of the poorest pedant; and when a Christian church in a Christian metropolis is selected as the fittest depository for these outrages . . . there must have been something most unsound in the tone and manners of the age.[10]

Naked figures, *putti* (described by one polemicist as 'fat lugubrious boys, who are so much wrapped up in their grief as to be negligent of all other apparel . . .'), Greek or Egyptian styles, and inappropriate symbolism were all thoroughly castigated by writers of the mid-nineteenth century. Markland referred to mural tablets (of which, admittedly, there was an excessive rash in the first quarter of the nineteenth century, when everyone aspired to such a memorial) as 'marble excrescences', 'sepulchral fungi', and 'stone tumours'. The main problem was that such monuments were devoid of Christian symbolism, and some commentators felt that the character of churches was being wrecked by a 'medley of sepulchral placards' composed of 'braggart heathen allegories'. Commonplace 'monuments and tablets' were 'needlessly multiplied', and this 'excess' had to be restrained. On the walls of many churches the multiplicity of tablets ensured that not only was every vacant space filled, but that portions of the original structure had been 'shamefully mutilated' to accommodate them. Female figures embracing partially draped 'heathen urns' came in for universal denunciation.[11]

The mighty voice of *The Ecclesiologist* was raised against the larger tombs, including urns, sarcophagi, railed enclosures, broken columns, and mural marbles. By 1845 many seventeenth- and eighteenth-century features were being replaced by the 'Catholic symbol of the blessed Cross, the glowing Memorial window, or the consoling and inspiring portraitures of Saint and Angel'.[12] Pagan grandeur was to be replaced by over-'restored' and scraped Gothic.

Even greater horrors were experienced by Ecclesiologists who ventured into the churchyards and cemeteries. Many Victorian memorials were painted, so that the faces of cherubs were pink, and fleshy tints contrasted with the cream of the stone and the blacks and reds of the lettering. Wooden crosses were advocated by *The Ecclesiologist*, but for stone memorials, crosses, or ledger-stones incised with the cross were recommended. Memorial-brasses were to be encouraged as 'Catholick art', despite the fact that there was a respectable historical precedent for them. In all cases, monuments were for the church, and burial was to take place outside, except for 'benefactors' who were to be allowed interment inside the building.[13]

Sepulchral vaults were not felt to be 'Christian', however, as these were 'pues for dead men' and thus extended the pew system to the dead. The building of vaults in churchyards was a 'monstrous abuse', as it extended the rights of private ownership to a churchyard which was the property of the parish. The construction of brick vaults in churchyards was blamed firmly on the 'Dutch Usurpation'.[14]

A moral and 'Christian' outlook discouraged expenditure on tombs. Money would be spent on beautifying churches, and on building chapels, schools, almshouses, and hospitals. Markland and others saw that sculpture could well be discouraged, and so busts and memorial statues would be made and exhibited in institutions or the premises of learned societies.

Despite such early successes, 'Christian' funerary art never quite replaced pagan elements. This is not surprising, since Dissenters viewed things Gothic, and even the symbol of the Cross, as indications of Popery. In Scotland, Wales, and Ulster, for example, a classical tradition persisted in funerary art which still persists today. State funerals remained obstinately classical, while even royal tombs stayed clear of Gothic for the most part.[15]

The Goths did their best to destroy a classical tradition that was firmly embedded in funerary art. Yet even Gothic tombs had derived from classical precedents, as I have demonstrated, and so the best of Gothic had not a little of Greek and Roman principles embedded in its architecture of death. Gothic and 'Christian' apologists first copied, then interpreted, and produced monuments that were indubitably High Victorian, but not mediaeval by any stretch of the imagination. Even urns were to be designed to resemble reliquaries to match the décor in Gothic churches in an attempt to flee the heathenish shapes of classical containers.

Such fervour only succeeded in destroying the vigour of classicism. Angels became curious parodies of classical figures, totally sexless and oddly repulsive. The smiling angel of Bernini's Ecstasy of S. Teresa is an Eros, an incredibly vital work, but the expressionless Victorian angel is depressingly vapid. *Putti*, once mischievous children, almost caught with their fingers in the jam, as at Wallfahrtskirche Neubirnau, became angelic cherubs, hideously smirking among the tendrils of marble ivy and Gothic thorns. The symbols, and the eternal verities of an ancient classical tradition that was related to designs for death going back thousands of years, were suddenly and violently abandoned. They were replaced by marble hearts, by plastic ash-containers, and by the well-tended and excessively coloured rose-garden.

There were forlorn attempts to revive good standards of funerary design. The beautiful carvings of Eric Gill, Gilbert Ledward, Edmund Ware, David Kindersley, George Friend, and others, attempted to restore classical lettering and the refinements of seventeenth- and eighteenth-century carving to monumental design in the inter-war years, but popular taste insisted on the mass-produced excrescences so familiar in burial-grounds all over Britain.

Where a classical tradition never truly succumbed to Gothic blandishments, as in Italy, funerary art and architecture remained vigorous and inspiring. The sculpture of the Staglieno in Genoa is startling and superb, while the cemeteries of Milan and Rome can still provide us with admirable examples of an architecture of death worthy of the name. The Neoclassical element in French monumental art also remained healthy, and the cemeteries of Paris contain many fine tombs and sculptures. German funerary art was vigorous and chunky, especially in the twentieth century, when rural, wooded cemeteries were developed. Scandinavia also favoured a design for death where nature was dominant, and memorials are almost lost in the woods and flowers. In the seventeenth and eighteenth centuries, however, Campo-Santo styles of cloistered graveyards with sepulchres set behind cloistered arcades were planned in Scandinavia, in Central Europe, and the Mediterranean lands. Central Europe evolved designs of great elaboration, and a tradition of Baroque ironwork to mark graves is still very much alive in Austria, Bavaria, and Switzerland. Spain, Portugal, Italy, and Greece favour walled cemeteries that are villages or even towns for the dead, with cloistered walks, marvellous sculpture, and buildings to serve as chapels and memorials.

The architecture of death is perhaps the purest architecture of all, as it lends itself to the creation of objects in space, quite set apart from the rest of humanity, and providing strong statements that appeal to the hearts and minds of mankind. Many designs are so grand and formal that they become unforgettable images graven on the consciousness. The awesome grandeur of the Ossuaries at Verdun, and of the war cemeteries, is an example of how buildings that truly celebrate death transcend the ordinary and become sublime. The great mausolea and tombs of Islam, of Egypt, of prehistoric Europe, of Greece, of Rome, of the Middle Ages, of the Renaissance and Baroque, and of the last three centuries are also supreme creations of architecture, and all have common elements of form and of content.

To be concerned with death and with its celebration is not 'morbid'. It is proper to reflect on a certainty of life. All healthy and vigorous civilizations of the past have apprehended the significance of death, and have responded to beliefs and cultural requirements in the architecture of death. The dead of many cultures were buried or burned, and were supplied with needs for an after-life. The Romans ensured that tombs were endowed for upkeep, and that libations would be poured for the dead. Funerary gardens supplied produce for funeral feasts and income for repairs. The Christians buried their dead in expectation of a Resurrection and Last Judgement, while the Egyptians built their tombs to withstand the ravages of time until the call to a new life was heard by the inhabitants of their necropoleis. Old customs died hard, and even as late as the nineteenth century, rich mourners dropped their mourning-rings into the vaults at funerals. The riderless charger walking behind a gun-carriage at a funeral is a reminder of the time when the horse would have accompanied its master to an after-life. Funerary and mourning customs, like the architecture of death, have had surprisingly constant themes, perhaps reflecting Sir Thomas Browne's remark that the 'certainty of death is attended by uncertainties, in time, manner, places.'

The neglected cemeteries, poorly designed crematoria, and abysmal tombstone designs of the present insult life itself, for death is an inevitable consequence of birth. By treating the disposal of the dead as though the problem were one of refuse-collection, society devalues life. The architectural memorials of great cultures are works that, by their sublime equalities, express something of the infinite. Such architecture transcends the prosaic. Creativity and vigour characterize a true celebration of death. We could learn much from the funerary architecture of the past if we are to give new significance to a celebration of life in our own time.

Fig. 1 *Finis* (*Author's Collection*)

Notes

Chapter 1   *The architecture and artefacts of death in ancient cultures*
1   *Ethic.* iv, 67
2   *Epistulae Morales* lib. xi, Ep. 3
3   *Tusculanae Disputationes.* 1
4   Psalm 90, verse 12
5   *De Rerum Natura* lib. iii. See also King, C. W. *The Gnostics and their Remains* London 1887 p. 179
6   Brunton, G. 'Burial Customs', in Engelbach, R. (editor) *Introduction to Egyptian Archaeology* Cairo 1946 pp. 199–244
7   Walton, J. 'Hog-back tombstones and the Anglo-Danish house' *Antiquity* 28, 1954 pp. 68–77
8   Herodotus *History* v
9   See Glob, P. V. on *The Mound People* and *The Bog People.* Various editions
10   Wooley, C. L. *Ur Excavations* London 1934, and *Excavations at Ur* London 1954
11   Jones, Gwyn *A History of the Vikings* London 1968
12   Homer *The Iliad* Book 23
13   Lauer, J. P. *L'Histoire Monumentale des Pyramides d'Egypte* Cairo 1962
14   Grinsell, Leslie, V. *Barrow, Pyramid and Tomb* London 1975 pp. 101–109. This is a remarkably erudite survey of the subject with full coverage of selected tombs, described in detail
15   *Exodus* 1, verses 9–11
16   Lauer, *op. cit.*
17   Description of Maes Howe and Runic inscriptions in the volumes of the Historical Monuments (Scotland) Commission
18   Marwick, Hugh *Ancient Monuments in Orkney* Edinburgh 1952
19   There is an excellent description of Maes Howe by Professor V. G. Childe in the *Proceedings* of the Society of Antiquaries of Scotland 1954–6 pp. 155–172
20   For barrows and other tombs, see Daniel, G. E. *The Prehistoric Chamber Tombs of England and Wales* Cambridge 1950; Childe, V. G. *The Dawn of European Civilization* London 1957; Corcoran, J. X. W. P. 'The Cotswold-Severn Group, in *Megalithic Enquiries in the West of Britain* edited by T. G. E. Powell, Liverpool 1969. See also Eogan, G. 'Excavations at Knowth, Co. Meath' in *Antiquity* 41, 1967 pp. 302–4; 43, 1969 pp. 8–14; and the same author's 'Report on Knowth' in the *Proc. Royal Irish Acad.* 74(C), 1974, pp. 11–112

For details of the burial customs of the Scythians see Herodotus, whose *Histories* describe in gory detail the mass-slaughter that accompanied the burial of a Scythian king. The killing of immense numbers of horses and of servants must have had an adverse effect on the economy. There is a very full account of pyramids, barrows, and other tombs in Grinsell, Leslie V. *op. cit.*

Chapter 2   *Graeco-Roman funerary buildings, cemeteries, gardens, and sculptures*
1   Wace, A. J. B. *Mycenae: an Archaeological History and Guide* Princeton 1949
2   Higgins, R. A. 'The façade of the Treasury of Atreus at Mycenae' Papers of the British School at Athens 63 pp. 331–6
3   Wace *op. cit.*, to which work I am much indebted
4   Kurtz, Donna C. and Boardman, John *Greek Burial Customs* London 1971 p. 22, and pp. 123–7. This is by far the fullest account of the subject, and is admirably illustrated

5   See Casson, S. *Macedonia, Thrace and Illyria* London 1926
6   See the remarkable collections in the British Museum, including the drawings by Scharf. See also Kurtz and Boardman *op. cit.* pp. 283–333
7   See Cook, B. F. *Greek and Roman Art in the British Museum* London 1976
8   Jeppesen, Kristian *Paradeigmata. Three Mid-Fourth Century Main Works of Hellenic Architecture Reconsidered* Jutland Archaeological Society Publications Vol. IV Aarhus 1958. This volume contains Jeppesen's reconstructions of the Mausoleum in the light of his researches. See also Jeppesen, Kristian 'Neue Ergebnisse zur Wiederherstellung des Maussolleions von Halikarnassos' in *Istanbuler Mitteilungen* 1976 pp. 47–99
9   Lawrence, A. W. *Greek Architecture* London 1957
10 Benndorf, O. and Niemann, G. *Das Heroon von Gjolbashci-Trysa* 1889–91
11 Kurtz and Boardman *op. cit.* pp. 300–3. This book contains a comprehensive bibliography. I acknowledge my debt to this splendid study
12 See also Vermeule, E. *Greece in the Bronze Age* London 1964; Dinsmoor, W. B. *The Architecture of Ancient Greece* London 1950
13 Toynbee, J. M. C. *Death and Burial in the Roman World* London 1971 pp. 11–24
14 See Dennis, George *The Cities and Cemeteries of Etruria* London 1883, Vol. I p. 452, and Gray, Mrs Hamilton *Tour to the Sepulchres of Etruria in 1839* London 1841 pp. 301–305
15 Toynbee *op. cit.* pp. 39–61 et. seq.
16 Hare, Augustus J. C. *Walks in Rome* London 1897 pp. 267–70
17 Merivale, Charles *History of the Romans under the Empire* 1864
18 *Mille pedes in fronte, trecentos cippus in agrum hic dabat: heredes monumentum non sequeretur*
19 Igel is described by Baedeker as 'an inconsiderable village'
20 Toynbee *op. cit.* pp. 172–200
21 *Ibid* pp. 201–46
22 *Ibid* pp. 210–81
23 *Ibid*, to which I am indebted
24 Which might be translated thus:
    'Here, thrown together, are many of the saintly; the bodies of the holy ones are enclosed within revered sepulchures, and their precious souls are within the palaces of heaven'
25 Karl Baedeker's *Rome and Central Italy* (Leipzig & London 1930) has been an invaluable guide, companion, and mine of information, as has Augustus J. C. Hare's *Walks in Rome* (London 1897). The latter is essential as a delightful and entertaining companion to the wonders of the Eternal City. Other sources are the collections in the British School in Rome; Sir Banister Fletcher's *A History of Architecture on the Comparative Method* (London 1954); H. Heathcote Statham's *A History of Architecture* (London 1950); and the many occasional papers in various learned journals dealing with the funerary architecture of classical times. *Etruscan and Roman Architecture* by Axel Boëthius and J. B. Ward-Perkins (Harmondsworth 1970), is a useful volume. Toynbee's excellent book (*op. cit.*) gives a full account of funerary customs, architecture, and artefacts throughout the Empire, and is graced with an exceedingly full bibliography. My own very large collection of books, pictures, and drawings provided valuable source material.

Chapter 3   The flowering of funerary art in the Middle Ages
1   Knight, Charles *London* London 1841–4, Vol. 5 p. 163
2   Cutts, Rev Edward L. *A Manual for the Study of Sepulchral Slabs and Crosses of the Middle Ages* London 1849
3   Greenhill, F. A. *Incised Effigial Slabs. A Study of Engraved Stone Memorials in*

Latin Christendom c. *1100* to c. *1700* London 1976

4   Boase, T. S. R. *Death in the Middle Ages. Mortality, Judgement and Remembrance* London 1972 p. 92. This is a remarkably succinct, readable, and well-illustrated account of the subject

5   Blore, Edward *The Monumental Remains of Noble and Eminent Persons* London 1826

6   Crossley, Fred H. *English Church Monuments AD 1150–1550* London 1921

7   For full descriptions of the tombs in Westminster Abbey see the *Inventory* of the Royal Commission on Historical Monuments, Vol. 1 *Westminster Abbey* London 1924. See also Boase *op. cit.* pp. 59–126

8   For exhaustive details, see Weber, E. Parkes *Aspects of Death in Art and Epigram* London and Leipzig 1914 pp. 56–68. Similar epitaphs, contrasting the scents of the flowers of the world with the stink of decay, were not uncommon. See also Boase *op. cit., passim*

9   The *Danse Macabre* is also a theme in *Les trés riches heures de Jean De France, duc de Berry*. See Weber *op. cit.* pp. 28–48 for illuminating detail far beyond the scope of the present work. I am grateful to Mrs Penelope Jessel for introducing me to Widford Church.

10 The Latin inscription pointing out that the corpse was once what the onlooker is and what the onlooker will one day be like the corpse, is obviously admonitory. The famous frescoes of S. Maria Novella include a skeleton above which is the inscription *Io fu ga quel che voi sete e quel chi(:)son voi aco sarete* (I was what you are, and what I am you will become)

11 See also Styan, K. E. *A Short History of Sepulchral Cross-Slabs with Other Emblems found thereon* London 1902
    Markland, J. H. *Remarks on English Churches and on the Expediency of Rendering Sepulchral Memorials Subservient to Pious and Christian Uses* Oxford 1843

12 Lindahl, Göran *Grav och rum* Stockholm 1969

Chapter 4   *The Renaissance and Baroque periods of funerary architecture*

1   See the chapter on 'The Development of the Individual' in Burckhardt, Jacob *The Civilization of the Renaissance in Italy* trans. S. G. C. Middlemore Vienna and London n.d.

2   Burckhardt *op. cit.* Such melancholy was also familiar to Irish, English, and German observers of the ruins of their own pasts

3   See Carl Baedeker's *Northern Italy* and Augustus Hare's *Venice*. For a very full critique see Clark, Kenneth *The Nude* Harmondsworth 1956

4   Colleselli, Franz *The Court Church and the Tomb of Emperor Maximilian in Innsbruck* Tiroler Volkskunstmuseum Innsbruck n.d.

5   See especially Esdaile, K. A. *English Church Monuments 1510 to 1840* London 1946

6   See Hibbard, Howard *Bernini* Harmondsworth 1965

7   Jameson, Anna Brownell *Monastic Orders*

8   Taine, Hippolyte *Voyage en Italie* Paris 1866

9   *The Dictionary of British Sculptors 1660–1851* by Rupert Gunnis, London, n.d., is indispensable. Lawrence Weaver's *Memorials and Monuments Old and New: Two hundred subjects chosen from seven centuries* London 1915, is also useful

10 For an account of late-eighteenth- and early-nineteenth-century memorials see Penny, Nicholas *Church Monuments in Romantic England* New Haven and London 1977

Chapter 5   *The burial crisis; overcrowded churchyards; first modern cemeteries*

1   Evelyn, John. *The Diary*

2 *Ibid.*

3 *Proceedings in Reference to the Preservation of the Bunhill Fields Burial Ground* London 1867

4 See Wilkinson, Theon *Two Monsoons* London 1976. See also Chetwode, Penelope 'Monuments to Empire Builders' *The Architectural Review* August 1935

5 See Nilsson, Sten *European Architecture in India 1750–1850* London 1968

6 Graham, M. *Journal of a Residence in India* Edinburgh 1812

7 Wilkinson, Theon 'Crumbling Monuments of the Raj' *Country Life* 2 September 1976. I am greatly indebted to Mr Wilkinson for all his help. See also Curl, James Stevens *Mausolea in Ulster* Belfast 1978

8 Marion, John Francis *Famous and Curious Cemeteries* New York 1977

9 *The Belfast Telegraph*, 25 July 1936. Reference kindly provided by Miss Wendy Johnston

10 My thanks to Mr Denis F. McCoy, who accompanied me on an exploration of the Edinburgh cemeteries. I am also grateful to Mr Desmond Hodges who first showed me Grey Friars

11 Mr John Gerrard kindly told me about these graveyards

12 Fuhrmann, Franz *Salzburg and its Churches* Vienna 1950

13 Speer, Albert *Inside the Third Reich* New York 1969

14 S -A. . . . P. *Promenade aux Cimetières de Paris, aux Sépultures Royales de Saint-Denis, et aux Catacombes* Paris n.d.
See also Marty (author) and Lassalle (lithographer) with Rousseau (architect): *Les Principaux Monuments Funéraires Du Père-Lachaise, de Montmartre, du Mont-Parnasse et autres Cimetières de Paris Dessinés et Mesurés Par Rousseau, architecte, et Lithographiés Par Lassalle, Accompagnés d'une Description succincte du monument et d'une Notice historique sur le personnage qu'il renferme, Par Mary* Paris, n.d., and Normand Fils *Monumens Funéraires choisis dans les Cimetières de Paris et des Principaux Villes de France Dessinés, Gravés et Publiés Par Normand Fils* Paris 1832

15 See Bibliography

16 Much information concerning the French cemeteries and monuments comes from Normand Fils' *Monumens Funéraires choisis dans Les Cimetières de Paris et des Principales Villes de France*, published in Paris in 1832. Most of the best funerary monuments in New York, Washington, and other cities were more or less taken from this French volume that concentrates on the monuments of Père-Lachaise. The great Parisian cemetery therefore influenced American cemeteries in detail as well as in overall terms

17 For detailed information concerning Moghul tombs, see Volwahsen, Andreas *Living Architecture: Islamic Indian* London 1970

Chapter 6 *Mausolea from the Renaissance period to the twentieth century*

1 Burckhardt, Jacob *The Civilization of the Renaissance in Italy* Vienna and London n.d.

2 Craig, Maurice 'Mausoleums in Ireland' *Studies* Winter 1975 pp. 410–23

3 For details of Michael Shanahan and the building of Downhill, see Rankin, Peter *Irish Building Ventures of the Earl Bishop of Derry 1730–1803* Belfast 1972

4 See Potterton, Homan *Irish Church Monuments 1570–1880* Belfast 1975. See also the lists published by the Ulster Architectural Heritage Society. See also Curl, James Stevens *Mausolea in Ulster* Belfast 1978, for a fuller account, with photographs, of these mausolea and other tombs

5 See Freeden, M. H. von *Balthasar Neumann Leben und Werk* Munich 1963. This includes a useful biography and bibliography. I am also indebted to Dr von Freeden for his kindness in discussing Neumann's work with me

6   See Downes, Kerry *Hawksmoor* London 1959

7   I am indebted to Dr Maurice Craig for help with the monuments in and around Dublin

8   Stroud, Dorothy *The Architecture of Sir John Soane* London 1961. See also Summerson, John 'Sir John Soane and the furniture of death' *The Architectural Review* March 1978 pp. 147–55. I am indebted to Sir John Summerson for permission to quote from this essay

9   Rosenau, Helen *Boullée and Visionary Architecture* London 1976

10 Rosenau, *op. cit.* p. 106

11 See Rosenau, Helen 'The Engravings of the *Grands Prix* of the French Academy of Architecture' *Architectural History* Vol 3 1960

12 See Curl, James Stevens 'Mozart considered as a Jacobin' *The Music Review* August 1974. See also Köppen, Karl Friedrich *Crata Repoa, oder Einweihung der ägyptischen Priester* Berlin 1778. For further information, see von Born, Ignatz *Journal für Freimaurer* Vienna 1784; Kneisner, F. *Geschichte der deutschen Freimaurerei* Berlin 1912; and Friedel, J. G. *Geschichte der Freimaurerei* Leipzig 1861. There is an excellent essay by Pevsner, Nikolaus and Lang, S. on 'The Egyptian Revival' in Studies in *Art, Architecture and Design* London 1968 pp. 213–35

13 See Blackburne, Harry, and Bond, Maurice *The Romance of St George's Chapel* Windsor 1976

14 See Curl, James Stevens 'A Victorian Model Town' *Country Life* 9 March 1972

15 Colvin, H. M. *A Biographical Dictionary of English Architects 1660–1840* London 1954 p. 680

16 I am grateful to Mr John Morley for showing me this extraordinary building

Chapter 7   The development of British cemeteries in the nineteenth century

Much of the information in this Chapter is taken from the Minutes of the Cemetery Companies, where I have been able to locate these.

1   With the exception of my *The Victorian Celebration of Death* Newton Abbot 1972

2   Briggs, Asa *Victorian Cities* Harmondsworth 1968 p. 59

3   For further information concerning literary influences on the Gothic Revival, see Clark, Kenneth *The Gothic Revival. An Essay in the History of Taste* London 1962

4   Allom seems to have been in the van of cemetery promotion. He prepared drawings with H. E. Kendall for the Kensal Green and Brompton competitions

5   James Ewing of Strathleven (1775–1853) was the author of a *History of the Merchants' House of Glasgow* and Lord Dean of the Merchants' House from 1815

6   Loudon J. C. See *The Gardener's Magazine* of 1842 and 1843

7   *The Morning Chronicle* 10 June 1830

8   Published in London *c.* 1842, although the *designs* had been exhibited earlier

9   2 and 3 William IV *c.* 110 Local and Personal

10 See Kendall H. E., Architect *Sketches of the Approved Designs of the Chapel and Gateway Entrances, intended to be erected at Kensall Green for the General Cemetery Company* London 1832

11 Vol. CII, Part ii p. 245

12 P. 84 of the Minutes of the General Cemetery Company. See also p. 96 of the Minutes. John Griffith's obituary appears in *The Builder* vol. 55, 1888 p. 345. I am indebted to Mr Howard Colvin for information

13 *The Gentleman's Magazine* Vol. CIII, Part i p. 169

14 See J. W. *Illustrated Guide to Kensal Green Cemetery* London *c.* 1858

15 Walford, Edward *Old and New London* London 1887

16 *Cemetery Designs for Tombs and Cenotaphs*, by Stephen Geary, Architect. Founder of the Cemeteries at Highgate, Nunhead, Peckham, Westminster, Gravesend, Brighton, etc. London 1840. This book contains twenty-one designs engraved by B. Winkles, and was published by Tilt and Bogue, of Fleet Street. See also *A New Work on Monuments, Cenotaphs, Tombs, and Tablets, etc, etc, with their details drawn to a large scale, by which the Workman can erect each design with facility* by E. W. Trendall, Architect. London *c.* 1840. Mr Colvin first showed me this book.

17 Bunning, J. B., Architect *Designs for Tombs and Monuments* London, John Williams Library of Arts 1839. This is a series of designs, all of which are disappointing when compared with Bunning's later work

18 17 December 1856

19 Knight, Charles *London*

20 6 and 7 William IV, *c.* 129 Local

21 Wilson, J. B. 'The Story of Norwood'. Unpublished

22 Article in *The Architectural Review* Vol. CXLVII no. 876 February 1970

23 6 and 7 William IV *c.* 136 Local

24 Quoted from the original Act

25 Cansick, Frederick Teague *A Collection of Curious and Interesting Epitaphs* London 1872

26 Curl, James Stevens *The Victorian Celebration of Death* Newton Abbot 1972. See also the Minutes of the West of London and Westminster Cemetery Company

27 Lloyd, John H. *The History, Topography and Antiquities of Highgate, in the County of Middlesex* Highgate 1888 pp. 494–5

28 Curl, James Stevens 'Highgate. A Great Victorian Cemetery' *Journal of the Royal Institute of British Architects* April 1968

29 The Minutes of the London Cemetery Company, now held by the London Borough of Southwark. See Curl, James Stevens 'Nunhead Cemetery' *Trans. Ancient Monuments Soc.* n.s. 22 1977

30 Prickett, Frederick *The History and Antiquities of Highgate* London 1842 p. 80

31 Loudon, J. C. *The Gardeners' Magazine* 1843

32 6 Vic. *c.* 36

33 The Minutes of the London Cemetery Company

34 *The Builder* 17 Aug. 1861 p. 560

35 Pp. 2–35 of the Minutes of the West of London and Westminster Cemetery Company, now in the Public Record Office

36 I Victoria, *c.* 130 Local. *An Act for establishing a Cemetery for the Dead Westward of the Metropolis by a Company to be called 'The West of London and Westminster Cemetery Company*

37 Pp. 39–44 of the Minutes

38 The Minutes p. 70

39 Obituary in *The Builder* Vol. 33 1875 p. 402

40 10 and 11 Vic. *c.* 65 Public

41 13 and 14 Vic. *c.* 52 Public

42 15 and 16 Vic. *c.* 85 Public

43 22 Dec. 1866 p. 938

44 5 Jan. 1867

Chapter 8 *John Claudius Loudon and the Garden Cemetery Movement*

1 Gloag, John *Mr Loudon's England* Newcastle-upon-Tyne 1970 p. 17

2 Loudon, J. C. *The Gardener's Magazine* 1842 p. 666

3 Loudon. *op. cit.* p. 200

4   Loudon, John Claudius *On the laying out, planting, and managing of Cemeteries, and on the improvement of Churchyards* London 1843

5   Loudon, J. C. *The Gardener's Magazine* 1843 p. 93

6   *Ibid.* p. 94

7   *Ibid.* p. 96

8   *Ibid.* p. 100

9   *Ibid.* p. 100

10 Blair, Robert *The Grave* Edinburgh 1826

11 Picton, in *Arch. Mag.* Vol. IV p. 430. Quoted in Loudon *op. cit.* p. 101

12 Strang, John *Necropolis Glasguensis; With Osbervations* (sic) *on Ancient and Modern Tombs and Sepulture* Glasgow 1831

13 Loudon, J. C. *The Gardener's Magazine* 1843, p. 105

14 *Ibid.* p. 105

15 Strang *op. cit.* p. 63

16 Loudon, J. C. *The Gardener's Magazine* 1843 p. 148

17 *Ibid.* p. 152

18 *Ibid.* p. 153

19 *Ibid.* p. 156

20 *Ibid.* p. 222

21 Alison, Archibald *Essays on the Nature and Principles of Taste* Edinburgh 1811 1, pp. 24–5. See also Hersey, G. L. 'J. C. Loudon and Architectural Associationism, *The Architectural Review* Vol. 144 1968 pp. 89–92.

22 I am indebted to Miss Melanie Simo for information regarding Bath and Southampton

23 Loudon, J. C. 'Report on the Design for a Cemetery Proposed to be formed at Southampton by authority of an Act of Parliament and under the Direction of the Mayor and Town Council' 31 Aug. 1843 Southampton Civic Records Office

24 6 and 7 Victoria, 1843

25 Appendix to *Report on the Sanitary Conditions of the Labouring Population,* 1842. Loudon reviewed the *Sanitary Report* of 1842 in *The Gardener's Magazine* Vol. VIII 1842 p. 472. He obviously knew Vetch's diagram of a drainage system for a town, and may have borrowed the ideas in planning the Southampton Cemetery drainage system. I am indebted to Miss Melanie Simo for pointing this out to me

26 *The Hampshire Advertiser* 9 May 1846

27 Loudon *op. cit.* 1843 p. 591

Chapter 9   *Some great nineteenth century cemeteries in Europe, America and Australia*

1   Strang, John *Necropolis Glasguensis; with Osbervations* (sic) *on Ancient and Modern Tombs and Sepulture* Glasgow 1831

2   Curl, James Stevens *The Victorian Celebration of Death* Newton Abbot 1972

3   See Potterton, Homan *Irish Church Monuments 1570–1880* Belfast 1975

4   *A Guide through Glasnevin Cemetery* Dublin 1879. See also Sheehy, Jeanne *J. J. McCarthy and the Gothic Revival in Ireland* Belfast 1977

5   Marion, John Francis *Famous and Curious Cemeteries* New York 1977

6   *Ibid.*

7   Fitzgerald, Edward *A Hand Book for the Albany Rural Cemetery, with an Appendix on Emblems* Albany 1871

8   See also Laughlin, C. J. 'Cemeteries of New Orleans' *The Architectural Review* Vol. 103 No. 614 Feb. 1948

9   Mitford, Jessica *The American Way of Death* London 1963 Waugh, Evelyn *The Loved One* London 1948

10 Eaton, Hubert *The Comemoral* Los Angeles 1954

11 See Lichino, V. *Camposanto. 50 vedute di Genova* Genoa n.d. See also Baedeker

12 I am indebted to Mr David Walker for information

13 Much valuable information concerning cemeteries is contained in the guide-books to great cemeteries like the Staglieno. Karl Baedeker's *Handbooks for Travellers* published in Leipzig before the First World War are packed with information. Augustus J. C. Hare is always a delightful and useful guide

14 Chadwick, Edwin (of Poor Law Reform fame) *A Supplementary Report to Her Majesty's Secretary of State for the Home Department from the Poor Law Commissioners on the Results of a Special Inquiry into the Practice of Interment In Towns, 1843*

15 In Vol. XVI of 1840

16 Vol. III 1845 p. 588

17 *The Builder* Vol. III 1845 p. 83

18 *Ibid.* pp. 69, 82, 92, 110

19 Knight, Charles *London* Vol. IV p. 163

20 *Ibid.* p. 164

21 The Builder Vol. III 1845 p. 197

22 *Ibid.*

23 *The Builder* Vol. IV 1846 p. 395

24 Health of Towns *An examination of the Report and Evidence of the Select Committee*, etc. Signed by James Edwards. London 1843

25 Lane, Charlton *To the Parishioners of Kennington, Stockwell and South Lambeth—on How to Meet the Cholera* London 1854

26 13 & 14 Vic, *c.* 52. Public

29 *The Builder* Vol. IX 1851 p. 443

28 See Extramural Burial *The Three Schemes* London 1850

29 Buckle, E. G. *A Station of the Cross* Goulbourn n.d.

30 *The Metropolitan Burials Act* 15 & 16 Vic, *c.* 85

31 See *Plans and Views of the City of London Cemetery at Little Ilford in the County of Essex formed under the direction of the Commissioners of Sewers of the City of London from the designs and under the superintendence of William Haywood, Architect* 1856

32 *Plan of the City of London Cemetery at Little Ilford in the County of Essex* London 1855

33 47 & 48 Vic *c.* 72

34 48 & 49 Vic *c.* 167

35 50 & 51 Vic *c.* 32

Chapter 10 *The development of cremation*

1 Robinson, William *God's Acre Beautiful; or, The Cemeteries of the Future* London 1883

2 Richardson, Dr *On the Disposal of the Dead* London 1875. See also Parkes, A. E. 'Disposal of the Dead' in *Practical Hygiene* 1873

3 Lloyd, John H. *The History, Topography and Antiquities of Highgate, in the County of Middlesex* London 1888 pp. 494–95

4 Browne, Sir Thomas *Hydriotaphia, or Urne Buriall* London 1658

5 Amos 6, verses 9 and 10. See also 1 Samuel 31, verses 12 and 13

6 Browne *op. cit.*

7 Jamieson, Dr. F. 'The Origin of Cremation' *Proceedings of the Royal Society* Edinburgh 1817

8 Loudon, J. C. *The Gardener's Magazine.* 1843 p. 591. I am grateful to my friends, Miss Melanie Simo and Mr John Gloag, for discussing this with me

9 Wylie, W. M. *Burning and Burial* London 1858. See also Cobbe, C. *Burning of the Dead, or Urn Sepulchre, etc.* London 1857

10 Martin, Colonel T. *Cinerator for Use of Brahmins* Poona 1864

11 Hemsworth, H. W. *Incineration by State Regulation* London 1870

12 See note 2

13 Thompson, Henry 'Cremation: The Treatment of the Body after Death' *The Contemporary Review* Jan. 1874

14 Grindon, L. H. *Cremation Considered in Reference to the Resurrection* London 1874. See also Haweis, Rev. H. R. *Ashes to Ashes: A Cremation Prelude* London 1875. For *La Lumière as Lais* see Langlois' *La Vie Spirituelle en France au Moyen Age* Paris 1928 pp. 66–121

15 Tegg, William *The Last Act* London 1876

16 *Atti della Cremazione di Alberto Keller* Milan 1876

17 Bond, Peter Bernard 'The Celebration of Death. Some thoughts on the design of crematoria' *The Architectural Review* April 1967. I am grateful to Mr Bond for permission to quote from his lucid and humane work

18 Haweis *op. cit*

19 See also Delves, H. C. 'The Disposal of the Dead' *The Journal of the Town Planning Institute* Sept.–Oct. 1952 pp. 261–5; Whittick, Arnold 'Planning and Cemeteries' *Town and Country Planning* Feb. 1952 pp. 81–6; Thompson, Sir Henry *Cremation in Great Britain* London 1909; Eassie, W. *Cremation* London 1875; and *The Transactions of the Cremation Society of England, 1877–1912*

20 See Jones, P. H., and Noble, G. A. *Cremation in Great Britain* London 1931; *The Cremation Committee Report; The Joint Conference of Cemetery and Cremation Authorities* Folkestone 1935. The publications of the Cremation Society provide valuable sources of material. A very full Bibliography may be found in Jones, P. Herbert, and Noble, George A. *op. cit.*, also published by the Cremation Society. I am grateful to Mr Kenneth G. C. Prevette, General Secretary of the Cremation Society of Great Britain, for kindly providing information

Chapter 11   War cemeteries and memorials

1 Adshead, S. D. 'Monumental Memorials and Town Planning' *Journal of the Town Planning Institute* Vol. III No. 5 1917

2 *Hansard* Vol. 134 No. 23 p. 1029 (14 Feb. 1945)

3 *Hansard passim*. See also note 7

4 *Commonwealth War Graves Commission Fifty-Eighth Annual Report* 1977

5 Stamp, Gavin *Silent Cities* London 1977. I am indebted to Mr Stamp for help and information and for permission to quote from his work

6 Stamp *passim*

7 Whittick, Arnold *War Memorials* London 1946 p. 9 *et seq.* Mr Whittick's perceptive writing on memorials and on funerary art has been a considerable inspiration, and I acknowledge my debt to him

8 *L'Ossuaire de Douaumont* Edité par le Comité de l'Oeuvre. J. Varcollier, Hélio-Lorraine Nancy 1960

9 Weaver, Laurence *The Scottish National War Memorial* London 1927

10 Curl, James Stevens 'Victorian Garden Village, Port Sunlight, Merseyside' *Country Life* 16 Dec. 1976

11 I am indebted to the *Commissariato Generale Onoranze Caduti in Guerra* of the *Ministero della Difesa* in Rome for information on Italian War Cemeteries and memorials

Chapter 12   Buildings to celebrate individuals and national events

1 Burckhardt, Jacob *The Civilization of the Renaissance in Italy* English edition translated by S. G. C. Middlemore. Vienna and London n.d.

2 *Ibid.*

3 *Ibid.*

4 See Rosenau, Helen *Boullée and Visionary Architecture* London and New York 1976

5 *Walhalla. Amtlicher Führer* Herausgegeben vom Landbauamt Regensburg. Regensburg 1976

6 Whittick, Arnold *War Memorials* London 1946. This is an admirable book, full of good sense, humanity, and intelligent observation. Mr Whittick has been a sensitive observer of monumental and memorial design for many years, and I acknowledge my great debt to his ideas and to his studies

7 See *The Architectural Review* July 1968 pp. 65–6

8 *Ibid*. Dec. 1967 p. 411

9 *Ibid*. Jan. 1963 p. 186

10 See *Architectural Design* April 1965. I am deeply grateful to M. G.-H. Pingusson for helping me with material

11 See *Domus* Feb. 1965

Chapter 13   *Epilogue*

1 Bodl, M. S. Rawl, B. 376, ff. 351–2. Mr Van-Brugg's Proposals about Building ye New Churches

2 See Pugin's *An Apology for the Revival of Christian Architecture in England* London 1843

3 *New Scientist* Vol. 78 No. 1099

4 Pugin *op. cit.*

5 *The Ecclesiologist* Jan. 1845

6 *Ibid*.

7 Trollope, Rev. Edward *Manual of Sepulchral Memorials* London 1858

8 *Ibid*.

9 Markland, J. H. *Remarks on English Churches, and on the Expediency of Rendering Sepulchral Memorials Subservient to Pious and Christian Uses* Oxford 1843 pp. 88–9

10 *The Quarterly Review* 1842

11 See Trollope, *op. cit.*; Markland, *op. cit.*, and especially *The Ecclesiologist* for vitriolic comment

12 *The Ecclesiologist* Jan. 1845

13 *Ibid*.

14 See *The Ecclesiologist* Nov. 1845

15 See also Blair, George *Biographic and Descriptive Sketches of Glasgow Necropolis* Glasgow 1857. *The Ecclesiastical Art Review* is also useful. For an indication of the longevity of classicism see Curl, James Stevens *Mausolea in Ulster* Belfast 1978

Bibliography I (Books in the Author's Collection)

Ready to be any thing, in the ecstasy of being ever,
and as content with six foot as the *moles* of Adrianus.

SIR THOMAS BROWNE (1605–1682): *Hydriotaphia*

Act of Parliament. *An Act for establishing a Cemetery for the Interment of the Dead Southward of the Metropolis, to be called 'The South Metropolitan Cemetery'*. 6 and 7 William IV. 28 July 1836. All the private cemeteries were founded by authority of similar Acts of Parliament. See Text Notes for details.

A. P. *Souvenir du Cimetière de Gênes* A remarkable booklet with thirty-seven photographs and descriptions of the Staglieno, Genoa. *c.* 1910. This booklet has been updated and published as *Camposanto di Genova. 50 Vedute* V. Lichino & Figlio, Genoa. No date

Andrews, William *Curious Epitaphs Collected from the Graveyards of Great Britain and Ireland, with Biographical, Genealogical, and Historical Notes* London 1883

Andrews, William *Curious Epitaphs* London 1889 (An updated version of previous ed.)

Bakewell, Joan, with Drummond, John (Ed.) *A Fine and Private Place* London 1977

Barker, Rev. Thomas B. *Abney Park Cemetery: A Complete Descriptive Guide to every part of this beautiful Depository of the Dead* London 1896

Batsford, Herbert *English Mural Monuments and Tombstones. A Collection of eighty-four photographs of Wall Tablets, Table Tombs and Headstones of the 17th and 18th centuries; the subjects specially selected by Herbert Batsford as representative examples of the beautiful and traditional types in the English Parish Church and Churchyard, for the use of Craftsmen and as a guide in the present revival of public taste; with an introduction by Walter H. Godfrey, FSA* London 1916

Benes, Peter *The Masks of Orthodoxy. Folk Gravestone Carvings in Plymouth County, Massachusetts, 1689–1805* Amherst 1977

Białostocki, Jan *Vom heroischen Grabmal zum Bauernbegräbnis* Mainz 1977

Bickley, Francis *True Dialogues of the Dead* London, 1925

Blair, George *Biographic and Descriptive Sketches of Glasgow Necropolis* Glasgow 1857

Blair, Robert *The Grave: and Other Poems* Edinburgh 1826

Blake, William *Illustrations* to *The Grave* executed by Louis Schiavonetti. London 1808

Blore, Edward *The Monumental Remains of Noble and Eminent Persons, Comprising the Sepulchral Antiquities of Great Britain* London 1826

Bloxham, Matthew Holbeche *Fragmenta Sepulchralia. A Glimpse of the Sepulchral and early Monumental Remains of Great Britain* An unpublished fragment, printed at the University Press, Oxford, between 1840 and 1850

Boardman, John–See Kurtz

Boase, T. S. R. *Death in the Middle Ages. Mortality, Judgement and Remembrance* London 1972

Bond, Francis *An Introduction to English Church Architecture From the Eleventh to the Sixteenth Century* In two Vols. London 1913

Bond, Peter Bernard 'The Celebration of Death. Some thoughts on the design of crematoria' *Architectural Review* April 1967

Boutell, Rev. Charles *Christian Monuments in England and Wales: An Historical and Descriptive Sketch of the Various Classes of Sepulchral Monuments which have been in use in this Country from about the era of the Norman Conquest to the time of Edward the Fourth* London 1854

Boutell, Rev. Charles *The Monumental Brasses of England: A Series of Engravings upon Wood, from every Variety of These Interesting and Valuable Memorials, Accompanied with Brief Descriptive Notices* London 1849

Briggs, Asa *Victorian Cities* Harmondsworth 1968

Brighton Art Gallery and Museum *Death, Heaven and the Victorians* Catalogue of Exhibition 6 May–3 August 1970

Brindley, William (and Weatherley, W. Samuel) *Ancient Sepulchral Monuments Containing Illustrations of over Six Hundred Examples from Various Countries and from the Earliest Periods down to the end of the Eighteenth Century* London 1887

Briscoe, John Potter *Gleanings from God's Acre: being a Collection of Epitaphs* Edinburgh and London 1883

Britton, John *Cathedral Antiquities, Historical and Descriptive Accounts, with 311 Illustrations* Five Vols. London 1836

Brown, James *The Epitaphs and Monumental Inscriptions in Greyfriars Churchyard, Edinburgh* Edinburgh 1867

Browne, Sir Thomas *Hydriotaphia. Urn Burial; with an Account of Some Urns found at Brampton in Norfolk*, Ed. Sir John Evans London 1893. Also another edition by Greenhill, W. A., including *The Garden of Cyrus* London 1929

Brusin, Giovanni (with De Grassi) *Il Mausoleo di Aquileia* Milan 1956

Budge, E. A. Wallis *The Sarcophagus of Ānchnesrāneferāb, Queen of Āhmes II, King of Egypt, about B.C. 564–526* London, 1885

Burckhardt, Jacob *The Civilization of the Renaissance in Italy* Translated by S. G. C. Middlesmore Vienna and London n.d.

Cansick, Frederic, Teague *A Collection of Curious and Interesting Epitaphs,Copied from the Monuments of Distinguished and Noted Characters in the Ancient Church and Burial Grounds of Saint Pancras, Middlesex* London 1869

A Collection of Curious and Interesting Epitaphs, Copied from the Existing Monuments of Distinguished and Noted Characters in the Cemeteries and Churches of Saint Pancras, Middlesex London 1872

A Collection of Curious and Interesting Epitaphs, Copied from the Existing Monuments of Distinguished and Noted Characters in the Churches and Churchyards of Hornsey, Tottenham, Edmonton, Enfield, Friern Barnet and Hadley, Middlesex London 1875

Also these three volumes in the Large Paper Editions of the same years

Christison, D. *The Carvings and Inscriptions on the Kirkyard Monuments of the Scottish Lowlands, Particularly in Perth, Fife, Angus, Mearns, and Lothian* Edinburgh 1902

Bibliography

Clark, Kenneth *The Gothic Revival, An Essay in the History of Taste* London 1962

Clarke, Basil F.L. *Church Builders of the Nineteenth Century* Newton Abbot 1969

Colvin, H. M. *A Biographical Dictionary of British Architects 1600–1840* London 1978

Commissariato Generale Onoranze Caduti in Guerra *Sacrari Militari* Rome Various dates

Cook, B. F. *Greek and Roman Art in the British Museum* London 1976

Connor, Arthur B. *Monumental Brasses in Somerset* Bath 1970

Crook, J. Mordaunt *The Greek Revival. Neo-Classical Attitudes in British Architecture 1760–1870* London 1972

Crossley, Fred. H. *English Church Monuments A.D. 1150–1550. An Introduction to the Study of Tombs and Effigies of the Mediaeval Period* London 1921

Curl, James Stevens 'The Architecture and Planning of the Nineteenth-Century Cemetery' *Garden History* The Journal of the Garden History Society, Vol. III No. 3 Summer 1975

Curl, James Stevens *Mausolea in Ulster* Belfast 1978

Curl, James Stevens 'Nunhead Cemetery' *Trans.* of Ancient Mon. Soc. 1977

Curl, James Stevens *The Victorian Celebration of Death* Newton Abbot 1972

Cutts, Revd. Edward L. *A Manual for the Study of the Sepulchral Slabs and Crosses of the Middle Ages* London 1849

Dagley, R. *Death's Doings; consisting of numerous Original Compositions, in Prose and Verse, the Friendly Contributions of Various Writers; Principally intended as Illustrations of Twenty-Four Plates, Designed and Etched by R. Dagley* London 1826

Davey, Richard *A History of Mourning* Published as an advertisement, by the House of Jay, Regent Street *c.* 1890

Davies, Gerald S. *Renascence: The Sculptured Tombs of the Fifteenth Century in Rome* London 1910

Dennis, George *The Cities and Cemeteries of Etruria* Two Vols. London 1883

Downes, Kerry *Vanbrugh* Vol. XVI of *Studies in Architecture* London 1977

Drummond, James *Sculptured Monuments in Iona and the West Highlands* Edinburgh 1881

Drummond, John – See Bakewell, Joan

Edwards, I. E. S. *The Pyramids of Egypt* London 1972

Esdaile, Katherine A. *English Church Monuments 1510–1840* London 1946

Fairley, W. *Epitaphiana: or, The Curiosities of Churchyard Literature. Being a Miscellaneous Collection of Epitaphs. With an Introduction giving an account of various customs prevailing amongst the ancients and moderns in the disposal of their dead* London 1875

Fairweather, Barbara *Eilean Munda. The Burial Island in Loch Leven* Glencoe n.d.

Freeman, Albert C. *Antiquity of Cremation and Curious Funeral Customs* London n.d.

Freeman, Albert C. *Crematoria in Great Britain and Abroad* London *c.* 1905

Fisher, Major Payne *The Catalogue of Most of the Memorable Tombes, Grave stones,*

Plates, Escutcheons, or Atchievements in the Demolisht or yet Extant Churches of LONDON from St. Katherines beyond the Tower, to Temple-Barre London 1668, privately reprinted and edited by G. Blacker Morgan, 1885

Fisher, Major Payne *The Tombs, Monuments, &c., Visible in S. Paul's Cathedral (and S. Faith's Beneath It) Previous to its Destruction by FIRE A.D. 1666* London 1684. Privately reprinted and edited by G. Blacker Morgan

Fitzgerald, Edward *A Hand Book for the Albany Rural Cemetery, with an Appendix on Emblems* Albany 1871

Gell, Sir William, and Gandy, John P. *Pompeiana. The Topography, Edifices, and Ornaments of Pompeii* London 1852

Gillon, Edmund V., Jr. *Victorian Cemetery Art* New York 1972

Gloag, John *Mr Loudon's England. The Life and Work of John Claudius Loudon, and his influence on architecture and furniture design* Newcastle-upon-Tyne 1970

Grassi, Vigilio de – See Brusin, Giovanni

Gray, Mrs Hamilton *Tour to the Sepulchres of Etruria in 1839* London 1841

Greenhill, F. A. *Incised Effigial Slabs. A Study of Engraved Stone Memorials in Latin Christendom, c.1100 to c.1700* Two Vols. London 1976 These invaluable volumes contain a very full bibliography on the subject of monumental brasses and other incised slabs

Green-Wood Cemetery *Green-Wood* A small collection of selected views, engraved and printed by the Photo-Engraving Company, 67 Park Place, New York. New York 1891

Grinsell, Leslie V. *Barrow, Pyramid and Tomb. Ancient Burial customs in Egypt, the Mediterranean and the British Isles* London 1975

Gunnis, Rupert *Dictionary of British Sculptors 1660–1851* New Revised Edition London n.d.

Hare, Augustus J. C. *Epitaphs for Country Churchyards* Oxford 1856

Hartland, Frederick D. *Tapographia, or A collection of TOMBS of Royal and Distinguished Families. Collected during a Tour of Europe in the Years 1854 and 1855* Privately printed in 1856

Havergal, Revd. Francis T. *Monumental Inscriptions in the Cathedral Church of Hereford* London 1881

Hennessy, J. B. *Stephania. A Middle and Late Bronze-Age Cemetery in Cyprus.* London 1963

Hollis, G. and T. *Monumental Effigies* Walworth 1840

Holloway, Harold *The South Park Street Cemetery Calcutta* Calcutta n.d.

Holmes, Mrs Basil *The London Burial Grounds. Notes on their History from the earliest times to the Present Day* London 1896

Johnston, J. I. D. *Clogher Cathedral Graveyard* Omagh 1972

Jones, Barbara *Design for Death* London 1967

Jones, P. Herbert (with Noble, George A.) *Cremation in Great Britain* London 1931

Justyne, William *Guide to Highgate Cemetery* London *c.* 1870 (This is a rare example of Victoria ephemera, and contains advertisements for sculpture and undertaking establishments)

Bibliography

Kurtz, Donna C. and Boardman, John *Greek Burial Customs* London 1971

Lagrèze, G. B. de *Pompéi, Les Catacombes, L'Alhambra* Paris 1872

Lassalle – See Marty

Light, Alfred W. *Bunhill Fields* London 1913

Lindahl, Göran *Grave och rum* Stockholm 1969

Lindley, Kenneth *Graves and Graveyards* London 1972

London, Corporation of *Proceedings in Reference to the Preservation of the Bunhill Fields Burial Ground* (This contains a reprint of Edmund Curll's *Inscriptions on the Tombs in the Dissenters' Burial-Place, near Bunhill Fields* London 1717) London 1867

Loudon, J. C. (Ed.) *Gardener's Magazine* New Series 1835–43

Macklin, Revd. Herbert W. *Monumental Brasses* London and New York 1905

Maeterlinck, Maurice *Death* (tr. by Alexander Teixeira de Mattos) London 1911

Marion, John Francis *Famous and Curious Cemeteries* New York 1977

Markland, J. H. *Remarks on English Churches, and on the Expediency of Rendering Sepulchral Memorials Subservient to Pious and Christian Uses* Oxford 1843

Marriott, Rev. Wharton B. *The Testimony of the Catacombs and of Other Monuments of Christian Art, from the Second to the Eighteenth Century, concerning questions of Doctrine now Disputed in the Church* London 1870

Marty (author) and Lassalle (lithographer) with Rousseau (architect) *Les Principaux Monuments Funéraires Du Père-Lachaise, de Montmartre, du Mont-Parnasse et autres Cimetières de Paris Dessinés et Mesurés Par Rousseau, architecte, et Lithographiés Par Lassalle, Accompagnés d'une Description succincte du monument et d'une Notice historique sur le personnage qu'il renferme, Par Marty* Paris n.d.

Miller, Thomas *Picturesque Sketches of London Past and Present* London 1852 (Contains an early description of Highgate Cemetery)

Mitford, Jessica *The American Way of Death* London 1963

Morgan, G. Blacker —See Fisher, Major Payne

Morley, John *Death, Heaven and the Victorians* London 1971

Nichols, John Gough *Description of the Church of S. Mary, Warwick, and of the Beauchamp Chapel, and the Monuments of the Beauchamps and Dudleys: also of the Chantry Chapel of Isabella, Countess of Warwick, in Tewkesbury Abbey* London n.d.

Nilsson, Sten *European Architecture in India 1750–1850* London 1968

Noble, George A. —See Jones, P. Herbert

Norfolk, Horatio Edward *Gleanings in Graveyards: A Collection of Curious Epitaphs* London 1861

Normand Fils *Monumens Funéraires choisis dans les Cimetières de Paris et des Principaux Villes de France, Dessinés, Gravés et Publiés Par Normand Fils* Paris 1832

Pagan, James *Sketch of the History of Glasgow* Glasgow 1847

Palliser, F. and M. A. *Mottoes for Monuments or Epitaphs Selected for Study or Application* London 1872

Penny, Nicholas *Church Monuments in Romantic England* New Haven and London 1977

Pettigrew, Thomas Joseph *Chronicles of the Tombs. A Select Collection of Epitaphs, preceded by an Essay on Epitaphs and other Monumental Inscriptions, with incidental Observations on Sepulchral Antiquities* London 1902

Potterton, Homan *Irish Church Monuments* Belfast 1975

Prickett, Frederick *The History and Antiquities of Highgate, Middlesex* London 1842

Puckle, Bertram S. *Funeral Customs, Their Origin and Development* London 1926

Rankin, Peter *Irish Building Ventures of the Earl Bishop of Derry* Belfast 1972

Ravenshaw, Thomas F. *Antiente Epitaphes (from A.D. 1250 to A.D. 1800) Collected & sett forth in Chronologicall order* London 1878

Richardson, Edward *The Monumental Effigies of the Temple Church with An Account of Their Restoration, in the Year 1842* London 1843

Rimmer, Alfred *Ancient Stone Crosses of England* London 1875

Robertson, D. S. *A Handbook of Greek & Roman Architecture* Cambridge 1929

Rogers, Rev. Charles *Monuments and Monumental Inscriptions in Scotland* In Two Vols. London 1871–2

Rosenau, Helen *Boullée & Visionary Architecture* London 1976

Rosenau, Helen *The Ideal City. Its Architectural Evolution* London 1974

Rosenau, Helen *Social Purpose in Architecture. Paris and London Compared 1760–1800* London 1970

Rousseau — See Marty

Rushen, Percy C. *The Churchyard Inscriptions of the City of London* London 1910

St. A . . . , M. P. *Promenade aux Cimetières de Paris, aux Sépultures Royales de Saint-Denis, et aux Catacombes, etc.* Paris *c.* 1820

Sculpture Centre, The *Sculptured Memorials and Headstones Designed and Carved in Sculptors' Studios in British Stones* Paperback Edition, Jan. 1937 Hardback Edition, September, 1938

Sheppard, F. H. W. (Ed.) *Survey of London. The Parish of S Mary Lambeth* Vol. 26 London 1956

Sheppard, F. H. W. (Ed.) *Survey of London. Northern Kensington* Vol. 37 London 1973

Snow, William *Sepulchral Gleanings; or, a Collection of Epitaphs, Ancient, Modern, Curious, Instructive, and Moral; As actually and accurately taken from various parts of England; including those in the vicinity of London and Westminster, forming a complete Mirror of Mortality, and calculated (in an unusual degree) to promote the cause of Virtue and Religion; the whole collected, digested, and alphabetically arranged* London 1817

Southey, Caroline *Chapters on Churchyards* Edinburgh and London 1841

Stamp, Gavin *Silent Cities* London 1977

Stephenson, Mill *A List of Monumental Brasses in Surrey* Bath 1970

Stewart, Aubrey *English Epigrams and Epitaphs* London 1897

Stone, Mrs. *God's Acre: or, Historical Notes relating to Churchyards* London 1858

Stothard, C. A. *The Monumental Effigies of Great Britain; Selected from Our Cathedrals and Churches, for the Purpose of Bringing Together, and Preserving Correct Representations of the Best Historical Illustrations Extant, from the Norman Conquest to the Reign of Henry the Eighth* London 1817

Strang, John *Necropolis Glasguensis with Osbervations* (sic) *on Ancient and Modern Tombs and Sepulture* Glasgow 1831

Styan, K. E. *A Short History of Sepulchral Cross-Slabs, with Reference to Other Emblems found thereon* London 1902

Sullivan, F. A. *Sullivan's New Text-Book on Embalming and Sanitation* Kalamazoo and London 1901

Taylor, Joseph *The Danger of Premature Interment, Proved from Many Remarkable Instances of People who have recovered after being laid out for dead, and of others entombed alive, for want of being properly examined prior to Interment. Also a Description of the Manner the Ancient Egyptians, and other Nations, Preserved and Venerated their Dead, and a curious Account of their Sepulchral Ever Burning Lamps and Mausoleums. Likewise the pernicious effects of burying in the body of Churches, and confined Church-Yards pointed out, whereby many valuable lives have been lost to the Public, and their Friends. Selected from Historical Records* London 1816

Tegg, William *The Last Act, being The Funeral Rites of Nations and Individuals* London 1876

Tirard, H. M. *The Book of the Dead* London 1910

Toynbee, J. M. C. *Death and Burial in the Roman World* London 1971

Vallance, Aymer *Old Crosses and Lychgates* London 1920

Vincent, W. T. *In Search of Gravestones Old and Curious* London 1896

Wake, Henry Thomas *All the Monumental Inscriptions in the Graveyards of Brigham and Bridekirk, near Cockermouth, in the County of Cumberland, from 1666 to 1876* Cockermouth 1878

Walford, Edward *Old and New London* London 1887

Weatherley, W. Samuel—See Brindley, William

Weaver, Lawrence *Memorials & Monuments Old and New: Two hundred subjects chosen from seven centuries* London and New York 1915

Weber, F. Parkes *Aspects of Death in Art and Epigram* London 1914

Whittick, Arnold *War Memorials* London 1946

Wilkinson, Theon *Two Monsoons* London 1976

Wright, Geoffrey N. *Discovering Epitaphs. Being a collection of some of the most curious epitaphs and memorials gathered together* Aylesbury 1972

BIBLIOGRAPHY II (Other sources)

Abdul-Qader, M. M. *Development of the Funerary Beliefs and Practices . . . in the Private Tombs of the New Kingdom of Thebes* Cairo 1966

Abshoff, Fritz *Deutschlands Ruhm und Stolz. Unsere hervorragendsten vaterländischen Denkmäler in Wort und Bild* Berlin *c.* 1901

Addy, S. O. 'House Burial' *J. Derbys. Archaeol. Soc.* 1918–20

Alison, Archibald *Essays on the Nature and Principles of Taste* Edinburgh 1811

Alken, Samuel, And Sala, George Augustus *Folding Panoramic View of the Duke of Wellington's Funeral which took place on 18 November 1852*

Angeli, Diego *Mino da Fiesole* Florence 1905

Anonymous. *The Burials Question Further Examined from a Layman's Point of View. Is there a Grievance?* London 1880

Anonymous *The Cemetery. A brief appeal to the feelings of society on behalf of Extra Mural Burial* London 1848

Anonymous *Extramural Burial. The three Schemes* London 1850

Ashbee, P. *The Bronze Age Round Barrow in Britain* London 1960

Atkinson, R. J. C. 'Wayland's Smithy'. *Antiquity* 39, 1965 pp. 126–33

Austin, Edwin *Burial Grounds and Cemeteries: a practical guide to their Administration by Local Authorities, etc.* London 1907

Bendann, E. *Death Customs. An Analytical Study of Burial Rites* London 1930

Berchtold, le Comte Léopold de. *Projet pour prévenir Les Dangers Très-Fréquens des INHUMATIONS précipitées* Paris 1791

Bertin, Georges *Le Cimetière d'Auteuil* Tours 1910

Boase, Frederic *Modern English Biography, containing many thousand concise memoirs of persons who have died between the years 1851–1900* London 1965

Bode, Wilhelm *Florentine Sculptors of the Renaissance* London 1908

Born, Ignatz von *Journal für Freimaurer* Vienna 1784

Boëthius, A., and Ward-Perkins, J. B. *Etruscan and Roman Architecture* Harmondsworth 1970

Bowker, A. & Son *In Memoriam, or, Funeral Records of Liverpool Celebrities* Liverpool 1876

Brunton, G. 'Burial Customs' – See Engelbach, R. (Ed.)

Bryan, W. R. *Italic Hut Urns and Hut Urn Cemeteries* Rome 1925

Buchheit, Gert *Das Reichsehrenmal Tannenberg. Seine Entstehung, seine endgültige Gestaltung und seine Einzelkunstwerke* Munich 1936

Builder, The An invaluable source of material. Various dates

Bunning, James Bunstone *Designs for Tombs and Monuments* London 1839

Burger, Fritz *Geschichte des Florentinischen Grabmals* Strasbourg 1904

Cemetery and Crematoria Superintendents, National Association of *The Joint Conference of Cemetery and Cremation Authorities* Folkestone 1935

Chadwick, Sir Edwin *A Supplementary Report to Her Majesty's Secretary of State for the Home Department from the Poor Law Commissioners on the Results of a Special Inquiry into the Practice of Interment in Towns* London 1843

Childe, V. G. *The Dawn of European Civilization* London 1957

Cleaveland, N., and Walter, Cornelia *Green-Wood and Mount Auburn* New York 1847

Coffey, G. *New Grange* Dublin and London 1912

Cole, Hubert *Things for the Surgeon. A History of the Resurrection Men* London 1964

Bibliography

Contemporary Review, The January 1874

Corcoran, J. X. W. P. 'The Cotswold-Severn Group'. *Megalithic Enquiries in the West of Britain* Ed. by T. G. E. Powell Liverpool 1969 pp. 13–106

Cottrell, Leonard *The Bull of Minos* London 1962

Coussillan, Auguste André *Les 200 Cimetières du vieux Paris par Jacques Hillairet* Paris 1958

Cremation Society, The *Transactions* 1877–1912

Croydon Weekly Standard, The 25 November 1865

Curll, Edmund *The Inscriptions upon the Tombs, Grave-Stones, &c. in the Dissenters Burial Place near Bunhill-Fields* London 1717

Daniel, G. E. *The Prehistoric Chamber Tombs of England and Wales* Cambridge 1950

Delves, H. C. 'The Disposal of the Dead' *Journal of the Town Planning Institute* Sept–Oct 1952

Dickens, B. 'The Runic Inscriptions of Maeshowe' *Proc. Orkney Ant. Soc. 8*, 1930

Dufresne, D. *Les Cryptes Vaticanes* Paris n.d.

Eassie, W. *Cremation* London 1875

Eaton, Hubert *The Comemoral* Los Angeles 1954

The Ecclesiologist Various years, but especially 1845

Edwards, James, *et al. Health of Towns. An examination of the Report and Evidence of the Select Committee; of Mr MacKinnon's Bill and of the Acts for Establishing Cemeteries around the Metropolis* London 1843

Emery, W. B. *Archaic Egypt* Harmondsworth 1961

Engelbach, R. (Ed.) *Introduction to Egyptian Archaeology* Cairo 1946 pp. 199–244

Eogan, G. 'Report on Knowth, Co. Meath' in *Proc. Royal Irish Acad.* 74(C), 1974, pp. 11–112

Evans, E. E. *Prehistoric and Early Christian Ireland: A Guide* London and New York 1966

Evelyn, John *Diary* various editions

Fischer von Erlach, Johann Bernard *Entwurf einer historischen Architektur* Vienna 1721

Forest Lawn Memorial-Park Association *Art Guide of Forest Lawns* Los Angeles 1956

Friedel, J. G. *Geschichte der Freimaurerei* Leipzig 1861

Frothingham, A. L. *The Monuments of Christian Rome* New York 1908

Fuchs, Werner *Das Marine-Ehrenmal* Wilhelmshaven 1960

Garstang, J. *Burial Customs in Ancient Egypt* London 1907

Geary, Stephen *Cemetery Designs for Tombs and Cenotaphs* London 1840

General Cemetery Company. The Minutes of the Company, still in their possession and held in their Harrow Road offices. The Company had offices at 95 Great Russell Street, Bloomsbury

Gentleman's Magazine, The Various years

Glob, P. V. *The Mound People* Trans. Joan Bulman London 1974

Godwin, William *An Essay on Sepulchres, or, a proposal for erecting some memorial of the illustrious dead in all ages on the spot where their remains have been interred* London 1809

Green-Wood Cemetery *Exposition of the Plan and Objects of the Green-Wood Cemetery, An Incorporated Trust Chartered by the Legislature of the State of New York* New York 1891

Grinsell, L. V. *Belas Knap Long Barrow* HMSO London 1966

Haestier, Richard *Dead Men Tell Tales* London 1934

Hagger, J. *Monumenta, or, Designs for Tombs, Wall-Monuments, Head-Stones, Grave-Crosses, &c.* London 1868

Hallam, Arthur (Ed.) *The Burial Reformer*, later the *Perils of Premature Burial* Various dates

Haweis, Rev. H. R. *Ashes to Ashes. A cremation Prelude* London 1875

Hawkes, Jacquetta (Editor) *The World of the Past* London 1963

Haywood, William *Plans and Views of the City of London Cemetery at Little Ilford in the County of Essex formed under the Direction of the Commissioners of Sewers of the City of London and under the superintendence of William Haywood, Architect* London 1856

Haywood, William *Plans of the City of London Cemetery at Little Ilford in the County of Essex* London 1855

Hemp, W. J. 'The chambered cairn of Bryn Celli Ddu' in *Archaeologia* 80, 1930 pp. 179–214

Henshall, A. S. *Chamber Tombs of Scotland* Edinburgh 1972

Higgins, R. A. and others 'The façade of the Treasury of Atreus at Mycenae', in *BSA* 63, 1968 pp. 331–6

Hillairet, Jacques—See Coussillan, Auguste André

Hood, M. S. F. *The Minoans* London and New York 1971

Jamieson, J. 'The Origin of Cremation' *Proceedings of the Royal Society* Edinburgh 1817

Jones, Gwyn *A History of the Vikings* London 1968

Jowett, Jane *On Burial, Death and Resurrection* sold by Jane Jowett, 3 Camp Lane Court, Water Lane, Leeds, and by W. and F. G. Cash, of Bishopgate, n.d.

J., W. (Justyne, William) *Illustrated Guide to Kensal Green Cemetery* London *c.* 1858

Keller Family *Atti della Cremazione di Alberto Keller* Milan 1876

Kemper, Friederike *Denkschrift über die Nothwendigkeit einer Gesetzlichen Einführung von Leichenhäusern* 1856

Kendall, H. E. *Sketches of the Approved Designs of a Chapel and Gateway Entrances intended to be erected at Kensal Green for the General Cemetery Company* London 1832

Kneisner, F. *Geschichte der deutschen Freimaurerei* Berlin 1912

Knight, Charles (Ed.) *London* London, 1841–4 and later editions.

Lane, Charlton *To the Parishioners of Kennington, Stockwell, and South Lambeth—*

On How to Meet the Cholera London 1854

Köppen, Karl Friedrich *Crata Repoa, oder Einweihung der ägyptischen Priester.* Berlin 1778

Langley, Batty *Gothic Architecture improved by Rules and Proportions in many Grand Designs of Columns, Doors, Windows, Chimney-Pieces, Arcades, Colonnades, Porticos, Umbrellos, Temples and Pavilions, &c* London 1742

Lauer, J. P. *L'Histoire Monumentale des Pyramides d'Egypte* Cairo 1962

Laughlin, C. J. 'Cemeteries of New Orleans' *Architectural Review* February 1948

Ledoux, C. -N. *L'architecture considerée sous le rapport de l'art, des moeurs et de la législation* Paris 1804–46

Lerici, C. M. *Italia Sepolta* Milan 1962

Lewis, Revd. Thomas *Seasonable Considerations on the Indecent and Dangerous Custom of BURYING in Churches and Churchyards, with remarkable OBSERVATIONS historical and philosophical. Proving that the Custom is not only contrary to the Practice of the Antients, but fatal, in case of INFECTION* London 1721

Lloyd, John H. *The History, Topography, and Antiquities of Highgate, in the County of Middlesex* Highgate 1888

London Cemetery Company, The Minutes of the Company. Apparently only parts of the minutes, from about 1860, survive and are held by the London Borough of Southwark

Loudon, John Claudius *On the laying out, planting, and managing of Cemeteries and on the improvement of Churchyards* London 1843

Loudon, John Claudius *Encyclopaedia of Cottage, Farm and Villa Architecture and Furniture* London 1833

Loudon, John Claudius (Ed.) *The Gardener's Magazine and Register of Rural and Domestic Improvements* 1826 onwards. The volume for 1843 contains *On the laying out, planting and managing of Cemeteries and on the improvement of Churchyards* in serial form

McDowell and Partners *Victorian Catacombs, Nunhead Cemetery, Southwark. Building Surveys and Structural Report* Claygate Esher 1976

Mylonas, G. E. *Mycenae and the Mycenaean Age* Princeton 1966

Morning Chronicle, The Thurs. 10 June 1830

National Philanthropic Association, Fifth Report *Sanitary Progress* 1850

O'Kelly, C. *Illustrated Guide to New Grange* Wexford 1967

Oncken, A. *Friedrich Gilly* Berlin 1935

O'Neill, H. E., and Grinsell, L. V. 'Gloucestershire Barrows' *Trans. Bristol and Gloucestershire Archaeol. Soc.* 79, 1961, pp. 1–15

Ó Ríordán, S. P., and Daniel, G. E. *New Grange* London and New York 1964

Pallotino, M. *The Necropolis of Cerveteri* Rome 1957

Petrie, W. M. F. *Pyramids and Temples of Gizeh* London 1883

Pevsner, Nikolaus *A History of Building Types* London 1976

Pfister, Rudolf 'Die Kultur des Friedhofes' *Baumeister* March 1948

Piranesi, Giovanni Battista *Diverse Maniere d'adornare i Cammini* Rome 1769

Pope, Alexander *Moral Essays* London 1733

Prevette, Kenneth, G. C. *The Cremation Society's Handbook and Directory of Crematoria* Maidstone 1975

Pugin, A. W. N. *An Apology for the Revival of Christian Architecture in England* London 1843

Quarterly Review, The 1842

Rice, T. T. *The Scythians* London and New York 1957

Richardon, E. *The Etruscans* Chicago 1964

Robinson, William *God's Acre Beautiful, or the Cemeteries of the Future* London 1880

Scharfe, Siegfried *Deutschland über Alles. Ehrenmale des Weltkrieges* Leipzig 1940

Sala, George Augustus—See Alken Samuel

St Johns, Adela Rogers *First Step Up Toward Heaven* London 1959

Scott, Sir George Gilbert *Consecration versus desecration. An appeal against the Bill for the desctruction of City churches and the sale of burial grounds* London 1854

Seeger, Karl von *Das Denkmal des Weltkriegs* Stuttgart 1930

Society of Antiquaries of London, The *Proceedings* London 1921–present

Society of Antiquaries of Scotland, The *Proceedings* Edinburgh 1851–present

Thomas. E. *The Royal Necropoleis of Thebes* Princeton 1966

Thompson, Sir Henry *Cremation in Great Britain* London, 1909

Thompson, Sir Henry *Modern Cremation. Its History and Practice* London 1891

Timbs, John *Curiosities of London* London 1885

Times, The 1830s and 1840s

Trendall, E. W. *A New Work on Monuments, Cenotaphs, Tombs and Tablets, etc. etc. with their details drawn to a large scale, by which the Workman can erect each design with facility* London c. 1840

Trollope, Revd. Edward *Manual of Sepulchral Monuments* London 1858

Truth-Seeker, A. *Cremation considered in reference to the Resurrection* London 1874

Wace, A. J. B. *Mycenae: an Archaeological History and Guide* Princeton 1949

Walker, George Alfred *Gatherings from Grave-Yards, Particularly those of London, with a concise History of the Modes of Interment among different Nations, from the earliest Periods; and a Detail of dangerous and fatal Results produced by the unwise and revolting Custom of inhuming the Dead in the midst of the Living* London 1839

Walton, J. 'Hog-back Tombstones and the Anglo-Danish home' *Antiquity* 28, 1954 pp. 68–77

Waugh, Evelyn *The Loved One* London 1948

West of London and Westminster Cemetery Company, The. Minutes, now in the Public Record Office, PRO Works 6/65, 2–35

Whitehouse, R. 'The rock-cut tombs of the central Mediterranean' in *Antiquity* 46, 1972 pp. 275–81

Williamson, R. P. Ross. 'Victorian Necropolis—the Cemeteries of London' *The*

Bibliography

Architectural Review October 1942

Wilson, J. B. 'The Story of Norwood.' Unpublished MSS, in the Members' Library, County Hall, London

Wooley, C. L. *Excavations at Ur* London 1954

Woollacott, Ron 'Brief Guide to Nunhead Cemetery' *Newsletter 4* of the Peckham Society Feb–Mar 1976

Index